Peter Biddlecombe is a travel-hardened businessman. His much-acclaimed first book, *French Lessons in Africa*, described his travels through French-speaking Africa, and has been followed by five more gloriously funny accounts of global business trips: *Travels With My Briefcase*; *Around the World – On Expenses*; *I Came, I Saw, I Lost My Luggage*; *Very Funny – Now Change Me Back Again* and *Faster, They're Gaining*, all of which are available from Abacus Travel.

He is the first travel writer to have visited and written about over 125 different countries.

A Nice Time Being Had By All

PETER BIDDLECOMBE

An *Abacus* Book

First published in Great Britain in 1999
by Abacus

A CIP catalogue record for this book
is available from the British Library.

ISBN: 0 349 11145 6

Typeset by Solidus (Bristol) Limited
Printed and bound in Great Britain
by Clays Ltd, St Ives plc

Abacus
A Division of
Little, Brown and Company (UK)
Brettenham House
Lancaster Place
London WC2E 7EN

CONTENTS

Introduction

Why am I always the one being had?

Take buying tickets. How come I'm always the only one on the flight paying full fare? Everybody else has either got a Supersaver-this or a Super-supersaver-the-other or knows this travel agent who gets bundles of tickets off his brother-in-law who knows someone in Moscow. Come to think of it, why am I also the only one in the world never to get an up-grade? Everyone else seems to get them all the time, yet you can bet your life they don't spend a fraction of the money I spend on airlines.

And what about airport taxes? Why am I also the only one to pay my airport taxes in full, even when there's no airport tax - another favourite dodge of the travel trade.

But the real propeller heads, as far as I'm concerned, are the airlines, the biggest con merchants of all. They pretend they love you: they make out you're the most important person to them in the whole world. Nonsense. Look at the way they treat you.

Take checking in. I recently got bounced all over Gatwick by Virgin Airlines. The reason? Some menopausal, congenitally dysfunctional fag-bag who looked as though she did her training in Zeppelins accused me of daring to take on board just over 7.5 kilos of hand luggage - which I must explain wasn't just hand luggage, it was also all my gear for a two-week swing through the States.

'You're only allowed to take 5.5 kilos,' she barked.

You know me, I'm never unintentionally rude to anyone. It doesn't do my post-traumatic traveller's stress disorders any good. So I started out quietly.

'But it's hand luggage,' I said. 'I've just come back from Miami on Virgin. I've just come back from Kuala Lumpur on Virgin. I had exactly the same stuff. They didn't say anything. And don't forget, I haven't got any other luggage at all.'

'Only 5.5. kilos,' she glared, a thin sprinkling of ice beginning to form on the moustache on her upper lip.

'Okay,' I said. 'I'll take out 2 kilos and carry them under my arm. The rest is hand baggage: 5.5 kilos.'

'You're only allowed one item of hand luggage,' she growled.

'That is only one item. The rest, books, papers, documents, I'm carrying under my arm.'

'That's two items.'

'Nonsense.'

'Well, sir,' she sneered, pointing an arthritic claw at a pile of chairs on the edge of the horizon, 'if you would like to go and sit down over there and think about it ...'

Now that really got me.

'So you mean to say there will be nobody on this flight carrying more than 5.5 kilos of hand luggage and nobody carrying more than one item of hand luggage?'

'No, sir. They're the regulations.'

Well, what could I do? I took out my 3.5 kilos of books and papers and documents and checked in my mere 4 kilos of baggage, which, I hasten to add, was in an unlocked, unprotected canvas bag.

It goes without saying that there were a million guys on the flight with four, five, even six, items of hand luggage. One even had three big cardboard boxes of stuff, while others had hand luggage far, far heavier than mine. Now tell me what's fair about that. Yet again

I'd been had. I was forced to give in: the others got away with it.

There was also, incidentally, one guy on the flight, a Rasta, who was carrying a four-foot walking stick the size of a tree trunk. As soon as he sat down one of the Virgin hostesses did rush up to him and say she would have to take the stick and put it in the hold. He screamed and shouted at her so much she beat a hasty retreat and didn't make any other attempt to remove it. Neither did anybody else.

Yet I recall once, on British Airways, this fully paid-up member of the aeronautical gerontocracy going bananas because I was reading the *Financial Times* as we came in to land. It was, she wailed, a dangerous hazard, and if I didn't put it down immediately she would call the pilot. Neither of which seemed particularly sensible ideas at the time. I gave in and stuffed it in the back of the seat in front of me.

Other people, of course, get flights on which, when they come in to land, they are told to return the stewardesses to an upright position.

But what happens when I do as I'm told and take not only just hand luggage, but exactly the right weight of hand luggage? I still get bounced. Take the last time I flew with American Airlines. I checked in at Gatwick. I was going on the usual swing: thirty-three cities in ten days, or whatever. Because the planes are always late taking off, because they're always late arriving, because whenever I go anywhere near Miami they always lose my luggage or stick it on a flight to Timbuktu, and because I knew that as a result I'd miss all my connections, and that my luggage, if it was ever found, would never catch up with me, I decided to take only hand luggage. And because of that previous encounter of a most unreasonable and unpleasant kind, I also decided – call me chicken if you must – to take exactly the right weight of hand luggage.

Were they grateful? Did they upgrade me for being

the first person in aviation history to obey the rules? Did they throw air miles at me in gratitude? Did they hell.

'Why are you visiting so many places?' their sad-faced, snivelling chief security gonk sneered at me.

'Because American Airlines is such a fantastic airline and flies to so many places,' I smiled sweetly back at him.

He glared. 'Which countries are you visiting?'

'What do you mean, which countries am I visiting? You've got my ticket, you know better than I do where I'm going.' It was becoming difficult to maintain the smile. Damn it. I spend a fortune with these guys. I'm the customer they make a big fuss about caring for.

'Can you prove who you are?'

My God. 'Can I prove who I am? You've got my passport. That's who I am, unless—'

'I mean who you *really* are. Have you got any business cards, any letter heads?'

I'm sure Her Britannic Majesty's Government will be thrilled to hear that in the eyes of American Airlines' security chief, a British passport stands for nothing. A dog-eared business card is far, far more credible. Then came what he considered the killer question.

'Four shirts? You can't possibly live on four shirts for a week.'

You would have been proud of me. Instead of strangling the guy on the spot like any other halfway self-respecting American Airlines Advantage cardholder would have done, I took a deep breath.

'First,' I said as calmly as I possibly could, 'it's nothing to do with you whether I live on four shirts or four hundred. It is nothing to do with you what I pack or do not pack in my luggage. Secondly – this might come as a shock to you – but there are such things in America as hotels. With laundries.'

Well, that was it. I was pulled out of the line and escorted to the security zone. My bag was unpacked. Grubby fingers tore everything to bits. My clothes were unfolded, flattened, pawed over, re-folded and unfolded and pawed over again. My razor was switched on, switched off and put through the X-ray machine several times. The bag itself was X-rayed and re-X-rayed. And obviously there was nothing wrong. Then some old sticker was slapped on my bag and I was left to shuffle off to the departure lounge.

And as if that was not enough, just as I was about to board their plane, zonk, the whole thing happened again. I reckon it was touch and go whether I was going to get the rubber-glove treatment too.

I was taken out the back by two more security gonks and once again my bag was unpacked and all my stuff was manhandled. But this time I got the full body search as well. I had to take my coat off, I had to take my jacket off – they even wanted me to undo my shirt and take my tie off. Still, of course, nothing.

I do realise that by telling you all this I will get some secret black mark against my name in the American Airlines computer so that whenever I check in with them anywhere in the world, I'm going to be given the twice-over. But, I ask you, is that the way to treat a regular business traveller, let alone one of their so-called privileged cardholders? It's not as if I was breaking any rules. In fact, I was *sticking* to the rules. It's not as if I refused to co-operate, either, although at one stage I got pretty close to it. Sure, security is security, that I understand. But look at the daft things they do in the name of security, and then I'll try to calm down.

First, what's the point of asking all those damn fool questions like 'Is this your luggage?' 'Did you pack it yourself, sir?' 'Has anyone given you anything since you met that strange man with a beard and a raincoat outside in the car park this time last year?' You can say whatever you like – how the hell are they going to know whether what you're telling them is true or not? Surely there's no point in asking questions unless you can check the answers. The whole thing is a total nonsense.

Second, if security is so vitally important to American Airlines in London that they have to create virtually all the apparatus of a police state, how come that in America, where there are far more people travelling to far more places far more often than anywhere else in the world, they don't bother about it at all? Do they think that all the nuts and psychos and terrorists confine themselves to Europe? I think we should be told.

So, what do I have to do to avoid being bounced by American Airlines in future? Take more hand luggage than I'm entitled to? Ring up their security chief beforehand and ask him how many shirts he thinks I should take with me? Forget the whole damn lot of them and take another airline?

Then there's the flight itself. I've paid more money than anybody else on the plane. I've probably flown with the airline so much I've practically bought the damn thing. Yet who's the one squeezed between two fat ladies and surrounded by a pack of howling kids? Who's got a mass of work to do and the only overhead light in the whole plane that's on the blink, not to mention an air nozzle jammed on frozen? Then this great hulk in the seat in front of me suddenly jerks back his chair. Not only does all that bat guano they call food go all over me but now I can hardly take my pen out of my pocket.

So if you're game for shooting out a couple of tyres on a 747 or, even more dangerous, kicking in a couple of check-in desks or security zones, I'm with you. Provided that we start with Row A in Gatwick's South Terminal.

Then there's everything that happens, or rather doesn't happen, when you get to wherever it was you were going in order to find out why you didn't want to go there in the first place. In fact, faraway places are well named. Not only are they usually far away from decent living conditions, fair wages, the rule of law, justice, honesty and integrity, they are usually also far away from a hassle-free existence.

For example, there are taxi drivers who are not really taxi drivers. Chauffeurs who are not really chauffeurs. And people meeting you who are not the people who are supposed to be meeting you. And that's only at Heathrow.

Then there are the people you meet while you're there. You've flown halfway round the world to meet a certain businessman who then tells you it's not really his company, he's standing in for his brother-in-law and what's more they've changed their minds anyway. Then there is the lawyer who's no more a lawyer than an empty champagne bottle and the fixer with a multi-million-dollar deal in his pocket who, believe me, is on first-name terms with everyone including the President but sleeps under a plastic sheet in whatever empty house he can break into. It almost makes you want to lose the will to live.

But the most glorious travel cons of all are the tourist cons. Crystal City, Texas. Broccoli Capital of the World. Come on. Abu Simbel. It's about as genuine as an indoor ski mountain. The Mayan Temples at Chichinitsa. They're about as authentic as a documentary on Channel Four. And as for traditional villages, authentic visits to native craft centres and, God help me, *evening folkloriques*, they're no more real than a genuine 22-carat Inca key ring. They are show business. In fact, they're worse than that. They are degrading show business: degrading for the poor guys who have to throw themselves through the hoops, hip-hop on stilts, or make yet another genuine 200-year-old tribal mask. Although to be fair I don't suppose most people would recognize a genuine African tribal chief, let alone an Arab, if he crept up from behind and goosed them.

As for the made-up cons – the Historic Rivers of Russia;

the Golden Spires of Europe; Great Railway Journeys of the World – they're a load of old hooey thought up by some marketing bod for the Sunday supplements. All praise to Chris what's-his-name. He deliberately refused to climb all seven of the world's most famous summits because he didn't want to be associated with the marketing of them.

Now let's consider the biggest con of all – eco-tourism. In a phrase that even the greenest green would understand, what a load of old garbage. I ask you, how can you possibly even mention the word when, wherever you look, 'eco-tourism' has been responsible for not only choking the Inca Trails with rubbish, but producing piles of litter in the Himalayas almost as high as Everest itself, as well as destroying whole colonies of flamingoes on the Galapagos Islands so that an airport could be built to make it easier for even more tourists to destroy everything else as well. To me, the only responsible eco-tourist is the eco-tourist who stays at home. Not that for one moment would I imagine that his home is strewn with rubbish, or that he would be prepared to dig up his garden for a new airport to be built so that millions of tourists could tramp all over his organic potatoes in order to admire the wildlife that had once been there.

Goodness me, it's no wonder that the older I get – I'm now $87\frac{1}{2}$ – the more I suffer from travel psychosis.

A few months ago when I was in Kazakhstan, I got back to my hotel after the usual round of meetings. There, standing in the middle of reception bawling their heads off, was a bunch of eco-tourists, beta-blockers coming out of their ears. All were dressed, I'm serious, in white shorts, bush jackets, pith helmets and boots the size of a duck-billed platypus, as if they had just stepped out of some 1930s travel guide to the tropics. It was too much for me. I came over all cold. (A bit like the time my wife said she wanted to come with me on my next trip.) I immediately fled to my room, emptied the mini-bar and then called reception and asked them to get me the hotel doctor, fast. But fast.

The hotel doctor, I must tell you, saved my life.

He didn't turn up.

But - the final con - I still had to pay for his services.

Peter Biddlecombe
Up the Khyber Pass.
Near the border with Afghanistan.
Negotiating to buy a counterfeit AK-47.
To end it all.

St Petersburg

Some people will do anything not to leave St Petersburg. Even when they've been invited to dinner by frail, delicate Russian princes with long, curly eyelashes who love nothing better than cruising Nevsky Prospekt in their mother's dresses; plied with cakes and Madeira laced with cyanide; shot twice in the back, four times in the courtyard; had their head smashed to pulp; been bound tooth and nail and wrapped up in a blue curtain; bundled in the back of a carriage; driven to Krestovsky Island and thrown in the icy River Neva. Even then, full of arsenic, riddled with bullets, head smashed to smithereens, he still did everything he could to free himself, so determined was he to stay. Either that or he really was as bad as people say and God was trying to put off meeting him as long as possible.

That, of course, was Rasputin.

I, on the other hand, couldn't wait to get away. Not because anyone tried to fill me full of arsenic, shoot me in the back or tie me up and wrap me in blue curtains. Worse luck. Nor because I couldn't stand St Petersburg. I thought it was fantastic. In fact, I wouldn't mind going back there again, especially in June or July to see their famous white nights, when the sun barely dips below the horizon so it never gets dark and the street lights don't have to be switched on - well, the two that work anyway. No, my reason for leaving in a hurry was the

British. There was (run for cover, lock up your daughters, even your dogs) a British trade mission, or rather the remnants of a British trade mission, in town.

I'd tried being French. But, *mon Dieu*, that didn't work. As soon as I said, '*Zut. Alors. Les perfides sont arrivés,*' I was tumbled. My mistake – I was talking to them in French, which no real Frenchman would ever dream of doing. Especially if they knew they were there on business and likely to grab even a single sou that rightly belonged to La France. I'd tried being Dutch but after just six and a half hours in the downstairs bar at the super-swish Grand Hotel Europe being wined and dined and entertained by everyone this side of the tulips I just had to buy a round. Which immediately blew my cover. I even thought of trying to be, God help me, American and bragging about… about… about… but very quickly gave up the idea. To no avail. However much I protested, the good old Brits insisted that I join them, become one of them and join in the usual round of hand-shaking and flag-waving with them on behalf of the old country.

'You must. You *must.*' An eager middle-aged young man kept jumping up and down in front of me. 'Everybody thinks that we no longer manufacture anything, that we ship it all in from Taiwan. You must help us convince them we don't.'

'Okay,' I gave in. A sucker to the end.

'By the way,' I said to this guy. 'Who are you with?'

'Sony,' he said.

Before heading for St Petersburg, I'd been in Ekaterinburg way down in the Urals in Western Siberia. It was their worst winter on record. It wasn't chilly. It wasn't frosty. It was one single, solitary, solid block of ice, which may or may not be the reason why when in the 1720s Peter the Great – who else? – founded the place as his base for building guns, cannons and all manner of weapons for killing, maiming and generally destroying men's lives, he named it after his wife, Katerin, whom he regarded as Catherine the Great Block of Ice. Inevitably, though, she thawed out for plenty of others when he wasn't around. Once when Peter (who was obviously not so great in some departments) found out that she was up to no good he had the poor guy's head chopped off, stuck in a jar of surgical spirit and put in her bedroom. As a present. By then it was too late to change the name of the place, re-do all the signposts, alter all the maps and reprint all the postcards. Even in those days Intourist was slow and inefficient. All I can say is it was just as well she wasn't called Gladys or Hilda. It was bad enough freezing to death without being somewhere called Gladysburg or Hildaburg.

The third largest city in the country after Moscow and St Petersburg and probably the third most expensive as well – a simple one-room flat that nobody can afford costs over US$100,000 – Ekaterinburg is also the cultural capital of the Urals, the capital of Sverdlovsk Economic Region and, of course, the centre of the Greater Urals Economic Region which covers the *oblats* of Chelyabinsk, Perm, Kurgan and Tyumen as well as the two tiny republics of Bashkortostan and Udmurtia. If all that is not sufficiently riveting for you, it is also the town that has more 24-hour pizza delivery services than anywhere else in Russia, as well as being the place where the tzars were killed. It has even witnessed the rise and stumble and still further rise and stumble to power of Boris Nikolaevich Yeltsin. Born just outside in Butka – it rhymes with vodka – this is where he learnt his politics, where from 1976 to 1985 he was head of the Sverdlovsk regional party and, most important of all, where he learnt to drink.

Take a bow, Ekaterinburg. Oops. Mind you don't fall over.

I went there to check out opportunities for British business. When I got to the Consulate-General's office in Gogol Street and they gave me a 24-page briefing which contained four pages on bars, hotels and restaurants and just three paragraphs on Opportunities for British Business, I decided there and then to give up. Especially when half the hotels listed were in the middle of blocks of flats, contained no more than four or five rooms including a sauna, and insisted on cash in advance. Wasn't it Gogol, by the way, who wrote comic stories about government civil servants? Wonder what made them pick that address.

Instead of packing my hot vodka bottle and heading back to the sun, I thought I'd try to take advantage of the unique contribution the town has made to the latter half of the twentieth century and try to find out if I could also be taught to drink like a fish and still survive double pneumonia, quintuple heart bypass surgery, two attempted coups and a dunk in a lake in the village of Uspyenskoye, 24 miles outside Moscow, whether he was pushed by his very own secret servicemen, as he said, or not.

In the old days, I mean before glasnost and perestroika, Ekaterinburg didn't exist. At least not officially. Like Chelyabinsk, Tomsk, Ktasnoyarsk, this was one of the hidden, closed, unknown towns until 1960 when on May Day Garry Powers was snooping overhead in his U2 spy plane and the Russians shot him out of the sky, thus destroying the big summit conference which was about to begin in Paris. For three hundred years Russia's engineering, industrial and energy powerhouse, at the time it was full of nothing but top secret munitions plants, top secret biological warfare establishments and, of course, massive top secret vodka deposits. Come the last war, as soon as Stalin realised that his ex-colleagues' decision to position all these key establishments close to the borders in the Ukraine and Western Russia was not exactly a good idea, especially with Hitler casting his beady little eye on them, he had them all virtually uprooted and stuck a million miles from everywhere in the middle of the Urals which, with Europe on the left and Asia on the right, stretch two thousand kilometres from Kazakhstan in the south way up practically to the Arctic. Though why they call them mountains, I have no idea. They barely hit two thousand metres anywhere. Obviously there must be a Texan influence somewhere in the background. I'm not talking about garden shed operations either. Some of these plants were big, big time, often employing as many as 80,000 people. Of course, 79,998 were administration and only two guys were actually doing any work but they were still some operation.

Today, however, the place is not worth a roll of film, let alone losing a spy plane over. The town itself is Identikitski Sovietski Cityski No 9. Well, everything to do with Yeltsin has got to be one over the eight, hasn't it?

The main street is in the shape of a hammer. The Hotel Iset at the end is, I swear, shaped like a sickle. I should know. I was staying in the curved sickle bit which meant I spent my life there going round and round in semi-circles. Although credit where credit is due, I didn't have to lock the door to my room the whole time I was there. Multiple coats of paint did the trick.

Just out of the hotel, up the main hammer of a street on the left is the Opera House, where for just 100 roubles or the outrageous sum of US$3 I sat practically in the middle of the stage for yet another rousing production of *Il Trovatore.* Outside facing it is a statue of Yakov Sverdlovsk, who, on the night of 16 July 1918, decided to shoot for the Tzars, starting with Alexei and Maria, the youngest. For he was the guy who ordered the killing of Tzar Nicholas and his family in the basement of the house owned by Nikolai Ipatev on Voznesensky Prospekt. I don't know who the sculptor was but he seemingly had a wicked sense of humour because Sverdlovsk, who was obviously a big fan of royalty, privilege and inherited wealth, is pointing at the cellar as if to say, 'They're down there. Get on with it. I'll go and put the samovar on.' I only hope he didn't have too tough a time in the camps. Sverdlovsk went on to have even greater shame heaped on him. He had the town named after him. Which it remained until 1991 when it reverted back to Ekaterinburg.

I don't know about you, but having been to Ekaterinburg, having read the reports of the murders, the bayoneting, the petrol not to mention the acid baths, I cannot believe all this Anastasia business. It's just not possible. It's not as if a couple of guys just turned up out of nowhere and started firing blindly into the room and then went off for a drink; then maybe one of them could possibly have survived. But these guys were professionals. Well, maybe not at killing Tzars and Tzarinas and the Russian royal family, but at killing people. There was a whole gang of them and they knew what they were up to. For Anastasia to have survived would have meant all of them agreeing to it: it's just not possible.

Further up the street, past one vast monolithic slab after another (the big, smudgy, dirty, green building on the left was Yeltsin's office when he ran the place. You can tell by the pile of empties that are still waiting outside to be collected) is the head of the hammer or rather, the main square. Most people say the statue in the far corner shows Lenin complete with regulation waistcoat and overcoat pondering the dilemmas between anarchy and democracy, personal dictatorship and governmental chaos, parasitic capitalism and the price of a *pelmeni*, a meat-filled Siberian dumpling. Don't you believe it. Look carefully. He's waving his hand in the air and grandly proclaiming that the run-down old building on the corner that the local council refuses to pull down is where his baby brother Dmitri focused his attention not on establishing a mighty Communist empire but on surviving as a poor, humble photographer – which, come to think of it, means both of them must have been responsible for putting innumerable people up against walls and shooting them.

Today this historic monument is suitably honoured by the Russian people with a giant ten-foot high sign proudly proclaiming 'Konica Films and Cameras'.

Further down is the River Iset where, not that you'll believe me for a second, I actually for the first time in my life walked on water. Well, all right then. It was frozen solid. There was enough ice there for a good few vodkas for President Yeltsin. But it was still walking on water.

Just before you get to the square, if you turn right by the Comedy Theatre and up a couple of blocks, is, if you must know, where I tried to walk on ice – and fell over. Just opposite the house where they shot the Tzars, or rather where the house used to be. In 1977, the year after Yeltsin took over as the local party boss, suddenly one night it was flattened to the ground on the orders of the big boozer himself. Secret orders, he said. In a sealed envelope. From Moscow. In fact, so secret were they, nobody else ever saw them.

Make a Tzar trek up there today and the site has been cleared and levelled. All that's there is a tiny shoe-box of a chapel, an open shelter, a stone slab, a simple cross and the occasional Tzar-struck old lady actually kneeling in the snow and ice, praying and kissing the cross. But be careful of the ice, especially opposite the grand old Church of the Ascension where I did my descending trick. Suddenly I was surrounded by fallen women. The reason? Yeltsin had invited Chancellor Köhl and President Chirac to visit his home town for some big conference or other. Were they all running around agonising over how they were going to repay Russia's US$100 billion of foreign debt, where they were going to find almost US$10 billion in unpaid wages and what on earth were they going to do about the US$12 billion backlog in pensions owed by both the public and the private sectors? No way. They were all running around turning the thick snow and sludge over so that the white side was on top. As a result everybody was sliding and skidding all over the place. Not to mention, as far as the select one or two were concerned, skating on very thin ice.

The officials were also having great fun trying to decide which way up they should fly their proud new Russian flag. They might have known how to keep the red flag flying but they had no idea about their horizontal red, blue and white affair – or should it be the opposite, white, blue and red? A huge mountain bear of a man, 20 foot, 30 stone, nothing but thick, long black hair – he could have been either the head of Russian security or a Russian Orthodox priest in civvies – was adamant. It was red, blue and white. Red was always on top. A tiny, shrivelled-up sparrow of a woman, who for some reason or other had three tiny white kittens cuddled up together inside some filthy shopping bag, said, as women usually do, the exact opposite. The correct way to fly it? I hate to say it but the little old lady was right. White on top. Blue in the middle. Red underneath. How do I remember? Easy. White on top is the snow that blanketed everything that fateful night. Blue the colour of their veins. Red the colour of their blood seeping into the Russian soil.

The highlight of the two presidents' visit was going to be a quick trip to the Ural State Technical University where Yeltsin studied and later qualified. Known as the UPI, Uralsky Politekhnichesky Institut, Russian for Cut the crap, open the bottle, you've got to admit, it must have been a damn sight more fun there than studying Classical Greek with blokes in dresses. Maybe I should have gone there instead. Most students when they go to university are only interested in getting one, maybe two degrees. Yeltsin, I was told, was absolutely dedicated to getting no less than the full 65 degrees. Night after night after night. Year after year after year. They say that when he finally left for Moscow he didn't leave his heart behind in Ekaterinburg. He left his liver behind instead.

But that's not what he is most remembered for as

student, party chief and governor. Well, apart from being a real *muzhik*, in other words one of the lads, taking the tram to work every day, visiting all the local factories, nuclear warhead assembly plants and not missing a single official dinner held anywhere in the town, his big achievement was closing down Sverdlovsk-17 (cough, cough), the big biological weapons plant where one day because of a tiny, insignificant failure in all their 100-per-cent fail-proof security systems (cough, cough), a tiny, insignificant amount of gas just happened to (cough, cough) escape into the atmosphere. What gas was it? Anthrax (zonk).

This very nice man I met in a white coat who said he worked for a pharmaceutical and vaccine company called Biopreparat looked straight at me with his third eye and assured me it was perfectly harmless. When I asked him why the Russians hadn't opened up any of their other biological weapons sites at Kirov, Sergiyev Posad and the big new one at Strizhi to international inspection, as everybody else had done years ago, the eye positively spun round and round like a roulette wheel. Luckily his third leg stopped him falling over.

Well, I say the place is not worth a roll of film. The only things worth photographing in Ekaterinburg today are the architectural delights of Factory No 9 which manufactures guns, which wasn't allowed; those in the El Dorado nightclub which was not allowed either and Garry Powers' old spy plane which was allowed but wasn't there. For a long time I'd been told it had been exhibit number one in the Military History Museum. Unfortunately when I went to see it, I got a negative. It had gone. Where it had been taken nobody could tell me. They couldn't even show me a photograph of it either.

The frightening thing, however, is that Ekaterinburg could have been the equal of London, Washington, Tokyo, Bonn and, of course, last of all Paris. Had the coup attempt in Moscow in 1991 succeeded Yeltsin had apparently already not only drawn up plans to make Ekaterinburg his capital in exile, he'd already selected which of the old Second World War bunkers was going to be his headquarters. The one with all the vodka in it.

Having 'done' Ekaterinburg, the sensible thing would have been for me then to fly back to St Petersburg. But you know how I love the challenge of travel. I decided to go by train.

For years I'd been told I just had to try the Trans-Siberian Express. For years I'd read books about it. An adventure, I was told. Exciting, I was told. The thrill of a lifetime, I was told. Nonsense. It was boring b-o-r-i-n-g, zzzzzzzzzzzzzz.

First of all, there's no such thing as a Trans-Siberian Express. There are a million different lines criss-crossing Russia east of Moscow. The whole mishmash is grandly called the Trans-Siberian Express. Second, whatever train you get, the last thing it is is Express. It's like the Channel Tunnel train from Folkestone to London. It trundles. It stops. It trundles again. The whole thing is practically covered in cobwebs. For the first time you actually realise that Russia is twice as big as the United States. As a result it takes ages. From Ekaterinburg to St Petersburg is about 1,500 miles. It took me practically 36 hours, at an average speed of 40 miles an hour. See what I mean about trundling. It probably would have been quicker to walk. Furthermore, I reckon I spent six whole years staring at the same patch of snow, the same two trees and the same pile of wood. There was so much snow that not only was I unable to see the big white obelisk which is supposed to mark the divide between East and West, Europe and Asia, I couldn't even see the Urals.

The only good thing about the train was the restaurant car. Not because of the food. Which wasn't. But because of the drink. The smallest measure they served was a carafe. Of vodka. I reckon I did about 60 miles to the carafe. If the journey had been any longer I'd have needed a quintuple heart bypass operation myself by the end of it.

I arrived in St Petersburg about the same time as Rasputin called in at Yusupov Palace for a quick snifter with Prince Felix, who he must have reckoned, with his long curly eyelashes and his taste for sashaying around town in his mother's dresses picking up sailors, was the unlikeliest hitman in history. Which just goes to show how wrong a self-proclaimed, superhuman, infallible evil genius with psychic powers can be. Although I must say when I discovered that, as an old man, Prince Felix ended up living in exile in Paris, plastered with mascara, changing his wig three times a day before breakfast, lunch and dinner and, worst of all, hanging out with the Windsors, I did feel just a tiny shred of sympathy for old Rasputin and the enormous efforts he made to stay in St Petersburg. After all, apart from the fact that it's the last place on earth any self-respecting, sensible, practical person would ever want to build a city (in the middle of a desolate, rain-sodden swamp on the edge of the River Neva, where it curves round to meet the Gulf of Finland, unless of course you're Peter the Great and your motto is Never say Neva), I'd say that even at four o'clock in the morning, in a raging snow storm in the freezing cold, it really is without doubt one of the great cities not of Russia but of the world. Actually, in many respects it's too good for Russia. It's glamorous. It's extravagant. It's palatial. It's... it's fantastic. It would be better off in Austria or in the Czech Republic or maybe even down the road in Sussex.

St Petersburg has 44 islands, 60 rivers and 576 bridges. Practically everywhere you turn there are fabulous fancy wedding-cake palaces, huge cathedrals and churches. My favourite has got to be St Isaac's: when they built it they discovered that the dome designed by a French architect wasn't wide enough for the pillars underneath to support it. The city has massive broad avenues, enormous squares, triumphant arches includ-ing, the most famous of all, the golden arches of

McDonald's, not to mention a million tiny, cramped, dingy back streets and mile after mile after mile of not just nineteenth-century but twentieth-century slums. Take just the Nevsky Prospekt. Four kilometres long, six lanes wide, it must be one of the grandest streets in Europe. Talking of prospekts, incidentally, there were no titled ladies of society with or without tiny gold Chanel buttons awaiting me when I checked in at the hotel. Instead the only thing I could hear was the sound of my serious, hardworking, dedicated fellow country-men knocking back life-size glasses of vodka; sliding and slipping and slurping all over the bar, trying to persuade a whole bunch of serious St Petersburgers to play something they called Pass the Pickled Egg, which involved a row of people passing a pickled egg from mouth to mouth; telling long, complicated jokes about if all the girls working in Reception were laid end to end…; and finally, the climax of the evening, every-body howling away at the top of their voices:

If you love the Ayatollah, slap your head
If you love the Ayatollah, slap your head
If you love the Ayatollah
If you love the Ayatollah
If you love the Ayatollah, slap your head.

Which certainly made a change from that other well-known song beloved of British trade missions around the world, *The Hole in the Elephant's Bottom*. As if that was not enough, when the bar closed they insisted on marching everyone either to their waiting cars outside or along the corridors to their rooms while chanting continuously the final rousing chorus of that well-known traditional English song: *En-ger-land, En-ger-land, En-ger-land*. In other words, meet your typical British trade mission. Or rather, remnant of. I tell you, if we had had a shred of influence left in the world, we would have finally lost it that night. But then on the other hand Dostoevsky did say St Petersburg was for the half-mad. Except these guys were behaving as if they were rip-roaring, way-over-the-top, one-hundred-per-cent totally British insane.

Not, of course, that this was the first British trade mission I'd come across. I've seen them all before. In Europe I remember one whisky-sodden ambassador staggering into an official reception just as we were all about to leave.

'Dashed bad luck. So looking forward to...'

An assorted collection of flunkies helped him to the nearest chair.

'F-fab-fabulous job you chaps doing. Al-al-always admired our trades people. N-n-need m-m-more like...'

Then he fell fast asleep. We crept out trying not to interrupt his no doubt glorious dreams of how he single-handedly reversed Britain's decline as a major exporting nation.

Benefit to British exports: nil.

In the Middle East, the chairman of the local Chamber of Commerce was so impressed by the leader of another British trade mission I was on, he named a goat after him. Our leader, would you believe, was impressed. I felt sorry for the goat.

Benefit to British exports: nil.

In the Far East, the high spot of yet another mission was a photograph of our leader, obviously bombed out of his mind, his arms around a couple of waiters, twiddling a cocktail stick in front of his nose in a decidedly unmacho manner.

Benefit to British exports: nil.

But the most hilarious, sorry I mean the worst, most degrading, insulting behaviour of all, was again in the Far East. For some reason I cannot now remember I got tied up with a mission doing the usual round. It was jointly led by three men who wherever we went, whoever we met, insisted on announcing themselves as Ben, Doon and Phil McCavity. It was hilarious, I mean, grossly offensive to our hosts. We'd no sooner arrive anywhere, at the Chamber of Commerce, at the Central Bank, in a minister's office, than everybody was bowing and scraping and repeating, again and again, Ben, Doon and Phil McCavity. It was a riot, I mean, the most stupid, childish, senseless thing you could imagine.

Wherever in the world you come across a British export mission, you can always guarantee two things.

First, ambassadors, commercial attachés even temporary, assistant, junior, part-time, semi-retired secretaries of commercial attachés, will go on and on about missions being the most important thing in Anglo-wherever relations – yet they can hardly drag themselves out of the bar long enough even to give you the name and number of the local Chamber of Commerce, let alone tell you the important people to meet and companies to visit.

Second, before you arrive, wherever you're going, the local British Embassy will assure you the place is calm, quiet, safe, secure and, absolutely old chap, *totally* stable. What's more, they are desperate to do business with Britain. What! When you get there you find the place is in uproar. Students are taking to the streets. Troops are lurking around every corner. Taxis are out on strike. Buses have stopped running for fear of being stoned by not only the students but the taxi drivers as well, who are frightened they'll take their business away from them. And farmers are bringing in their tractors to blockade every street in town. You go to the official mission briefing in this huge luxury house you think can only belong to the ambassador. But it doesn't. It's the second commercial under-secretary's house. The ambassador's home is even bigger with, so confident is he of the peace and stability of the place, walls that are two foot thick, doors of reinforced steel and windows made of bazooka-proof glass.

Then in swans the ambassador.

'I'm sure this…this…this situation won't inconvenience you too much,' he smarms, his car outside the door, his driver at the wheel, the engine running, as he goes on to explain he's got this urgent appointment with somebody or other in the middle of the country and must leave immediately.

'I'm terribly sorry about this,' the assistant-deputy-under-trade-counsellor twice removed rushes to apologise, as the door slams behind the ambassador and we can't help but notice his car head off, not to the centre of the country, but to the airport and the midday flight back home.

'This little matter,' oozes the assistant, deputy whatever who has been in the office for all of three months, 'we only had confirmation that it was going to take place two weeks ago. If we had had any earlier notice we would naturally have informed you of the situation.'

Two weeks ago! We were all still at home two weeks ago, listening to the wife going on about how we spend all our time travelling the world enjoying ourselves. If we'd known about this, er, little matter two weeks ago we wouldn't have bothered to waste our time and hard-earned money dragging ourselves halfway across the…

Does anyone say a word? Does anyone admit it is now a complete waste of time being there? Does anyone ask the oh-so-simple question: so if you knew about it two weeks ago why the hell didn't you tell us instead of sitting around drinking pink gin at the British Club and doing nothing? Not on your life! Everybody just plods back to the bus, back to the hotel to spend the rest of the visit hiding under the table while the students and the riot police battle it out. Except, that is, for the Jewish mother and son. There is always a Jewish mother and son on every trade mission. Believe me.

Momma immediately rushes off to the students

offering them an instant deal in Israeli-made tear-gas shells, anti tear-gas sprays, tin helmets, body protectors. Delivery guaranteed in 24 hours. Negotiable credit terms. Knowing Israeli Momma's, she is also bound to offer them a container load of tomato ketchup so that they can smear themselves all over with the stuff, get their photographs in the world's press and wait for public opinion to draw the necessary conclusions about how their peaceful demonstration was ruthlessly put down by the authorities.

The son, on the other hand, races off to the riot police and offers them a special price on everything from Israeli-made handcuffs and CS-gas canisters to special armoured shields and rubber bullets. Delivery guaranteed in 24 hours. Negotiable credit terms.

Having done that, both then rush back to the hotel to start phoning – to place the orders; to arrange delivery; to get you-know-who in Tel Aviv to call you-know-who the other end to arrange against all rules, laws and regulations to let an emergency flight land at the far end of the civilian airport in the middle of the night on the basis that otherwise it might be difficult to organise for his personal security service to renew their contract at one minute past midnight that night which might create all kinds of problems. In addition, you can bet your life they also make contact with the agricultural attaché in the local Israeli Embassy and warn him that there is an acute danger of the local farmers blocking the streets of the capital with all their US, German and Russian-built tractors. And if this happened they would obviously be severely damaged if not completely destroyed, which would subsequently mean big orders for new tractors if not for huge quantities of spare parts. If he could persuade the farmers to buy Israeli-made tractors...

Benefits to British exports: nil.

As for the typical members of the typical British trade

mission, the vast majority of them apparently want nothing to do with trade. Well, apart from certain sectors of the after-dark cash trade. As for the mission, their only mission is to avoid as much as possible anything to do with the poor, unfortunate country they're visiting and to get bombed out of their minds as quickly and as cheaply as possible. Invariably this means they hit all the lunches and dinners and cocktail parties and embassy receptions they can get to, arrive early, stay as long as they can, then head for the nearest, cheapest local boozer.

It's not always the trade missioners who are bombed out of their minds. Once on one of my regular swings through South America I happened to pop into a hotel bar around eleven o'clock one morning to find it packed solid with members of a British trade mission waiting for the local British commercial attaché to turn up to give them an intensive in-depth breakfast briefing. Come lunchtime he stumbled into the bar. He'd had a hard time the night before, he mumbled apologetically. He'd slept in. He'd rushed to the hotel and straight into the first conference room he came across where, would you believe, he'd spent the whole morning giving his breakfast briefing to the rival Danish trade mission which was staying at the same hotel. He only discovered his mistake, he told us, when at the end he finished speaking and they not only started asking far more serious questions than he usually got from visiting British missions but they spoke better English as well. Hence the old joke, 'What's the difference between a British ambassador and a supermarket trolley? They both have minds of their own. But you can get more food and drink into a British ambassador.'

As for the trade missioners themselves, they're always the same.

There are the innocents: the guys who not only do dummy runs to the airport to make sure they don't miss the plane but take their mother with them as well to check the timing. Worse still, they insist on telling you about it again and again and again the whole length of the mission. There are the colonels, who over a long and illustrious career across the world's continents have progressed steadily from captain, major, colonel to junior export sales assistant, and are still knocking at preferment's door. They are invariably as dull as a Toc-H lamp, were it not for the perpetual shine from their one and only suit which they wear morning, noon and night. Their only interest seems to be spending meeting after meeting sitting with their dirty black plastic briefcase on their knees surreptitiously sliding out their thumb-stained *Abridged Ritual: The Masonic Handbook* for another quick flip-through.

There are the eager young graduates who although they've only hung up their satchels all of two, maybe three months before, are already the world's greatest leading experts on everything under the sun. They are also so conceited that on their birthdays you can bet your life they send their mothers cards saying, Congratulations. One such eager young graduate I shall never forget. He was trying to sell copies of *Three Little Pigs* to Arab countries.

There are the smarmy know-alls who invariably head for the nearest minister, banker, ambassador or, heaven help us, commercial attaché they spot and proceed to crawl so far up their backsides they end up practically cleaning their teeth.

There are the crossover queens who seem to be intent on extending the hand of friendship perhaps further than most of us would ever dare imagine. They go around forever sipping tiny glasses of Tanqueray Gin, shrieking about having a rear entry visa, advising everybody they meet to keep in touch with themselves and offering mouth-to-mouth resuscitation to all and sundry. 'Man, woman or dog,' they keep screaming, 'throw it on the bed.'

But, lest you are tempted to despair at the quality of

the mighty British export machine, let me assure you the backbone of any trade mission, the guys without whom no trade mission, or at least no British trade mission, would be possible are the boozers. The guys with the overdeveloped right arms. The guys who wear cloth caps in the plane, insist on trying to find a parachute for the drinks trolley and tip the pilot on the way out. The guys who walk around all day with a spare pair of what they call drinking trousers, brag about how they won the VD and scar, convert the coffee machine in their room to a gin-and-tonic maker with a thirty-minute cycle and think nothing of having three steaks washed down by two lobsters for breakfast.

Oops. I almost forgot.

Last and certainly the least comes the chairman or the leader of the mission. No matter who they are or where they come from or how many times they've visited the country before, somehow or other they manage not just to communicate their total ignorance of the market and their complete inability to sell anything, they positively flaunt it.

The mission, or rather the remnant of the mission, in St Petersburg was no exception. When I saw them the following afternoon in the hotel lobby – none of them was in a fit state to get up in the morning – the innocent guy was slumped in a corner playing with his money belt; the Colonel was re-fighting the Battle of El Alamein with some poor helpless hotel porter which by my calculation must have made him all of $8\frac{1}{2}$ at the time; the eager young graduate was studying an *Economist* intelligence report on Russia that was so out of date I reckon in its usual authoritative way it was forecasting that the Tzar was safe and rumours of a revolution were greatly exaggerated. The smarmy know-all turned out to be a lawyer. Or at least I think he was. All I know was he kept on telling me he was an expert on the Marriage Act. The crossover queens were prancing around with the doormen. 'If you'd had a shave this morning, I'd have given you a big kiss,' they were squealing. As for the chairman, he was fulfilling the chairman's role perfectly. He was nowhere to be seen.

As is my luck I got buttonholed by one of the boozers. He was filthy. He smelt like a couple of breweries. Russian breweries. He was swearing and cursing and chasing all the women in sight. That apart, I'm sure he also had his faults. He told me he was called Fingers. He was also, he said, chairman, vice-chairman and chief usher of the DBA Society.

'DBA Society?'

'Dodgy Blondes Appreciation Society.' He nudged me with a half-empty bottle of vodka. 'By 'eck. That always gets 'em.'

He surveyed his colleagues.

'Useless,' he said. 'They can't take the pace. As for the chairman, we've got to wait another hour for him before he's late.'

He wanted me to do the rounds with them. Not for my expert knowledge of Russia and the Russians. Not for my vast knowledge of Russian industry and how it operates. Not even for my still wider experience of all the best bars and clubs in town. He wanted me to help make up the numbers. What could I do? Desert my fellow countrymen and let the French ... In any case I learnt a long time ago that trade missions are a fabulous way of making money. Whenever we go to a lunch or a dinner or some kind of reception I always take bets among both members of the mission as well as among our poor, unfortunate hosts as to how long the speeches will last; how often they'll mention Mrs Thatcher; how often they get the name of the leader of the mission wrong; how long he'll actually stay awake to hear the speeches. Indeed, so successful have I been that many's the time I've paid for the whole mission out of my winnings. Now if that doesn't deserve a Queen's Award for Exports, I don't know what does.

Then, of course, it occurred to me.

'Hey, why do they call you Fingers?' I asked him.

'Because I'm hanging on to my job by my fingertips. Why else?'

Why else indeed.

I said I'd join them – and I immediately called the travel agents and asked them to book me on the next available flight out. Which obviously meant I had to reschedule all my own important meetings, like seeing the sights.

I'd read a lot about St Petersburg and, of course, Peter the Great. About how all 6 feet 7 inches of him loped around Europe disguised as an ordinary sailor called Peter Mikhailov. Except that Mikhailov means leader of his people. About how he worked as an ordinary carpenter in the Dutch shipyards in Zaandam although reports and pictures and engravings at the time show him in powdered wig, frock coat and buckled shoes, which to me says a lot about Dutch shipworkers at the time. About how he came to London in January 1698 when he was 25 years old insisting that he be treated as an ordinary ruler of an ordinary country that at the time was the biggest in the world; that the visit remain secret and that the king, William III, pick up the tab. Which obviously proves he did at least learn something from his visit to Holland. And about how the new skills he picked up not surprisingly in Deptford in South London made him more of a rock Tzar than a real Tzar. For he not only virtually destroyed Sayes Court, where he stayed, he also, far more seriously as far as the English are concerned, completely wrecked the garden hailed by Samuel Pepys himself as this 'most beautiful place...a lovely, noble ground', and in particular a glorious 40-year-old, 9-foot high, 400-foot long holly hedge by running backwards and forwards through it with a dwarf sitting in a wheelbarrow.

Come on. You don't mean to say you believe all this stuff about him being a worker, a man of the people, the second greatest carpenter in the history of the world?

He was a maniac. The cost of his three-month stay in Deptford: broken chairs; smashed windows; stained carpets; one bedstead 'broke to pieces'; three beds smashed to smithereens; not to mention three wheelbarrows – exactly £350 in total, according to none other than the great Sir Christopher Wren himself, who in between building churches was also the Court Surveyor at the time.

Did Peter pay up? Of course he didn't. I told you he learnt a lot from the Dutch. But at least he left with an example of the latest British technology: a 6-foot-6-inch long leather coffin studded with brass nails. He wanted it as an example to his fellow countrymen. First, because there were a number he preferred to see dead. Second, because the custom in Russia was to be buried in single hollow tree trunks which meant his beloved navy was rapidly running out of wood.

Once he got home and unpacked – so that's where the other wheelbarrow went – he did what all great men do when they get back from visiting Europe. He ran around cutting everybody's beards off, beheaded 1,500 men, strangled 700 others, and cut off the ears and noses of another 400 as part of the entertainment at a special banquet to celebrate his return. That out of the way, he immediately started building a European city all of his own. Before you could say 'forget the damage he did to Sayes Court, it always pays off in the end,' 640 Dutch engineers, craftsmen and artists were pouring in. Clogs unpacked, they immediately set about doing what they're renowned for throughout the world: draining marshes, digging canals and avoiding buying anyone a drink. St Petersburg, don't forget, was originally called Sankt Pieter Burkh, so Dutch was the place and everything in it.

But it was not to last. Somebody told Peter about some fancy place in Florida, surrounded by water, with an art gallery the biggest attraction in town and he promptly renamed it St Petersburg. Then the Italians turned up. The Dutch got the heave-ho, presumably because they didn't buy their round of drinks. The Italians, no doubt as a result of their traditional charms not to mention their traditional way of doing business, then took over. Which, of course, is why today the city is known the world over as the Venice of the North and not the Amsterdam of the North.

Wander around St Petersburg today and I'm always surprised it hasn't got skid marks all over the place. For just 22 years after turning over the first sod it was finished. So too were hundreds of thousands of other poor sods. Because in his drive to build a European city and open up Russia to the civilising influence of the West, Peter adopted a deadly Asian approach to the matter. Heavily armed recruiting gangs were sent out all over Russia to ship back all the poor Russian peasants, Swedish prisoners of war and poor unfortunates who couldn't buy them off to enlist in the great enterprise. Come 1722, built, paved and lit, the city was proclaimed the Imperial Capital of Our Holy Mother, Russia. Trouble was nobody wanted to go there apart from a couple of billion mosquitoes in summer and a little chap called *giardia*. What the Great Peter forgot, or maybe what his great Dutch builders failed to tell him, was that in any big city in the world it is possible to pick up nasty little parasites that can cause, among other things, headaches, bloatedness and diarrhoea. In St Peterburg's case these are called *giardia*.

Peter's wife, like all wives, was the first to criticise. 'St Petersburg,' she declared, 'will stand empty.' The aristocracy moaned. There was no way they wanted to leave the big village of Moscow so Peter had to lay the law down. He issued an imperial edict ordering 1,000 aristocratic families, not to mention another 1,000 businessmen, bankers and traders, to move in. Doctors and nurses he didn't have to tell. They could see the opportunities for themselves. But once Peter was dead and buried (no doubt in a single hollowed-out tree trunk) everybody promptly rushed back to Moscow again, led by his wife, now Tzarina Catherine, no doubt clutching the head of her lover still in the jar of surgical spirit.

Having done my homework and in the process become the world's greatest living authority on St Petersburg I naturally wanted to do the town. I wanted to see the tiny two-room log cabin where our man of the people, our son of the soil, the second greatest carpenter in the history of the world, sat in his scruffy clothes, slurping his kraut soup, supervising the building of his European city. I expect he was just far enough away from the river so he couldn't see the thousands of his poor workers who were dying on the spot like, well, mosquitoes, from lack of food and shelter and being promptly swept out to sea. Or where he couldn't hear the screams of his son, Alexei, whom he had ordered to be beaten to death in the Peter and Paul Fortress for conspiring against him. At the same time he could put his feet up at the end of a busy day banning stone buildings the length and breadth of Russia, throttling the occasional adviser and dream of fireworks and for some reason, dwarves and dwarves' weddings.

I wanted to take in the Peter and Paul Fortress or to give it its unofficial name, the Russian House of Literature. Dostoevsky was imprisoned there. So was Gogol. In fact all the best guys were. In Russian literary circles it was said you were not worthy to be considered in the same breath as Tolstoy let alone Jeffrey Archer unless you'd served your time there.

I wanted to visit the Taurida Palace built by Catherine the Great who, as she got older, looked more and more like a battleship for her lover, Prince Potemkin, who was so moved by her death that he threw a ball for 300 guests to mark the occasion. Afterwards her son, Tzar Paul, turned it into stables. Why they call him mad, I have no idea. It seems a perfectly sensible idea to me.

I wanted to call in at Our Lady of Kazan, the Bernini-look-alike designed and built to be the third largest cathedral in the world, which under the Communists became instead the world's largest museum of atheism and is now the world's largest museum of religions and religious development.

I wanted to pay my respects at the Big House on Liteing Prospekt where for so many people their prospekts were zero. Once in there, if you came out at all you were either dead or on a one-way ticket to the camps.

I wanted to wander round the same dirty back streets full of grime and punishment like Dostoevsky, who at one time or other lived and drank glass after glass of freshly brewed tea in practically every street in the city – unlike Gogol, who wished he could have moved around as much but had so much trouble with his haemorrhoids it took him all his time to hobble backwards and forwards to the chemist. Pushkin wished he hadn't done any wandering at all: when he got back from one particular probe into all kinds of exciting and desirable places he discovered his wife, Natalia, was having an affair with a French soldier. He promptly challenged the man to a duel, lost, staggered home, collapsed on a couch and like any good storyteller spun out his dying for two nights and a day. Where was his home, or rather first-floor flat? Round the corner from the Cathedral of the Spilled Blood, which to me looks like a first draft for St Basil's Cathedral in Moscow. Worse still, in the true tradition of Russian literature, it was later discovered the affair was false. Pushkin's wife was as faithful to him as any other wife. The French soldier had been paid to make out she wasn't. The guy down the road in the big house overlooking the river made the whole thing up because he was after Natalia and naturally wanted Pushkin out of the way.

I wanted to go to the last flat Dostoevsky stayed in in Kuznechny *perelok*, just up from the market where he wrote *The Brothers Karamazov*. There is still a cup of tea on his desk, made fresh every day. Beside it is his personal icon: his box of tobacco. Also some note from his daughter, no doubt insisting he give up smoking or she would sue him for all his royalties under some passive smoking law or whatever. The area around Sadovaya metro station he used as the setting for *Crime and Punishment* – not that Raskolnikov, the murderer, would dare go down there today. With or without his axe.

I wanted to check out all the other dives where Mussorgsky, Borodin, Turgenev, Glinka and Rimsky-Korsakov, not to mention Tchaikovsky, Wagner and Berlioz, used to hang out, as well as the amputated nose which Gogol claimed had developed a life of its own and spent all its spare time wandering around town. Well, he did have haemorrhoids, didn't he?

But it was not to be. Instead, for the sake of the balance of payments, I dragged myself from meeting to meeting.

Wait a minute. Was that the Smolny Institute, the school for ladies-in-waiting built by Catherine the Great in 1764, which was Lenin's first headquarters while he was dictator-in-waiting? And that statue there. Wasn't that Dzerzhinsky, the founder of the KGB? And the Astoria Hotel. Wasn't that where Hitler planned to hold his Victory dinner? They even had the invitations printed. Instead for 900 days and at the cost of over a million lives they denied him the pleasure. Hey, hold on. That must have been the Aurora, the most destructive ship ever built. It fired just one shot, a blank, on the night of 25 October 1917, sank the Russian royal family and launched the start of the October Revolution. And, of course, I wanted to visit The Hermitage with its 1,500 rooms and 2.8 million exhibits, including more Rembrandts and Picassos and dusty corridors than you can imagine.

But first, of course, I insisted on doing those things that a man who spends his life dragging himself around the world for a living has got to do: pay a courtesy call on the powers that be. In this case the Kazans, the

Malishevs, the Tambovs and last but not least, the Vorkytins. In other words the four Mafia gangs that virtually control the place. Who mentioned Chicago in the Thirties? All I will say is, if you're invited to a St Valentine's Day party next year, think about it.

How do you find them?

Easy. Up Nevsky Prospekt from Moscow Station to Aprokhim Bridge where all the horse statues seem to prove that you don't have to whisper in horses' ears to tame them like Monty Roberts says. You've just got to take all your clothes off, which obviously, according to Russian practice, scares the hell out of them to such a degree that they immediately start eating out of your hand. Hopefully. Then turn left by that fancy-looking store where an old lady spends all day long trying to sell the same greasy old picture of Stalin. Welcome to the world of Dostoevsky. The unbearable stench from the drinking dens has gone. The old pros have swopped their old, green-coloured three-storey houses on the canal for mobile phones and the Grand Hotel Europe. But the place is still full of scaffolding, bricks, dust and dirty, stinking courtyards. During the Nazi siege, which killed ten times as many people as Hiroshima, this was also where, would you believe it, traders having run out of cats, dogs, rats and even old boots actually bought and sold human flesh, so desperate were people for anything to eat in order to survive.

Now go up to any of the women standing around with a picture of a gun stuck on her coat. She will tell you who to talk to. A word of advice – it helps to break the ice a bit if you talk about the odd consignment of gas guns or Kalashnikovs. If you mention you might also be in the market for the odd assassination at US$5,000 a shot – oops. Sorry about that – they might even invite you in for a drink. Another word of advice. Whatever you do, sit facing the door.

When I was there I met one guy who looked like what they call an ex-SpetsNaz, a commando in the

Russian Special Forces. He was doing a roaring trade in secondhand police sirens. Slap them on the roof of your car, he told me, and you are guaranteed to get home from work twice as quickly. Going to work? Don't be daft. No Russian ever rushes to get to work.

So having paid my respects to the powers that be, I attended my usual round of meetings: in this case, a string of computer software companies doing roaring business in the West via the Internet. Within a couple of hours I was filing in with the rest of the trade mission to some confidential, top-level meeting with a bunch of Russians. We all sat down around this big table. It was obvious who was the chairman of the Russian delegation. He was confident, smartly groomed, sitting in the middle of his colleagues. Our chairman, who looked like a colonic irrigator, was sitting at the end by the corner with his briefcase open on top of the table looking as though he was having labour pains.

The Russian chairman spoke first. He welcomed us, felt sure we'd enjoy ourselves, was confident we'd all do business and make money. All in beautiful, faultless English. Our chairman didn't actually want to say anything. He looked as though he was dreaming of the first flight back to Milton Keynes. In the end he managed some toe-curling drivel.

'Lay gentlemen,' he began. 'Donchaknow...'

Then I lost him.

It was so bad the Russian interpreter didn't even bother to translate.

The meeting was then thrown open for discussion. Nobody said a word. Silence. Absolute total silence.

'Well, gentlemen,' said the Russian chairman after a while. 'You've come all this way. You say you want to help our country. You requested this meeting.'

Silence. Even more total silence. The chairman disappeared up his own insignificance. The Colonel got out his Masonic handbook and started to flick through it. Fingers mumbled something like, 'Well flap my haddock'. The interpreter, who was obviously being paid by the hour, seized on this and soon we were off on some rambling discussion about fish.

Mr Smarmy Know-all got out his nail clippers and started a full-scale manicure.

While all these momentous events in the history of Anglo-Soviet relations were taking place, I'm ashamed to admit my only interest was in who was going to be the first to fall asleep.

Eventually the Russian chairman looked at Fingers.

'Does that answer your question?'

'By 'eck,' he mumbled. 'I'm spinning plates here.' Now we were off into a round tour of the Russian ceramics industry.

Suddenly the Colonel stood up and crossed himself.

'Spectacles, testicles, wallet and watch,' he intoned deeply. Everybody looked at each other, wondering what on earth was going on.

'A custom in our country,' he murmured, collapsed back into his chair and returned to his first love, his Masonic handbook. I was terrified about what would happen if he reached the bit about the leather apron and standing on the chair on one leg.

The Russians, meanwhile, continued their in-depth analysis of the ceramics industry.

Mr Eager Young Graduate now stood up. 'Boots,' he proclaimed. 'I want to splash my boots.'

The interpreter was thrown. 'Boots? Splash? I do not understand. Polish, no. Shine, no.'

''Eck. He's got girl's bowels, 'e 'as,' mumbled Fingers.

Mr Eager Young Graduate began to edge his way towards the door. As he got to where Fingers was sitting, he caught his coat on the other man's chair.

'Catch your frock again?' asked Fingers.

'Always have problems whenever I wear dresses,' he grinned back sheepishly.

The Russian chairman looked at the interpreter. The interpreter looked at the Russian chairman. The Russian chairman looked as though he was about to sympathise with the British chairman about the road accident he was going to have the following week.

'What about the ball gown?' Fingers continued, as the Young Graduate went past him.

'No. That's different.'

'Don't have to get on buses in a ball gown, eh?'

The Russian chairman leapt to his feet, glaring at the British chairman.

The British chairman, suddenly, unbelievably, galvanised into action, glared at Fingers.

'I think,' he said, slamming shut the top of his briefcase on the table, 'you owe an apology...' Trouble was, as he went to stand up he realised he'd also slammed the end of his tie in the briefcase as well. The whole place collapsed in howls of laughter. Everybody headed for the bar. In the lead, arms around each other's necks, howling and screaming at the tops of their voices, were the Russian chairman and Fingers.

Then somebody mentioned the Nevsky Melody nightclub. Now I don't know about you, but the last place I want to be at eleven o'clock in the morning is in a nightclub. Even the Nevsky Melody nightclub where everybody is so poor they don't seem to be able to afford to wear anything more than the kind of G-string you don't find on a balalaika.

Boring businessman that I am, I went back to visiting more software companies. But I couldn't manage to avoid the official British mission reception that evening, which I must say did us proud: French wine, Dutch cheese, German sausages, Italian pizzas, tiny Danish pastries, open Scandinavian sandwiches... The missioners, as you would expect, lived down to their reputation. They looked like a bunch of six packs chasing a container-load of vodka.

Mr Innocent looked severely deformed. He'd obviously found somewhere else to hide his money bag. He was also carrying one of those tiny fold-up umbrellas which all evening he kept putting down on the table in front of him whenever he was eating or drinking anything. He was frightened to leave it in the cloakroom, he said, in case it was stolen.

Colonel Colonel went around barking at everybody 'JB' which I thought meant something to do with judges and bribes. Apparently it meant 'jacket button'. It's the top secret, hush-hush way lodge members make sure they help each other to maintain their high standards. After that he switched to barking 'FHB' at everybody which conjured up even worse things in my mind. But again I needn't have worried. This stood for 'Family hold back', reminding lodge members to let their guests get their sticky paws on the grub first. Within ten minutes, however, all the missioners were following him around barking 'NC' (nut case).

Mr Eager Young Graduate, obviously determined to fit in, was sashaying around in a pink voile shirt, silk tie, lightweight blue blazer, olive linen trousers and bespoke crocodile-skin loafers. Mr Smarmy Know-all, his hair dyed jet-black to within an inch of its life, sat in the corner studying an armful of Scrabble books.

The Crossover Queens, when they were not asking the Russians in turn which they fancied, French or Italian, were giggling with the waiters about some newfangled peppermill they'd discovered. 'If you're going to have any success,' they were telling them, 'you've got to take the top off, turn it upside down and screw it.' At least, I'm pretty sure it was a peppermill they were talking about.

The chairman, true to form, arrived too late to welcome any of the guests. His tie, I noticed, was still torn from the morning and he was smelling of Dettol.

As for Fingers, he was looking half man, half bucket of vodka. He was swaying around everywhere with a parcel under his arm, smelling to high heaven of mints.

'What's in the parcel?' I asked him.

'A spare pair of trousers,' he winked. 'Just in case.'

He spent most of his time approaching all the women,

leering at them, 'Who's your Daddy, then?', complaining that his putter wasn't working and telling them he was a 'mattress tester', and if they would like him to test theirs he'd be only too happy to oblige. 'Like a day out at Ripon Races,' he grinned at me.

True to trade mission receptions I've been to all over the world, within twenty minutes the booze had run out and within twenty-five so had the food. So it was back to the hotel bar ... 'Last one at the bar drops his trousers,' shouted Fingers. As one, the missioners turned, wheeled about, trampled the guests aside and made for the bus waiting outside. On the way back to the hotel Mr Innocent, apart from being sick everywhere, kept putting his arm round the driver's shoulder and telling him he loved him.

The following morning, early, I was off to that fabulous baroque green and white Italian wedding cake, The Hermitage. Or in other words the Winter Palace, the Little Hermitage, the Old Hermitage, the New Hermitage and the Theatre Hermitage. How anyone could think of storming this lot I have no idea. It's not as if it's a single building, there are five of them, all scrolls and columns and fancy mouldings, linked together, stretching maybe half-a-mile along the banks of the Neva. Apart from that the buildings are on the far side of an enormous square the size of about five polo fields. I'd have been exhausted by the time I had staggered across the square to the column in the centre, commemorating Alexander I's defeat of Napoleon, let alone have the strength to race across the other half, go chasing up the stairs and then start throwing furniture out of the window. Not that I wouldn't have done my duty to the cause. If I'd have had the chance I'd have headed for the imperial wine cellar and seen what damage I could do there. Not that I would have broken a single bottle. I'm not stupid.

I don't know about you, but I'm always amazed The Hermitage is still standing. You would have thought that one of the first things the Bolsheviks would have done when they took over, along with ordering a whole planeload of the very best champagne and caviar direct from Paris, would be to have got rid of the whole thing. Just think. All that stone work. They could have used it to put up even more statues of Lenin all over the place. Not that this wasn't suggested at the time. The poet Vladimir Mayokovsky called The Hermitage 'a dead mausoleum full of dead works' and suggested that the whole place should be turned into a macaroni factory. But what seems to have saved it was the very first Conference of Peasants which took place there in 1918. Instead of using chamberpots they used all the genuine Sèvres vases which obviously made a deep impression on them. The penny dropped. They realised it was to their convenience to keep it. So instead they decided to get rid of the various directors instead. Well, when I say get rid of, I don't mean they retired them, stuck them in the House of Lords and gave them television programmes all of their own. I mean that one by one they were arrested, thrown in gaol and even executed which might, of course, account for the fact that today it is obviously one of the world's greatest museums.

The big question now is, in a world where 'satisfactory condition' means nothing is falling down and 'renovation' is a bunch of women slapping great dollops of handmade cement on to anything that's crumbling, will it survive capitalism? With its budget already cut by a fifth, whole areas of the building are already looking the very picture of distress. Which may or may not be a bad thing. With its 1,500 rooms, 2.8 million exhibits on show (which is less than 5 per cent of what they've got – the rest is hidden away in the cellars) everybody kept telling me that 2 minutes per exhibit would take me exactly 10 years 7 months 5 days 4 hours and 37 minutes to see the lot. I did it in 20 minutes. Of course, it took me 10 years 7 months 5 days 4 hours and 17 minutes, 3,000 doorways, 1,000 acres of malachite walls and gilded ceilings, 275 miles of dusty corridors, 523 signs saying

'Don't speak loud', 117 marble staircases, 250 wrong directions from 7 bored guides and 3 visits to that damned peacock clock to find the exit. On the other hand, of course, if the whole lot had been on display you could be born and die in the place and still not see everything. My only chance is that if the place carries on crumbling the way it is now the next time I'll be able to do it in 15 or maybe even 10 minutes - with or without all the treasures the Red Army lifted from Germany at the end of the war, and which are still also supposed to be hidden away in the basement somewhere.

So how did I do it in 20 minutes? Easy. Up the main staircase to the sparkling gold and white Pavilion Hall with all the columns and galleries and chandeliers, Catherine the Great's hanging garden in the background and the huge, ornate peacock clock in the centre, which I can assure you is nothing like the real thing. The peacocks we have at home shriek every five minutes morning, noon and night. They don't just drive me mad, they drive the whole village mad as well. So much so that I no longer get any Christmas cards from anybody south of Watford. This clock only makes a noise when the left toadstool hits the hour, which is far more civilised.

So, the peacock clock out of the way, go across the staircase, past some early Italian paintings to Room 214. Here there are two fantastic Leonardo da Vincis, the only ones in the whole of Russia. One looks like an early da Vinci, all sweet and light and innocent. The other, obviously the older, looks wiser, more worldly, more dark and sombre da Vinci.

Now a quick dodge to the right. Oops. Mind the crowds. This is the busiest hermitage I've ever been in. Here are some Titians and I must say a rather fetching Judith by Giorgione, sword in one hand, dress cut way above the knee showing far more leg than you would have thought appropriate for a woman in her position.

And what's that? It looks like a room straight out of

the Vatican. Except there are no Swiss guards lying around dead.

Now back a bit. Here's the only Michelangelo in Russia. It's a marble statue of a boy.

At the end of the corridor are your Rembrandts. The one with flowers and fruit in her hair and a couple of miles of heavy curtain all round her is Mrs Rembrandt, which shows you what a bundle of laughs she must have been.

Back through room 249 with more Dutch painters. Forget the Rubens. Look out for my favourite, the hunting picture by Paulus Potter which I'm surprised has not been adopted by the anti-hunt brigade. Goats and bears and wild boar are grilling and roasting dogs on the spit, with deer and rabbits looking on enjoying the show. All very X certificate Beatrix Potter.

Down the stairs. There's a huge statue of Jupiter in room 107. Then there's the Kolyvanskaya vase, which was carved out of a single piece of stone so enormous it took more than 150 horses to drag it all the way here from Siberia. Obviously if they had stuck it on the Trans-Siberian Express we'd all still be waiting for it.

Back up the stairs. A quick look at the Russian military display. Judging by the weapons factories I've visited all over Russia, this lot represents their very latest technology.

Now upstairs to the nineteenth and twentieth century and your Cézannes and Van Goghs, your Gaugins and Monets. To think Van Gogh's sole ambition in life was to 'find the means to mount an exhibition of my work in a café'.

Next, would you believe, is a whole room of Picassos – where it suddenly struck me. If, like Russia, you owed over US$100 billion in foreign debt, practically US$10 billion in unpaid wages, not to mention US$12 billion backlog in pensions, wouldn't you sell the lot of them and start paying off some of the bills? If that is too drastic for you, how about adopting the Russian way and doing a deal with some of the gentlemen in long, leather jackets and big Mercedes? They could arrange for some Russian art students to copy secretly all the paintings and then sell the copies. Plenty of people have bought fake paintings in the past. Why shouldn't they buy fake Picassos now? That way you have the best of both worlds. You have the money to start paying off some of the debts. You've created jobs for Russian art students. And you've still got the original paintings.

Don't worry though. There may be room after room of French painters but the British are not totally ignored. In a tiny little room I stumbled on while desperately looking for the exit I came across what The Hermitage boasts is a wide range of painting showing the genius of English painters, featuring such famous names as George Dawe, Thomas Lawrence, Christina Robertson, George Hayter, William Allan, George Morland, John Hoppner and a whole string of other names I'd never heard of including the one and only Joseph Wright of Derby. All I can say is if the Russians think these guys are the cream of English painting some middleman somewhere made an awful lot of money.

So, unless you're interested in the Green Frog dinner service which Catherine the Great commissioned from Wedgwood, which has just been delivered, that's it. Exactly 19 minutes 53.7 seconds. Time for a quick one. Last one at the Caviar Bar pays the bill.

But if it's class you're after, forget The Hermitage. For Peter the Great's gilded throne, for the Tzar's dinner service depicting Russian peasant life in 24-carat gold, for the famous Fabergé egg highlighting 300 years of the Romanovs, for the Fabergé pen used by Tzar Nicholas II to abdicate in 1917, in fact for the biggest collection of Romanov dynasty treasures, you must go to that world centre of culture and excellence, the way-out, Brazilian-style, Rio All-Suite Casino Resort just off The Strip in Las Vegas. Don't ask me how or why or wherefore. All I know is it's all there. And it's not freezing cold. And it doesn't cost you US$10 to get in. And just round the corner you can get all the free drinks you can swallow.

If, however, that's a bit too far to go, try the Russian Museum just down the road from The Hermitage, which to me was a revelation. I always thought the Russians jumped straight from the icon to those enormous Stalinist social realism posters. Not so. In between, they actually had some decent artists and painters – well, compared to George Dawe, Thomas Lawrence, Christina Robertson and all the other geniuses of English painting on show in The Hermitage, anyway. What's more, the building is also more modern, more up-to-date, better laid out than The Hermitage. It opens earlier. It closes later. There are even plastic flowers stuck outside in the garden in front. Oh yes, and it's easier to find the exit. The other good thing about the Russian Museum is that it's just round the corner from that other centre of cultural life in St Petersburg, the Caviar Bar in the Grand Hotel Europe.

The cultural life in St Petersburg is not what it used to be. In spite of all the black leather jackets around, I didn't see one assassination all the time I was there. Once I must admit I thought we were in for some excitement when a guy came into the Caviar Bar, smooth hair, camel-hair coat draped over his shoulders, black and white spats, and sat in the far corner, facing the door chatting away non-stop into his mobile phone. In Italian. But nothing happened. Or at least nothing happened while I was there. Maybe afterwards, who knows? It's also nowhere near as expensive as I was expecting. However much caviar they shovelled on to my plate and however many vodkas I had, it always seemed somehow cheap. Of course, on the other hand, that could have been because of the number of vodkas I had and the amount of caviar they shovelled on to my plate.

For real St Petersburg culture, you have to go to the Literary Café which is famous throughout the world, not because it was the hang-out of practically every famous Russian writer who has been banned or deported to Siberia but because this is where they invented Beef Stroganoff. There. I knew you'd be impressed. Count Stroganoff apparently staggers in there one evening on his way home. 'Okay,' he says to the head man. 'I want something new, something tasty and something fast. And if I don't get it in ten minutes you're a dead man.' Or words to that effect.

What do they do? They give him this huge mash of stuff together with great lumps of reheated yesterday's meat which shows you how far standards have changed in St Petersburg over the last few years. Go into, say, that place next door to the Okoshki Art Kafe on Ulitsa Bolshaya Morskaya and ask for something to get the juices going and the last thing you'll get is a huge mash of stuff and reheated yesterday's meat. Although I don't know.

I popped in there late one evening – the Literary Café that is, not the you-know-where – for a Baltika beer, a cup of moose-lip soup and a couple of caviar sandwiches. All I can say is, whatever I was expecting it wasn't. Instead of leather-bound Russian classic it was more cheap Jeffrey Archerski paperback, if you see what I mean. Although to be fair everybody I met was talking about literary things: how literally everybody was starving to death.

I'd no sooner slumped into one of the chairs by the window than a rather smart-looking guy at the next table leant across and told me he was a professor at the Conservatoire; his salary – barely US$100 a month. He lived in a room six metres by two metres with four other people. One of them, an old lady they took in from the streets, spent every day begging at Moscow Station.

'I was born in St Petersburg. I went to school in Petrograd. I married in Leningrad. Now I am starving to death in St Petersburg,' he grimaced. To make ends meet he worked nights supervising a boiler in some new big office block. 'At ten o'clock I turn the boiler off. At four o'clock I turn the boiler on. It is not intellectual but I earn more than I do at the Conservatoire,' he grunted.

A young guy with him, who looked like a teenage Rasputin (long hair; intense eyes; big boots. Whether he had the other qualifications I cannot say, although I noticed he wasn't having any cakes or Madeira) joined in.

'You know what a communal flat is?' he asked me. 'I was brought up in a communal flat. There were six of us in our family. We lived in one room. There were four other rooms on the same floor. We all shared the same kitchen. We all shared the same toilet. Every morning we had to time everything to the second. Everybody had to go to work or to school. If anyone took longer than they were given, even a second longer, everybody was in trouble.'

An old lady now shuffled up to us. She offered to help me fight my way through the menu which was about as long as *War and Peace* and chock-a-block with spelling mistakes. She kept on and on to me about, of all things, being a vegetarian.

'I'd like to be vegetarian. But we would die if we eat only vegetables in Russia. We must eat meat. You don't understand this. I like Greenpeace. But can we support Greenpeace in Russia? We must kill animals. We must have furs. How can we keep warm if we don't have furs?'

Whatever it was she ordered for me, it wasn't new, it wasn't tasty and it definitely wasn't fast. In fact, come to think of it, I couldn't even tell you if it was meat or vegetables. All I know is that after a couple of glasses of sweet Georgian wine, not only could I not taste anything, I couldn't care less either.

Another guy who looked like a defrocked Orthodox priest, who was either studying a Japanese-English-German Dictionary of Mechanical Engineering or carrying it around with him so that he could burn it page by page throughout the winter to keep warm, now joined our happy literary band and immediately made with the verbals. His father, he said, was also suffering but in a different way. During the early days of *perestroika* he had bought a house in Spain. But the taxes were killing him. So he decided one morning to just up and leave and come back to St Petersburg.

'What are the Spanish going to do? Search all over Russia for him?' he shrugged.

He'd now got a tiny house in the countryside. He had pigs and goats and grew his own fruit and vegetables which kept the whole family going. Trouble was his daughter liked the sunflowers he gave him and now that was all she would eat.

'My wife, she is angry. She says it is wrong for a daughter to reject her mother's milk. But what can I do?'

No idea, my friend. I don't know anything at all about that kind of thing – and to be frank, I don't want to either. Another glass of axle grease, please.

Another guy I met who was knocking back lashings of vodka, sweet Georgian wine and axle grease told me he was the son of a carpenter. He had tried to get into the navy. Instead he ended up in the air force in the parachute regiment. He spoke English, French and German. But he said he couldn't get a full-time job. Instead, whenever he could he worked as an interpreter for a local firm of way, way up-market estate agents. Whenever they had their hooks into a big client, he had to go around with them and show them what was on offer.

'Such luxury in my city you cannot imagine. Flats and apartments I have seen better than the Tzar's Palace. You could not believe such things are possible.' He waved his empty glass in the air. Where did he live? I wondered. In a huge nineteenth-century mansion, divided into a million tiny flats, or rather rooms.

'*Sans* lighting, *sans* water, *sans* decoration, *sans* furniture, *sans* privacy, *sans* everything.'

'But are you happy?'

'Of course I'm happy,' he grinned 'Don't you know the

Russians are only happy when they're sad?'

We had another round of whatever it was. As we finally, in the early hours of the morning, stood outside on the pavement, shook hands and said our *dasfid-anyas* while some young guy was desperately trying to take photographs with a tiny, broken-down, bellows camera – no flash gun, probably no film either – of a bunch of Germans heading down Nevsky Prospekt he said, 'In St Petersburg we've seen off all the -isms. Tzarism. Marxism. Communism. Nazism. Now we are succumbing to the worst -ism of all.'

'Vegetarianism? Feminism?'

'Tourism,' he grinned.

I get back to the hotel just as – oh joys of joy – the British mission is leaving. The easy way. By car to the airport. Not Rasputin's way, wrapped in a blue curtain, in a sack in the Neva. They are not just out of their minds, they are out of their skulls.

'A great success for British exports,' exclaims the chairman, whose looks have improved dramatically. He now looks less like a colonic irrigator and more like an undertaker. Fingers, whose sole purpose in life I thought was to serve as a warning to others, has just landed out of the chaos of pure possibility some enormous export order. He is not just on Cloud Nine. He's in the ether. Something to do, the chairman tells me, with power stations. Supplies. The whole of Russia. With an order like that in the bag they had decided there was no longer any point in staying. They were off. Back to their lodge meetings, their favourite bars, oh yes, and their homes.

They start loading their luggage the traditional trade mission way: by removing all the airline stickers and hotel labels and tags from their suitcases so nobody back home, especially the wife, knows where they've been. All of them that is except Mr Innocent, who true to his name is collecting as many labels and tags as he can and slapping them all over his suitcases, his holdalls and his Harrods carrier bags. One day, he'll learn. One day.

I congratulate Fingers on landing such a big...

''Eck,' he slurs. 'You don't believe that. Only told them that so I could come on another mission.'

'You mean there's no...'

'Sure, there is. But nothing that big. Sophisticated though. Me and the guy who was chairman of that meeting, we're going to buy cheap perfume in India, stick it in expensive bottles, sell it all over Russia.'

'So what's sophisticated about that?' I wondered.

'We're going to supply it in boxes of 144. But we're only going to fill up 120 bottles. That's what's sophisticated about it,' he laughs.

As the coach pulls away, what do I hear echoing down the street?

Rule, Britannia,
Britannia, rule the waves
Britons, never, never, never shall be slavs.

Tehran

In the Name of God

*To the Supreme Leader of the Islamic Revolution,
Hazrat Ayatollah Khamenei*

Let me Congradulate you on the nineteenth Anniversary of freedom, independence and establishment and thriumph of the hoLy regime OF Islamic Republic and announcing my sincerity to the Honourable Status of the Leadership. HeartFelT felicitations to the Supreme Leader, the GuardiansHip of SuprEme Jurisprudence, the WonderFul, Unique PlenipotentiAry of the Muslims, AyaTollah Seyed Ali Khamenei on my very happy, very auspicious and very surprising return, complete, intact and unharmed from What will obviously be my first and last visit to the crAdle of mysticism and the source of bravery and martyrdom of 100,000 people and self-sacrifice of millions of revolutionaries whose per-CApita income is today, under your carefuL Leadership, about One-third of what it was two decades ago under the cruel rule of the dastardly monarchy. Well, very happy and auspicious as Far as I was concerned was my visit. Surprising, perhaps even amazing as Far as oTHEr people were concerned seeing as I was there For what seemed like hAlf a lifeTime, travelled two million miles, criss-crossed - oops, I mean criss-crescented - the country a thousand times, visited every single city, town and village, met and spoke to literally everybody from tramps and beggars all the **WA**y down to the mullahs and their deadly friends, the Basij al-Mustadhifeen all without a single drink. For me, I mean. I was told again and again they had plenty of their own stashed away. Only trouble was they had obviously run out of that natural **C**ourtesy **A**nd generosity of which I read so much in the Rubaiyat, that g**L**orious boozer's bib**L**e **OF** yours about Omar Khayyam, which has had such an in**F**luence on my life. Literary, of course.

Oh a hundred **TH**ousand apologi**E**s, O Supreme Leader. The lack of alcohol has a**F**fected my br**A**in. Or what's lef**T** of it. **W**h**A**t I meant was I was honoured to be the recipient of such unique hospitality wherever I went throughout your glorious country of Islam, the household of the Prophet, the thriumph of all thriumphs, which will forever be hailed as a turning point in the history of the world for its unique actions and achievements that are so beyond words that they are truly unutterable if not unspeakable. But don't worry. I won't tell the Ministry of Information. I don't want to get anyone into trouble. Well, that's what I was told by so many of your grateful subjects. On the other hand, it crossed – I mean crescented – my mind that the very least I should do before the world is humbly to acknowledge in the traditional Iranian manner that it is now my bounden duty and destiny to exert my utmost efforts to recall and commemorate for you the glorious achievements I experienced of all the human kind of the Islamic Republic of Iran, the household of the Prophet, the thriumph of all thriumphs, especially as a Nation you have now decided on the increasing importance of your touristic capacities at the international level. In other words, as I understand it, you now want to take bookings instead of hostages.

Now, however I must congratulate you on how, starting on Khordad 15, 1342, you manage to keep Iran, the household of the Prophet, constantly in the news headlines - well maybe not quite as much as Richard Branson, but close - and therefore in the minds of tourists worldwide. It will certainly have, I assure you, a profound effect on the number of people who visit your country, the amount of money they spend and what they spend it on. So too will your unsurpassed attention to detail. For example, no sooner does everybody board an Iran Air plane anywhere in the world than they start saying their prayers, although why they should do so completely baffles me. As far as I'm concerned Iran Air is the safest airline in the world. Apart from the fact that every other person on the plane is a secret policeman, I ask you, who on earth is going to put a bomb on an Iran Air flight? Then there is how you are welcomed at Tehran Airport - not by policemen carrying guns, which can be so off-putting to first-time visitors, but by policemen with huge six-inch knives strapped to their belts, the blades glistening in the sunshine. Finally, there is the reassuring fact that wherever one goes there is always a tourist official either following discreetly twenty paces behind, sitting in a car (arms crescented) outside places you are visiting, or just aimlessly lounging around your hotel at all hours of the day or night, obviously ready to answer any questions or queries you may have. In fact, I think it is true to say that the only crude thing I saw throughout the whole of my visit comes in barrels and sells at US$2.50 below the price of North Sea Brent.

Glorifying the said achievements of the glorious Islamic Republic of Iran, the household of the Prophet, the thriumph of all thriumphs, I speak objectively and without reserve - nobody, I promise you, has tried to crescent my palm with rials - as far as I'm concerned Iran is the one country in the world in which I have no ties, flashy ties, boring club ties or just plain old greasy ties. Oh incomparable situation. Oh God preserve the ground realities from decay, I am more than pleased to share with you my appreciation of the glorious mullahs who all hate the Americans almost as much as the French do; the noble, martyr-fostering people of your country, the respected families of your martyrs; the liberals who believe in beheading and the conservatives who believe in flogging people first and then beheading them. Provided, of course, the censors don't get there first. In doing so, I humbly acknowledge to the world my faith in God's rule and the household of the Prophet. I acknowledge all your glorious, indescribable achievements which will live forever in the annals of time and, fingers crescented, I hereby single out for praise eight glorious mentionable events – eight because wherever I went I noticed an intense feeling of eight throughout the country – achieved by your peoples in the face of the Malahedeh to safeguard the ideals and values of the Islamic Revolution and to uphold the noble teachings of Islam.

First Mentionable Event

Let us all hail the Islamic Republic of Iran, the Household of the Prophet, the thriumph of thriumphs, for the greatest, most far-reaching revolution of modern times: the invention of dress-down days. Oh guardianship of jurisprudence – Or may I call you Juri, which I assume you prefer to being called Prudence? What faith. What dedication. Other people, admittedly infidels, may have taken the first hesitant steps, either deliberately or as a result of a night out with the boys: but it was the glorious Islamic Revolution that recognised how men devote all their lives to their wives and family and have so little time and energy left over to devote to themselves, their wellbeing and their own personal affairs, which has made this dressing-down a living, thriving, breathing institution stretching from Tehran, the throbbing heart of the nation, to the four corners of the country: and not for just one day only, but for the full seven days of the week from Shanbeh to Jom'eh.

I can imagine how the fever-producing rays of joy must have glittered in the hearts of your martyr-fostering businessmen (I mean, specialised and experienced elite) when they realised for the first time in history that being a Muslim means never having to shell out for a Marks and Spencer let alone an Armani, a Versace, a Boss, a Karl Lagerfeld or, if you're really desperate, a double-breasted dark blue number from Gieves and Hawkes. Instead, day after day they could turn up at the office looking like they'd just been dragged in by the Basij – even though I was told that to achieve the genuine, authentic, co-ordinated dress-down look complete with faded chinos and a special Friday linen-mix shirt often costs more than buying a stack of Ralph Lauren rejects. But I can assure you, you made the right decision. There is nothing quite like going into an office to discuss investing in the company to be met by the senior manager wearing a Barry Manilow T-shirt. Believe me, the impact it has on you and your decision is not, if I may say so, exactly a positive one. The pioneers of ignorance and prejudice, the profiteers, the uncommitted (not to mention the infidels acrescent the sea) so far only acknowledge your lead in this matters on just Jam'ehs which is why I know so many of your beloved followers refer to them affectionately as Jam'eh buggers. But I know this will gradually increase to include Doshanbey, Seshanbeh, Chahaarshanbeh and Panj-shanbeh as well. This means they will then be free to wear their suits and ties on only Shanbeh and Yekshanbeh, the two days of the week when the last thing they want to wear is a suit and tie. Nice one, Juri.

Verily I know their hearts were also beating fast when you launched on the awaiting world the other post-ironic fashion statement for which you are justly famous: the three-day designer stubble, not to mention the flattened-down back of the shoe, a skill which I must admit I lost all of 73 years ago but I am now hastily trying to recover. And what an authentic experience it is to appreciate the consequences of these two world-leading decisions. You no longer have to ask waiters for a menu: you can see what's available delightfully displayed all over their three-day growth. In one cafe I went to in Shiraz, where incidentally the last thing I could get was a Shiraz – another one of my gripes of wrath – I could immediately see the wide range of delicious food on offer: lamb kebab, chicken kebab and lamb and chicken kebab. Like dress-down days, these glorious disciplines have also been adopted by many sons of the Revolution, leaders of influence, opinion-formers and trend-setters throughout the world. Most of them, O Juri, are at present busy pretending to work in advertising agencies, design studios, television production companies and fashion houses with the exception for some reason or other of those working for Gillette, Philips, Braun and Old Spice although, I'm told, there's hope that the Old Spice agency will come across shortly. Something to do with the problems they're having getting a girl swimming around in a waterfall wearing the full chador. But the important thing is this crescent-fertilisation of cultures continues. Every day, you'll be pleased to hear, the numbers are increasing especially as, unlike you, we cannot afford the basic necessities of life: four wives, the oldest one to fetch the razor, the next oldest to run the hot water, the next oldest to work up a lather, and I forget what the youngest is supposed to do but it will no doubt come back to me. It won't be long, I feel sure, before we see other influential figures such as the Pope and the Dalai Lama joining the ranks of the great unshaved.

Either way, in case you think we're talking at crescent purposes and I am obsessed only with the trivial superficialities of the world, I must tell you I also hail the ground realities, the economic significance of your mentionable actions. How you destroyed the market for suits from the infidel West. How you throttled the market for cheap ties from the East. How you destroyed the market for imported razors, razor blades, shaving soap and a million different after-shaves (most of which I cannot help but notice are supplied by companies of the Great Satan) and as a result how today you all smell as though you've been dipped in a bucket of Chanel: the English Chanel. Then there are razor sockets. So thorough and so effective has been the extent of your glorious revolution, you will be pleased to hear that of all the hotels in your country in which I served a life sentence not one had a razor socket. By the end of my visit people were not only stopping me in the street and asking me the way to the nearest mosque, one morning, as I was trying to cross Revolution Square in Tehran, I was even given a banner and told to wave it in front of some television camera or other, which, of course, I did. Not for me to argue with people's inalienable right to help CNN transmit misleading reports. At the same time, of course, I can also see how by your glorious actions you have given your own local industries the potential to move in on these markets by producing specially designed scruffy suits, collarless shirts, blunt razor blades and shoes with the backs already crunched flat without attracting slanderous allegations from the world community of imposing import barriers, manipulating markets, giving unfair preference to domestic manufacturers and all the other base and unreasonable allegations the enemies of the Prophet make when the bars are closed and they've got nothing better to do. Much the same reasons I guess were behind your decision to have so many different police forces and non-police forces. Everyone needs different uniforms and non-uniforms. So nice one, Vicar.

Second Mentionable Event

Sacred rather than glorious to the second greatest event of modern times nurtured and given forth by the great Islamic Revolution is Women's Lib. In the time it takes for a quick squirt of Muslim Dior under the arms – well, it's hardly likely to be Christian Dior is it? – you gave women not only the liberty *not* to spend all morning trying to decide whether to wear green gloves with blue shoes and the rest of the day regretting it, you gave them also the freedom to dispense with such agonising decisions as whether to wear a hat, a scarf or a thick, gungy carpet of hair spray. For as the Prophet said, 'By all wearing the same clothes, women truly reclaim their own bodies as if they had been left in a left luggage locker for two thousand years which some of them look as though they have been. For when clothes are different, the emphasis is on the clothes. When clothes are the same, the emphasis is on the body.' Or if he didn't say it, he should have done.

All this reclaiming business is important but even more important, if I may say, O Juri, bearing in mind the imposed war with Iraq, you saved the whole of Iranian mankind from dying young from all the agony, heartache, crescent words and nervous energy they would have had to expend deciding there's nothing wrong with green gloves and blue shoes or was it blue gloves and green shoes? What the hell. All married mankind, therefore, salute and acknowledges your Juris prudence with grateful thanks for the extra half hour they can now spend every morning with the paper doing the crescent word because they no longer have to face the prospect of trying to force their wives to take the wrong decision about whatever it is they don't want to wear that day. Not that women can't see reason: it's just that they can't under-stand it. Instead, thanks to your practical wisdom and knowledge and understanding of one of the greatest mysteries of the modern world, the working of a woman's mind, all women have to do now is wrap themselves up in their long black veils, pull their headscarves down tight over their faces and that's it. No agony. No heartache. No fuss and bother about what goes with what. Although I was told on good authority (and I always believe everything I'm told on good authority) by those who live in such close proximity to the household of the Prophet that in a nation which gave the world so many heroic martyrs, many women, especially young women deeply concerned about the future development of Iran, struggling to survive on their own and with so little money to spend on the necessities of life, are forced to go around with nothing on under their veils. This is obviously a matter of critical importance to the socio-economic development of the Revolution, not to mention the future development and expansion of the Iranian lingerie industry which up until now has no doubt been living off the fat of the land. If it helps you, therefore, I am more than prepared to drop everything and, solely in the interests of the Revolution, investigate the matter as quickly and as thoroughly as I can and let you have my full report and proposals at your earliest convenience. Or at mine, if you wish. But please don't expect miracles. This is the kind of report that could take years to complete.

Let me also tell you, as a result of the success of this policy of yours, O Juri, you will be pleased to know that I have crescent-checked with a number of people who know more about these things than I do and I'm pleased to tell you that already there is growing enthusiasm in the West to follow suit. Admittedly at the moment, more men are in favour of it than women. But whatever they say and however much they protest initially, I think it's true to say that throughout history, whatever aspect of life you are talking about, women always have the freedom to agree eventually to whatever men suggest.

Funnily enough, I don't know why but this particular enthusiasm for the veil manifested itself almost spontaneously throughout the rest of the world during the recent World Cup when the glorious national team of the Islamic Republic of Iran, exhibiting all the gracious and humble virtues of the Prophet, allowed themselves to thrash the Great Satan. One only hopes the team were duly rewarded on their return. I'm sure I speak for the rest of the world when I say that we all sincerely hope it won't be long before they are all fully recovered and have the energy to be able to return safe and sound to their 44 wives and 88 children. So far I have only spoken about the positive advantages and benefits of your far-sighted policy of Women's Liberation. There are, however, disadvantages. Men no longer have the pleasure of suffering the sneers and snarls and grinding of teeth or stomping of feet or bursting into tears or slamming the phone down or throwing things through the window as they have done throughout history. At least, not in public anyway. What happens when the Iranian man gets home with his four wives I can only imagine, although to be honest it's probably better if I don't. I am, after all, of a certain age.

May I add – please don't tell the Ministry of Information this either – that I've never been anywhere in the world where I've had so many offers of help, of, how shall I say, 'friendship' (although all my life I've always believed that the only true sign of friendship was an unfolded US$100 bill). At first, I will admit, it was a bit intimidating. I thought I'd strayed into a cross between an old Bergman movie and a dress rehearsal of some post-modernist production of *The Raven*. Then the birds started chatting me up. Where was I from? Where was I staying? Did I like it? No mucking about with preliminaries. Straight to the point your Iranian woman, veiled or not. In the old White Palace in Tehran where, in the bad old days, people were three times as rich as they are now, and the Shah used to hold court downstairs, one of the heavily veiled assistants came up to me and thrust a 200 rial-note into my hand. Which in itself I thought was odd. After all it's normally the other way round. On the note, however, she had scribbled her name and telephone number. Naturally, I called her: it was the decent thing to do. But I couldn't get through. The lines were crescented. Another day, on my way back from Vank, the fantastic Armenian Cathedral in Jolfa where the worshippers are known as serious, sober, God-fearing Christians, I came across a shop selling some pretty racy gear – which could only mean that somebody was calculating the risqué and whooping it up somewhere. Don't worry. If I find out where you'll be the second person to know. As if that wasn't enough, this mass of black veils drifted up to me and started whispering to me what sounded like 'Sexy, sexy'. It turned out to be Sejzi, a two-donkey town on the edge of the desert. The mass of black veils wanted me to stop there on my way to Yazd to give her son some English lessons. I've never been able to turn down an invitation from a bundle of black veils so, of course, I agreed. As you would expect, I taught him all the usual boring phrases I'm sure he will find useful in years to come, such as:

'Like the tie. Pity it clashes with the suit.'
'What do you mean, it's blunt?'
'You have dollars? I'll give you a good rate.'
'Psst. You want a bottle of vodka, very cheap?'
'My little sister, she's around the corner. I'll go and get her.'

And the age-old favourites:

'Death to America'. (*Even though you and I know that America has just overtaken Germany and become your biggest trading partner. But don't worry. I can be discreet.*)

'Poodle of Israel.'

And, of course, the most popular of all:

'France is true friend of Islam, *n'est ce pas?*'

Aㅣl kinds of other things the veils offered me, as well as the hand or otherwise of friendship. In the enormous Martyrs' Cemetery, next to the huge Mausoleum of Ayatollah Khomenei just outside Tehran, this tiny bundle of black veils actually offered me not an apple but handfuls of cherries. She even told me what she said was a typical Iranian joke:

'Two soldiers going into battle. One asks the other, "What is the colour of blood?" "I don't know," he says. Bombs go off all around them. One turns to the other and says, "Well, if it's yellow I've been shot".'

Shortly after that, O Juri, for various reasons I can't quite recall at the moment, I spent the evening in the only pleasure zone I could discover in the country: the area between the polo club, the cricket club and the ski slopes on the north side of Tehran, *posht-e pardeh*. In other words locked, barred and barricaded in one of those big, big houses surrounded by high security walls and mountains of caviar. You may or may not have heard about what goes on there on the grapevine – or the Radio Bazaar as you call it – but I can tell you it is nothing like what goes on this side of the wall. Not only do the women not fall asleep in front of the television all night, there is also, you'll be pleased to hear, a lot of serious dressing-down going on as well. One woman in particular, who I think was writing a novel, kept offering to show me what she called her outline. When I said 'no' she got pretty annoyed about it, I can tell you, which was probably my fault. I told her I didn't like going to bed with a novel. Instead I preferred a good thriller. As if that wasn't enough, people kept getting up to all kinds of outrageous things that are *haram*, forbidden. Like comparing their un-Islamic watches; swapping names of un-Islamic hairdressers; making notes of streets where it's safe to walk your dog without having a passing mullah or *basij* lob a brick at it; riding bicycles round the yard; playing bridge; wearing sleeves with buttons at the wrist; playing chess for money; listening to dance music; drinking water; watching Batman on satellite television; sipping a Scotch at US$50 a bottle; and, horror of horrors, getting their moustaches wet while they trimmed their beards with a razor blade. They also told me, the shame of it, more jokes:

'Young Iranian boy and girl go to visit her parents in the country. On the way home, the car breaks down. They have to stay in hotel. Hotel is full. They have to share bed in hotel. Good Muslim girl says to good Muslim boy, "We are not married. I put handbag between us. You stay that side. I stay this side." Following morning, both wake up. Go to breakfast. Leaving hotel, wind catches girl's veil. It blows over wall outside hotel. Boy says, "Don't worry. I'll climb over wall and get your veil." Girl says, "You climb over wall! You couldn't climb over my handbag."'

One woman called, I think she said, Saliva, who seemed keen to extend more than the hand of friendship and co-operation, gave me some pretty compelling evidence as to why women wear trainers under their long black veils. She even offered me what she said was the ultimate pleasure any man could expect in this life: a Persian Gulf shrimp. Believe me, I did everything I could to appreciate her sincerities. Then she pulled it off. She just popped it straight in. The Persian Gulf shrimp, I mean. Just as I was about to have my third glass of that funny stuff with bubbles in.

Now here again, however, I detect your omnipotence-ship at work. You know and I know that you can only keep women under for so long. Sooner or later they break out and start going on and on about having needs of their own. You've only got to read the Koran, if I may be so bold as to suggest, to know about the mischief of weird women. So my guess is you only decided on all this veil business because of what, I believe, you call the prophet motive. You wanted to give your own home-grown textile industry time to catch up, because you know as well as the rest of the world that when you finally let them off the leash after so many years of stifling, monotonous conformity every single woman in Iran is obviously going to want to exert her individuality by wearing the same Calvin Klein T-shirt, Armani jeans and Versace look-alike. In this way, of course, your Juri is ensuring that by then your glorious Iranian textile industry will have built up not only the technology but also the stocks to be able to meet the demand rather than be swamped by cheap, foreign imports. Much the same I can see also applies to your glorious Iranian engineering industry. Again, once you loosen the leash, instead of continuing to produce valuable and essential goods such as advanced nerve gas, Shahab-3 medium-range ballistic missiles and nuclear bombs with or without help from Russia, they will have to swing completely into reverse and start producing such cruel items as earrings and nose rings and tongue rings and all other kinds of rings, not to mention nose pins, safety pins and – oh, I feel faint at the thought of it.

Third Mentionable Event

Rhapsodies of praise to the third greatest event of modern times nurtured and given forth by the great Islamic Revolution: a just society. O Great Jurisprudence, in so many aspects of modern life in Iran you are hailed before the world as being just. Just about civilised. Just about religious. Just about cultured. Forget Persepolis, where that so-called great expert on Persia, Robert Byron, boasted he was accompanied by a grumpy old Airedale and a wild sow which he seemed to think was a fun way of visiting the ancient capital of Persia. But, correct me if I'm wrong, I always thought wherever you see a wild sow you also see a wild boar not very far behind. However, be that as it may, as far as I'm concerned the hallmark of any great civilisation is the attitude of the Fitrah-oriented peoples to their rulers, their loyalty to their country, their freedom of expression and their theories about Lady Di. In all four respects, O Juri, you are a light unto the dark clouds smothering and consuming the rest of the world, helped, of course, by the fact that those great fire worshippers, the Zoroastrians, were running the place 2,500 years ago. Talk about being fired with enthusiasm – the fire has not been allowed to go out in their temple in Yazd for over 1,500 years.

Unless I'm wrong, you are already so civilised, so perfect, you have laid down so many rules and regulations for your people to embrace enthusiastically, that there is little for you to do to improve and civilise your society any further. Which is obviously why, nineteen years after the great, glorious Islamic Revolution, I couldn't help but notice that the only things your Parliament can find time to discuss were the use of pictures of women in the press, segregating men and women in hospital, banning the construction of any building over four storeys in Tehran, and the number of holidays members should be allowed to take. To visit their constituencies, of course. But for me the true height of civilisation, which I must admit I did not expect to find in of all places, Iran, was not as you call them 'tourist attraction centres', such as the wonderful, soaring, magical fourteenth-century entrance to the Jame Mosque in Yazd; the glorious Imam Square, four times the size of St Mark's Square in Venice, twice as large as Red Square in Moscow, in Estfahan nesf-e jahan (Estfahan is half the world: and we all know which half). It wasn't even all the pictures, paintings and cartoons of, oh my, isn't he just cute? Mickey Mouse and

Donald Duck and Pluto and all the other members of the irrepressible, happy-go-lucky Disney family. On shops. On stores. On walls. On a huge wall by the fun-fair in Shiraz. (Which explains the real reason for your undying hatred of the Great Satan. For you know that once you recognise the US you'll have to pay royalties and reproduction rights on the illegal use of all those Disney characters for the past eighteen years and you'll be bankrupt. You won't be able to afford one nuclear bomb, let alone a whole stack of them aimed at Israel.) No. The thing that amazed me more than anything was your obviously far-seeing decision to allow women not only to go to football matches, but to play football as well. Next thing we know you'll not only be allowing them to watch cricket but play it as well. As for Lady Di, whisper it not, but I was told on the very best authority by a Japanese-speaking Revolutionary Guard that her destiny was ordained from the beginning of time. After all, what do the letters DIANA spell out? Diana Dies In A Nasty Accident. I never argue with what a Revolutionary Guard tells me, Japanese-speaking or not. You think that's, how shall we say, interesting? I also met no end of Iranians who genuinely believe Ayatollah Khomenei and his merry bunch of mullahs were actually financed by the British, apparently because they wanted to get their own back on the Shah for double-crescenting them and kicking them out and replacing them with the Americans.

So far as being religious is concerned, any country that in the middle of an economic crisis can blow 56 million rials building a five-star, luxury hotel for ordinary pilgrims visiting the holy shrine of Imam Reza, the eighth Imam of the household of Prophet Mohammad in the holy city of Mashhad, has got to be a deeply religious country. In the old days your philos-ophy was simple: it was Khomenei or your life. Today, now that the mullahs have seized the moral low ground, you are far more sophisticated. Your theologians stand

among the highest in the world. For centuries Christian
theologians wrestled with such fundamental religious
problems as how many angels could fit on top of a pin.
The theologians of your religion, which according to
your famous Ayatollah Yousef Sanei is the 'religion of
freedom', have not only wrestled with but mastered far
more difficult and complex metaphysical problems
such as: When is a veil not a veil? When is black black
and not light black? How many strands of hair is a
woman allowed to show under her veil? Is 1mm the sign
of sanctity but 1.1mm the sign of blasphemy? Is a wig
hair, the hair of the woman who is wearing it, the hair
of the woman or women who provided it, or nobody's?
Must a woman wear stockings? What colour should the
stockings be? Can she paint one toenail red? Or two?
One on each foot? Or two on the same foot? What
happens if she is covered from head to toe by the
chador but completely naked underneath? One can
only admire the dedication of your holy priests and
theologians who wrestle with these problems and
thank Allah that, unlike so many of their counterparts
in the indecent, reactionary and decadent West, they are
not obsessed with sex.

Having one day finished all my meetings early you'll
be pleased to hear, O Juri, that having consulted the
budgerigar fortune-teller outside the prison, I mean
hotel, where I was completing my sentence, I mean my
stay in your glorious country, I decided to dodge off -
oops, I mean make a pilgrimage - to the holy City of
Qom hidden away between the Great Salt Desert and
the Kashan mountains. Now Qom is one of the places
I've always wanted to visit: the Vatican of Shi'ism, with
no fewer than 60 *hausas* or seminaries, the site of the
famous blue-domed shrine dedicated to Fatima, the
daughter of the seventh Imam, the sister of Imam Reza,
the eighth Imam of the household of Prophet Mohammad; the birthplace of your great Islamic Revolution;

and home to sixty thousand Allah-fearing revolutionary sanctities, *talibs* or students, *hojatoleslams* ayatollahs, religious jurisprudents, common or garden ayatollahs with white turbans, your real ayatollahs with black turbans who can trace their antecedents back to Mohammad and grand I-only-talk-to-Allah ayatollahs. All I can say is, if heaven is full of mullahs I don't think I want to go there. Qom, I discovered, was not just one huge religious training centre; it was also one huge religious terrorist training centre. Just outside town is the Fateh Ghani Husseini camp, which, like the ones at Imam Ali east of Tehran and another one, Qazvin, up towards the Caspian Sea, is dedicated to turning out graduates skilled in such practical, everyday pursuits as bomb-making and hand-to-hand combat. In the centre of town is the beautiful blue-domed Fatima Shrine which I wasn't allowed into, even though a whole string of dead bodies were being bounced round and round it shoulder-high by gangs of Revolutionary Guards. It was so empty I could have thrown a bomb in there without killing anyone I didn't know. At the outer gate I was told I was *nages*, dirty or unclean, which frankly I took as a compliment. At the Feyzieh *hausa*, the then unknown Ayatollah Khomenei wrote literally hundreds and hundreds of learned, erudite books interpreting and reinterpreting Islam, including the famous Tozih-el Masa-el all about the right and wrong way of looking at a woman; the fact that all women from the time of the Prophet hit the menopause at sixty, the rest at fifty; that it is okay, fellahs, to sodomise your neighbour's camel so long as you kill it afterwards; and that when one is doing 'one's business' it is imperative that you neither face Mecca nor point your bum at it, bearing in mind, of course, that your weight should always be on your left foot – but of course, we're not all savages, you know. Then one day he got himself all worked up and made his famous denunciation of what he called 'capitalisation', the law passed by the Shah which gave all

Americans absolute and total freedom to do whatever they liked without being subject to the laws of Iran in any way, shape or size. The following morning the Shah sent in the troops and the rest, as they say, is history. Had the Shah ignored the whole thing as the ravings of some out-of-touch theology lecturer, who knows, he might still have been in power today and the mullahs a nightmare waiting to happen. However, he nailed his colours to the crescent and had to live with it. Similarly, here the way was barred to me by another scruffy Revolutionary Guard with a greasy beard and filthy clothes. Yet again I was told I was *nages*, unclean. Yet again I took it as a compliment, especially as the whole time I was being lectured about not being a Muslim or dedicated follower of Islam he was busy heating the tiny cake of earth Muslims routinely put on the ground in front of them when praying, so that they can keep touching it with their foreheads. Not this guy. The more he heated it, the softer the cake of earth became, the more he would rub it furiously on to his forehead to create the prayer mark your serious Muslim only gets after literally years of continual praying. I did, however, have what I think you would describe as a very interesting conversation with a jolly Friar Tuck-like mullah about the sky being round and the earth being flat. At first, I'm afraid, I did tend to disagree with him. But as soon as we were joined by this particularly enthusiastic young man with a green band around his forehead and about two dozen twelve-inch knives in each hand, I very quickly saw the error of my way. Then, with every door locked and barred and bolted in a strange city, time on my hands and money in my pocket, there was only one thing to do: give in to temptation. I decided to treat myself to a tin of sohan, the sticky, sickly, sweet pistachio-brittle you see on sale all over the place. As I was fighting my way through all the *talibs*, *hojatoleslams*, ayatollahs, grand ayatollahs and Allah-only-talks-to-me ayatollahs and at the same time, for some reason or other, trying to whistle 'In olden days a glimpse of stocking was something shocking as Khomenei knows...', I suddenly realised that far from worrying myself silly about the sinister visage and ominous goals of reactionary intellectuals, I was in the one area which had remained untouched and uncorrupted by the infiltration of indecent culture, deceived arrogant elements not to mention hypocritic Western thought. In other words, I was slap-bang in the middle of the Las Vegas of the Islamic World. Holy City it may be, but in the time it takes to say Qom or rather Qom, Qom, Qom, Qom I could be married four times. As for the funeral, that comes later – or sooner I suppose, depending on how the wedding goes. I hailed another jolly Friar Tuck mullah. I was right, he said. In a country where thirty-something women professors need their father's approval for practically everything but a fifteen-year-old boy can go out and pick up whoever he likes, Come was the place to Qom. I mean, Qom was the place for Allah-fearing Muslims to come if they felt they couldn't wait until they died in order to sample the fruits of paradise; in other words, if they were after what he called quickie quickie 'marriages of enjoyment' as opposed to presumably the usual, longer, more drawn-out kind. Here, all you had to do was fill out a form saying how long you intended to enjoy your marriage – five minutes, five weeks, five months (not any longer surely) – shuffle off to the nearest Sharia court and bingo, you're ready to go. If that's the right word. I was so thrilled with the news that from then on, because of your people's instinctive, unwavering faith, the depths of their beliefs and their ability to know immediately what is right and wrong, whatever hotel room I stayed in I always changed the direction of the arrow pointing to Mecca. People less enlightened than yourself might just pass it off as some silly Christian practical joke worth paying no more attention to than the time it takes to say 'Such blasphemous action deserves fifty lashes or thirty years in gaol.' But you, I know, will be grateful. For it will help you to prove that your Allah-fearing people do not need to rely on outside symbols to support their faith. Instead they know instinctively from the depths of their heart what is the correct thing and what is not the correct thing to do. Much the same, I hasten to add, applies to Roman Catholics. Nobody has to tell us in which direction to turn to discover the foundation of our faith, the source of our beliefs and our spiritual home. We all know it's Cracow. All the same I'm glad I didn't live through the Reformation.

Don't try to deny it because I'm afraid it's true. When it comes to culture, most people think of Iran as some kind of upmarket knocking-shop full of water fountains, over-enthusiastic blondes and non-stop orgies. But then it's your own fault for publishing fantastic tales such as *The One Thousand and One Nights, Omar Khayyam* and those by James Moray. But not me. As far as I'm concerned, bearing in mind the only criterion is both unity and unanimous agreement on the general political and social targets imposed by a wholly unrepresentative minority, you're the most cultured nation on earth. I can quite honestly say I've never been anywhere where I've been bombarded with so much genuine, authentic, living, breathing culture – largely because I've never been anywhere else where three times a day sixty million men, veiled women and children wade through great mountains, huge buckets and enormous slabs of yoghurt plastered all over with lactobacillus, acidophilus, bifidobacterium and every other kind of culture you can imagine, both bio and rip-roaring, blood-and-thunder natural. Even though I'm married to a vegetarian and am thus not exactly unfamiliar with yoghurt (I only have to have it four times a day when I'm at home), the amount you guys consume quite turned me over. At first, I thought that in much the same way as you ensure everybody enjoys the highest possible level of culture by laying down what they read in the newspapers, what novels and books they read, what films they watch, what television programmes they see and even whom they entertain in the privacy of their own homes, this was your way of ensuring they maintained the same standards in their diet. Not that my poor, weak, pathetic white corpuscles would agree. Then I thought that because the main pillars of the great Islamic revolutionary intellectualism are knowledge, possibilities and aspired values, this was your way (under the umbrella of these values) to protest against Western cultural aggression, which everyone knows is far more dangerous than Western armies – not to mention Mossad, the CIA, enemies of the revolution, communists, royalists, spreaders of corruption, sexual deviants and readers of *Time* magazine. Then, of course, I realised. In a country where it is forbidden even to think of having a stiff Scotch, it's the only way to make certain you don't get the runs from eating all that delicious bacteria you see crawling all over the place. Yet another triumph of purposeful leadership in the face of the rightful and legitimate wishes of the suffering masses. I congratulate you. The other thing that struck me, apart from that charming *basij* and his wooden truncheon in Qom, was how eager you are to share your culture with everyone. You've only got to stop and ask the ordinary man in the street, the one with the three-day stubble, greasy jacket, scruffy old trousers, broken-back shoes and a mobile phone in his hand, who the old bloke is – the chap with the white beard and the black bandage round his head whose picture is plastered all over the side of every ten-storey building in town – and before you can say 'Islam is the language of freedom' he's taking you off to an in-depth lecture about the gentleman in question, at what I assume, judging by the furniture, is the local Adult Education Centre. Or it could have been the local Co-op Hall. Trouble was, unlike the evening classes back home where the lecturers can't wait to get out of the place and across the road to the local boozer, your lecturers are all so keen and enthusiastic, hurling the inquisitive mind into the abyss of despair and disillusionment in order to homogenise the perspectives of transiting into a stage of negation of foundations that it practically takes a letter from the acting British Ambassador before they let you go.

One Australian I met in Shiraz was not only even more amazed than me that he couldn't find his favourite national wine in Shiraz, he kept telling me that it was only because he paid the fees for his three-year course in full, in advance, that the lecturer agreed to let him go. He said he wasn't too upset about it because at least the accommodation was better than the hotel he was staying in. He didn't have to wait so long for his food either. Largely because it all came on the same plate. At the same time, there's no denying that a knowledge of Iranian history and culture certainly makes it easier to find one's way around the country. Stop anyone in any street in any town in the country and ask the way to the nearest mosque and they will tell you straightaway – left at the big poster of the two buddy Revolutionary Guards hugging each other in the sunset; second right at the cartoon of Mickey Mouse on the cash desk by the funfair; past the elegant tableau painted on the wall saying, 'Obedience to Khamenei is obedience to Imam Khomenei' and there it is right opposite the graffiti on the bridge saying Death to America. Once in Tehran the only way I could find my hotel was by finding first the notorious Evin prison where in the old days around-the-clock executions were the norm. 'You find the prison, my brother,' this three-day-stubble, greasy-jacket, scruffy-old-trousers and broken-back-shoes told me. 'Then up from there. Turn right. Along a bit is a funfair. Opposite the funfair is your hotel.' When I got there I found the hotel was called the Asadi, which means freedom. Great sense of humour you Iranians have got.

I noticed also how in your wisdom you have seen fit to increase the level of unemployment to a staggering ten million so that as many people as possible now have the freedom to pursue their cultural interests. In Shiraz, for example, wherever I went, whether to the shrine of Hafez, the literary giant of fourteenth-century Iran, or to the shrine of Sa'di, another famous Iranian poet, there were blokes wandering around with other blokes. In Persepolis in the Winter Palace I could hardly see the polished stone to the left of the door, which they say is the world's first mirror, for all the blokes hanging around all over the place. In Estfahan I went to Chehel Sotun, a fantastic fun palace built by Shah Abbas who founded the place for nothing but fun, Fun, FUN – I mean for outrageous, illicit, so-called entertainment. I wanted to see the famous portrait of one of his notorious banquets in full swing, which you may like to know is no longer covered with a white sheet to protect public morals as it used to be shortly after the great Islamic Revolution. Could I see it? No way. There were blokes all over the place. I saw blokes taking pictures of other blokes. I saw blokes going to the cinema with other blokes although I was told most Iranian films are best seen on radio. I saw blokes going for big dipper rides in the funfairs with other blokes. I saw blokes together on the banks of rivers. I saw blokes in a horse and carriage trotting around, laughing and chatting and joking together about obviously cultural matters like how much who had to drop whom so that they could dodge their one hundred per cent compulsory military service. US$20,000 I was told was the going rate. Don't pay a penny more. Such is the high level of cultural awareness and sophistication in Iran. But funnily enough I never saw any blokes arguing with other blokes about where to go, what to eat, what not to eat, what to drink, what not to drink and why on earth did you wear those shoes? I've told you a million times they don't go with the jacket. What I did notice, however, was the small but vital role that women play when they are allowed out in polite society. They can push in front of everything and everyone they like. Or at least the ones with moustaches can. At airports. At railway stations. At bus stops. At first I thought this was a French tradition the Ayatollah brought back with him from exile. But after the fifty-seventh time it happened in two days I realised it was as much part of your culture as keeping people trapped inside their embassies and throwing away the key. Not that I'm complaining for a single moment. Any time any black veil with a moustache carrying an AK-47 and chanting Death to the Infidel wants to push in front of me, she is more than welcome to do so. All that yoghurt provides a valuable opportunity for those in the international, scientific and intellectual circles within the province to consider researchable religions, new discourses, and all aspects of sociology and political science. In other words, it does the bowels a power of good.

Exactly the same thing applies to restaurants. You would never believe, for example, the amount of time I spent in what must be your most popular chain of theme restaurants. I say theme restaurants, because wherever I was they were all the same: the same crumbling, concrete floor, the same paint peeling off the same walls, the same plastic sheets over the same tables next to the same open toilet doors. Those were the cheap restaurants. In the expensive ones they close the door. Then just as you're about to scratch another notch on the plaster before it falls on the floor, two Revolutionary Guards, complete with beards, broken-backed shoes and scruffy green uniforms, burst in. The maitre d'hotel is easy to spot. He's the one with the rubber gloves. They throw the charge sheet, sorry, I mean the menu, down on the table. You study it. You can have whatever you like just so long as it's yoghurt and kebab: lamb kebab, chicken kebab or if you're in a five star restaurant, lamb and chicken kebab. You order yoghurt. Three hours later a glass of what I always assume was once some kind of orange juice is slopped on your table. Another two and a half hours later just as you are beginning to find yourself chewing the plastic sheet on the table they bring in the kebab. Whether it's lamb kebab, chicken kebab or lamb and chicken kebab can produce hours of endless cultural discussion. In one restaurant where I served a life sentence I ordered an orange juice and some bread. I got a yoghurt - see what I mean about culture - and a lamb kebab. Or a chicken kebab. Or maybe it was a lamb and chicken kebab. In another one, in the centre of the table was what looked like a thick, crumbling slab of rich, dark, treacle cake. Again and again while I waited and waited watching the guards, I mean waiters, picking up the salt cellars, banging them on the tables, testing them by shaking salt into the palms of their hands and then opening up the bottom of the cellar and pouring the salt back in again, I felt like cutting myself a slice. But I resisted. Which was just as well. It turned out to be the sponge they used to wipe down the table and goodness knows what else behind the closed door. The restaurant, I shall never forget, was called Salimy.

Fourth Mentionable Event

Even more glory to the fourth greatest event of modern times nurtured and given forth by the great Islamic Revolution: art transplants. Before the great Islamic Revolution everybody had their eyes on the ground. They were all making carpets. Pretty good ones as well. One book I read on carpets as well as on the train to and from London actually said that 'it would indeed be hard to dispute the Iranian claim to have produced the most elaborate, the most decorative, the most valuable and

the most superbly assured carpets in the world', although
as it then went on to say the most ancient carpets
known to exist were found 'nearly three decades ago at
Kizirik in south-eastern Siberia' maybe we should take it
with a lump of the salt the waiters kept recycling in that
Salimy restaurant. Either way they were good at carpets
and all because years ago some old Shah came back
from a visit to Paris where he obviously went to the
ballet and immediately decreed all women should wear
the tutu. Now Iranian women at the time being, how
shall I say, Iranian women, the only place for Iranian
men to look to try to hide their embarrassment was the
floor. As it was boring looking at a sandy floor all day
long somebody, glory be to Allah, came up with the
bright idea of fancy, intricate carpets. An industry was
born. (Although what would have happened if the old
Shah had been taken to the Crazy Horse instead of to
the ballet, goodness only knows.) Today, however,
nobody dares to trample over the glories of Iranian art
or anything else Iranian come to that. Iranian art has
been transplanted from the floor to the wall. You've
only got to dodge down any street to see splashed all
over the walls threats and slogans of such richness of
design and exquisite craftsmanship that I'm sure in
years to come it would be hard to dispute that they
were the most elaborate, the most decorative, the most
valuable and the most superbly assured threats and
slogans produced in the world and upon which the dust
of age will never sit. Not to mention leaflets, posters,
banners, paintings and huge display screens, each one
an eternal tableau, the colour of blood and brighter than
the line of light. In the old days, with all those tutus
swishing around at sixes and sevens, the policy was
obviously: if it moves or rather wobbles don't look.
Today, it's the other way round. If it doesn't move slap a
picture of an Ayatollah on it. If, on the other hand, it
moves, stop it from moving so we can still slap a picture
of an Ayatollah on it. Fail to do one or the other and

you'll be carpeted: turned into an exquisite pattern and trampled on.

Very much as you would expect, this has virtually turned the whole country into a living art gallery. Although if I may say, O Juri, I know that to you painting is, as you say, a whispered song which only the deaf can hear and the painter a dreamer who can listen to what the world has to see – or words to that effect – I honestly think that putting that huge poster of Ayatollah Khomenei above a road sign in Shiraz proclaiming Sa'di St was not necessarily one of your better ideas. Although, of course, I could be wrong. It can after all be seen by everybody on their way to visit the mausoleum of your famous thirteenth-century poet, Sa'di, not to mention He who is Himself the Creator of these Masterpieces and the One who says to those who paint their own faces red and the faces of their enemies yellow, Well done.

Even though you've tried to disguise it, I'm afraid you can't hide the real reason why this enormous transplant in the arts from the floor to the wall is of fundamental importance to the Revolution. Most artists, designers, painters, let's be honest, are troublemakers. By giving them so many huge pictures, paintings and even plaques and busts and sculptures to create, you are not only keeping them out of mischief and, therefore, very cleverly stopping them from annoying you, you are also by no doubt paying them handsomely for what they do ensuring their continued one hundred per cent support for the Great Islamic Revolution. The same goes for everybody working in all the equally important allied industries: printers, picture framers, photographic studios, fairy light manufacturers, ink suppliers, the vast Iranian drawing pin manufacturing industry. That's not all. Having developed such a successful policy for reducing social tension, creating employment and stimulating key strategic sectors of the economy, unlike other governments in the world who would by now be performing a sharp U-turn if not cancelling the policy altogether, I notice you are instead extending it to, as you say, that silent cry which talks to peoples of all colours and reveals the unknown beauties of the human soul. In other words, outdoor signs. I'm pleased to see that at long last you are replacing those lascivious signs of Queen Soraya's famous assets with speed bumps, all over the country. Allah help me, anyone would think you were still under the direction and guidance of the royal family. As for those obscene and depraved pictures of little boys and girls going to school together actually, actually, actually… I can hardly say it … *holding hands*: I can see you are ripping them up and destroying them just as quickly. Similarly on many road signs, especially by roundabouts, I couldn't help but notice that you are correcting some of the more excitable directions and angles and even replacing them with far more appropriate political slogans exhorting people simply to 'Keep Right'. Also I see that outside electronics shops you are replacing signs with the insulting message 'Philishave' with others saying 'Brother' – obviously exhorting people to remember that they are all part of the one Islamic family.

Neither are you, on the other hand, neglecting your duty to remind people of the glories to be won living up to and surpassing the ideals of the great Islamic Revolution. I was very pleased, therefore, to see that you have installed in key, strategic locations, very discreetly and very fashionably, a whole series of posters featuring undercover agents in dark glasses with the simple message, Police. In fact, so good is this series I wouldn't be surprised if it were to be copied by the undercover agents working for Mossad, the CIA, the enemies of the Revolution, communists, royalists, spreaders of corruption, sexual deviants and people who have trouble with their eyes for one reason or another. On the other hand, I must admit I didn't quite see the relevance of all those grubby signs in back alleys all over the place saying 'USA Certified Urologist'. Quite frankly if I ever have to go to a urologist as a result of all that yoghurt I will definitely not be going to one who is certified, whether it is in the USA or not. But if all the signs help to sustain the great Iranian art transplant, create work for designers and keep potential troublemakers off the streets, I'm all for it. As if that wasn't enough, you are also applying the same positive strategy to the humble printed word. Every day, millions of books pour fourth hailing the glories of the Revolution. The Contemporary History Studies Institute alone now contains over 130,000 books, 20,000 of them dealing with, I was told, contemporary history, not to mention three million pages of documents, one million photographs and more than a few rotten apples who will no doubt be purged sooner or later. As if that's not enough for artists, designers, printers, book binders and librarians to handle, I notice you are following your usual policy of keeping people out of mischief by insisting they now put the whole lot on the Internet which should in itself keep goodness knows how many more potential troublemakers stuck in front of their PCs. Then you are organising still more huge international congresses on Imam Khomenei and the Revival of Religious Thoughts, with participants from all over the world generating still more mountains of paper to be analysed and catalogued and sent winging into cyberspace. Caxton would have been proud of you.

Fifth Mentionable Event

The best vintage glory to the fifth greatest event of modern times nurtured and given forth (or fifth) by the great Islamic Revolution: the greatest wine industry in the world. I'm no expert. But I vaguely recall, through some kind of foggy haze no doubt induced by the cooling liquid in the fridge in my room in Yazd, that in the past Iran produced the odd bottle. Piton from Zanjan. Cabernet Sauvignon from somewhere in the Bashakerd Mountains. And I forget where Shiraz came from. I also seem vaguely to remember that the whole thing died out because being strict Shi'ites it was impossible for you to pray for Sunni weather to ripen the grapes. The result was that until very recently the whole place was like the Drunkard's Remorse come back with a vengeance.

However, I'm pleased to say that as a result of your far-seeing policies you have united the country as one. Wherever you go, whoever you talk to, you come across this sharp reduction of the scientific and reasoning strength of the community rendering it vulnerable to foreign factors, international shortcomings, low impact of the mass media and uncontrolled fountains of speculation, producing a total, undivided, unanimity of view. In other words, the country is full to overflowing with one wine after another. And, just as in France or Germany or Romania, or anywhere else for that matter, your best wines I came across not in the open but behind closed doors. Under lock and key. Whoever I met, businessmen, managers, workers, even bankers, would as one lock their doors, switch on the radio and in an oath of obviously undying loyalty mutter under their breath, 'Khomenei', while at the same time pledging their lives to the cause by licking the tips of their fingers and passing them backwards and forwards first across their tongues and then across their throats. Others, obviously less sophisticated, would signify the sanctity of all the grand ayatollahs, senior clerics and intellectuals of the Revolution by twirling their fingers in a circle around the top of their heads and shrugging their shoulders, as if to say there was no way they could ever expect to be as holy as you all. This I remember happened one particular evening when I was visiting my very good friend, whose name and address escapes me at the moment, when instead of showing some football match the television played yet another one of those glorious dreamy, dreamy tributes to Ayatollah Khomenei including the bed on the balcony scene which, I don't know why, always reminds me of the final party political broadcast by New Labour on the eve of a general election. On another occasion I was seeing a businessman, an ex-pilot, off at Tehran Railway Station. He kept saying to me 'Iran no good' and then mumbling something which I'm sure was 'without the mullahs'. But I may have been mistaken. It could have been, 'at football', 'at making nuclear weapons', 'at hiding them from the US spy planes' or anything. But rest assured, O Juri, he assured me he would never dream of going for a Shi'ite while the train was standing at the station. Or anywhere else for that matter.

O Juri, as if that is not enough, every day in your wisdom you are creating more and more wines than poor old Omar Khayyam could ever have dreamed of.

Unless I'm very much mistaken, everybody whines about something called a non-alcoholic malt beverage which tastes like it was made in somebody's washroom. But at least it proves one thing. There is soap in Iran: even if it's all in the non-alcoholic malt beverages. They whine about the orange juices which, even after years of sinking New Zealand Chardonnays are, I must tell you, grim. Because in many places there was nothing else on offer I drank so much of the stuff that by the end of my trip I could not only tell you which side of the pip it was grown on I could tell you who picked it, when, and how much curly hair she was showing under her veil. Trouble was when I got home I looked as though I had third-degree jaundice. Talking of jaundice, I don't know whether I should tell you this, but on one occasion I was actually offered a Whisky Mac in Bagh-e Eram, the Garden of Paradise in Shiraz. But as we were surrounded by a bunch of gardeners with scruffy jackets, open shirts, three days' stubble and mobile phones, I thought it best to decline. Instead, I accepted as graciously as I could this very cool looking Lively Lady they kept thrusting at me. Which I must say was a bit of a shock because I didn't think you guys did that kind of thing. Especially in public. Back home, apart from the fact that there are hardly any left, you are only ever likely to come across them in humid, hot-house conditions. As far as I was concerned, therefore, it was an opportunity not to miss. Temperatures, especially in the desert areas, were positively broiling – in some cases as high as 50-55 degrees Centigrade. The place was crawling with police, religious police, secret police and (who knows?) the odd suicide bomber. I'm sorry to mention this again, O Juri, but there was nothing else to cool me down. No Pimm's Number One. No vodka tonics. No glasses of chilled champagne. In any case, the Lively Lady is one of my favourite roses. Now pass me another yoghurt.

Goodness me, but the best wine of all was in the top restaurant in the country: the wooden shack on the top of the snow-capped Elburz Mountains just outside Tehran. The kitchens were out of action. Instead we sat at wooden benches, munching greasy hamburgers and drinking bottles of some kind of fizz. But I wasn't worried. Before we went there I insisted it was only fair, as it was truly one of the unique gastronomic centres in the world, to split the bill. They could pay for the food. I would pay for the drink. Either way it was worth it. The shed we had to go in to catch the cable car back to Tehran was, everybody told me, the next best thing to being inside a typical Iranian court room. It was enormous. There were metal barriers everywhere. People kept shuffling in all the time. There was only one exit – and that was down.

Here again, however, I detect your underlying strategy to stimulate and develop the agricultural sector. First, deliberately create a scare about the drinking water so that nobody, but nobody, is prepared even to go into the same room as a glass of water. Which you and I know is nonsense. All I can say is, I've drunk the water in hotels, throughout Iran. I've had salads in a million different restaurants. I've even had ice with my yoghurt and … if you'll excuse me, I'll be back in about two hours to explain why I always force myself to drink whisky whenever I go abroad just to kill off the bugs. But your approach is, I admit, interesting. I mean sixty million people drinking twenty-seven glasses of grape juice a day is one hell of a way to stimulate the agricultural sector. There is little time to drink such nasty, foreign imports as Coca-Cola. It also stops people from throwing up on all your precious carpets. And it must be one hell of a boost for the urology sector, which is probably why there are all those signs. Cup of tea, Vicar – I mean, Your Jurisprudence?

Sixth Mentionable Event

It's more glory still to the sixth greatest event of modern times, nurtured and given sixth by the great Islamic Revolution: suicide as an art form. Now I know you wouldn't want me to mince words so I'll tell you straight. In present circumstances, the agents of mysterious manoeuvres move contrary to the current with an ever growing speed, unchained by ignorance, free of pretenders of virtue and ever determined to release the trench between the cultural and political élites that fan the flames of enmity and opposition. In other words, you guys are the biggest bunch of frustrated martyrs I've ever come across. Everything you do seems somehow designed to kill you and everybody else as well. And I don't just mean your non-alcoholic malt beverage or the pile of barbari, lavash, sangale or even taaftun you're supposed to get through every day.

Take the way you drive. You may not believe in casinos but far more gambling takes place in even the smallest back street of the smallest town in Iran than in any game with a bunch of high rollers at any casino anywhere in the world. As for getting the juices going, nothing beats facing a truck head-on at 120 km an hour in the middle lane of a two-lane highway when nobody is going to give in. This happened to me on the way back from Persepolis to Shiraz. We swung out into the middle of this two-lane highway. Coming straight at us was this 200-ton truck. Faster. And faster. And... suddenly my driver swung off the far side of the road, careered around a car jammed under the back of a lorry, passed a body – a dead body – stretched out in the middle of the road and back on to our side again. Without slowing up. Without so much as a foot hovering above the brake pedal. Did I have faith then in God's rule and the Household of the Prophet? You bet your life I did. Crescenting the road, or even trying to crescent the road, anywhere in your glorious country is the biggest gamble I've ever come acrescent. In fact, come to think of it, which I'd rather not, it's like playing Russian roulette with a full barrel – only more dangerous. You don't just drive behind the car in front. You drive *underneath* the car or bus or truck in front. You don't believe in using your brakes. Ever. Instead, if the car or bus or truck in front slows up you immediately swing out and overtake. If there is a 40-ton truck coming straight at you it somehow seems to add to the excitement. As for traffic lights, turning left, turning right and all the other boring things people plan, think about, consider, you just do it. Whether the lights are in your favour or not. Whether there's a constant stream of traffic coming at you or not. And if you can do it at 70 mph on two wheels, so much the better. You don't believe me? Let me tell you about the time I was crossing one of the roads that lead into Iman Square in Estfahan when I all but joined the ever growing list of

Illustrious Martyrs to the Glorious Revolution. I was following my own personal please-let-me-survive Iranian highway code. I positioned myself the other side of about six Iranians who were also preparing to cross the road. Nobody would think twice about knocking me down, I reasoned, but to knock six or seven Iranians down just to get me might be just too much even for them. The traffic slowed to a steady 80 mph. A gap was coming up before this truck. We all stepped off the pavement together. Yaaargh. A motorbike coming in the opposite direction on the wrong side of the road, half on the pavement, half on the road, missed me by nothing at all. Did he stop? Not on your or rather my life. But I did see him make a mental note to add $27\frac{1}{2}$ points to his total of near-misses. The only reason I can think of for you guys driving so crazily is that somewhere in the Koran someone must have discovered a passage – obviously a fast passage – that says, 'So he threw down his rod, clambered on to his camel and hurtled into the sunset.' Which roughly translated suggests, 'The faster you go, the more you take with you, the better the place you get.' There can be no other explanation.

So you think I'm paranoid. Not at all. The mere fact that all Iran Air flights are prefixed IRA did not, for example, worry me one bit. The fact that nobody checked my bags either on the way in or on the way out of any airport did not concern me too much. What did concern me, however, was the fact that whenever I had a body check the soldiers or security guards would always sneeze all over me. Whether they were exercising some kind of Islamic freedom of expression or whether they were allergic to infidels, I don't know. Every time I tried to find out, a bunch of them surrounded me and hustled me through to passport control. I will admit I did have a few scares in your country. In Yazd I'd just been to the Shrine of the Twelve Martyrs. It's generally locked. But smile at the guy at Alexander's Prison next door and he will give you the key. I wanted to get to the Amir Chakmaqu Mosque and the Takieh-ye Mir Chakhmaq, a fantastic grandstand built in the shape of a, well, grandstand. The driver said he knew the way. We went up sandy back streets. We went down sandy back streets. We turned left. We turned right. We crisscrescented practically the whole of the old town. Then suddenly aaaaargh – don't ask me how – we're actually parked, engine running, on the carpets in the centre of this mosque all done up in its Friday mourning best. Imams came running from everywhere. But – Robert Byron would have been proud of me – I got out, told everyone my name was Bill Bryson and asked the way to Amir Chakhmaq. They couldn't have been more charming apart from one particularly fat mullah – all mullahs are fat – who the driver told me afterwards kept muttering 'May Allah burn his bones.' Another day in Shiraz I must have innocently strolled into some kind of special Suicides Anonymous service at the big Astenah Mosque. About fifty thousand blokes, all with black beards and black bands round their heads, suddenly turned to me and started chanting and slapping their chests and waving black banners in the air. Unperturbed, I gave them a quick twirl with my prayer beads, scratched my two-day-old beard and blew them all a big kiss which seemed to do the trick. Either way, I'm here to tell the tale. Now if you'll just stop trying to pull the pin out of that thing...

Seventh Mentionable Event

All glory to the seventh greatest event of modern times nurtured and given forth by the great Islamic Revolution: Cool Irania. Like Cool Britannia but more serious. Your arts are cool, if not frozen stiff. Your last two decent poets were Sa'di, the big traveller who wandered all over the Middle East, India, Turkey, Lebanon, North Africa (and no doubt he, like us all, got bounced many times by British Airways) and Hafez, the stay-at-home. Both died years and years ago which is obviously why you make so much fuss of them, especially Sa'di. Fancy building a pool complete with fish underneath his mausoleum. It's not as if he was even a minor Lakeland poet. When I went there, there was more debate about whether the fish were piranhas than about the poet's habit of behaving like a dervish and cadging whatever he could from whoever he could. However, if a comprehensive model of Islam is produced and its beauties learnt, credence will be given to the role accorded to your gardens. For they really are cool. In fact, I don't think I've been anywhere where the gardens are as cool and pleasant. If I may say so, O Juri, some of them could do with a bit of weeding but, I suppose, given the appropriate ambient there are not too many rakes in Iran. The gardens I liked best were in Shiraz, especially the big formal botanical gardens which, far away from the microphones, were full to overflowing with seeds of discord. The Royal Highness roses were, I noticed, growing quite happily alongside the Red Devil roses in the shade of – dare I say it? – a Petticoat palm. Really creative gardening that. I only hope it won't be too long before the gardener is fully recovered and back at work. The rock gardens always looked somewhat depleted wherever they were. Not of plants. Of rocks. What on earth people could do with the rocks I have no idea, although there must be some deep mystical connotation somewhere. I was so serious about checking out your gardens, I even went to pay my respects to the oldest tree in Tehran which at one time was home to a shoe repairer. But no longer. I was told he's got another branch elsewhere in the city.

As for your buildings, the serving tables of the Revolution, now they are really cool. Especially in the desert areas where they have their own cooling towers. (In fact, in some ways you could say that with the cooling system on the outside they were the inspiration for the anti-values of Norman Foster. Except I doubt whether so many people complain about having to live and work inside your buildings as they do in his.) I like the attention to detail. How the decoration on the doors to the women's quarters, for example, are different to the men's, or as one old man I met in the back streets of Yazd told me, 'Women have different knockers from men.' The towns and city centres are cool. I like the way you very cleverly turned all the millions of potholes and bomb sites and derelict areas into respected sources of emulation by converting them into traditional craft markets, where all kinds of people wearing traditional old clothes sell the basic essentials of life. I like the idea of charity boxes lining the streets looking like parking meters all connected, so I was told by many people, to a huge underground network of tunnels so that the money can go straight into the mullahs' pockets without anybody seeing. On the outskirts of town I like the idea of the cemeteries blending in with supermarkets – something we're not able to do back home because we were always told to drive the money-changers out of the temple. As a result our cemeteries and churches stand deserted, surrounded either by dirty bits of grass or gangs of drug addicts. Outside town, in the desert, I like the way that, Swiss-style, you've concealed all your F1-11 bombers in secret hideaways in the mountains rather than let them mar the landscape. Although why you've then written in the soil in huge white letters in Farsi exactly where they are, somewhat baffles me – although no doubt it's all explained in the Koran if I study it hard enough. But best of all, whether it's in town, on the outskirts or out in the desert, I just love the way you've made certain that the police control posts blend in with the environment. All along the roads, by hotels and factories even at Persepolis you would never guess that those rickety old green towers with eager young men staring at your every move and waving guns in the air (no doubt as a traditional form of greeting) were there solely for your protection. And, of course, the ultimate accolade of coolness: insignificant opposition grouplets don't want anything to do with even the idea of Cool Irania. Tony would be proud of you.

Eighth Mentionable Event

Lots more glory to the eighth greatest event of modern times nurtured and given forth by the great Islamic Revolution: The Nobble Prize for English. Nobody could possibly disagree with your success, unrivalled by any other nation in history, at nobbling the English language. One has only to pick up a newspaper, switch on the radio, talk to people hobbling along the street to marvel at the new dimension you have brought to the language of Shakespeare, Omar Khayyam and, of course, the Ayatollah Khomenei himself, who did not just nobble but supernobbled the language. Apparently his style of writing and speaking was so involved and convoluted and complicated that you only have to see a single sentence on the printed page, scrawled up on a wall or winging its way on some website somewhere, to know one possibly it written person in the world only could have that Americans shoot the camel to the Death. How eagerly Shakespeare, let alone Fitzgerald, would have given an Afghani counterfeit ten-bob bit to have had your skills and facility with the English language. Out would have gone boring stuff such as 'To be or not to be', not to mention awful, complicated, pretentious stuff such as, 'Myself when young did eagerly frequent Doctor and Saint, and heard great argument/About it and about; but evermore came out by the same door wherein I went.' I'm sure your moving finger would have writ far, far different things and then moved on to more important matters. After all, it's not that you speak or write English differently, it's just that you somehow use the words in a totally unexpected order. Like somebody speaking from cue cards that are all mixed up.

On the other hand, take your newspapers. One day I was positively gripped by the main story on page one which was all about the deciding strata in the community... how they are going about discharging their duties... how sages and thinkers 'have rendered their traditional circles impotent which as a result means emptying the system from humanitarian and virtuous people and to dig a big trench between the system and the cultural and political elites of the community and fan enmity and oppositions'. Real punchy stuff.

Unfortunately – I mean, fortunately – it's the same with radio. Everybody said their team did great at the World Cup or, in the case of you-know-who, *très bon*. What did you say, O Juri? 'In the name of God, the Merciful, the Compassionate. My dear ones. In tonight's honourable and brave game, which was technical and strong, you defeated strong opponents... This was a beautiful picture of the struggle of the Iranian nation in all... its revolutionary existence. A combination of intelligence, strength and dedicated and co-ordinated efforts in a paradise of remembering God and relying on him. It was this unprecedented struggle which bestowed victory and honour on our nation during the Revolution and in all the conflicts between the Iranian nation and the Great Satan. Tonight, once again, the strong and arrogant opponent felt the bitter taste of defeat at your hands. Be happy because you made the Iranian nation happy.' Poetry. Sheer poetry. Just what the fans on the terraces wanted to hear.

Such are your standards of education, the amazing thing is that Nobbled English is spoken by everyone. Whenever I visited a factory, for example, and simply asked what they did, the manager (with or without his Barry Manilow T-shirt) would invariably put his AK-47 down on his desk, adjust his body armour, look me straight in the eye, twirl his beads round and round and say, 'In the Name of God have a good taste and thought. With an appropriate climate one day it would be a strong economic pole in the country.' Which you have to admit lays it on the line. No ifs or buts. Straight to the point. The kind of guy you can do business with, though exactly what line of business I have yet to decide. The meetings would then continue in much the same vein, with a lot of transfactionals and socio-political relations and hands of friendships and co-operations all over the place. Then, when I finally dragged myself away, I would usually be told as I was being frisked on the way out – in case I had lifted some rusty nuts and bolts or smashed-up wooden pallets or even broken panes of glass – 'Regarding that you remind investors have welcome prominently the opportunities all too correctly after accurate specialist works. Let us not take your time any more but enjoy your views I hereby appreciate your helps.' In fact, wherever I went, I found people wanted to share their glorious love of Nobbled English with me. I can't, for example, remember the number of times groups of eager young men pushed up to me in the street to give what I now realise is the traditional Iranian greeting to strangers, 'You American? I'll cut your ...' As soon as I told them I was Canadian, which I gather is the traditional response, they seemed more relaxed and put their knives and iron bars away and started asking me if I could lend them US$150 for a bottle of Johnnie Walker, which was invariably being hustled by the brother of some Imam or other round the corner, no doubt to raise money to build some more mosques.

You will be pleased to hear, O Juri, it wasn't all one way. The least I could do, I felt, was to cultivate this love you have of the English language. In the hotels where I stayed I taught the Revolutionary Guards on reception useful phrases which I felt might come in handy some day.

'Okay, US$100. Now she looks like your wife.'

'Don't tell anyone, but the Ayatollah with four wives in Room 431 has a couple of bottles of Scotch he is happy to share with you.'

'Don't worry, you don't have to pay the bill.'

Then, to show my appreciation of the restaurants which for the first time in my life taught me the joys of constipation, I taught all the waiters to say:

'Well, that's all we've got.'

'What do you mean, it's green? That means it's fresh, doesn't it?'

'Are you going to finish this stuff, or do I give it to someone else?'

But, as you know, speaking Nobbled English is one thing. Speaking Nobbled English correctly takes a lifetime's dedication. So again, as a servant of the Revolution round the clock, wherever I got the chance I helped my brothers improve still further their impeccable use of English. A businessman kept saying to me as we headed uphill to his house in North Tehran, 'Careful. He *basij*, maybe. Smell like one.' Instead, you'll be pleased to hear, I taught him to say, 'Careful. He looks like a *basij*. He certainly smells like one.' In Qom, an ayatollah with a black turban (which meant he must have been a direct descendant of Mohammad) kept telling me, 'Friends with Israel, we are yes really. Because bomb we want help with, yes?' It took a long time but – you'll be proud of me as I know you are determined to free society from the evils of hypocrisy – by the time I left he was saying, 'It is a lie. Israel is our friend. We do not have a bomb. We do not want bomb. We are peace-loving people.' As for the ladies or, as you say, the damsels who poison the pure environment I'm afraid I didn't have much success. But then I never do. Although, come to think of it, I was able to introduce one particular disturber of society's tranquillity to the joys of English. She told me that her father was coming back shortly from the States, I mean Canada, and she wanted to impress him with her knowledge of English. As she seemed more interested in the practical side of things, I taught her what I thought were the five phrases which any Allah-fearing father would want to hear from his loving daughter:

'How long have we got?'

'Good. That's long enough.'

'Okay. Let's get on with it.'

'No, it's free.'

'But I was careful.'

I trust you agree with me. I wouldn't want the blade of the knife to start fighting the handle as you say, O Juri. But the Nobble Prize must without doubt go to the big, fat Friar Tuck Imam in Qom who told me in no uncertain terms that it was his ambition to penetrate as many women as possible in public life.

Believe me, in conclusion, O Supreme Leader, the Guardianship of Supreme Jurisprudence, the Wonderful, Unique Plenipotentiary of the Muslims, Ayatollah Seyed Ali Khomenei, I would like to say that as far as I am concerned there is no other country on earth like Iran. It is truly unique. It is very difficult for me to find the words to express what I feel about the mullahs and what they have done for the country which is totally beyond belief.

O Juri, many's the time people told me that because of your achievements which they thought were not of this world they couldn't wait to bury the lot of you with the dignity and reverence they felt you deserved so that you wouldn't have to wait for years on end to obtain the due reward for what you have done to Iran and its peoples. I don't think any fair-minded person could possibly disagree. After all, Iran is now a nation known and spoken of throughout the world.

O Juri, I honestly believe Iran has a great atmosphere all of its own. It has a great bunch of people who are prepared to list your achievements at the slightest prompting. It is also the greatest laxative in the world. For this continuing mercy a grateful people gives you eternal thanks.

Knowledgeable you are, O Juri, about all things. But it won't last. Like it or not, you will become more Westernised. Estfahan, for example, will become Westfahan. You will give in to women and begin making those far-reaching fundamental changes you have been dreading, not only in your attitude to them but also in the way you treat them. Kerman will be renamed Kerwoman; Kermanshah, Kerwomanshah and, of course, Susa, Susan. You will also have to relax all those silly rules and regulations about booze and cutting your beards with scissors instead of razor blades and clapping hands and enjoying life. What's more, I bet, Qazvin will become Qazvino. Shiraz will become so famous they will even name grapes and wine after it. So make the most of it while it lasts, sunshine.

Your humble and obedient servant etc. etc.

PS I've been thinking about that mosque in Yazd. Honestly, I didn't mean to drive through the middle of it. Perhaps you could put in a word for me with Allah. I'm sure He'll understand. Especially if, O Juri, you tell him it was a mistake. After all, from what I understand, it won't be long before you actually see him. Thanks.

PPS Somebody's just told me that if you take the first letter of each paragraph of this letter you come up with some silly message. Don't believe them.

PPPS The same applies to the capital letters in bold type at the start of this letter.

PPPPS Maybe you could give me the name of a goode printter?

Kaliningrad

You want to see the results of ethnic cleansing? Go to Kaliningrad, once a top-secret Nazi naval base, now a Russian one, which, in all honesty, should be called the Kalinin Fields. Even the statue of Mikhail Kalinin outside the main station I swear looks like Radovan Karadzic, the Bosnian Serb leader – without that enormous quiff, of course. The Mister Nobody of Soviet politics, Kalinin somehow managed to survive purge after purge after purge, so that when Uncle Joe was looking for a weak, innocent pliable president for the mighty USSR, he was about the only guy left. So good was he at surviving that he lasted, would you believe, from 1919 until his death in 1946. But check him out in the books and he's not there. It was the same in Kaliningrad itself. Nobody could tell me who he was, or what he did or did not do. The nearest I got to finding out was from a young manager in one of the factories I visited, who said he thought Kalinin was some kind of vegetable. Which I suppose he must have been to have survived with Stalin for so long. Like those who were Cabinet ministers under Mrs Thatcher. You mean you've forgotten the story of Mrs Thatcher taking the whole of the Cabinet out for lunch? Into the restaurant she bustles, sits down at the top of the table and orders herself a large steak. And the waiter says, 'The vegetables?' 'Oh,' she replies, as all the others jostle to sit as far away from her as possible, 'they'll have the same as me.'

Wedged up on the Baltic Sea between Poland and Lithuania, about half the size of nothing, Kaliningrad was originally Koenigsberg, the heartland of Prussia, the very heart of Bismarck's Germany and for more than seven hundred years the capital where the imperial dukes and kings of East Prussia lived, the guys with pointed helmets, shiny leather boots and rows and rows of medals. For many it was the golden age of German history. So dedicated were they to honour, duty, service, hard work, thrift, everything that we now despise, that they didn't believe in paying their civil servants. Instead, according to their constitution, they undertook to provide them with what they called an alimony or a retainer. The fact that the constitution was drawn up by the Junkers, rich landowners dedicated to such things as honour, duty, service, hard work, thrift and being 6 foot 6 inches tall was, of course, completely incidental. Apparently so determined were the Junkers to maintain their standards that they scoured the Baltic for anyone of the same height to be members of their Prussian Guard. Even the undertakers were instructed to make all coffins 6 foot 6 inches in length. Strangely enough, even though today the Germans still call the area *Das Nordlich Ostpreussen*, Northern East Prussia, people in both western and eastern Germany have been arrested and taken to court for calling someone a Prussian.

The turning point in the Junkers' fortunes came, I reckon, not when the Knights of the Teutonic Order practically destroyed the place in the thirteenth century, but when East Prussia became the first European power to sign a friendship treaty with the United States. After that it was downhill all the way. Frederick the Great gave way to the rule of law. The rule of law gave way to universal suffrage. Universal suffrage meant women in Koenigsberg had the vote long before women in Britain or even in the United States.

Today, wandering around Kaliningrad, which through-out the rest of Russia is known as a lawless enclave, it is practically impossible to see any trace of its once glorious past. The famous sixteenth-century Koenigs-berg Castle, headquarters of the Grandmaster of the Teutonic Order, official residence of the Dukes of Prussia, the scene of the coronation of Frederick I in 1701 and in 1861 of William I, has been flattened. The cathedral built in 1333 is now a shell held together with barbed wire and bits of boarding. They say it is being restored. All I can say is, it'll be a long time coming. Still it is without any kind of roof, while the front of the building, with its windows blocked in and some crude brickwork filling in the occasional hole, looks like a cheap backdrop to some horror movie.

The observatory, the academy of painting, the music school, the library (which once held over 200,000 books) - are all gone. The zoological museum, the botanical gardens - both totally wiped out. The ironworks, the engineering works, the brewery, the factories, the craftsmen who once built some of the world's finest pianos - all gone. All destroyed. All that's left of the university founded in 1544 is a single pinkish lump of rock with a brief inscription, which even the most dedicated searcher after Kaliningrad's past - and there are very few of them, with the exception of the occasional determined Hungarian visitor - can easily miss. Early one morning on the way to my first meeting I saw an old man standing by it, weeping into an enormous red handkerchief. He was what they call a *Heimattouristen*, an old Koenigsberger come back to visit the scenes of his youth. Except there were no scenes left for him to visit. As for all the elegant streets and town houses where once Count von This polished his monocle and Count von That strutted up and down in his shiny boots, they too were all gone, buried, obliterated. Practically all that is left is the old Italian-style stock exchange on the banks of the River Pregolya, which has been painted a strange pastel blue and turned into some kind of exhibition centre.

But be careful, don't start blaming the Russians just yet. Huge chunks of the city were, in fact, destroyed by – guess who? – the British, in no fewer than 386 bombing sorties in August 1944, which killed over four thousand people. It's just that the Russians finished it off. First in a massive assault the following year. Then, as soon as the war and Potsdam were over, they levelled practically anything that was left standing. Any Germans who were still living there were then evacuated, sent to Siberia or just slaughtered. The children were sent all over Russia and the Ukraine, where they were given local names and farmed out to local families. Some estimates talk of no fewer than two million men, women and children being forcibly uprooted, subjected to the most horrific treatment or killed in probably the biggest single ethnic cleansing operation of all time.

We've had Schindler's List; somebody should now make Kaliningrad's List. The terror, the horror, the cruelty was no less than that inflicted on the Jews and others in Krakow or Auschwitz by the Germans. Not once, the whole time I was there, did I see even one droopy Prussian moustache, let alone catch the slightest trace of a German accent.

'There are no German people here,' an old Russian soldier told me. 'Maybe in the villages, in the countryside, but I don't think so. You can try to find them, but I don't think you'll be lucky.'

Instead, all you see is Wigan on a wet Wednesday afternoon. Covered in slush, the ultimate in desolation and dejection. The buildings are all standard-issue brutalist Soviet towerblocks surrounded by standard-issue brutalist Soviet single-storey buildings. The biggest of them all, the Communist Party headquarters, built, as you would expect, on the site of the Royal Palace, started falling to bits before they even finished it. The foundations started to shift, like the foundations of the once great Russian Communist Party itself. Walls began to crack, windows broke. It was decided it was too dangerous to use. Our Leaning Tower of Pisa, the local Communists used to call it. The Monster, the non-Communists call it, because if you look closely at the different balconies that stick out at odd angles you can see two eyes and one huge Cherie Blair letter-box mouth.

As for offices and factories, they are more outside than inside. In one factory I went to, the window frames had no windows, the walls were bare breezeblocks, the doors had long since been taken down and chopped up for firewood.

Then there are the roads. The main roads look like side roads. The side roads look like country lanes. And the country lanes look as if they never existed. One day I visited a string of derelict factories. It was like going back into the dark ages. We went up and down muddy tracks. We waded through ankle-deep mud. It was more like a cross-country run than an industrial tour. As if that were not bad enough, the whole place is so badly polluted you think you're driving around all the time with a filthy windscreen. The River Pregolya, which flows – or rather tries to flow – through the centre of town is as black as soot. I was going to slice it up and bring some home, but I couldn't find a knife strong enough to cut the stuff.

On the other hand, think positive: it's the best place in the world to try to find out what makes the Russians tick because there are so many people there from so many different parts of Russia. Believe me, it's even better than walking down Larnaca High Street or lounging on the beach in Dubai wondering who's going to murder whom next. From Moscow, from St Petersburg, from Siberia, from the Volga region, from all over the Caucasus, from the Urals, even from Vladivostock they come. Not to mention Latvians and Estonians and Lithuanians and Poles and Ukrainians and

Belorussians. Because when Stalin shipped the Germans out, he shipped other nationalities in. In fact, the local Kaliningrad town council says it is home to over thirty different nationalities, although, surprise, surprise, it doesn't say how or why.

Not that this is in any way the promised land. Life is rough, tough and basic, very basic. The kind of place to go if you want to toughen yourself up before joining the Marines or going to Scotland for the weekend. With an average meal in an average restaurant costing a month's salary, most people find their own entertainment: sitting at home watching a samovar come to the boil. Others claim a visit to the post office takes some beating.

With nothing else on offer one evening, I went back home with the manager of a local factory to have dinner with his family. He had a string of degrees and professional qualifications. He wasn't the big boss but one of the little bosses, in charge of a whole manufacturing plant employing around fifty or sixty people. We drove past the Monster. In the background was the shell of the old cathedral. We turned on to a side road which very quickly became mud and pulled up in front of a crumbling block of flats, maybe ten storeys high. The whole place was filthy, full of broken-down old cars and dustbins with piles of rubbish heaped up against the wall. Dogs, most of them big German shepherd dogs, were around. Kids were howling and squealing and crawling and playing in the mud. We went up to their flat: two tiny rooms which they shared with his wife's parents who, because I was coming, had gone out.

'Where have they gone?' I asked.

'Out,' he said. 'It's what we have to do. There is no room.'

Out, I assumed, meant walking the streets, hanging around the railway or freezing to death in a shop doorway.

We ate our meal sitting on the edge of what were obviously cheap bunk beds. In the centre were two wooden boxes. This was the table. On one wall were a couple of cheap pictures which looked as though they had been torn from a magazine, stuck on some cardboard and hammered into what little plaster there was. From the ceiling hung a single lightbulb. No shade. Judging by the light it threw off, it couldn't have been more than forty or maybe sixty watts.

'In the West, they have nice toilets. But what can they teach me about morals, about ethics, about philosophy? Nothing. I prefer my life here,' said the manager's wife, another graduate with a string of qualifications in engineering, before I had hardly set foot in the place.

I asked the manager how much he earned a month. About US$100, he said. Was it enough?'

'We live. We often wonder how we live, but we live.'

'Do people ever complain?'

'Maybe, as we say, in the kitchen we complain. But we always say, "Things will get better." We hope.'

'You must choose,' his wife said. 'If I want something I stop eating. I want a coat for the children, for a week I don't eat.' Judging by how thin they both were, they obviously didn't eat very much or very often.

But at least this couple had a degree of choice. At a children's hospital I visited the following morning the children had no choice. Whether they had anything to eat or not depended on their parents, who already had to pay for their medicines, their injections, their syringes and their clean linen. 'You mean there's not enough money to feed the children?' I asked one of the administrators, a gentle, white-haired old man who told me he was with the Soviets' 159th Division, which marched into Kaliningrad on 4 April 1945 after the two-month siege.

'We have beds for three hundred children,' he explained. 'We are trying to keep as many in use as possible.'

'So how many are in use?'

'About a hundred and thirty.' He shrugged his shoulders in despair. 'What can we do? We have no money.'

'So the more people look after their children, the more you can look after?'

'*Da*,' he nodded. 'It's not right, but what can we do?'

Stop the big guys – including even, would you believe, the Russian Central Bank itself – from sending billions of dollars of foreign currency reserves out of the country and into a mass of secret offshore bank accounts. That is what they should do for a start. But even in their new-style Russian democracy they don't stand a hope in hell.

Later I discovered that even to get into the hospital, a child didn't just have to be seriously ill, his parents also had to know one of the doctors, or, better still, one of the staff. Then, with varying degrees of persuasion, the kid was in. 'Of course it's wrong,' I was told. 'But that is the system. That is the only way we know.'

The following morning, at another derelict factory, another manager told me that one old woman who lived near him was so hungry, that she actually killed her husband, a certain Nikolai Dalonov, chopped him up into little bits and put him into cans, which she kept in the fridge. She was slowly eating him bit by bit. And one of the secretaries let slip that the man I had had dinner with the previous evening also had two young children. They too had been thrown out in the cold with his wife's parents so that I could be entertained in the two-room flat.

Yet the amazing thing is, Kaliningrad is the super, super, top, top-secret Russian naval base. Until *perestroika* and *glasnost*, it was easier to get into Tibet and take tea with any number of Chinese-backed Dalai Lamas than it was to get into Kaliningrad. There were no direct flights. All road crossings were blocked. Trains from Berlin and the West had been suspended long ago.

Trains from the East were possible – the only problem was getting into the East in order to catch them. Today, however, the only secret is the extent to which it is disintegrating, although you'd never think so. For the Russians still behave as if it is the second most secret place on earth. Everywhere there are soldiers – some say as many as 100,000, one tenth of the entire population. But the crazy thing is, you hardly ever see them, probably because they're too busy trying to keep their tanks from falling to bits. Collapse of the Russian empire or not, to the Eleventh Army, Berlin is still only six hours away – by fast tank.

What you do see is the navy. All over the place. Crowded on to the railway station. Blocking up the streets. Wandering around the main square. Staring up at the Monster, their white hats and long black tassels blowing in the breeze. Torpedo boats are tied up along Muscovsky Prospekt. There are naval higher colleges for, I was told, the commanders of Russian warships in the twenty-first century, and presumably naval lower colleges for the commanders of Russian submarines in the twenty-first century. If, of course, they can find the money by then. Not for the warships or the submarines – governments always find the money for them. I meant the money for the commanders' bus fares to get to their warships and submarines. In the civil port, I saw mile after mile, or rather fathom after fathom, of ships and submarines, but (nobody say a word to Moscow) they were rotting and rusting away to nothing.

Port officials I met claimed they handled over 2,000 ships and over 3.5 million tons of cargo a year. Whether they do or do not, I have no idea; all I can say is that if they do, they must be the best, most efficient, most organised people in the world. Because the place is an absolute, total mass of great enormous tankers, ordinary old steamers, cargo ships, barges and tugboats. Some of them looked as though they had been there since the days of Peter the Great. Many of them looked as though they had actually rusted themselves together into solid lumps and were now slowly sinking into the sea as one. One boat, which might have been a passenger liner a long, long time ago, looked as though it was actually melting with rust. The funnel had virtually unpeeled itself on to the top deck, and the top deck had started to collapse on to the deck below. All the rails and other bits and pieces had folded themselves inwards. Soon all that would be left was another filthy heap jutting out to sea. Even as we were looking at it, a great lump of the hull suddenly came crashing down on to the edge of the wharf.

Out of what looked like a stack of wood waiting to be burnt now came a tiny, shrivelled-up old man with three of the thinnest Alsatians I've ever seen. They were so thin they could hardly summon up the energy to bark. Which is unusual. Most animals (and people, come to think of it) take an instant dislike to me. The old man turned out to be the Baltic's, if not the world's, greatest authority on the Soviet Navy. Kaliningrad, he told me, had been the home of the Russian fleet ever since Peter the Great came there disguised as Peter Mikhailov to work as a foreman and learn the nuts and bolts, or rather the hammer and nails, of the business. Which was a great idea. I only wish some of our other leaders and politicians would do the same thing so at least they would have a rough idea of what they are talking about. Take Mrs Thatcher, for example. What would the health service be like today if she had worked as a nurse rather than playing at shops?

For the old man, the greatest day in the history of the world was 7 May 1703, when Peter the Great attacked and captured his first two Swedish ships, the *Gedan* and the *Astrid*, in the mouth of the River Neva. It was the birth of the glorious Russian tradition of smashing foreign ships to kingdom come. After that came the Northern War (1700–21); the Battle of Gangut Peninsula (1714); the Battle of Esel Island (1719) and the great and glorious War of Aland Islands (1720), which finally secured Russia's access to Europe. After that came Khios Strait and Cesme Bay (1770); Kerch and Tendia Island (1790); the Dardanelles, Aphon (both 1807) and Navarin (1872). As for seamen, the greatest were Kruzenshtern, Lisiansky, Golowin, Lasarev, Bellinsgausen, Nevelskoy and some guy called Popov, who invented the radio telephone for ship-to-shore communication, presumably because it was the only way captains could make sure the KGB were waiting on the dock to arrest any troublemakers who didn't laugh at their little jokes.

Having seen what there was of the civil port, I wanted to see the naval port just outside the city of Baltyisk, the once top, top, top, top, top-secret Soviet Navy port and home to their Baltic fleet and all their latest and most up-to-date naval vessels. Not that I was particularly interested in the ships: what I wanted to see was 2 Street 6. Why? Because, as if I hadn't got enough to do, the shocking Becker, an exotic, debauched, pink-cheeked, middle-aged, cherubic, top of the fops who claims he is a pretender to the Libyan throne and a thousand other things besides, but looks more like a drop-out from *Brideshead Revisited*, had asked me if I could take a look at the old family mansion for him.

I first met Becker a million years ago somewhere or other in the middle of Francophone Africa which he practically had eating out of his hand. Wherever he was he would arrive like an old-fashioned ambassador and immediately attract the same deference and respect. At least to his face. Afterwards and in private people would be more direct – after all, this vision in a soft denim suit, a white shirt and with a tiny red handkerchief tied tightly around his neck is not a slight welcomed by everybody.

With malicious glee Becker would then happily gatecrash anything from presidential press conferences to the opening of some dreary factory addressing everybody in the most gloriously theatrical mixture of upper-class English and God knows what kind of French. Then there were his naval stories. I've forgotten how many times I've heard him regale African Ministers and assorted dignitaries with his stories about the navy. 'But my dear Monsieur le Ministre, *écoutez-moi* for a minute. No, don't listen to him. I have something much, much more important to say.'

He would give a little squeal of delight at the thought of telling a favourite story.

'There we were, Monsieur le Ministre, all at sea. All *sur la mer*. For three weeks. *Trois semaines*. What happens? What happens?'

He assumes a mock serious air. We all drop our knives and forks and lean forward. An enemy attack? Bombs? Submarines? Death? Disease? Famine?

'I'll tell you what happens,' he says and gives a quick schoolboy grin. 'We run out of water. Can you imagine? We run out of *l'eau*.'

We all draw a deep breath at the enormity of their suffering. And don't forget we are invariably in a country that has been suffering a drought for maybe five or ten years; which has seen hundreds and thousands of its people dying for lack of water.

'We run out of water.' We all take another deep breath.

'So what happens?' They begin to die like flies? No, worse than that.

'They issue orders banning all officers from taking a bath.' My God. Don't they know how to suffer, these British dogs of war.

'Can you imagine? No daily bath.' He rolls his eyes up to the heavens. 'Well, I ask you. It was preposterous. Absolutely preposterous.' Preposterous. Not to have a bath every day. We're in a country where probably nobody has ever even thought of having a bath every day.

'Well, of course, I agreed,' he purrs. 'Had to, because of the men. But there was no way I was going without my bath. So what did I do?' We all lean forward once again.

'Monsieur le Ministre, I'll tell you what I did.' The Ministre leans even further forward on the table and practically topples the whole thing over.

'I decided I was going to have my bath whatever they said.'

Shock. Horror.

'And what happened?'

This is the bit that I like.

'Monsieur le Ministre, I will tell you what happened.' He leans back in his chair. 'What happened was, I was discovered.' Fantastic. Serves him right.

'The Chief Petty Officer came in, saw me in my bath. Immediately he reported me to the Captain. The Captain made me run around the deck ten times in my running shorts. In front of all those able seamen. Can you imagine?' I try not to. Everybody else begins to relax their elbows.

The final scene, he milks to the last drop. He leans back in his chair, gives that catchy schoolboy grin, then adds: 'But it was worth it. It was worth every embarrassing minute.' He pauses. 'One just can't go without one's daily bath.' He looks at everybody. Absolutely not, Robert. Impossible. Perish the thought.

When I gave up going to French Africa, he started sending me letters from all over the world regaling me with his malicious views on everything from Graham Greene's 'romping with Lord W ... (Harry to me)', to why the scenes of the first-class deck in the film *Titanic* were all wrong – 'The deck chairs were made of teak! They should have been made of navy blue matelassé tied with linen ribbon. First-class passengers on their verandah sundeck would certainly *not* expect to sit on/ lie back on hardwood *teak*!!' Then there were all the boring – I mean heroic – tales of his naval ancestors, the legendary Beckers of Baltiysk: Captain Master Mariner Frederic Thomas Becker, some cousin or other Becker who was officer commanding at the School of Navigation, and another Becker whom luckily I can't remember, but who no doubt ran the whole world from there. Even though he had served in the British Navy himself, probably for no other reason than that he thought the uniforms were so pretty, he had never been able to go there himself because of - nudge, nudge - intelligence and - wink, wink - security. Know what I mean, old chap.

I say, writing me letters. Becker's idea of writing letters is to grab whatever is close to hand, a wrapper from the *International Herald Tribune*, a back number of *The Times*, a copy of *Le Monde* - the non-diplomatic edition, of course - and scrawl indiscreetly all over it. Not just from left to right like any normal person, but up and down the gaps in the print, along the margins and even all over the envelope as well. I got a Ghana Police Service Christmas card from him once which I had to read like a twisted, old-fashioned gramophone record. He started in the centre of the page and then went round and round in circles until he rambled off the edge with the final flourish, 'Hoots. Toots. Robert'. Hoots! Toots! Robert! He is the last person in the world who needs to sign his letters. I've only got to see the envelope with the scribbles shooting off in all directions and immediately I know who it's from.

But I got my own back. For a long time Becker lived in France, so I used to send him letters from all over the place, especially from different parts of Russia or Eastern Europe, addressed to Son Excellence Colonel Becker, General Becker, K.G. Becker. In the end, triumph! The letters were opened before they were delivered. By whom we do not know, but whoever it was should go back to spy school, because it was all so obvious. The seal was always torn and crumpled. In some cases, the thing was hardly resealed at all.

All the same, as soon as I knew I was going to Kaliningrad, I agreed to go and look up the family pad for him even though I knew from bitter experience that whatever you do or do not do for Becker is highly dangerous because he invariably plays fast and louche with whoever he comes across. In fact, dealing with him is a bit like using a lump of Semtex to start a fire. You're lucky if you escape with your wallet or your life, whichever is the more important to you. Especially when he breaks into his poor little Beckstein routine.

It was not, of course, the first time since I started dragging myself round the world trying to earn a living that somebody had asked me to go and take a look at something, to visit somebody or even to deliver something please. As a result I've been up mountains, down dales, along filthy back streets, across rivers and lakes I wouldn't normally dream of going near in a million years. I've also conveyed lumps of Cheddar cheese to finance ministers, and a pair of – what do you call them? – shoe trees, to a traditional African tribal chief way in the north of Togo because he had problems keeping his one and only expensive pair of Church's shoes in good shape in the heat and humidity of his wooden hut. I've even dragged myself up and down country lanes and villages in the far north of Lithuania helping some chap look for his family home. When we finally found it I nearly froze to death pacing around outside while he came to terms with the fact that it wasn't the palatial mansion he expected but a tiny, collapsing old shack.

Becker, however, is different. He's like something out of an early Evelyn Waugh or, worse still, a Stephen Fry novel – outrageous, filthy-minded and absolutely hilarious. He has this glorious *de haut en bas* patronising lolling hauteur, and complete moral indifference if not excitement at anything even remotely breaking the rules, like an eighteenth-century toff who has somehow strayed out of the pages of a Georgette Heyer novel. To him young people are always 'vulgar' and 'cowardly'. Friends are always 'horrid'. People eat smoked salmon 'so disgracefully fast'. Claret is always *wunderschön* and for throwing over people, even senior Foreign Office officials (I've seen him do it a number of times, even during discreet Whitehall lunches). Champagne is always '*delish!*'. And if he makes a spelling mistake in a letter or a fax it's because 'like my schoolmate, Palmerston, I spell like a gentleman, not like a clerk'.

Wives hate him, if that's not putting it too mildly. To them he is the original guest from purgatory, if not from hell. He invariably arrives days late, insists on being the centre of attention from the moment he staggers into the house and stays for weeks on end, by which time they are showering him with goodbye presents – usually suitcases. Come dinner the very first evening, and he positions himself at the centre – what am I saying? At the head of the table – rolls his eyes and in that slightly high-pitched, plummy, Martini-soaked voice, launches himself into Lecture 27a, 'The Beckersteins of Koenigsberg', or whatever he calls them, 'The family, history of, from the year dot'. Immediately they're screaming for his blood – but inwardly, because once he's off, he's off. Nobody can get a word in, which makes everybody even madder. As a result, wherever he goes he leaves behind him a whole string of broken families. The merest mention that he might, just, perhaps, by chance be dropping in for a drink, let alone dinner, some time between now and the end of the millennium is enough to send wives screaming for the hills. My own wife, for example, has not only totally forbidden me to bring him within a million miles of our place, she has accorded him the glorious honour of being permanently enshrined at the top of her personal hate list, a position which, until Becker came back for dinner with friends one unforgettable Friday evening, was reserved solely for me.

Through no fault of our own (honestly) we were late leaving London. The trains were up the creek. Instead of going to Buxted we had to go to Lewes, queue up for a taxi to Buxted, and so on. We finally arrived home to the kind of welcome written in six-foot high stalactites that says, 'You did this deliberately. This is all your fault.'

'Look, I'm sorry. The trains were—'

'Soup or pâté?'

'Please, if I may, I'll have—'

'You'll have what you're given. If you haven't got the decency to be home...'

Everybody else had obviously been sitting at the table staring at each other for an hour and a half.

'Let me introduce you to—'

'Well, what's it going to be, then? Or do we have to wait another three hours before we can start dinner?'

'Sorry. I thought I said I'll...'

A visible iceberg was forming in the centre of the table. Becker was oblivious of the whole thing. He smiled his best choirboy smile at everyone. 'Oh,' he purred, 'pâté. I do love pâté. You can't get it, you know, in France.' Then he was off on some long and involved nonsense, or, as he would boom, *mise en scène*, about how the French don't know anything about food; that they are all snobs; that he should know, he lived there for three hundred years until the mayor threw him out. Presumably in another glorious *mise en scène*.

Absolute total silence. Nobody said a word. Nobody was biting. Still he carried blithely on. 'Lamb! Oh, how lovely,' he gurgled as the next course was thrown down on the table. Then - don't ask me how he did it - he was going on about Navarin, Navarino, Admiral Codrington blowing the Turkish fleet to pieces and Peter the Great. 'In Peter the Great's victory of 7 May 1703, I think, he captured two ships of four hundred tons, the Swedish *Gedan* and *Astrid*. And at least the Neva didn't have to have a name change.'

Absolute total silence. Relishing his own discomfort, he ploughed on. 'My family come from Baltiysk when it was called Pillau. Kaliningrad was then Koenigsberg and was the old chief Baltic town of the kingdom of Prussia. The two towns work in tandem, like Edinburgh and Leith. Russia wanted them so as to dominate militarily and by sea the southern Baltic. The Germans fled from the advancing Red Army by sea, a sea that is not meant to freeze over all winter long.'

The silence was now not only totally deafening, it was also clutching at my throat.

'I have a letter with a curious oilskin outside. It was sent by one sailor to another, Riga to Memel, to my great-grandfather's Russian ship *Bertha*. Remember the big gun that shelled Paris in the First World War? Well, Memel was at that time in the Prussian kingdom, 1857. In Memel they put their stamp on the cover and duly delivered the letter in Riga to Frederic Thomas Becker, Schiffe *Bertha*, which is a funny way to write "ship" in German. I had the old German translated and the old boy writing to F.T.B. goes on about their ships, the vagaries of trade, the newspapers and thanking him for some fur rug present.'

Nothing seemed to make any difference to him. On and on and on he went. With the cheese and port, it was the Baltic Festival of the Fleet, the mining of the Koenigsberg Canal, and 'why do the Nazis concentrate so on the male bottom?' By now even I was nodding off. The early start, the long day in the office, the journey home, the drink, Becker and ... and ... and ... zzzzz.

'The Germans – did I tell you? – evacuated Pillau by sea as the Russian Army moved up and shelled it. Being Russians, they continued shelling long after the Germans had left and so pulverised the city they had already marked out for themselves. Again, very Russian.'

Suddenly I woke up to find him banging his empty port glass on the table. I filled it up to the brim.

'The Russians, you see, wanted Koenigsberg and Pillau as warm-water ports. Neither are meant to freeze over in the winter. Leningrad and Kronstadt do, Helsingford and Stockholm do. Even Oslo is hopeless in winter. So Kaliningrad and Baltiysk have strategic importance. Walter by the way, did I tell you, was another one of my gorgeous relatives, he was a—'

I grabbed on to the table to stop myself falling off my chair. 'Oh, go on!' he bellows. 'You know how you love listening to stories about them.'

'Yes, yes. Yes, of course, Robert,' I could hear myself mumbling.

'Well, he was a cousin of Fritz, did better than him at KBC no less, and kept his money to the end. Katie Boyle has most of it. She got her father to marry Walter's old trout in 1928. Fritz gave her away and the service had to be in Yugoslavia. It was on the clear understanding that she handed over all the Walter money immediately. He had been made a count by Mussolini.'

Whoa. I'm falling off my chair again.

'You will be pleased to hear that I am a friend of Admiral Schneider-Rings. He once made me stand up before the visiting Dartmouth training squadron and explain that a bottle of Mateus Rosé is based on the shape of a buck's testicle.'

I'm nodding my head vacantly up and down.

'Did I tell you at least three generations of Beckers were born in Baltiysk, owned ships and had the grade of master mariner? One was commandant of the Navigation School in Pillau. Another of the family went and started Becker Paints in Stockholm. You see the plant as you go into Stockholm Harbour. But now there are no Beckers on the board.'

Zzzzz.

'*Coffee!* You want coffee?'

'Ahhhh, where am ... Oh, yes, please. Thank you.'

'Well, it's over there.' With the coffee came liqueurs. I filled Becker's glass with cognac. To the brim.

'Oh, yes. Cognac,' he said, taking a huge gulp. 'That reminds me, I was once nearly killed with a Russian. Did I tell you? It was over Lomé. The Fokkering engine caught fire and blew up and yet we landed at Lomé and drank all of a bottle of cognac together. He only got slightly cross when I held his hand. It's a very funny story in retrospect. He was so interesting about fighting the Germans. They used to bathe in the river with them and only start fighting again if a Communist or a Waffen SS general came nosing around.'

Zzzzzzz.

Crash. Knives and forks and plates and everything else were now being thrown in a heap in the middle of the table. But he was still at it.

'Obviously, sloppy old Moskva couldn't do better than thirty-one knots. But the Kiev Class had just been commissioned and they had twice the engine power of the Moskvas, same as the old Lexington Saratoga 1925 Class that made sea passages of over thirty-two knots before the First World War. But forty knots is out of the question.'

Zzzzzz. Wha—! What's that? The door coming off its hinges, pictures smashing to the floor. My god, what the hell is he on about now?

'Of course, I shall be buried in my grandfather's eight-seater *laundrette* in the churchyard where the *hoi polloi* have been forbidden burial for fifty years. I love being related to the most cruel man in Saxon history.'

I know this will come as a surprise to you, but Becker did not go down very well. Nobody could say anything to anybody else, he just completely and absolutely dominated everything. To me the whole thing was hilarious – his glorious history of the Becksteins, the wonders of the ancient world of Prussia – he actually lives up a creek, near some old gunboat sheds in Gosport at the mercy of a bunch of what he calls vandal-Vikings who keep throwing his prized petunias in the water.

The following morning there was no shortage of volunteers to drive him to the station. Not just because they wanted to get rid of him: it was also because nobody wanted the job of shifting all the empty bottles piled high on the table, stuck behind the cushions and generally scattered around the room.

In spite of all this, or maybe because of it, as soon as I finished my rounds in Kaliningrad, I decided to go and have a look at 2 Street 6.

First I discovered that you can't just turn up and take a look, you need a pass. A director of one of the companies I was visiting told me he regularly went inside the naval port on business and he could get me in. He called his contact. Where did I want to go? 2 Street 6 Baltiysk. Why? Because it was the family home of a friend of mine. Well, what else could I say? If I told them the truth they would never let me in. Name? Becker. Initials? K.G. It wasn't true – I just wondered if they would notice. A pause. The guy says, okay, no problem. Turn up at the gate, there'll be a pass waiting. I thank him profusely and promise to bring him a bottle of whisky on my next visit. But when I get to the gate, no pass. Nobody knows anything about it. Nobody has heard of any phone call. Who did I think I was? If I didn't turn round and go straight back where I came fromski, they would arrest me and throw me in jailski.

At first I thought it was all bluff. The driver told me they hadn't been paying their electricity bills. Again. At one time, would you believe, this top, top, top-secret, secret, secret Russian naval base did not have enough money to pay their electricity bills (around US$2 million) and the local power company cut them off, paralysing everything: their radar stations, their communication systems, their missiles and their own military airport.

But it was for real. They thought I was a security risk. Which was crazy, because if I'd got a boat from across the water in Gdansk in Poland I'd have seen everything: the narrow channel running all the way up to Kaliningrad Bay; the tiny island; the dilapidated lighthouse and then, strung out for all the world to see, hundreds of warships, the might of the Soviet Navy. Except, I was told by someone who did make the trip, most of them were out of action. Many were listing badly, a number had been beached, some were on scaffolding. Others had odds and ends hanging off them. A radar dish here, a bunch of aerials there.

I must admit that, on the basis that a Kaliningrad jail couldn't be much worse than the Kaliningrad hotel I was staying in, I was tempted to argue. Especially as it would have meant not seeing Becker again for maybe twenty or thirty years. But of course I gave in. With an afternoon to spare, therefore, I did the only thing anybody can do in Kaliningrad: I went back to work. Or, at least, back to the guy who said he could get me into the naval port in the first place.

He was rushing off to a meeting with a group of other businessmen. They were trying, he said, to draw up plans for the future. Kaliningrad was one of 89 similar regions or *oblats* in Russia. If they stayed the way they were, they would continue going downhill. If they broke free, they could set up on their own, become the Hong Kong of the Baltic. The trouble was, most people in Kaliningrad were arch left-wingers, Communists, even Stalinists. They had voted solidly for Zhirinovsky and his non-liberal, non-democratic Liberal Democratic Party in the Russian presidential elections. As if that wasn't bad enough, many of them wanted back the northern coastal strip either side of what they call the old Hanseatic port of Memel, where Thomas Mann spent his holidays and Hitler harangued the population in the town square, which the Lithuanians and the rest of the world call Klaipeda. It should never have been given to Lithuania in the first place, they say. They also wanted to be part of Russia, not stuck out on their own on the other side of Lithuania. The great motherland should be an undivided whole, not split by a matter of a couple of hundred miles. In any case, whenever they sent anything through Lithuania to Russia, surprise, surprise, it never arrived. Even whole convoys of the Russian Army regularly disappeared into thin air: arms, equipment, even the soldiers themselves.

Others – a minority, of course – disagreed. Kaliningrad

had a population of only one million and hardly any natural resources apart from amber. And even that is smuggled across the border to Lithuania, where, with practically every other street stall creaking with the stuff, it is sold at around US$5 a gram, not much less than the price of gold. If they were on their own they could exploit their amber resources, which are among the biggest in the world, creating a lucrative business.

But before he solved all these problems, the guy had to pick up his daughter from school. Would I like to go with him? I hesitated. Schools are not exactly my thing. But I was glad I did, because I discovered that in Kaliningrad schoolchildren are taught nothing about their past. For them the world began in 1917. Then came the Great Patriotic War when Stalin liberated their city from the Nazis. They had never heard of Koenigsburg. They had never heard of the Prussians. And, I know you're going to find this hard to accept, but they had never even heard of 2 Street 6, Becker or any of his flipping Becksteins.

Yerevan

You're not going to believe this.

I'm way up in the middle of the Caucasus Mountains. The lesser Caucasus, to be precise. Around me is miles and miles of nothing. The main roads across the mountains are out of action. They have been subjected to so many raids and attacks that nobody uses them any more. Instead I've been forced to take the side roads which are treacherous - smashed and broken and pot-holed. Somehow they seem to cling to the edge of the mountains rather than go across the top of them.

The car I'm in is a wreck of an old Lada which keeps heaving and wheezing and choking and breaking down every ten minutes because of what the driver, who looks like a retired Cossack, keeps telling me is bad benzene from Romania. Already I've lost count of the number of times we've juddered to a halt and he's dismantled the whatdyacallit and pumped air into the whatsit with the foot pump. The first time he did this I wondered what the hell was going on. With all the bumping and shaking and swerving caused by the state of the roads, I thought that either all the microphones behind the dashboard had broken loose and he was trying to find them and reconnect them again, or it was some kind of Russian voodoo. But whatever he did seemed to do the trick and we chugged on for another couple of miles before stopping so that he could repeat the process all over again.

Eventually we get to the Armenian border, which is a bit like Killarney meets the Himalayas. We putter slowly up to the customs sheds. One looks like some huge converted water pipe which has been blocked up at either end. The other looks like an upmarket container that has fallen off the back of some jazzy Italian truck. All around us are young soldiers, Kalashnikovs at the ready.

I go into the container office. Inside are two more soldiers. One, a shy young man sitting at a battered old desk. The other, a big burly bloke with a beard, who looks like an extra in a Tolstoy novel. I hand my passport to the shy one at the table and begin to assume the usual grovel-grovel attitude. The big burly guy grabs it, flicks the pages over slowly and there and then, I promise you, promptly detains me – to drink a bottle of cognac with him. Armenian. Eighteen years old. The best. Why me? Why a bottle of cognac? Why the best? I don't know. All I know is I was more than willing to oblige. Usually it's the other way round. I'm the one walking through signs saying 'Alien' and handing over my bottles of cognac and wine and whisky and champagne to customs officers all over the world. This was the first time in my life that one was actually offering me a drink, free, gratis, and for nothing.

To refuse, I thought, would be unwise for all kinds of reasons, not to mention a touch discourteous. So – cheers! First we drank and toasted each other. Zunk. Straight down. No touching the sides. Then – cheers! – we drank and toasted the guy at the table. After that it was cheers! cheers! cheers! To all the other guards and soldiers on duty, not to mention Armenia, Britain, Mrs Zacha, the whole world. They were miles from anywhere, he kept telling me. They never had anything to celebrate. In fact, he admitted, they hardly had any contact with the outside world at all. They were so high up in the mountains they didn't have radios. They didn't even have radio contact with their army headquarters back in Yerevan. For all they knew Amenia could have been invaded, with the Russians once again grabbing all the best seats at the opera.

All the time we were busy drinking and toasting each other and everyone else's health, the big chief, I remember, kept grabbing my hand and shaking it again and again as if he was looking for some secret Masonic inflection. If he had found one, God only knows what would have happened to me.

'Winston Churchill. He drink bottle of Armenian brandy. Ten year old. Every day. He good man. Cheers.'

'Cheers.'

'Khrushchev. He drink vodka. Brezhnev. He drink Armenian brandy. He good man. Cheers.'

'Cheers.'

'Gorbachev. He not drink. Phah.'

'Phah.'

Suddenly the door of the container opened. In came another group of young soldiers. One was carrying a saucepan. The other had glasses and cans of beer. Everything they now put down on the rickety old table. '*Shashlik*,' said the big chief. 'You have *shashlik*.' What could I say?

One of the soldiers thrust a huge doorstep of bread at me. I broke it open, filled it full of *shash* and washed the whole lot down with more brandy. And to think of the years I've spent being delayed and pushed around by other customs officers for all kinds of crazy reasons. In Lagos, because I didn't have a spare pair of glasses. In Algeria, where I had to spend the night sleeping under a Land Rover. In Brazil, where because I was travelling on a business visa they tried to charge me twenty-five per cent tax on all the business they thought I had done in the country. In Atlanta, for simply asking if anybody ever came to the States for pleasure. At Gatwick, where on my way back from quick trips to Amsterdam, Paris, Brussels or wherever, many's the time I've been held up for hours on end by customs controls which have not only been abolished but which, according to the Travellers' Charter produced by HM Customs and Excise itself, are supposed to work 'quickly and tactfully'.

Eventually, the bottle empty and the *shash* well and truly licked, it was time to leave. Except this time (not that you'll ever catch me saying a word against Armenian brandy, especially when I get it free and from a customs officer high in the Caucasus) *I* was heaving and wheezing and choking as badly as the Lada. Which was probably just as well. Because from then on, every couple of miles I was forced to stop, again and again and again: not by the Lada but by the police. To drink still more cognac.

Barely a couple of miles into Armenia, high on an open ridge that felt like the top of the world, I was detained for the second time. I was the first Englishman they could remember coming their way. Virtually on the edge of the mountain, with cattle ambling everywhere, I was detained again. At the bottom of a valley, streams rushed past yet again. At another – hic – stopping place, one of the soldiers, a young chap, told me he had only another ten months to go. Then he was free. He wanted to go into business and become a millionaire. He stopped me, he said, because he wanted some contacts. For my trouble, we had a couple of beers.

Then once more it was chug-chug, splutter-splutter, hic-hic, through more fantastic scenery: sweeping hills, broad valleys, winding, twisting roads crammed full of cattle lumbering backwards and forwards, and more and more old-fashioned electricity pylons disappearing into the distance.

The next time we were stopped it was because of the car. One of the soldiers said the whatsit needed cleaning out with the foot pump and proceeded to do it for us. The driver was so pleased he didn't have to do this himself that he sank two whole bottles of beer non-stop. I had what was left of some kind of unspecified bottle which could have been cheap Armenian vodka. On the other hand it could have been some of that bad benzene from Romania. It was difficult to tell the difference.

The next thing I remember after that is going through this enormous, long, long road tunnel which looked as though it had just been hewn directly out of the rock. There were no supports, no struts, no lining, nothing. Or if there were I couldn't see them. There was no lighting either. It was pitch black except for the weak, flickering lights of the occasional Lada. The whole place was flowing with water. There was water running down the walls. There was water all over the road. At first, I thought I was having some kind of nightmare, but I quickly realised it was for real. There were even huge potholes inside the tunnel.

The final stop came just as we hit the outskirts of Yerevan. Initially I thought it was a speed trap. One of the policemen looked as though he was waving some kind of gun or sensor at us. But none of them were worried about the speed we were doing, they wanted to talk. And drink brandy. Armenian brandy. A tall, thin man with a pencil moustache showed me the sensor they used to check the speed of cars and trucks bombing along the road, except it didn't work. It was jammed permanently on sixty-nine kilometres an hour. 'We stop motorists. We show them the reading. They pay us money so we don't fine them. It is good business. Yes?' he grinned.

'Yes, of course,' I replied. 'Very good business.'

'Hic.'

'Hic.'

When Colin Thubron came this way, for him it was not cognac but wine. He whined the whole time like he usually does that the police were impossible, that he got stopped no less than twelve times. Can you imagine that? A guy who keeps count of how many times he is stopped by the police? No wonder he never seems to enjoy himself. Worse still, they wouldn't allow him even to step off the edge of the road.

Not me. As far as I'm concerned Armenia and I were made for each other. Zzzzz.

Yerevan is your typical enormous, rock solid, four square, Soviet-style city, built to last a million years or whenever the brandy runs out, whichever is the longest. It is full of vast buildings, long wide streets, and squares that are so huge they are in different time zones. And masses of monuments. They're everywhere.

The holocaust memorial, built in 1957 to commemorate the Armenians who died in pogrom after pogrom throughout their history, is about the size of a football pitch. First you walk what seems like miles between two far walls. On the walls are the names of the twelve provinces they lost to the Turks when the worst atrocities took place. At the end are two newly dug graves. Then you come to the memorial itself, a massive open globe split into, again, twelve parts. Inside it is the eternal flame, to keep alive the memory of the millions who lost their lives in the pogroms, which many Armenians believe are comparable in their horror to those suffered by the Jews, but which have somehow conveniently been forgotten. Except, irony of ironies, they can no longer afford to keep the flame alight. In the bad old days, of course, they could. To make up for the lack of the flame, hidden loudspeakers, under the control of a chubby ex-newspaper photographer, blast out stirring traditional Armenian music.

Alongside the globe is this enormous thing that looks, I suppose, like a tent peg or needle, but split in two from top to bottom. What does it mean? I have no idea. Some people say it stands for Armenia, which at one time stretched all the way from the Mediterranean in the west to the Caspian in the east. But not for long. For most of its existence, Armenia has been virtually a plaything between, to the north, the Russians; to the east, the Mongols; to the south, the Kurds and Persians; and to the west, the Turks. Today nine-tenths of the country may have been lost to other nations but what is left remains intact, united, still striving for a better future – with its feet firmly on the ground. Others say the monument symbolises the Armenian people. They may have lost millions of their countrymen but they are still a united people. With their feet firmly on the ground.

Sitting on the steps of the memorial was an old man, who looked as though he had fought against not only the Russians but the Mongols, Kurds, Persians and Turks as well. He told me it didn't mean a thing. It was built in 1956, strongly against the wishes of Moscow, but the Armenians went ahead just the same. In order not to upset anyone any further, however, they decided not to include any inscriptions or dedications. 'We know what it looks like. But we don't know what it means,' he said.

I asked him about the two newly dug graves. He said they were those of soldiers who had died fighting on the borders between Armenia and Azerbaijan. 'We know what to say,' he repeated. 'But we also know what to think.'

The monument to fifty years of Soviet power, however, is brilliant. There's no doubt in my mind what it symbolises. It symbolises what happened to Armenia under the Communists. It starts at the top of the hill with this huge area of nothing. From there, it descends lower and lower by an elaborate series of staircases about a mile wide until it reaches the absolute bottom of the hill. Here, hunched over a table, staring at a blank sheet of paper, is your typical, thick, huge, stolid, impassive, unthinking figure of a Soviet planner.

Some people, of course, will try to tell you that the monument should be read the other way round. That with Soviet power and might and planning one can start at the bottom and soar to the tops of the mountains and that the guy with the blank piece of paper is none other than Alexander Tamanian, the famous Armenian planner and architect who practically designed Yerevan and most of its famous buildings. But don't listen to them. They are revisionists or reconstructionists or whatever you call them.

In any case, Tamanian was no great shakes as a planner or an architect. When he drew up plans for Yerevan he said it was for a city of 150,000 people. Today it has around 1.5 million. As for his architectural abilities, have you seen his combined Opera and Ballet Theatre? To me it's a glorious example of the art of the ultimate compromiser. It is based on the design of a seventh-century cathedral but inside it is half opera house and half ballet theatre. And it looks like it. On the other hand, it is nowhere near as bad as the Sports and Concert Hall which, from a distance, looks like a first draft for the Sydney Opera House. Up close, though, it's in about the same state as the cultural life of Australia: broken down, derelict, beyond hope.

For monument overkill, however, you must go either to Republic Square or Independent Square depending on which map you look at, which taxi driver you get and who you're with. It has got the lot. The size: it's about ten miles wide. The buildings: they're massive. There's the National Art Gallery of Armenia, all eight storeys of it; the fourth largest museum in the old Soviet Union, the History Museum, the size of Red Square and the third largest museum in the old Soviet Union. The Literature Museum, which is, you can bet your life, the biggest of the lot. It's certainly bigger than our local library. The Armenia Hotel, which is so huge that if you call room service and order a boiled egg for breakfast, by the time it gets to you it's a chicken Kiev. But for all its size, I'll say one thing. The hotel still manages to have more old men in greasy uniforms sitting on chairs staring out of windows all day long, not to mention those fancy KGB ladies sitting on every floor watching everything you do, than it has guests.

But what I like most about Independence or Republic or Indepublic Square or Whatever-they-call-it-square is what's not there: the giant bronze statue of Lenin. On the left of the Armenia Hotel, on that wide strip of grass, is where it had stood since 1948. Come April 1991, however, down it came – and so did the world commodity markets. I'm not saying it was big. It was just that traders feared that if it was melted down and off-loaded all in one go it would create such a glut that prices would come crashing down all over the world. But they needn't have worried. Armenians being Armenians, there was this heavy debate about whether they should have pulled it down or not because regardless of the politics or all that the Russians had inflicted on Armenia, it was in itself a great work of art and as such, no matter what it did or did not represent, it should have blah, blah, blah. Then, would you believe, they had the same debate about the plinth. The statue was gone, but why not keep the plinth? The plinth didn't represent anything. It was just a plinth. In any case, regardless of politics etc., etc., it too was a work of art blah, blah, blah. But in the end it went as well, not for any particular aesthetic reason but because as one guy told me as we were sitting outside the hotel one evening sampling the brandies, 'We needed all the building blocks and materials we could get. It was cheaper to knock it down than go out and buy them.'

The argument now is what should be put in its place. I'm betting on General Antranig, the big Armenian national hero. But it will probably be Michael Jackson or maybe even Mrs Thatcher. I have been known to be wrong on the odd occasion.

My favourite monumental building, one for which I am prepared to forgive them everything (well, apart from the Sports and Concert Hall), is the Matenadaran. From the outside, it looks like any other solid, implacable nuclear-bomb-proof Soviet museum. Inside, it contains the most amazing collection of Armenian books and manuscripts you can imagine. There is the *Homilies of Mush*, weighing in at twenty-eight kilos as

the biggest Armenian coffee table book of all time.
Which as luck would have it is about the same size as
the biggest Armenian coffee table in the world. It has a
fabulous collection of saints' biographies, *Odes and
Sermons*. Written around 1200–1202, it consists of more
than six hundred pages. Each page is a separate calf skin,
so you can imagine the amount of blood, sweat and
tears that went into its production – unlike today, when
most books look as though they were produced on the
back of an envelope dipped in a glass of champagne.
Then there is a little – by comparison – sixteenth-
century book on smelting gold. There are seventeenth
century medical books prescribing all kinds of remedies
for all kinds of occupations: for shoemakers suffering
from back-ache a handful of this kind of herb; for textile
workers suffering from arthritis, a handful of that kind
of herb. I forget what the cure was for tourists. All I
know is it looked uncomfortable which pleased me
immensely.

But of all the thousands and thousands of books
there, my favourite is a little one tucked away in the far
cabinet by the window on the first floor. In it the author
not only proves conclusively that the earth is a globe
with Jerusalem at the centre and Spain, Russia, China
and Africa around the edge, he also comes up with
irrefutable evidence that it is carried on the backs of
elephants, blown this way and that by the wind. Clever
guys, these Armenians.

Now if that's not too much for you to take in, how
about this? Behind the Matenadaran, in the mountains, is
an enormous tunnel. Not for guns, or trains that always
run three or four hours late, but for the whole of the
contents of the building. Within minutes every single
manuscript, book and sheet of parchment can be tucked
up safe and sound inside the mountain to be preserved
forever. At least, that's the theory. How they will achieve
this is another matter. One man, who looked as though
he could remember when Jerusalem was the centre of

the world, told me the whole building was on rollers. At the press of a button it would roll back into the mountains. But I'm sure he'd been at the brandy.

Okay. That's the big-big stuff. Now for the not-so-big stuff. The Martyrs' Monument. The Mother Armenia Monument. The I-can't-remember-the-name-of-them-all monuments. Not to mention about 207 churches; one railway station; a restaurant called Karap, which boasts unashamedly of their famous Karap cuisine as well as their Karap specialities, such as their pizzas of which they are justly proud; and a string of snack bars called Smak, which I thought I just had to check out for my friends who went to public school and are all now lawyers and accountants and members of the soon-to-be-defunct House of Lords – especially as the advertising proclaimed: 'Speciality Smak. What, you haven't heard of it? Don't lose a unique opportunity to try it.'

Then there are the statues – down every street, round every corner, in the centre of every patch of green. In the empty space outside the railway station. There they are: artists, writers, composers, musicians, soldiers, Mothers of the Nation. Probably Mr Karap himself. One looks like an eighteenth-century troubadour on heat. Another has a paint brush and palette in his hand. And a good few others seem distinctly ill at ease. About the only statue they haven't got is one to the poor, unsuspecting, foreign investor: probably because they haven't come across one yet.

But more important than all the monuments, all the museums and all the other million and one cultural things going on, is the fact that the place is literally flowing with drink – at street corners, in every avenue and boulevard. Water fountains, I mean, everywhere. But be warned, they're not all the same. The water varies from district to district. Not, of course, that I am an expert – I don't touch the stuff. No, that is what I was told by some poor, unfortunate old man doing what must be one of the most depressing jobs in the world:

tasting the waters. Up in the surrounding hills, near the hospital and the big television station, the water he reckoned was clean and fresh and crisp. Down around what is the main street, Abovian Street, it was also very good, as were the fountains around Republidence Square. All of this comes from natural springs. Near the Holocaust monument, however, and in what was left of the old industrial parts of town, it was rough – warm and insipid. Sometimes even a bit cloudy. Where that water came from he didn't seem to know.

For those not drinking water, there are about as many places selling Coca-Cola. I don't think I've been anywhere in the world where there are so many people selling so much Coca-Cola – on every street corner, outside every shop, inside every shop, halfway up every stairway, down in every basement. Coca-Cola fridges, Coca-Cola tables, Coca-Cola umbrellas. Coca-Cola plastic crates blocking the pavements. Whoever the Coca-Cola agent in Armenia is, he is going great guns. One day he'll be rich and powerful, probably even running the whole show. Coca-Cola, that is, not Armenia. There's not enough money in Armenia.

As for the people themselves, if you really want to meet and talk and laugh and chat and drink with Armenians, forget Armenia. Go to Venice, or Jaffa or Paris or Tampa, Florida, especially Ybor City. Like the Jews, who also scattered to the four corners of the world, you will find Armenians all over the place. Gee whizz, they're even in Buffalo City, New York, where I discovered that there are so many of them they actually have two Armenian churches side by side. I don't know about you, but to me whoever they are, wherever you meet them, they always look like chess champions, classical musicians, top mathematicians or Nobel Peace Prize winners. The fact that throughout history so many of them really have been chess champions, classical musicians, top mathematicians and Nobel Peace Prize winners, does, of course, help.

Who was doctor to the harem of Akbar the Great? (The great what is not recorded.) Who was best man to Richard the Lionheart; the mother of the 'Polish Byron' Slowacki; and the designer of the first Soviet MiG jet? An Armenian.

Who was the first person and the longest serving member of the Politburo to denounce Stalin; the brains behind *perestroika* and – most important of all – the first to produce yoghurt in the United States. You got it.

And who, according to *The Guinness Book of Records*, is Mr Memory Man? Not only can he remember the names and addresses of thousands of people lost during the big earthquake in Armenia of 1988, he can also recall word for word thousands of words dictated to him over a five-hour period in no less than twelve different languages. I can't remember.

It is the same in Yerevan. Everybody you meet is a professor or doctor or theoretical physicist. Not only that, they can speak 53 languages as well. The old man sitting under an umbrella all day long outside the food market by the underpass in Mesrop Mashtots Avenue trying to sell half a dozen eggs – he used to be a professor of physics. The old lady trying to haul herself into one of their twelfth-century trams by the dilapidated Hotel Ahi – she was a professor of cardiology. The three young guys trying to mend a fridge on the pavement by the Institute of Linguistic. (Well, that's what they call it.) They're all chemists of one kind or another. Try and get a cab along Sayat Nova Avenue, and you have to wait for the drivers to finish their game of backgammon before they'll even look at you. Go into an office, the security guards are playing chess. Clamber on to one of their overcrowded buses somewhere along Terian Street and you can bet your life that not only is everybody reading a book, they are reading something by Shakespeare. In fact so hooked are they on Shakespeare that they actually call their kids Richard and Henry and Antony. Outside on the steps of the Parliament building I met a Brutus. At the television studios I met a Hamlet. I won't tell you the name of the guy I met at the state bank.

In fact, as far as I'm concerned, Armenians are owed a whole string of Nobel Prizes. Their literature and theatre goes back over two thousand years. They were getting rave reviews from Plutarch even before *The Phantom of the Opera* opened in the West End, which tells you how old they are. They developed their own alphabet while we were still trying to lift the Romans'. They were putting up fancy buildings and churches involving complex design and construction techniques while the rest of the world was still trying to put one brick on top of another. Three hundred years before we did, they were building hospitals, making anatomical studies, developing their own medicines and even carrying out autopsies. They even opened the first genuine cafés in Vienna and Paris while we were still trying to make a decent cup of tea and some toast without burning it.

By comparison, even Einstein is lightweight. Actually I don't think it will be long before they're running the world. There will be an Armenian Director-General of the United Nations, Secretary-General of NATO, President of the European Union. Goodness me, the French might even allow them – honour of honours – to be something like a vice-president of one of their local table tennis associations. Well, fair's fair. They might be great guys capable of running the world but *mon Dieu*, they still lack the greatest qualification of all. They're not French.

Some people maintain that the reason the Armenians are so talented is because, like the Jews, they know they're God's chosen people. They know that whatever they do they're right. Don't you believe it. I reckon it's because Old Armenian is the only language in the world composed of only capital letters. So, obviously, generation after generation of writing only in capital letters has given them this enormous sense of superiority over the rest of us who use capital letters only from time to time. And then More likely Than Not in all thE wRong plaCes.

But for some reason or other, maybe because they are so smart, God doesn't seem to favour them much. When you look at their history, you have to admit that bearing in mind they are the oldest Christian nation in the world – they were up and running in 301 – He's thrown everything He can at them.

All over the Caucasus there is beautiful, rich, glorious, fertile farm land. What have the Armenians got? Rocks. Rocks. And still more rocks. They've got no natural resources. No coastline. No nothing. Even then they've now got less than one-tenth of the rocks they started out with. The rest of them are in Ottoman, Turkey, as they say. In Russia. In Iran. In wherever. As for the one-tenth they have still got, even that seems to want to do nothing but move as well. For all the time they are at the mercy of one earthquake after another. The big one, of course, was in December 1988, when Gumri (up in the north, towards the border with Georgia), the main industrial part of the country, was practically 80 per cent destroyed, 24,000 people were killed and 500,000 left homeless.

During my first trip there, the earth carried on moving for me as well. There was a three-pointer in Yerevan itself; two four-pointers, one in Stepanakert and another out near Amasra on the border with Turkey; a five-pointer in Vanadzor; and the climax a five- to six-pointer on the Richter scale about 15 kilometres northwest of Ijevan. By the end of the trip I was positively out of breath.

As for the Armenians' big national symbol, the one thing they see literally looming over them, staring them in the face every day of their lives, Mount Ararat, which they call the greatest mountain in the world (it's on their flag, on their coat of arms, and even means 'mountain' in Armenian) doesn't actually belong to them any more. It's in Turkey.

Then, of course, there were the massacres – in 1604, 1890, 1909, 1915 and 1916.

Even when the Russians moved out and they were finally left on their own, what happened? Just as they needed a bit of breathing-space to get themselves sorted out, the electricity flowing regularly and the heating and lighting in working order, He hurled at them the roughest and toughest winter He could come up with. Not only were they burning the furniture, they were chopping down practically every single tree in the country for wood to keep warm.

What is more, He seemed to conspire with the Russians to ensure that the Medzamour nuclear plant was no big-deal leaving present either. It is one of the most dangerous ever designed. Slapbang in the centre of an earthquake zone, it can't withstand earthquakes. It lacks the dome-shaped concrete containment vessel that is standard on any Western design. The result is that if there's any leak of radiation, before you can say Chernobyl it's goodbye Yerevan which is just thirty-five miles away. Every nuclear expert you can think of is opposed to it. Yet the Armenians have got it up and partly running because they say they have no altern-ative. Without it they have no power at all. With it, they still only have power about four hours a day. What choice do they have?

As far as I can discover there's only one thing He hasn't yet thrown at them but I'm sure it won't be long now - and that's tourists. The Armenians may think they've suffered enough already. Wait until they get kids clambering all over their precious manuscripts, old women of all ages shuffling in and out of the National Art Gallery looking for a cup of weak, milky tea and gangs of yahoos causing chaos in bars and restaurants the length and breadth of the country by demanding warm pints of beer and great big plates of fish and chips.

Maybe it is because they reckon God has got it in for

them so much, that they seem to be doing everything they can to get into His good books before they are all swept aside yet again by the coming flood of tourists. I don't think I've been in any other country in the world which has not only so many churches but so many *khachkars* as well. You don't know what a *khachkar* is? To look at it quickly you would think it was a Celtic cross. But look again. Every one is slightly different, has different images, different decorations, different styles. They are all over the country, in churches, in church yards. As you drive along a country lane in the middle of nowhere, with Mount Ararat naturally in the background, suddenly there's another one staring you in the face.

Then there are the relics. Now I admit I'm no expert on relics, apart from the in-laws, but the Armenians seem to have got the lot.

A lump of Noah's old Ark? They've got it. As for the whole thing itself, every single one of them is convinced it is still buried under the icecap halfway up what still should be Armenian Mount Ararat. What's more, they've got CIA satellite photographs to prove it. If only the Turks were reasonable and gave the mountain back to them they would have the Ark dug up and on show in no time at all.

The vine Noah planted so he could at least have something to drink after all his increasing and multiplying? That's at Arghuri on the edge of the mountain. Or at least, it was. It was destroyed by an earthquake in, would you believe, 1840.

The spear that pierced the side of Christ? Not just a bit of it – they've got the whole thing, with, mysteriously, the shape of a cross cut out of the middle. His cloak? The one the soldiers cast lots for because they didn't want to tear it up into strips? That they've got as well. The nails? Ditto. Fragments of the cross itself? Well, what do you think? The shroud? Turin may have it now, but guess who had it first.

Finally, while we're on the subject of relics, they reckon

they've also got Mrs Noah. She's buried at Marland.

Now, you wouldn't normally find me chasing bits of old fingers, a toenail here or an eyelash there. There are normally far more important things to do. Like ... well, never mind. But these relics I just had to see. One day between meetings, therefore, I decided to skip my world tour of Yerevan's monuments, museums and statues, and take a trip out to Etchmiadzin, the old capital, at the foot of Mount Ararat. The right side, of course, not the Turkish side. This also, in case you didn't know, is the site of the Garden of Eden. Peach trees. Apricot bushes. Watermelons. I saw plenty of them. There were also plenty of vine leaves, although not particularly large ones I will admit. Whether that has any significance or not I couldn't discover. As for apple trees, I couldn't find one. Neither did I see any serpents.

Now Etchmiadzin, as everybody knows, was founded by Noah himself once all the flood waters had subsided, which probably accounts for the fact that it had two car parks, two attendants, two cafés, two guys hustling postcards and two stalls selling Coca-Cola. But whatever you do, don't run away with the idea that the Armenians accept the whole story of the flood, lock, stock and waterbarrel. Or rather the whole story of everything going in twosies, twosies into an arky, arky for forty daysies, daysies to survive the floody, floody as – I'm not kidding you – I once heard everybody singing at the tops of their voicy voicies at some happy-clappy service I once had the misfortune to stumble into somewhere in the Staties Staties. In fact, the Armenians will tell you straight there's no way they believe the floody, floody, I mean the flood, covered the face of the earth destroying everything and everyone. What they say is that the flood covered the face of the earth and destroyed everything and everyone: except for the Armenians. They all managed to clamber above the fifteen-cubit line, the height of the floods, and on to the top of – guess where? – Mount Ararat and several other mountains in the Caucasus which are higher still. There they sat until it was all over.

If you try to persuade them otherwise, you will not succeed. What's more, they will tell you, they also knew that Christ was going to be born way before anybody else did. As soon as they heard about some kind of strange star heading in their direction, twelve of their wisest men clambered to the top of Mount Ararat and waited and waited and waited. As soon as they saw it, three of them followed it to Bethlehem. The Three Wise Men were, you guessed it, Armenian.

In fact, trying to budge them from any of their beliefs is like trying to budge St Etchmiadzin Cathedral itself, because if anything looks as though it was built to withstand another flood, it's Etchmiadzin Cathedral. It is rock solid, four-square, built to last to the end of time or the day Turkey, out of the kindness of its heart, hands Mount Ararat back to Armenia. Inside it is stern, unyielding, implacable – with the exception of the high altar, which to me with its two fancy pink columns on each side looks somehow more sugary, flippant Italian than solid, intellectual Armenian.

In front of it, in the main area of the church itself, is another simple, square block of an altar which is where Christ himself is supposed to have descended – what am I saying? This *is* where Christ himself came back to earth – in AD 320. Hence the name, Etchmiadzin: 'Where the only-begotten descended.' Although why Christ, after promising that He would only return at the end of time should in the relatively short space of three hundred-odd years suddenly have changed His mind, nobody could tell me. I can only assume it was some kind of thank-you present to the Armenians for becoming the number one Christian nation in the world.

Facing the cathedral, through the huge, rock solid, four-square Gate of King Tiridates is the Pontifical Palace which, to be honest, looks a bit like Buckingham

Palace designed by an Armenian priest. It has the same bland exterior, the same three divisions, but with more arches and twiddly bits. Inside, I was told by an old lady who has dined many times with the Catholicos, in other words the Armenian Pope, it is sumptuous. Full of treasures, rich settings, fine furniture, wonderful paintings. In fact, maybe it was so rich and so lavish that Christ Himself couldn't resist the temptation to come back for a quick look to see how His teachings were being put into practice by the world's first Christian country.

All around, facing both the church and the palace, is the presumably less lavish accommodation for the monks for this, they tell you, is not only the centre, the heart, the headquarters of the Armenian Church worldwide, it is also very much a working monastery.

Go across the border to Turkey – if you dare – and the monks in Cilicia will tell you they are also the centre, the heart, the headquarters of the Armenian Church. They say they were in existence first and that when Etchmiadzin was established it was a breakaway, against the wishes of Cilicia. But you know what the Turks are like.

All I know is, both sides believe the same things. Well, roughly the same things. Christ was God only. Not God and Man. There is no such thing as Purgatory. When you die it's either Heaven or Hell. No temporary reprieve, no halfway house. No spiritual health camp to qualify for the top deck. To sign up for all this, all you have to do is be baptised three times, baptised three times, baptised three times. All the same there must be some reason why there are these two Armenian churches side by side in Buffalo City, New York, and not one.

For me, the best part of the visit was to the Treasury at the back of the church. It was fantastic. There in row upon row, shelf upon shelf, in one magnificent display cabinet after another, were millions of gold, silver, pearls and other precious stones, thousands of gorgeously decorated chalices and gold caskets and a whole array of dazzling church vestments. At the end of one room was an enormous urn made of gold and silver, about three foot high and three foot across. In here, every seven years, they prepare the precious oils used in sacraments and services throughout the Armenian world.

Did I see the lumps of Noah's old Ark; the spear; the cloak (even though there is supposed to be another one exactly the same, not only in the cathedral at Trier but also in the old church at Mtkzhet next door in Georgia); the nails; and fragments of the very cross itself? What do you think? But I did shake hands with the guy who looks after them. A tough-looking farmer type with a neat black beard and a grip like a vice. So where were they? I didn't dare ask Mr Nice Guy with the Iron Grip. I thought he might bring tears to my eyes. Instead I asked one old lady who looked as though she could be an Armenian nun but wasn't. They don't believe in them. Religion, they believe, is too important to be left to the likes of women. All she said was, 'on the way home,' which I must admit came as a complete shock to me. Because I had absolutely no idea they had all been transferred to somewhere between Gatwick airport and the village of Waldron in East Sussex. Later when I was boasting about this to a group of Armenians, I discovered that what she really meant was, 'on the way home to Etchmiadzin from Moscow where they have all been on display'.

Not seeing the relics was a bit of a disappointment. But not half as much of a disappointment as one famous American explorer, Carveth Wells, had when in the 1930s he travelled all the way from Leningrad to Moscow through the Ukraine, across the Caucasus Mountains into Georgia and Armenia because he wanted to climb Mount Ararat and search for Noah's Ark. The poor dear forgot to get a Russian exit visa into Turkey and had to turn round and go all the way back to Leningrad without ever having set foot in Turkey, let alone on Mount Ararat. Being American, instead of keeping quiet about it and trying to disguise the fact he was a Charlieski, he wrote a book about it all so that he could advertise his ignorance to the world.

What I did see, however, were plenty of other bits and pieces, I mean relics, of saints and holy men. This did make me wonder how which bit of what is selected to be preserved as a relic. I can understand, for example, why the finger of the right hand of poor St Gregory the Illuminator, who spent all his life illuminating one hand-written bible or prayer book after another, was preserved.

On the other hand (genuine, not artificial), what on earth would be cut off me, to be preserved and venerated for all time, as an example of my way of life?

Leaving Armenia was almost as easy as entering it, except that I left by air not by road and there was no booze. Or at least if there was, the pilot of this filthy, falling-apart Russian whatever-it-was wasn't sharing it with the rest of us, which was a pity. With a bottle of Armenian brandy inside us, I'm sure we would all have been much more relaxed and far less worried about adding to the piles of relics scattered everywhere.

I arrived at the airport an hour before departure. I'd no sooner gone through the door than I was greeted by a keen young man who led me to a small, overcrowded office with an enormous electric fan which was blowing bits of paper all over the place. Another young man led me to the bar where we drank Coca-Colas. A young woman then arrived and led me straight to the departure area. Did I check-in? I couldn't tell you. Did I go through Emigration? I don't think so. Was there a security check? Search me. As for my boarding pass, I was only given that as we were being led down the steps of the departure area to the bus outside. Even then my name wasn't on the boarding pass. All it had on it was a scribbled 'l' which I naturally assumed was a sign of the innate respect and high esteem in which I am held by the Armenian customs authorities.

Cheers.

Tbilisi

'Ladies and gentlemen – and Sasha.

'No, seriously, Zaza, Manana, Jura, Shota, Giorgi, Vlad, I mean Vladislav, Lado, Kakhi and Sasha. Funny that, how every Georgian dinner party always has nine people. Must be something to do with you guys always being one over the eight.

'No, no, Zaza. It's nothing to do with anyone putting anything over anyone. It's an English joke. Well, at least I thought it was. Though in my opinion, the ideal number for a small, quiet, intimate dinner is two: me and the wine waiter.

'Now what I'd like to say is, it gives me great pleasure – and I hope it always will. Yes. Yes. Manana, thank you very much. That's very kind of you. I'll bear it in mind. No. What I mean is, as it's the custom here in Georgia for toastmasters or *tamadas* as you call them, to stand up and make long, rambling toasts during practically every meal you have, I feel it's only right that I get my own back... er, that I should subject you, or rather honour you, with the same kind of long, involved, rambling speech that I have had to put up with, I mean that I have been privileged to hear, again and again during the 63½ glorious years of drinking wine I have spent in your fantastic country since I arrived here one very strained and very throbbing liver ago. Some people say they have Georgia on their mind. I have Georgia buried

143

deep inside what's left of my liver. I'm not saying you guys drink a lot of wine. Goodness me, I've gone through life on the basis that you can't trust anyone who doesn't slug back two bottles of the stuff at a time. It's just that I've never ever seen so much wine disappear so quickly anywhere in the world. I mean I've been to the odd bash or three in my time. But I've never seen anything like the way you guys down the stuff. If they were handing out medals for putting it away by the bucketful you would win the gold medal every time. As for me, I reckon it's going to be a good couple of weeks before I can get back on to solids again.

'Oh yes. A toast. A toast. Quick, quick. Glasses raised. To the 63½ glorious years of drinking your wonderful wine I have spent in your marvellous country since I arrived a couple of hundred gallons ago.

'Okay, so first I would like to thank Manana for, as she says, the many services she has rendered me. Not least the preparation – no, Manana, please don't jump up and down like that. I don't know why, but it reminds me of a couple of highly strung Caucasian ponies chasing each other round and round a field. Now, as I was saying, I would like to thank – She's doing it again! She's doing it again! – Manana for preparing this glorious traditional Georgian meal. Finding, let alone slaughtering, and then preparing three sheep, two wild boar, two pigs and half an ox for a gathering of just nine people is no mean achievement. In between everything else. Not to mention the preparation of six buckets of sturgeon with walnuts, three washbasins of pork *shashlik* with pomegranates and half of what looks suspiciously like an old Russian soldier's helmet of roasted mushrooms. Which is probably about the first time it has ever had anything as substantial in it in its life.

'No, no, please, no cheering. You'll wake the neighbours up. And Lado, please don't throw your hat up and down like that, you'll only get it hooked on the... Oh well, we'll get it down later.

'Now, what was I saying? Oh yes, preparing this superb meal. I do know from experience what's involved. Many's the time I've got home from a long, boring, exhausting swing through half a dozen dull, miserable, pathetic countries – not like Georgia, of course – and had to wrestle with the polythene film on the top of yet another Marks and Spencer shepherd's pie and then, as if that's not enough, had to work out which button to press to open the microwave oven.

'So, a toast to Manana. Long may she continue to render her services to visiting businessmen. Especially me.

'Hey, this is fun. I'm beginning to enjoy this. Why can't we have dinners like this at home?

'Now Sasha. When I first saw him, I thought to myself, this guy is a wonderful, warm, kind-hearted typical Georgian. Of course, he was slumped over the wheel of this fantastic Lada at the time, completely bombed out of his mind. I say fantastic Lada, because I think it was the first time in my life I had ever seen a Lada with not only four wheels but four doors as well. It's true. And the fact that one door was actually in the boot is just a minor detail. It had four doors, and four doors is four doors in any language.

'Okay, okay. A toast to the Lada. To the greatest car that never moved.

'Oh, I must just tell you how we got to the hotel, or rather the guest-house, or wherever it was he took me. Well, after about half an hour I managed to wake him up. Then it must have taken me, what, another half an hour to persuade him to sit in the right seat of the car for driving. At first he wanted to sit in the back seat with me. I know that was naturally being very Georgian and very courteous, but it didn't exactly seem very practical. After that it was just a matter of pointing him in the right direction. Now, I'm not saying for a moment he was incapable. What I'm saying is I was incapable. Incapable of letting go of the dashboard. Incapable of blinking. Incapable of breathing.

'So Sasha. I would like to propose a toast to Sasha. To the most exciting... No, no, don't bother to wake him up. Well, not unless you think he's going to break the soup plate with his head in it like that.

'Now, about Tbilisi. To me, Tbilisi is incredible, although as far as I'm concerned it should still be called Tiflis. No, no, Manana, I said Tiflis. *Tiflis.* Yes, I know you're... Oh, never mind. I think it was very unfair of you guys to change the name. Just think of all the jokes... Yes, yes... I know I shouldn't make fun of ... all I said was... Well if that's your ... *Put that chair down, Vlad. Vlad, if you don't...* Yes, all right then, a toast to the peace and friendship between our two... Cheers. Cheers.

'To me Tiflis - waaaagh, I mean Tbilisi, is a very pretty little town. It's in a marvellous location, on the bend of a river with mountains all around. Lots of long, wide avenues or boulevards. Masses of tiny cobblestoned streets. Carved wooden balconies. A genuine old walled city. I know you've got around one, one and a half million population. But somehow it seems smaller. I reckon it's about the prettiest town in the whole of the Caucasus.

'No, no, honestly, I mean it. I really think it's... No, Manana, honestly, you don't have to thank me every time I... Oh, well. Yes. Thank you. That was very, ahem, how shall I say, refreshing.

'Now you've made me forget where I was. Oh yes, the Caucasian ponies. No, that's not right. I was talking about Tbilisi. The other thing that amazes me about Tibs is that I know you've had the odd one or two barrels of problems over the years: like bombs going off all over the place, three or four civil wars, I forget how many, Russian subversion. As well as banditry, the Mafia and political chaos. Big problems in Abkhazia and South Ossetia. Industrial production is virtually on the floor, the infrastructure has practically disintegrated and energy supplies are a joke. Inflation is a staggering 15,000 per cent. International reserves, zero. Tax returns, practically nothing. Soldiers marching up and down in the middle of the night singing sad songs about how much they love Georgia.

'No, thank you, Kakhi. We don't want to hear *My Georgia Moma* just yet. Later. Have another drink.

'Well, in spite of everything, Tibs doesn't look as though it has suffered that much. The other amazing thing is that throughout all this, the civil wars and the complete collapse of the industrial sector, foreign investment in Georgia has been completely unaffected. It has continued at exactly the same level as before: zero.

'Seriously though, I think you've done a fantastic job. The Metekhi Church, for instance. It's still up there, looking down on Tbilisi, protecting everything that staggers. Also it's a church once again after its time as first a prison and then a theatre – both functions, incidentally, designed to keep their victims firmly in their places for an agreed period of time. The statue of Vakhtang Gorgasali, the King of the Karthli, on horseback alongside it is, I think, fantastic, even though to me it is too big, too solid, too dramatic. It looks as if it was designed by some guy who specialises in historical strip cartoons for kids' comics. Sioni Cathedral is still there, the seat of the Patriarch of the Georgian Orthodox Church. To me, it's a nice old church. From the outside, it looks somehow small and squat and squeezed. Inside, it is high and lofty and full of space with, I must say, some jazzy, modern paintings, which came as a bit of a shock. Incidentally, I couldn't help but notice that in all the churches I've been in even the cross is shaped like a vine.

'As for Rustaveli Avenue, it's great fun. Nobody should come to Tifs, I mean Tibs, without walking up and down Rustaveli Avenue at least a million times. Everybody else does. All those open-air bars and cafés and restaurants. I reckon the Georgian *nouveaux riches* go there to be seen by the rest of the Georgian *nouveaux riches*. I notice there is even a Salon Thé Luxe. Well, that's what they call it. One day last week, after a somewhat light session the night before (we only drank three barrels of wine – each) I managed to drag myself out of bed at the crack of noon so I staggered in there for a cup of coffee. On one side were some dirty old tables, a fluorescent light, a fan. At the other end of the room were two guys with oxyacetylene cutters wrestling with something on the floor. It could have been a Danish pastry, I suppose or maybe a cheese and cucumber sandwich, I don't know. Either way, I didn't exactly feel like anything to eat after that so I went and had one of your Lagidze fruit drinks instead. Well, I thought I'd better before Coca-Cola take them over or run them out of town.

'What else do I like doing in Rustaveli Avenue? Whenever I get the chance I like wandering up and down looking at the book-stalls, which all seem to be run by university professors. Sometimes it's difficult, I agree, as the pavements are piled high with water melons. Tell you what I did buy, though. I bought a copy of Rustaveli's very own *The Night in the Panther's Skin* which is, I'm pleased to say, the most interesting, exciting and thrilling book I think I've read today.

'The old Edwardian-style Hotel Tbilisi is still gutted, although, to be honest, it doesn't look any different from some of the hotels I have stayed in in Scotland. Come to think of it, it looks like many a Scottish hotel the day after Burns' Night. The Parliament building, which I remember was built by the Soviets on the site of not one but two churches, is still there. To look at it today you'd never guess the two wings had been gutted, the outside walls were once as black as hell and some of the fancy decoration on the front shot to smithereens. But then, you would have thought people would know the last thing you do is attack a Communist Party building. Even I know these massive Communist monoliths were built to last forever. Hand grenades, rocket launchers, a couple of Scud missiles – none of them would make the slightest difference. Probably wouldn't even blow the windows out. As for the Soviet hotels, the office buildings and, of course, the blocks of flats, you might as well save your ammunition. There's no need to attack them. They're all going to fall down of their own accord before long anyway. I see you've also cleared up Freedom Square. However, I couldn't help noticing that the Hotel Iveria is packed to overflowing with refugees, Georgians who fled the troubles in Abkhazia. And some of the flats had those huge television satellite dishes and lots of fancy carpets hanging over the balconies. One floor, I was told, is still open to visitors. They're charging US$10 a night. I must try it next time. I'd like to experience luxury living for a change.

'No, no, Manana. Thank you very much. It's very kind of you. Maybe the time after next, then.

'At the top of Rustaveli near the Dom Kino, by the Georgian Academy of whatever, you'll never guess what I discovered. A British pub. Some Brit has set up a mini-brewery in one of the old buildings there at the back and is teaching you guys to drink beer, British beer. What do you think about that, then?

'Okay. So a toast to British beer – with Georgian wine. Cheers, cheers.

'Look, I know you're having it tough now, but don't forget you guys were once wallowing in what I remember the *Financial Times* referring to as "sybaritic, cultured prosperity". Or was it, "arthritic, cultural pomposity"? I can't remember. Two hours in this place and my brain doesn't understand me any more. All those sunny Black Sea resorts, all those fruit groves, those wonderful vineyards, all your lush tea plantations. Per head of population you were the wealthiest guys in the old Soviet Union. Sure, times are hard now. But speaking with all the authority of someone who's only been here for 63½ gallons, I'm convinced things are getting better.

'You know as well as I do that only a couple of years ago, literally only a couple of years ago, you needed a wheelbarrow to buy a loaf of bread. I mean a wheelbarrow load of money to buy a loaf of bread. It took no fewer than five, yes five, million of your fancy coupons to buy one US dollar. And, even worse, my old *babushka* told me the price of bread increased practically three hundred times in a single month.

'No, Manana, I didn't. She was ... oh, never mind.

'Now look at you. You're back to normal. Well, practically normal. Inflation is down from 15,000 per cent to 16 per cent to whatever it is now. The economy has swung from minus minus whatever to, somebody told me, 12 per cent. Which is unbelievable. And the heating is back on at the ballet and the opera. Which must have been a thrill for everyone in their little tutus.

'Now, instead of knocking back the tiny $2\frac{1}{2}$-litre drinking horns you're back on the grown-ups' 10-litre drinking horn, which I must tell you makes our yard of ale look like kid's stuff. Then, of course, there are all the incidentals. No longer are there thugs wandering around your lush, expensive Metekhi Palace (or rather the Metacky Gin Palace) up on the hill, shooting up reception. No longer are there dead bodies in the foyer. Although judging by the prices they charge, there's still a great deal of armed robbery taking place in the bars and restaurants. And nobody has taken a shot at old Sher— sorry, I mean your glorious President Eduard Shevardnadze, for at least a couple of years. Acutally, I think the worst thing that's happened to him recently was when the leader of Abkhazia suddenly turned up unannounced at his office and wanted to be friends. That, I think, shocked him more than the car bomb. Talking of bombs, how come you see so many tyres bursting all over the place? I was walking back down Rustaveli the other day and it was like the Alamo. The amazing thing is that nobody takes any notice, although the man in the gun shop below the State National Singing and Dancing

Ensemble told me he is still doing a nice line in Colt
Detective Specials.

'At the same time, I admit that it is tough trying to live
on, what, US$100, US$200 a month. If you're that lucky.
You still see the old and the poor and the crippled sitting
all day long crouched over scarred wooden tables or
crates trying to sell a handful of sunflower seeds. The
other day, for instance, I saw this desperately poor old
lady outside the Georgian Academy of Science selling
men's socks: one at a time. Or rather trying to sell men's
socks one at a time. You see many old men, wearing
their medals, sitting all day long by these old-fashioned
weighing machines or playing their accordions in the
still dark and damp and dingy subways. Others you see
take over a whole street or a part of a street and appoint
themselves dictator-in-chief of everything they can get
away with – parking, reversing, stopping to ask directions.
Even car washing, if they can find some young kid to do
it for them and the car doesn't cave in from the sudden
impact of half a bucket of filthy water.

'As I said, I know you've got problems. Big problems. I
know for every shop you've got called Ici Paris or Ciao
Ciao there are a million still run by women wearing
funny old-fashioned white hats and coats and aprons
with nothing, or practically nothing, on the shelves. You
can hardly walk down the street for wires and cables
where people are nicking electricity off the public
supply. I've discovered why all the subways and
underpasses are so dark. People are using all the electric
sockets for themselves, for their stalls, for their shops
and even for their flats. You are also the centre of the world
for not only paintings of Sunsets over the Caucasus but
also for St George and the Dragon. If I see another of
either I think I'll go bananas.

'No, no, Manana. Bananas, *bananas*. I didn't say I was
going to Manana's. You're the only Manana in my life.
Oh, never mind – have another bucket of wine.

'I know that if you want to do a simple thing like

make a phone call, first you have to find a telephone that works and then queue up for hours on end in the street to use it. For long-distance calls you have to trudge down to your old Soviet-style telephone exchange, queue up for hours on end, hand over your life's savings and then they put you through to the wrong number. Which reminds me of the railway station. I know that if you want to get a railway ticket you have to practically get down on your hands and knees and shout through this tiny little window covered in net curtains at some fat old *babushka*, then stroll out and get on your train; whereas at home, all we have to do is stroll into this rather smart booking office, get a ticket and then wait three hours because the train is late or delayed or cancelled because there's the wrong kind of rain or leaves or snow on the line.

'But let's be positive. You don't have popcorn machines. You don't have mobile telephones. You don't have Mercedes blocking up the street, and I think I've only seen one Mercedes all week. All your huge, crumbling old buildings are still huge, crumbling old buildings and not trendy little gallerias or a million tiny offices with light, airy atria crawling with pot plants and modern paintings. And your police are still very friendly. At least, whenever I'm driving around town they keep stopping me and then insisting on apologising for any inconvenience and wishing me a nice day.

'No, Shota, put that bottle down. It's still half full. In any case, you know what I'm saying is true. Give it two or three years, give people time to make a little money, just enough to splash a bit of paint around, to get the old Polyfilla out, and you won't recognise this place. Look, I've been all over Eastern Europe. I've seen countries the day after the Russians moved out. I've also seen them a few years on. Believe me, it is amazing the changes that take place. I know it's tough now. I know people are suffering and I know people are going hungry. But slowly, slowly money will begin to come back into the economy.

Slowly, slowly things will begin to change. For the better. Women will begin to wear better clothes. Somehow, don't ask me how, they'll find the money for make-up and other things. Slowly, slowly they will want the front door painted. Slowly, slowly they'll want the inside of the flat painted. They'll want a new kitchen. They'll want things like new tables and chairs. The poor fellas will go along with it. They'll work every hour God gives them. But slowly, slowly they'll do everything they want to do. Of course, the blokes will still go around like tramps and down-and-outs. But that's the same story the world over.

'Oh yes, Zaza, yes it is. You've only got to look at me to see that most Western husbands are down-trodden, down-at-heel, miserable, pathetic wretches. No, honestly, Manana, I'll be all right. I don't need any special attention at the moment, thank you. Especially not in this condition. No thank you … I don't want another half bucket of … Well, okay then. Just a half. No, a half. Oh, well. I didn't really want a half. I was only being polite.

'Sasha. I was talking about Sasha. No I wasn't, I was talking about Giorgi. No, Georgia. The old brain keeps going fuzzy.

'I'll tell you what I like about your Georgia. First, I like the people. No, no, it's true. I mean it. No, no, no. Put me down! I don't want to be carried … carried round the … room. You might … No, no. I'll be all right. Honest. My leg always looks like that when I throw myself off somebody's shoulders because of a chandelier looming in front of me. Yes. That's perfect. Another bucket of whatever will make me feel as right as rain. No, I promise you, leaning up against the dresser like this is really very comfortable. I know I might look funny with one leg in the bottom drawer and the other twisted behind me but I'll be fine, I assure you.

'Now, what was I saying? Oh yes. The people. It's the people that make Georgia St George, was a lucky man to be born here and not in England, or the Lebanon, or Syria or any other place that either boasts they have his birth certificate or claims him as their patron saint. I love the way you make life simple. In any other country in the world I've got to learn a million things before I can even ask the time of day. Here, you've only got to learn one word: *gagimarjot*, cheers and you're in. That's it.

'No, no, Jura. Put me ... Oh well, at least my leg's the right way round again. Cheers, Jura. A toast to Jura.

'Listen, let me tell you, I love the way whenever I go into offices and shops you still have crucifixes and holy pictures on the wall. I also love the way women still wear black here if there's a death in the family. Not just for a big death but even the death of a distant relative. Nowadays the first thing any woman does in the West if there's a death in the family is to go out and buy a new outfit and then collect the insurance. Jura, please don't choke - it's true, I promise you. When I die I've got no illusions. Nobody takes any notice of me now I'm alive; nobody is going to take any notice of me when I'm dead.

'No, no, Manana. Please don't cry, it's true. Oh, okay then. A toast to happiness. To happiness. Cheers. Cheers. Cheers.

'But I've noticed that women wear black less and less. I don't mean, not so often: I mean, less and less of it. Some of the women you see obviously find it very difficult to hide, how shall I say, their feelings.

'Tell you what: I also love the way you Georgians never want to disappoint anyone. Yes, thank you, Manana. I didn't exactly mean it that way. But thanks all the same for the thought. What I meant was your way of always agreeing with everyone, always promising everyone the world. Yes, yes, Manana. Thank you. Very kind of you. Thank you very much, I'll bear it in mind. And the way you always say you have something when you don't. No, Manana, I know you've got it. You don't have to tell me.

'I mean, go into a bar, order a drink. People will be only too happy to stop whatever they're doing and come and join you in case you are feeling lonely or downhearted. Go into a restaurant. Ask for a bottle of your excellent Tsinandeli, which I genuinely think is one of the best wines I've ever tasted. Especially after the seventh or eighth bottle. They will always say they've got it. Then, when you've ordered your meal and they've just served the first dish, they will always tell you that unfortunately they've just sold the last bottle. You then order a bottle of Khvanchkara or Superavi or even a bottle of Regina Tamara, your red champagne. Then, when you've practically finished, hey presto, they discover they've got another case of Tsinandeli left after all. By which time, of course, it is nearly closing time so all the waiters are only too happy to come and help you finish the lot.

'Stay in somebody's house instead of a hotel and that's great fun. Most of the places I've stayed in are always the same. Lots of thick heavy furniture, good carpets, lots of paintings. A grand piano in the corner. Piles of books. And, as you'd expect, lots of wine. Trouble is, whenever I stay in anybody's home, they keep throwing their daughters at me, which, I must admit, makes a change. Stay with a family in Kyrgyzstan and they keep throwing their wife at you. I won't tell you what they keep throwing at you if you stay in somebody's house in Oman. All I can say is I hope you don't have a camel as a pet.

'Come, come, Lado, there's no need to take that attitude. How was I supposed to know your wife comes from Kyrgyzstan? I'm sure she's a very friendly lady. It's just that ... Oops. Can somebody pick him up? No, don't bother. Leave him there.

'And another thing. I love the way you can still go into some shops and there alongside the electronic calculator is an abacus which is used to double-check the calculator. Fantastic.

'Okay. A toast to Georgi. No, I mean Georgio. No, no, I mean Giorgia. It doesn't matter: to whatever we want to drink to. Long may it whatever whatever.

'Now, Vlad. I must tell you about Vlad. I reckon he's one of the Vladdy best Georgians there ... No, no, Vlad. You don't have to, I won't be offended if you don't. Oh well, at least there are no photographers present. I hope. Yes, I know, Manana. But it's different when blokes do it. Especially to each other. Well, I think it is.

'Oh yes, I was telling you about my trips outside Tibs. Nothing but miles and miles of potholes. Great piles of cars and trucks and buses everywhere. Churches and monasteries around every corner. Dying Ladas being towed backwards and forwards by stringy bits of rope to be brought back to life for another five hundred years. Cattle strolling around everywhere. And pigs: I've never seen anything like them. Some of them were about the size of a pony – enormous. For a moment I thought, this is *Animal Farm*. It's all come true. The pigs are taking over.

'A slice of pork, anybody? There's plenty left.

'And books. Everybody seems to be reading something by Tolstoy or Dostoevsky or Chekhov or some other Russian classic. Apart from one girl I met. She told me she was reading a modern American novel: *The Catcher in the Rye*. When I told her it was about a million years old, she naturally didn't believe me. Women never do. Apart from you, of course, Manana. Thank you very much. But at least it wasn't Jeffrey Archer. Although I don't suppose it will be long before everybody is reading his books instead.

'Gori was great fun. I know I shouldn't say that because it was the birthplace of The Great Unmentionable. No, I don't mean my mother-in-law. Or even Gregory Peck's father. I mean S-t-a-l-i-n. Shh. I never said that. All the same, it was still interesting to see how you – Okay, okay, I apologise. It wasn't you. It was your Soviet masters. But it was still interesting to see how he was treated. At first he was the big hero. Your Soviet masters built this enormous kind of Uncle Joe Theme Parkski. Also a gigantic museum about the size of Buckingham Palace. You filled it full of all kinds of paraphernalia: porcelain from France, glass from Germany, samovars from the Ukraine, silk paintings from China, plus practically every photograph that was ever taken of him. And a single postcard proclaiming, 'In all honesty I must tell you I do not deserve half the compliments that come my way, signed: J Stalin'. The actual house, or rather the shack, where he was supposed to have been born (appropriately enough in the room on the left) was put in the park inside this kind of temple thing. Then the train he travelled in was parked on its own little track alongside the museum. Then quite suddenly, you disown the guy. He is even removed from the Soviet Union's own official history of the Communist Party. Not that I blame you for one moment. I must say, though, that it is somewhat ironic that the guy who virtually created the Soviet Union and the guy who virtually dismantled it were both Georgians.

'It's crazy when you think about it - how come this poor Georgian peasant kid, the son of a shoemaker, became probably the greatest tyrant the world has ever known? Being completely impartial and objective. I blame the mother, of course. If she had been a good Georgian mother with the interests of her Georgian son at heart, she would have made certain he grew up to do something useful in his life. Like become a bus driver. As my mother always wanted me to be. 'Why do you want to go into business?' she always asked. 'Why don't you become a bus driver? You'd be much happier.' Instead Mrs Stalin, or Mrs Dzhugashvili, as the old ladies in the museum told me she should be called, let him go his own way. First he went to the local seminary to train as a priest. Then he obviously had some kind of reverse blinding red flash and changed sides to become a revolutionary. After that followed trouble with the police, arrest, deportation to Siberia or wherever, return to Gori, robbing the Tiflis stagecoach, more trouble with the police, a touch of spying for the Tzar's secret police, Moscow and finally his name up in lights. Red lights, naturally. Now you're desperately trying to downplay the whole thing. There aren't even any signs pointing to the house, let alone the museum. There isn't even a sign pointing to the sole remaining statue of Stalin left in the whole world, in the main square.

'Yes, Zaza. I know we don't make much fuss of the birthplace of the greatest dictator of the English-speaking world, Mrs Thatcher. But, believe me, it will come.

'By the way, what about Beria? He was Georgian, too. How come such a relaxed, boozy, friendly people as you lot produced two of the, how can I put it tactfully? most inhuman monsters of the twentieth century? It's amazing. You're full of fun. You're relaxed. You're not really interested in anything apart from drinking and drinking. Okay, Manana, I admit there are one or two other things *you* might be particularly interested in, but generally speaking...

'Because— No, no, Jura, put that bottle... Shota, if you as much as... Because as far as— Giorgi, I'm warning you. If you do that... Because as far as I'm concerned— Zaza, that's not exactly ladylike, is it? As far as I'm concerned, it means there can no longer be any badness left in Georgia. You've used it all up. Which is why today Georgia is such a wonderful, beautiful country full of wonderful, beautiful people and...

'Another toast to Georgia. Those wonderful, those beautiful, those... Now how am I going to get my jacket? No, it doesn't matter, I was only joking. There's no need to... no, no. Watch where you're— The table won't— The wine. *The wine. Mind the—* No, no, that's okay. I can get them cleaned. It's just that I don't fancy walking down the street with them like this at the moment. Thank you, Manana, it's very kind of you to offer, but I'd prefer to keep them on at the moment, if you don't mind. Right. Another toast to Kakhi for getting my jacket down from the chandelier. To Kakhi. To the best mountaineer in the whole of Georgia. No, the Caucasus. No, the world.

'Hey, I've just remembered something else about Gori. In the grounds of the museum I met this old boy. He told me he was an engineer. He had been in the Soviet Army. "Communism is very good for individual, very good for many people," he told me. But, he added, "It has many negative moments." The negative moments, as far as he was concerned, were the loss of his father and most of his family in the Great Purges. The collapse of Communism, he went on, had produced few if any positive moments. He'd sold the family piano. He'd sold his paintings. He'd sold his furniture. Now he was planning to sell his house. "It is difficult. Communism was good to us. But now…" he said. As I said goodbye to him, I noticed this kid sitting on the steps outside the museum. He was reading a book on Windows '96.

'After Gori I went to Uplis-Tsikhe, this third-century cave town, hewn out of the soft limestone rock overlooking the River Kur, which I reckon is a million times better than Machu Picchu, the Aztecs' secret hideaway high in the Andes. Not only were there all kinds of elaborate buildings carved out of the rocks, there was even a theatre, complete with baffle boards in the ceiling. Now the Aztecs never had that. As I was clambering over the rocks, I met this other old comrade, as one does. He told me London was his favourite city. "I know it very well indeed," he said. "I like Sherlock Holmes Plaza. It is my favourite street." He kept singing "Everybody Loves Somebody Sometimes" and the Beatles' "Yesterday", because, he said, of their "polyphonic harmonies," which beat me. I just thought they were good tunes.

'I also like Mtskheta, the old capital, just up the road

from Tibs. To look at it, you'd think it was the typical drive-through town - broad streets, a couple of monuments, nothing very exciting. But you'd be wrong. This is one of the oldest cities in the world. It has been around for four thousand years, give or take a century or three. It's also where they virtually invented Georgian, or at least Georgian handwriting, which as we all know was devised all those years ago with the Internet in mind. There are no capital letters: it's all lower case.

'As for the eleventh-century Cathedral of Sveti, it's fantastic, just what a cathedral should really look like. Huge pillars. (One, I noticed, with grapes all over it.) Icons and candles everywhere. Gee whizz, it's even got a scale model of the Holy Sepulchre in Jerusalem. Not that I'm the only one who thinks so highly of it - so did the King. To show his appreciation, he chopped the architect's arm off as soon as it was finished so he couldn't build another one like it. Hence the carving of a single arm way up the top of the outside wall, warning architects the world over that if they ever get any work in Georgia to get it written into their contracts that if they do a good job, there is no way that at the end of it they should be rendered harmless.

'Way up in the mountains overlooking the town is the Dzhvari Monastery. Or rather the church of the Dzhvari Monastery. I went there too. It was great fun. There were a couple of freelance monks outside offering to show people round but when you asked them a question, they didn't seem to know the answer. Funny, that.

'I tell you the other thing I like about Georgia. You see, you've got me going now. I like - what do I mean, I like - I *love* the wine and the food and, I must confess, the boozing. Or should I say the terribly civilised approach you have to enjoying yourself and entertaining your neighbours. Now, I'm not saying you're a bunch of boozers. But I've never come across anybody, not even the French, who are as fond of their wine as you are. Drink it by the glass? No way. You glug it back by the bucketful. A glass of wine? Zonk. Gone in a flash. A bottle? Zonk. My liver has been on the end of some pretty serious drinking in its time, but nothing like this. Not that I'm complaining. All I hope is that my tiny, fragile white corpuscles can keep up with you all. I've only got to stop someone in the street and ask them the way and they're insisting we go and get bombed out of our minds. I go into someone's office, even at ten o'clock in the morning and out come the glasses, soon to be filled to overflowing with wine. I go to one of the big Ministries, I'm hardly past the security guards before everybody is thrusting glasses into my hand and proposing toasts to my health, to the success of the meeting, to my safe return home, to my next visit to Georgia, to further successful meetings. By the time we've finished all the toasts I've forgotten what the hell the meeting was supposed to be about anyway.

'Yes, yes, okay, Jura. Goodness me, even Sasha's woken up. A toast to Georgian men. Long may they do whatever they do. Yes. Yes, Manana. Thank you. That was very kind of you. Thank you. I shall bear it in mind. Okay. Okay. Another toast to "Long may they do whatever they… Aaaargh! Watch out for Sasha. He's going to— Oh well, I'm sure you can get another Ming vase.

'In fact, the boozing is so serious that once there was some kind of mix-up with the security guards at one of the Ministries I went to and for some reason or other I ended up attending the wrong meeting. Instead of meeting some official in the finance department, I ended up with some deputy-under-secretary to the Minister for Protocol or something. I only discovered the mistake about half an hour after I reached his office and all the toasts had finished and we finally got down to business. By the time I found the right office, the official had gone out to lunch. So I went back to my friend in Protocol and we finished another barrel. Trouble was, as we were now friends, every time we had a glass, he insisted on us standing up, linking our arms together and then – zonk – another bottle hit the dust.

'Afterwards – I don't know what on earth possessed me – I clambered up on top of the roof of Sasha's Lada. Which I'd be the first to say was stupid. But what on earth it was that possessed Sasha to then drive the damn thing all the way back to my hotel was even more stupid. I could have dropped the bottle of wine I was drinking out of.

'Quick. A toast to Sasha's Lada. Long may it drive safely.

'The greatest thing of all, to me, are your traditional Georgian dinners. I don't mean official banquets or business dinners. I mean your ordinary, simple, everyday meals. Like this. Which, correct me if I'm wrong, started on Monday. Last week. And with a little bit of luck should be finished in time for my next visit. I've read about Old Testament dinners where thousands of cattle were lined up and slaughtered and priests slaved day and night to prepare the food for the table. They've got nothing on this. I know my appetite is insatiable – no, Manana, not that kind of appetite – but just look at those rolled crêpes filled with mincemeat. They're enormous. One slice is about the size of a dinner plate. Talking of plates, look at the plates of chicken; those great bowls of green peppers; all those cheeses; the piles of fried aubergine. Goodness me, that mountain of pressed beef, those buckets of *shashlik*, those heaps of baked potatoes. All that cornbread. And what's that? Sturgeon with pomegranates. And look at that enormous stew bubbling away over there. I bet you've thrown everything in there. You must have halved Georgia's annual cattle production at a stroke for this meal. Or rather at the swing of an axe. We're the ones who are going to get the strokes if we eat this lot.

'I suppose it's not really surprising that you're so good

at entertaining, because if you've been producing wine for five thousand years, way before the Egyptians even thought about it, then you've obviously got over five thousand years of experience of eating and drinking. So the law of something or other says you must be better at it than anybody else on earth.

'Agreed? Agreed. So a toast then, to the greatest drinkers in the world. To the Georgians. Long may your livers continue to throb.

'I'll tell you one other thing that amazes me about the Georgians. Here you are, eating and drinking and getting trashed out of your minds every night of your life, and the crazy thing is you will all live to be a hundred. Quick. I can feel another toast coming on. To me becoming a Georgian and to living to be a hundred. Cheers. Cheers. Cheers.

'As I was saying, or trying to say, it's no wonder Georgia is such a wonderful country, because as far as I'm concerned it's God's own country.

'I think it was Jura, or was it Manana? I can't remember. I get so confused. No, no, Manana. I was joking. English joke. No, no, you don't have to prove...Oh well. There we are. There is a difference after all. Which reminds me, you know the story: God is sitting on top of this mountain. He's just created the world. So he summons everybody for the big share-out. Everybody comes, apart from the Georgians. They're too busy eating and drinking. Eventually, when they turn up about three days – oh sorry, Jura, I forgot – when they turn up three weeks late, it's all over. God starts to tell them off. But when the Georgians, who are bleary-eyed and swaying about, tell Him they are late because they had been toasting His good health, He relents and gives them the land He had kept back for Himself: Georgia.

'Another toast. To Georgia: God's own country.

'No Zaza, leave Sasha there. I know he looks dead. But I'm sure he'll be fine. Where was I? Oh yes, the

Georgians. They're warm. They're colourful. They're exciting. Yes, Manana. I know you are. But later, Manana. I know it's getting very hot in here. But do you have to…? You'll catch your death of—

'Quick, a toast to Georgian ladies. To—

'No, Manana. I did not make you drop it. As I was saying, Georgia has these two big problems at present: inflation and stability. Inflation. Everything is getting more and more inflated day by day.

'Okay, a toast to inflation. Long may it last. No. What I mean is, long may the measures put into effect to control inflation last. And stability. Long may we have stability. Not just in the, how shall I say, younger and more vigorous sectors of the economy, but also in the more mature sectors as well. It's a pity that you're stuck in the Caucasus where you're overlooked and ignored. With your history, your architecture, your style, your *joie de vivre* you should be in the centre of Europe. That way you'll get the recognition, the reputation, the praise that you deserve. I tell you what, as soon as I get home - if I can remember where it is. Wait a minute, I've got the address written down on a bit of paper somewhere - I'm going to send a postcard to the President of the European Union proposing that we swap Belgium for Georgia. After all, what has Belgium done to improve the lot of the world? Sure, they gave us Simenon and Magritte and waffles. But, I ask you, what is that alongside Tsinandali and Khvanchkara and Regina Tamara and a couple of bottles of Enisseli cognac and meals that last six or seven hours at a time?

'Shota, will you please pick Kakhi up off the floor. I know it's a laugh, but he could choke. Undo his top button and roll him over on his side. That's better. He won't wake up for at least three hours, I know, but at least he'll wake up in time to drive you home. We hope. And incidentally, take that vodka bottle away from him. It's not nice to see a grown man sucking on a vodka bottle like that, especially when it's empty.

'Oops, who moved the floor? Now what was I talking about? Oh, never mind. Shota. We haven't had a toast to Shota yet.

'Well, that's four of us still cape, capable of s-st-standing. Not bad, eh? Yes, Manana. I know you can't wait to... but hang on a minute.

'Have we really drunk all that wine? You'll have to go out and plant some more vines first thing tomorrow morning. If we can shift fifty-three bottles of booze between the nine of us, what could the real professionals do?

'So, Zaza, Manana – Manana? Manana. Are you still... Oh, never mind. In c-con-conclusion, then all I would say is, it's no wonder your toasts go on and on and on. This Arab guy, Agnes Al Umari, reckoned that in the Middle Ages if you wrote to any king in the world, you just said, Dear Sir, or something like that. If you wrote to the G-G-Georgian King, however, you had to say, "May God make permanent the felicity of the exalted presence, the presence of the great monarch, the hero, the bold, the lion, the illustrious, the attacker, the dauntless, the enthroned, the crowned, a scholar in his community, just to his subjects, the successor of the Greek kings, Sultan of the Georgians, treasure of the kingdom of the seas and gulfs, protector of the homeland of the knights, the heir of his fathers in thrones and crowns, bulwark of the lands of Rum and Iran, offspring of the Hellenes, the quintessence of the kings of the Syrians, the successor of the sons of thrones and crowns, the strengthener of Christianity, supporter of the religion of Jesus, the anointed leader of the Christian heroes, who glorified Jerusalem by sincere purpose, the pillar of the sons of baptism, the helper of the Bab who is the Pope of Rome, the lover of the Muslims, the best of close companions, and the friend of Kings and Sultans."

'And we thought the Hapsburgs were pompous. By the time you've said all that, there's no room to say anything else, is th-th-there?

'T-t-talking of time. Goodness me, is that the time? Almost twenty past three. Oh well, it shust goest to roof, You can alwaysh rely on me to be thrite on the... the night. Now, you don't want to listen to me r-r-rambling on and on and on any more. We've got some s-s-serious d-d-drinking to do. So all I would like to say is. N-n-nobody in their right livers, I mean minds, should ever come to G-G-Georgia on b-b-business. It would be an insult to the warmth and generosity and hosh-hosp-hospitality of the Georgian people. Instead they should come to G-G-Georgia for pleasure.

'A f-final t-toasht, then, Shashy Shanana, Shuri, Shoti, Shiorgi, Shladi, Shlado, Shaki and Shashi ... Shashy! Shanana! Shuri! Where are you? Oh you're down there. Well, all right then. I shall now p-p-propose my shfinal toasht. Glasshes. Yours. Pleashe to raise: shto Georgia and the Sch-Georgians. Shcheers. May your cupsh shnever runneth under. Shcheers. Shcheers. No, wait a minute. Shanother toast. T-T-To Sctibbslisi. What schrdink ish t-t-to a shdrunk. Scheers...'

Chisinau

Look, *mio amico*, I don't care what you say. To me, Moldova is Russia with an Italian accent. *Capisce?*

The towns and cities look Italian – well, designed by Italians and run by Russians. There are huge public offices; big, impressive government buildings; beautifully decorated palaces; enormous, open piazzas; fountains and statues. Also, Gigolis all over the place: the Russian car, that is, the one that for some reason or other never really took off in the West.

As for the villages, way out in the middle of nowhere, even they look like Tuscany before the Brits moved in and ruined it: there are rolling hills, deep valleys, vast smooth lakes and huge forests. Tiny, run-down, dilapidated old houses. Rough roads and tracks. Wells in the street. Over-elaborate shrines on every street corner. Cattle and geese and goats and chickens everywhere. Huge, huge fields of apple trees that go on for mile after mile after mile, and endless trucks full to overflowing with apples.

As if that isn't enough, there are smaller fields of sunflowers – eat your heart out, Van Gogh – that go on for half-mile after half-mile after half-mile. In fact, you can hardly go anywhere in the country without somebody throwing an anchor out of the window of their Lada, juddering the thing to a halt and leaping into the nearest field to return with great armfuls of the things. Not to take home and paint, but to eat. The seeds, they say, are good for you. You spend so much time picking the bits out of your teeth you've got no time to get up to anything that's bad for you.

The clincher, apart from the fact that Moldovans queue up like the Italians, is that their bank notes all contain spelling mistakes. Admittedly in Ukrainian, one of their three official languages, but a *mistako* is a *mistako* in any language.

As for the Moldovans themselves, they're all dripping with chains and crosses and all kinds of jewellery; riding around on the backs of old Vespas; eating ice cream like it's going out of fashion; waving their hands in the air, gesticulating like mad and touching you and prodding you and squeezing your hand all the time. And that's just the men.

Don't ask me why, but the more I go there the more I find I'm becoming like them. No sooner am I trying to find my luggage and have my first ice cream than I'm going around practically patting the kids on the head – and I hate kids. Even when they're parboiled. What's more, I find I'm even beginning to sound like them. Not that that is difficult, of course. To speak Moldovan all you have to do is down a couple of gallons of apple juice, guess the Italian word for whatever you want to say and change the ending. YouthinkImadakiddinyou? Not at all. Industry is *industrie*. Factory is *fabrica*. Hydro-electric plant is *centrala idroelectrica*. It's the same with the more important, far more practical, words. Menu is *meniul*. Wine list is *lista de vinuri*. Champagne is *samparie*. I'm sorry, I've got a lot of work to do in the office this evening is *Fantezie Exotica*. And, you didn't tell me your husband is the Moldovan weight-lifting champion, is *Larniverdeci, Moldova Pronto*. Most times, *multumiri*. I find it works very well. Other times, particularly if you try to adopt a Sicilian accent, you find you can spend an enjoyable few hours studying the Moldovan approach to *asistenta medicala*.

In theory, admittedly, Moldova should be as Russian as a forged US$100 *bancnota*. Tucked away in the bottom south-east corner of *Europa* virtually surrounded by the Ukraine on the *nord, est* and *sud* with Romania *on de udder side*, I mean the *vest*, it started off as Bessarabia – although what on earth it had to do with Arabia, goodness only knows. I can only imagine Lawrence of Arabia dropped by one day and what with all those flowing *roba blancas* and everything, the people who thus far had spent all their lives up to their eyes in apples and sunflowers promptly nicknamed him Bess Arabia and somehow it stuck. As with anything to do with Lawrence, the country had been fought over, trampled on, bits chopped off, bits added and traded backwards and forwards so many times it's impossible to work out what was what and whose was whose and for how long. A bit like, I suppose, the Middle East: after Lawrence.

All I know is that their big hero is Stefan cel Mare – no, not Stefan the sailor, Stefan the Great – the King of Moldova. Between 1447 and 1504 he beat off the Poles, the Hungarians, the Khan of the Crimea and, it is rumoured, the IMF as well. After that it was back to being a political *fotbal* being kicked around by all comers: the Turks, the Hungarians and, of course, the Russians who in 1812, to the sound of cannon-fire, marched in and made it Russian. Romania next door protested and complained. But it wasn't until 1939 that the issue was finally settled. Everything, but everything, belonged to Russia.

In theory, out went the Moldovans' heritage, their traditions and their language. In came everything Russian, their language, their Cyrillic script and, of course, their people, Russian people. Not to mention a whole bunch of Ukrainians and Romanians as well. But little Moldova, the *bambino* of all the old Soviet republics – it is about 200 miles long and 100 miles wide, roughly the size of Wales, with a population of between four and five million - managed to remain fiercely Moldovan. So much so that when the Soviet Union finally began to fall apart, it was the first of the republics to unilaterally ditch Russia and all things Russian, including the Cyrillic script, and set up on its own with its own language as the official language at last. The statue of their beloved Stefan the Great they moved back from the far corner of Kishinev's Central Park to pride of place. They even gave him back his sword, which had disappeared under the Russians. They changed the name of the capital back from the Russian, Kishinev, to the Moldovan, Chisinau. For the first time in their history, Moldova was Moldova, or at least the bits the Russians said were Moldova were Moldova. The people were Moldovans. The language they spoke was Moldovan. Not even the Great Stefan cel Mare achieved that.

Although - and I warn you now, watch out for the landmines, we're treading on dangerous ground - one part of the former Moldova is today more Marxist-Leninist-Stalinist then either Marx or Lenin or Stalin ever were. Welcome, comrades, to the glorious ever Socialist Republic of Trans-Dniester - Trans, either side, Dniester, the River Dniester - a long, thin sliver of land, about the length and width of Lenin's scarf, along their *nord est frontiera* with Ukraine.

If Moldova is Russia or what used to be Russia with an Italian accent, then Trans-Dniester or what used to be Moldova is today Russia with not just a Russian but a thick Marxist-Leninist accent. Actually, give or take North Korea, it's probably the last totally unreconstructed one-hundred-per-cent Marxist-Leninist state in the *totale mundo*. Their flag is a hammer and sickle (what else?) with a red star. Their bank notes, or rather coupons, apart from the spelling mistakes - it obviously runs in the family - carry not the image of some long dead Trans-Dniesterian hero but the mounted figure of the old Tzarist General Suvorov, favourite of Catherine the Great and infamous in Russian history for the way his troops practically hacked Bessarabia to bits in 1790. Even the President, Igor Smirnov, is the spitting image of Lenin.

While Moldova proper is heading hell for leather in an Italian kind of way towards a capitalist economy i.e. two steps forwards one day, one step back the next, Trans-Dniester, if only it had a clock that worked, is busy turning it back to the good old days of central planning, of Gosplan, of Gossnab and of Gossnothing-worksletsblameitallonthecapitalists. The result is a complete, total, no holds barred, Marxist never-never land. They never have any bread. They never have any meat. They never have any electricity, let alone water or gas. Nothing ever works. Not even the hidden micro-phones, thank goodness, otherwise I might not be here today to tell the tale. There's nothing in the shops: no food, no drink. The only place to find any decent food (in Trans-Dniester decent food is sausages) is, a classic Soviet trick, in the polling stations, whenever they hold one of their Mickey Mouse elections. That is if it hasn't all been grabbed by the choirs of elderly women – another old Soviet trick – who go from one polling station to another threatening to sing old Soviet songs unless people vote the way they are told. Failing the sausages, the people have to stick with their normal everyday diet: fat, grease and on high days and holidays, fat and grease. As for drinks, their only hope is to find an illegal drinking den where everybody is racing to get bombed out of their minds on fake vodka made out of industrial alcohol before they go blind.

How people live I have no idea. Average salaries – if, that is, anyone can get a job and if they can, if they ever get paid – are around US$5 a month. Yes, a month. Pensioners? All they can do is whistle such stirring Soviet popular songs as 'Varschavuanka', 'The Red Csepei Works' and 'We Thank You Comrade Rakosy' while they slowly starve to death.

Originally, of course, it was all going to be different. It was going to be a Socialist Florida, or rather paradise. From the Ukraine, from Belarus, even from Russia itself flooded in old soldiers, pensioners, shattered old Siberian miners who year after year had struggled against impossible odds to fulfil their quotas as well as the clever guys who just bribed their managers to fill in all the necessary forms to say they had done. All of these people were lured to the good life by the promise of three-room flats, a mild, pleasant, sunny climate and relative peace and quiet. On top of that there was the promise of jobs and the possibility of earning a little extra on the side. Trans-Dniester, after all, was the business end of Moldova. They had most if not all of the heavy industry. The rest of the country had the odd shoe, textile, cigarette plant, but nothing big, nothing substantial.

Because of its location on the banks of the tree-lined River Dniester, the climate, and the relaxed atmosphere, there was also a booming tourist industry. People came from all over the Soviet Union to stay in the hotels and sample the delights of strolling innocently along the banks of the river, eating apples and sitting outside in the open air in November. The Prietenia Hotel in Bendery, or Tighina as the Moldovans call it, once rocked-and-rolled with honeymoon couples from all over Russia. As soon as they arrived they were greeted by staff in traditional costumes, who immediately thrust gifts of bread and salt at them and ushered them quickly into special honeymoon suites overlooking the river, with little white doves painted on the doors. What on earth they were expected to do with the bread and salt I have no idea.

When the big bust-up with the Soviet Union came in 1991 the Russians, who made up most of the 700,000 population of Trans-Dniester, decided they wanted to go their own way. They didn't want to be part of Moldova because Moldova was obviously going to be run by Moldovans not Russians. What is more, they were scared that if Moldova merged with Romania – at one time in its long, chequered history, it was a province of Romania – they were afraid that they would be even more of a minority. On their own, in their private little enclave between Moldova and Ukraine, with most of the heavy industry under their control not to mention the direct or indirect backing of Moscow, they thought they would be laughing all the way to the State Bank.

Instead, it all went horribly wrong.

Crossing the border at Kutchurgai is like going through Checkpoint Charlie in the old days. Hours and hours of hanging around. People walking around. Thick fog. At least I think it was. It was certainly lashing down with rain. I was in the back of a broken down old Paejero, which had so much thick, sticky, brown tape holding the windows together I could hardly see outside.

On the Ukraine side the crossing took time but at least it was organised. On the Trans-Dniester side it was crazy. We were herded in all directions by an endless string of heavies. They had no uniforms or badges, just bits of stick. Every single one of them stopped us. Each group looked at my passport and asked me questions I didn't understand and then waved me on to the next bunch, after the usual traditional exchange of courtesies. By the time I got through I was not only $3\frac{1}{2}$ cartons of Marlboro lighter, I'd say I'd bought the country three times over as well. Not that they believe in privatisation, obviously.

Once through, however, the road was quite good – smooth, wide and well-kept, although the fields either side were practically jungle. At least, the bits I could see through the sticky tape looked like jungle.

Tiraspol, the capital, was deserted. The roads were nothing but potholes, most of which were flooded. There was grass, even bushes, growing through cracks not only in the road but in pavements, on bridges, even in the sides of buildings. Dogs were sniffing around all over the place. Dilapidated cars, trucks, even tractors were everywhere. However, the enormous bronze statue of the President, or maybe it was Lenin, still stood proudly in front of the town hall or rather the Central Government building. Even though I drove up and down streets with names like October Revolution Street, Victory over Fascism Avenue and Five Year Plan Boulevard (where, you'll not be surprised to hear, U-turns are completely forbidden), the only signs of life I saw, if you can call it life, were long, silent queues outside the occasional shop where people with expressionless expressions were waiting to collect their meagre rations of cheap bread. Offices were practically non-existent. What few factories there were, were empty. In spite of all the stern portraits of Lenin everywhere – or were they pictures of the President? – the only business in town seemed to be money laundering: for drugs barons, for arms smugglers, indeed for anyone on the run with a couple of dollars to rub together. Mind you, if I was on the run with a couple of million dollars in my back pocket and the only place I could hide was Trans-Dniester, I'd give myself up straight away. Even Wormwood Scrubs must be better than that – at least there you eat three times a day.

Out of Tiraspol on the other side of town things were much busier. I spotted two bicycles, three horses, four old *babushkas*, who looked as though they had spent their lives walking on their corns rather than on the soles of their feet, and about seven thousand Russian soldiers. Not just ordinary Russian soldiers, mark you. These were smart, well turned out, young soldiers in crisp new uniforms from Colonel Lebed's famous Soviet, now Russian, 14th Army, fresh from the killing fields of Afghanistan.

The whole time I was there I think I only saw a couple of gnarled veterans – one carrying a briefcase as he ambled along a deserted back street somewhere in

Tiraspol, the other, looking the worse for wear, stretched out in the back of a truck as it went along a country lane.

Everyone says the soldiers are there to keep the peace. But everyone – the Trans-Dniesterians, the Moldovans and the rest of the world, which is busy looking the other way – knows they're really there as a symbol of Russian support for the breakaway province and a warning to outsiders to back off. Which, of course, they have done. While the champions of the Basques, the Catalans and the Kurds and even the Scots and the Welsh go on and on about small nations and their right to self-determination, nobody has said a word in favour of Trans-Dniester.

In Bendery on the Bendery of the River Dniester the only excitement was crossing the bridge, or rather the half of the bridge that was open to what little traffic there was, because this is where the fiercest fighting took place. Overlooking it, as a memorial to all those who died, is a tank parked on top of a slab of concrete, a jar of fresh flowers (although where the fresh flowers came from goodness only knows), a whole string of derelict buildings and another mass of smashed-up cars and trucks.

The Prietenia Hotel nearby now looks less like a honeymoon hotel and more like twenty-five years of marriage. The lobby needs a face lift. The lift no longer goes up or down; it's stuck firmly at ground level. The little white doves have long since disappeared, as have most of the doors, half of the phones and all the televisions. Open the door of one of the honeymoon suites today and all you'll see peeling off is the paint. There is still, however, a bed in the middle of most of the rooms which I suppose is all that counts. As for the bread and salt, I still can't think what it was for.

Yet in spite of everything, the deaths, the fighting, the wholesale destruction of people's lives on both sides of their Mickey Mouse border, one thing stands out above all else, more important than politics, more important than war, more important than people's lives. Trans-Dniester still plays in the Moldovan Football league.

Back in the real *mundo*, however, Moldovans are not exactly whooping it up, even though the *polici* do go around wearing what look like cowboy hats. The *capitala*, Chisinau, is your typical Stalinist, although strictly speaking it should be your typical Brezhnev, town. He of the big bushy eyebrows, the collection of fancy cars and the son-in-law was at one time the President of Moldova. The town is full of huge, faceless *sufocanta* buildings; long, wide *stradas*; massive monuments and statues and enormous wide open *plazas*. Which I have to tell you is a complete *disastore*, because you can't go anywhere safely: gangs of kids, without so much as a *scuzati-ma*, are skateboarding and rollerblading and doing their ollies and grinders and backside nolly kickflips all over the place.

I went to take a look at – whoosh – Ploshchad Pobedy, the huge Victory Square – whoosh – in the *centru* of town. Would they *respectate* my *distanta?* No way. Whoosh. Whoosh. Whoosh. Three kids zoomed right past me, with inches to spare. I wanted to exercise my democratic right to check out the old Soviet, now the Parliament building and *in imediata vecinatate* a poor comrades' Arc de Triomphe, built by the Russians in the nineteenth century to celebrate their *triumpha* over the Turks. But – whoosh – I failed. I surrendered to their wholly unjustified superior force and retreated to the *catedrala*, hoping for some *pace* and quiet. But in vain. Those kids on skateboards were kickflipping and hurling themselves off the top of the row of steps facing the *catedrala* and zooming about like bats out of *damnatione*. Whoosh, whoosh, whoosh – it was like walking out in the middle of *Starlight Express(o)*. Which, I gather, is the in-thing to do nowadays.

Did anybody complain? Did anybody as much as raise an eyebrow? Not at all. Not even when a bunch of kids came hurtling past the KGB *Konclava* near the top of Stefan cel Mare Boulevard. I told you they were like Italians. Their little *bambinos* can do no wrong. Even when they are wearing T-shirts saying McLenin.

Pushkin Park, on the other side of the square, was much more *sedato*. Lots of statues of old Moldovan heroes and old ladies sitting on benches. Also a couple of *Pavarottis* belting out what I assume were folk songs. No *bambinos* and no skateboards.

WacDonalds, further along, was even more *sedato*. Yes, WacDonalds. Some clever Woldovans, I mean Moldovans, decided the way to make a *molto grosso fortuna* was to set up a chain of fast-food outlets exactly the same as McDonald's but to avoid copyright and all the legal mumbo-jumbo involved by turning the famous golden arches logo upside down and calling themselves WacDonalds. The problem is, things haven't quite worked out as they planned. They are facing intense competition from a rival Moldovan chain called Mendy's. Or at least that's what I was told. But for what it's worth I don't reckon McDonald's have anything to worry about. Not so much because the hamburgers are, well, not in the same class, but the loud music belting out non-stop is bound to put people off. Not that their hotshot *Americano* lawyers will agree. They would probably prefer a five-year stint in Chisinau especially if, like Sylvester Stallone or some guy I met once in Vienna, their *mamma* comes from Moldova.

What with trying to fix meetings out in the Expo Park on the edge of town with Moldexpo (not the most attractive name for a company planning to bury the world in apples), as well as with the gloriously named Moldivi Con Bank, I only had time to check out some of the more important Italian *obsessiones*.

First there's the *famiale*. They'll do anything for the *famiale*. One day I was dragging myself around *fabricas* and timber-yards in Staseni, a small *urba* in the middle of nowhere. One of the *directores* had been in the Soviet Army based in Belarus so we were able to chat away about Minsk. At lunchtime he took me up to Capriana to see this fantastic fifteenth-century *monasteria* founded by not Stefan cel Mare but by Alexandar the Kind, which after years of *neglecto* the monks have started to *restoro*, I mean restore, to its *originale glorioso.* If he hadn't told me it was fifteenth century I'd have guessed anyway, what with the goats and chickens and geese roaming about. Not to mention the sea of mud. It was like something out of an Umberto Eco *novella.*

In the evening the manager insisted on taking me back to his *apartamente* to meet his wife and kids. We drove back to Chisinau, where on the edge of town there is row after row of your typical Soviet tower block. In Moscow, I was told, they call them Krush-chobys, because when Kruschev gave the go-ahead to build them it was on condition they were all exactly the same. Change a light bulb in the dark in a Khursuchoby in Siberia, they say, and you can change one blindfolded in one in the Ukraine. If you can get hold of a light bulb, that is.

Off the main *strada* we turned, up into the middle of all these enormous blocks. The *mini strada* was now pitted and potholed. What grass and shrubs and trees there were, were all overgrown. Up close, the blocks themselves were in even worse condition than they had looked from the main road. The outside cladding was crumbling like mad. In some cases there were gaping holes, in others whole chunks had fallen off. Windows were broken and patched up with cardboard or sheets of newspaper. Some of the balconies were piled so high with rubbish and sacking and bits of furniture they looked as though they were about to crash down on top of us. We now swung off the *mini strada* on to some kind of sandy track and dodged behind one of the blocks into a kind of courtyard. Well, I say courtyard; it was more a muddy patch of ground. We skidded to a halt in the far corner by an enormous row of bins. As I got out I was practically bowled over by the stench. It reminded me of the years of my life I wasted a million years ago canvassing council estates in and around south London. The same appalling conditions; the same stench; the same sense of hopelessness and despair.

Inside the building there was nothing. No floor, just bare concrete. No proper walls, just bare brick. No ceiling, just more concrete. No stairs. Well, hardly any stairs – the occasional lump of concrete jutting out of the wall. We decided to take the *elevatore* which was nothing but a metal box. No paint, no decoration, just a rusty, tin box. We creaked our way slowly up to the sixth, seventh, eighth floor. The box juddered to a stop. We got out. More of the same. Nothing. In the corner, however, was this enormous steel door which was shut flush to the concrete wall. The guy pressed the bell. Nothing. He pressed it again. Suddenly there was the sound of bolts being slid back and locks being unlocked.

The door opened. Inside it was a *revelatione*. A smart hallway. Carpets. Paintings on the wall. Leading off from the hallway a kitchen with all the essentials, bottles of wine, a bottle of cognac, glasses, oh yes and a sink and a fridge and an oven. Next to it was a sitting-room with a row of sofas, a television, a piano; then a small bedroom for the two children; and finally the main bedroom. Okay, it was hardly your latest David Hicks or even your Terence Conran, more 1950s Blackpool boarding house. But it was smart, clean, well looked after, not a speck of dirt in sight. I'm no expert on furniture and the cost of things but I can tell you in a country where the average wage is just US$30 a month this was not the kind of *comod* and *comfortabil* flat I was expecting the average kind of manager to have.

If I'm no expert on furniture, I'm even less of an expert on clothes. All I know is the wife and kids were well dressed. As for the guy, he was even better dressed, but only when he was not working. For some reason or other he insisted on showing me his wardrobe. It was about the size of a small wine cellar, chock-a-block with Italian suits.

Now I admit that maybe this man was earning way above the average but all the same it couldn't have been way, way above the average. Maybe his wife was also working. Maybe they had half-a-dozen part-time jobs each. Whatever. All I cay say is, they deserve all the credit and the success they can get. As if the flat was not surprise enough, I was then introduced to his two very *independenti* children: two daughters, one sixteen, the other nine. Both not only spoke Moldavian and Russian, they also knew some *Engleza*. Especially the sixteen-year-old, who was even going for private *Engleza* lessons. *Mamma mia*, he was as proud of them as any Italian *papa* would be. The only trouble is, he's going to be in for *mucho problemas* in years to come.

Then there's the wine. As befits a country that claims it has been producing *vino* for seven thousand years (which will come as a shock to both the Georgians who say they were the first to plant vines five thousand years ago and the Egyptians who say they were the first three thousand years ago) they've got literally mountains of the stuff. Believe it or not, they produce over a *millione* bottles a year. Which they sell under no less than 648 different labels. Except in their case the *vino* is not only on top of but also deep inside the mountains.

You think the caves and cellars under Rheims are *fantastico?* Let me tell you. You ain't seen nothing, as they say, until you see Cricova. Rheims has the equivalent of a village or a town underground. Cricova, the centre of Moldova's *vino* region, has a whole city underground. They don't just have caves and cellars and tunnels. They have subways which they even name after different *vino* varieties, such as Cabernet and Pinot and Feteasca, which stretch over 60 miles under the limestone hills and are big enough to take huge trucks and lorries. What am I saying, trucks and lorries? These things are practically bigger than the Eurotunnel. Just stand at the entrance and the *frig* air blasting out from deep inside almost knocks you over.

Go inside, and provided that there isn't a traffic *jammo* in Beaujolais Avenue, a diversion in Cabernet High Street, or a smash-up in Pinot Noir Lane, it is like a cross between a coalmine and, say, Toronto in winter.

Carry on along Gamay Way, turn left at Sauvignon Drive, and deep in the centre you'll find an army of no less than 850 men and women producing and bottling and storing over 1 million bottles of different wines, nearly 15 million bottles of champagne and another 2.5 million of other sparklers, which is not bad considering in the old days there wasn't a bottling line in the country. Then everything had to be sent to Moscow in huge tanks for bottling. Go past Zinfandel Corner and you'll see a huge stack of wines with a sign on top saying, 'Really rear specimens', which I assume means they're destined for Bottoms Up.

There is not just one set of tunnels or one complex. There are several. Drive round the area, drive through the rows and rows of vines, drive up to the huge transport and distribution centre which must handle millions of bottles every day, drive past the huge prison complex on the edge of the vineyards, everywhere you can see great gaping tunnels dug out of the surrounding hill ... Prison? Prison? You don't mean to say they use prisoners to ... No. It can't be possible. It would certainly upset the tender sensibilities of many a Moldavan wine drinker in the UK. Not to mention in the United States where people wearing jeans made in Chinese prisons tend to get funny looks. However, I had such a good time when I was there and so much wine (but then I do tend to like anything that's young and warm and fruity) that I promised not to mention it to anyone. So I won't. *Capisco.*

Then, of course, there is *fotball*. Moldovans are

passionate about their *fotball*. Trouble is, they're not much good at it. Two of their local teams even got beaten by that 1960s foghorn with the lacquered beehive, Helen Shapiro – and they were playing on their home ground as well. In the old days she might have been 'Walking Back to Happiness' but today she is striding *robusta* forwards for some mysterious Jewish Christian organisation out of Rochester, New York, called Hear O Israel which – don't tell the goys back at her old East End synagogue – believes Christ was The Messiah. When she turned up at the local *fotball* stadium in Chisinau to sing, she not only beat the two local teams into total submission, she also attracted a far, far larger crowd. Some people said it was up to two hundred times larger but that may have been an *exageratione*. On the other hand, it could have been not the loaves and fishes but the free pencils they were giving away.

As for probably the greatest Italian *passione* of all … wait a *minute*. I've just realised what the bread and salt was for.

At least, I think I have.

Damascus

As I was saying, Theopholos, the worst thing about Damascus is the leaving of it. The whole time I was there I just couldn't relax. I kept dreading getting into that rickety old wicker basket and being lowered down the side of the wall. It's not that I'm scared of heights, it's just that last time they got it all wrong. As far as I can make out they lowered the poor guy, no doubt on a whinge and a prayer, directly on to the edge of this 27-lane motorway that is so packed with traffic it would take more than a miracle to get across it alive. I don't care what the Acts of the Apostles say. I've been there. Admittedly when the Dead Sea was only sick, but I've seen what it's like. It's impossible.

The crazy thing is, of course, had they come back another, say, couple of hundred yards they could have lowered him to where the taxis stop and drop people off for the East Gate. That would have been far more sensible, especially as he was the kind of guy who did not like to busy himself in such profitless matters as trying to cross the road. But no. It had to be right by the Church of St Paul, a solid, squat, four-square block of a church that looks more like some huge prison cell, like say the one in Caesarea, than anything else. As for the furnishings they couldn't be more spartan. They're so spartan they look as though they came from a church jumble sale: funny old benches; two marble plaques (St

Paul being blinded, St Paul being lowered down the wall); and a single solitary icon which has practically disintegrated. In the centre is a small, square, solid altar, on top of which is a single solitary candle. No reference anywhere, you'll be pleased to hear, to A.N. Wilson. So his theories about St Paul being the founder of Christianity are not even rated here where it virtually all started.

The church itself is in the grounds of a school. Now, I ask you, what on earth possessed them to take the poor man there? Unless they thought that as he had just come across this was the best way to introduce him to a life of endless suffering and penance. Well, if that wasn't the reason, what was? Because he liked children? I very much doubt it, seeing all the agony and heartache he has created for schoolchildren for generations with his best-selling travel books – he's sold even more copies than Bill Bryson – as well as his theory of justification. Or was it to inspire him to write about the behaviour of children? In fact, I often wonder how different things would be today if St Peter had been in the basket and St Paul had gone to Rome and put even more words into God's mouth? Stricter? More austere? More intellectual? Women under the thumb? Obedient to their husbands? But then I suppose A.N. Wilson would be going on about St Peter being the founder of Christianity. On the other hand, it was probably just as well they didn't swap roles. The weight of St Peter would probably have brought the wall down as well and that would have put paid to the whole thing. Then A.N. Wilson would have nothing to go on about.

In spite of all this, or maybe because of it, Damascus should be heaven on earth. Literally. Squeezed between the desert and the mountains, they say it was the actual site of the Garden of Eden. In fact, don't laugh, but the Prophet Mohammad, on whom be the peace and blessings of Allah, not once in the whole of his life set foot in Damascus. He was scared in case it would prejudice his chances of getting into the real thing. Well, all I can say is, if Damascus is Paradise on earth it doesn't say much for the Muslims' idea of heaven which, according to my reading of the Koran, is 'a wine cup tempered at the camphor fountain which the just shall quaff' .

If I was bitter and twisted and cynical, I would say the Garden of Eden has nothing whatsoever to do with Paradise. It was, after all, the scene of the first row in the history of the world between husband and wife; the first occasion when, regardless of the consequences, a husband gave in to his wife for the sake of peace and quiet; the first time a wife made an enormous mistake and the husband didn't dare say a word about it, and therefore all the evil that has fallen on this world ever since is the fault of Syria. But I'm not bitter and twisted and cynical, so I won't say a word. In any case, I'm also scared of what my wife would say. To me, Damascus is nothing like heaven on earth; if anything, it's more like the hole the serpent crawled back into after he'd done the deed.

Take the city itself. By now - it's the oldest continuously inhabited city in the world - you would have thought everything would be organised. After all, it was at one time the capital of an empire greater even than the Roman Empire which stretched from Spain to Samarkand and far north into Russia. It was the crossroads, the stamping ground, even home, to practically all the great civilisations of the world: the Sumerians, the Akkadians, the Assyrians, the Babylonians, the Aramaics, the Canaanites, the Phoenicians, the Greeks, the Romans, the Byzantines and, of course, the Arabs. It was home to one of the earliest Christian communities in the world. In odd corners of Turkey there are villages, like Maalula, where they still speak your real Aramaic, the language of Christ, as opposed to Turoyo, the modern dialect. (Whether the inhabitants would understand Him, let alone agree with Him, if He came back today is doubtful.)

Wander around Damascus today in the grey dusk, which is virtually any time of the day or night, and instead of being one of the most striking and most glorious and most beautiful and most impressive and most inspiring heavenly cities in the world, it is pure hell.

The River Barada which flows, or rather is supposed to flow, through the middle of the city is clogged up with rubbish. In the past people have swooned over it. Genesis, backing up the idea that Damascus is heaven on earth, hails it as one of only four rivers that flowed out of the Garden of Eden. Even more important, Alexander Kingslake, who I reckon was the founder of the Bruce Chatwin School of Pseuds' Tourism, went all dewy-eyed about it. 'As a man falls flat, face forward on the brook, that he may drink, and drink again, so Damascus, thirsting forever, lies down with her lips to the stream, and clings to its rushing waters', he gushed into his obviously moleskin notebook. Not any more you wouldn't, Alex, my old fruit. Not if you didn't want to get bilharzia, malaria and every other kind of -aria you can think of. Today the Barada is more like an open sewer than anything else.

As for the streets and alleyways, they are choked with still more rubbish. Where there's no rubbish there are abandoned old cars, smashed-up trucks and enormous rusty buses and coaches. And then there are the people. Millions of them. At least half of whom are in military uniform.

Go to Martyrs Square, for example, which you would think would be kept as a national monument. No way. It is a mass of signs, loose cables, potholes, screeching brakes and soldiers. With machine guns, at the ready.

Go to the Hejaz railway station where Orance, as they call him around here, arrived on an away-day and tried to set the Arab world to rights. It looks as though the place hasn't been touched since.

Go into the famous Souk al-Hamadiyyeh. Now I

know every souk in the world is packed to overflowing, but this one is worse than that. Whenever I go there I can hardly see the butchers swinging their axes in the air and then smashing them – *thud* – straight through the middle of all kinds of strange-looking lumps of meat, puffing away merrily like chimneys all the while as cigarette ash falls everywhere. Neither can I see all the little boys thrusting their hands under the axes to grab various long, white bits of innards and washing them in buckets of filthy-looking water. Which, as you can imagine, is a big disappointment. What I do manage to see, however, are a million wizened old men who look as though they were at school with Adam, tucked away in a million tiny hideaways, stitching together a new pair of shoes every five or six hours or running up a thousand shirts or suits or whatever every couple of hours on aged Bradburys or even Ideal sewing machines, which were past it before Singer was even thought of.

As for the hotels, you can't get in them. Not for people, but for mountains of clothing, sacks of food and spices, piles of television sets and videos, crates of fruit, reels of cloth, bales of cotton, great slabs of strange-looking sweets and mile after mile after mile of gold chains. Damascus is a favourite of the Russians and, for some reason, of the Uzbekis. Whenever they hit town, and there are about six charter flights a week, every hotel they turn into a warehouse. Take the fantastic old Orient Palace opposite the railway station. It is justly famous for its ornate 1930s reception rooms, its marble staircase, its high-ceilinged rooms. I couldn't see any of these. Everything was hidden behind packing cases, cardboard boxes and those dirty great multi-coloured sacks that everybody seems to be able to lug on to planes at will – whereas I get bounced because I've got a briefcase and a tiny duty-free bag full of papers and files.

Complain? Who's going to complain? All that stuff is

good business. So you can't get to the reception desk to check in – so what? So there's no room for you? Sleep on the sofa. Provided that it is not also piled high with clothes waiting to be shipped out to Tashkent or Samarkand or wherever. Even if you do complain, you'll get nowhere. It's not that the people aren't friendly: the problem is they're too friendly. I promise you, wherever I went, wherever I was, anywhere in the country, I'd no sooner be out of the car than before I could say, 'Oops, there's the guy from the Mukhabarat still following me,' a soldier would saunter up to me as if he thought I was going to headbutt him or deliberately trip over his big, heavy boots and cut my head open, then without so much as a please or thank you, slump into the car and keep my seat warm for me until I got back.

But in this, the most Christian of all Muslim countries, the worst things of all, the things that really made it hell on earth, were the posters. I thought Gaza City was bad enough but it is unbelievable how many there are, of so many different shapes and sizes and in so many places, all over Damascus. Every one of them shows their long-time President, the gracious, witty, utterly inscrutable and eternally youthful air force general who seized power in 1970, Hafez al Assad. Ba'ath socialism, I always knew, was based firmly on belief in a command economy. That I used to think meant a crumbling public sector, employing 70 per cent of the workforce, spending more than half the national budget on the military; secretly unloading Katyusha rockets and no end of other military equipment from Iran Air 747s late at night at Damascus Airport for Muslim guerrillas in southern Lebanon; and shipping in counterfeit American currency to the Syrian-controlled Beka'a region. But having been to Damascus and all over Syria I now know I was wrong. A command economy is when everybody everywhere is commanded to pay for the most enormous uneconomic posters money can buy to be slapped up all over the place. I reckon the only things that keep the overblown state-run economy from crumbling even further into the dust are the posters.

At first you can see they started as small, postcard-size photographs to cover up patches of damp on walls and alleyways. Then as the damp spread and the walls began to crumble, bigger and bigger posters were needed to hold the walls together and stop them falling down. Now there are posters the size of ten-storey office blocks and they are on everything: shops, banks, government offices. And not just one poster either – quite often there are four, five, six of them, or a dozen maybe. All over the outside of buildings, of arches, of bridges, of doorways, of anything. As if that doesn't seem to make the point they are all over the insides as well.

At first, wherever I saw yet another poster of the President, I thought, there's another quiet, shy, ordinary mortal like the rest of us. But after a while the image gets to you. Wherever you go, whatever you do, whoever you're with, he's there, with that enigmatic smile, that funny-looking haircut. And what about those eyes? Staring straight at you, watching your every move, every second of the day.

After a few days of this, I tell you, I was going bananas. I couldn't begin to clamber over the piles of stuff in reception to get out of the hotel unless I had a clean collar and tie on. I couldn't dash across the road without making certain my jacket was done up properly. I couldn't go to a meeting without checking my shoes were not just clean but sparkling. I was even frightened to hit the Lebanese wine too much in case the eyes – those eyes! – saw me. Don't get me wrong, I wasn't getting paranoid or anything like that. It's just that by the end of my trip I was seeing that face in everything, everywhere, all the time. On the towel on the bathroom floor, soaking up the water from the leaking pipes. On the thick greasy pillowcase on the bed. In the stains on the tablecloth in the restaurant. Looking at me from behind a newspaper whenever I took a walk anywhere. Grinning at me as he climbed out of my car having kept my seat warm for the umpteenth time.

I went to look at the famous Roman arch on the Via Recta, the dividing line between Muslim and Christian Damascus. There it was, staring down at me from half a dozen posters all along one side of the arch. Late one afternoon I called in to take a look at Azem Palace, at one time home to one of the most famous governors of the city in the eighteenth century. I'm wandering around the courtyard which is full of orange and lemon trees and pools and fountains. Very pleasant, very civilised. I turn to go into one of the rooms which was dressed up like an arts and crafts museum. There. Staring at me. On the wall. That face.

In desperation I go to the National Museum. A spot of culture, I think, won't do me any harm. Take my mind off, well, things. I'm looking at a row of tiny statues in grass skirts dating back to the middle of the Third Millennium BC. I look at the last one. *Yaaagh.* There it is again.

I decide that there is only one thing that will do the trick. But that's not allowed in a strictly Muslim country. Instead I go for a good soap. I don't mean your television soaps, I mean the real thing: the full-blown, full-blooded, never-ending thousand-year-old Arab soap told by a traditional story-teller. Everybody knows the story by heart but they love to hear it again and again and again.

Somehow I ended up in this scruffy café in the old city, or rather, the older part of the old city. At the end of the room sitting in a high chair is this big fat man with a gold turban and a fancy jacket. For practically an hour, he regales us all with tales from *The Thousand and One Nights.* I didn't understand a word of what he said – if he had been speaking in English I probably wouldn't have understood a word either – but there we all sat, sipping our tea, enjoying the hookahs (as businessmen invariably do when they get together), hardly daring to breathe. The way this chap held his audience was amazing, especially when nearly everybody knew the stories. Many of his rapt listeners were even whispering the words along with him.

Just down the alley, second on the left, third on the right, I was told there was the All Nofara coffee shop, which had an even better story-teller. He not only had a wider repertoire, some of which it took him over a year to tell like some people go on about their weekend in Bournemouth, but he also had all the theatrical aids including a sword which he used to wave around whenever there was any action to illustrate.

The important thing is, did the story-telling cure my phobia? The answer is no. Desperate times call for desperate measures so I decided to take a look at the famous Crac des Chevaliers, hailed by Orance as the 'finest castle in the world'. I thought it would be bound to take my mind off, well, things. Unfortunately not: there were posters the whole way there. By the side of the road, down the middle of the road, on bridges – and not just one per bridge, but rows of them, along the whole length of every bridge I came across.

On the way, well north of Damascus, I'm afraid I just had to stop at Homs. Not because St Simeon the Fool said the girls from Homs, which was originally called Emesa, were as 'licentious as any in Syria'. Not because it was the home town of Deacon John, the Casanova of the Byzantine Church, who was not just in the habit, he was in the habit of going through all the married women in the place as well. (Now there's the subject of a travel-with-a-purpose William Dalrymple-type travel book for you). But because it's supposed to be the fun, fun, fun capital of Syria. Every country has its joke town or city or area. In Ireland it's Kerry. In Canada it's Newfies. In Belgium, it's the whole country. As far as Syria is concerned it's Homs.

I'm sitting in a café by the bus station. I'm no sooner shuddering with the taste of the first sip than one of the waiters comes up to me and sits down.

'Last night my daughter say to me, why England have crazy cows? I say, I don't know. Why England have crazy cows? Because, she says, they buy bulls from Homs on a Wednesday. Good. Yes?'

'Good,' I reply. Especially because the man sitting at the table next to me is laughing like a drain. A blocked Syrian drain.

Another guy comes up to me. He looks like he helped Orance blow up the Hejaz railway all those years ago. He sits down at the table with us and says that we should shoot all the mad cows because they are descended straight from the cattle in the Holy Land. At this, the two of them practically burst their sides. The man at the next table starts howling like a desert fox. I don't see what's funny about it but I join in as well. Well, it's better to be safe than sorry, isn't it? Especially with all those posters staring at you.

When I got back to the car, even the nice, kind, friendly soldier who's always there keeping my seat warm tells me a joke. In Homs, he says, they have the green, amber and red approach to crossing the traffic lights. Green means everybody shoots forward at the same time. Amber means they at least think about the consequences of shooting forward at the same time. Red means that everybody still shoots forward at the same time but when the Homs man is stopped by the police he leans out of the window and shouts 'Homsi, Homsi,' and the policeman lets him go. Laugh? I tell you I didn't stop laughing until I saw my next poster.

Ebla was just the same. But worse. Worse because this is where in the Tenth Millennium BC a bunch of Phoenician traders got together and invented what do they call it? Oh yes, writing. Just imagine, if it wasn't for them, how would we ever know that the management's had enough, dinner's in the dog and if we ever want to speak to her again she's at her mother's. I mean doesn't that make you feel grateful to them?

The Crac, when I finally got there, wasn't all it was

cracked up to be. Or down to be, bearing in mind the state it's in. If you read the books, look at the pictures, even talk to people who've been there, you get the impression that it is an enormous, impregnable fortress stuck somewhere in the middle of the desert that has somehow withstood the ravages of time. One book, I remember, even made a big thing, the way Sunday school travel writers do, about driving for hours on end into the middle of nowhere and then suddenly there it was: huge, vast, indomitable, glistening in the setting sun. No way.

The fortress stands on top of a hill, two minutes off the motorway to Tartus – which is a garbage dump with a beautiful beach alongside it, in the only gap in one long, solid mountain range that stretches practically 250 kilometres, all the way from Antakya in Turkey to good old Beirut. All around it there are crumbling, scruffy houses and shacks. Below them are rich, green fields, where herds of cattle graze, donkeys munch whatever they can get hold of, and old women and children make a big thing about looking after a few odd sheep.

As for the fortress being impregnable, that's a laugh. Four thousand highly trained, God-fearing, love-thy-neighbour, good Christian chevaliers or knights. Every one of them a trained killer. Every one of them ready to pour cauldrons of boiling olive oil on their non-Christian neighbours. Every one of them pledged to fight to the death for their God, their pope, their religion. In one of the finest, strongest, toughest, unconquerable castles ever built. What happened? They all caved in to Sultan Al-Malek az-Zaher Rukh ad-Dunya Wad-Din Abu al-Falt Baibars after less than a month. They had forgotten that with all those mouths to feed it was the easiest thing in the world for the Sultan just to sit back and starve them out.

The fortress is enormous, though. In fact, you wonder how on earth it was built. Everything about it is huge, massive, two sizes too big. The passageways inside are the size of railway tunnels. The refectories and kitchens and dormitories are the size of aircraft hangars. Even the stables for the horses are big enough to accommodate the Horse of the Year Show. About the only thing that seems to be the right size is the chapel, which is odd when you think it was built by the Crusaders. Or at least that's the story that was put around: it was actually built originally by the Kurds circa 1150. When the Crusaders arrived – not as the history books say to conquer the Holy Land but in order to give the Pope, who has already said sorry to the Jews, a reason to apologise to the Arabs come the Millennium – they tried to conquer it but failed. There is a bit of a dispute about what happened next. Some people say that they came back a second time and, because they learnt by their mistakes first time round, they succeeded.

I kept trying to ask one of the guides, a frail old Arab with hardly a tooth in his head, if that was true. But he kept grabbing my hand, shaking it and cackling, 'Everyone they say I look like Michael Jackson. Is right. Yes?' Another guide, who looked nothing like Michael Jackson, said the good Christian knights did a deal with the local people and, hey presto, it was theirs.

Either way, once the Crusaders had possession, they set about rebuilding and expanding it. The result is, it's really a fort within a fort, with a moat inside as well as outside. On the outside of one of the inside walls, if you see what I mean, you can still see the symbols of Richard the Lionheart who is about the only person who comes out of the story with any credit. Much as everyone looked forward to his arrival, he never actually turned up. Rumour was that, like the rest of us, he had big problems getting a Syrian visa. By the time it came through all the action was over.

Wander around the fortress today and you can see that it is crumbling to bits. Slowly, it's true, because of its massive size, but apart from one or two of the huge internal passageways it is definitely on the downhill slope. Hardly any of the floors or walkways exist any more: they are mostly earth and sand. Hardly any decorations have survived; there are only two bits of inscription left and one of them is the Exit sign. The stairways are crumbling, the famous round table has practically gone, the gates and portcullises are no more. The impregnable walls are covered in clumps of grass and creeper and there are even one or two trees growing merrily away inside the cracks. Part of the internal moat has caved in and the rest is full of rubbish. But what did I see plastered all over the outside of the outside wall? What did I see all over the wooden doors? What was all over the dilapidated wooden shack which served as a ticket office? Yes, you're right, him again.

In desperation, I decided to head for Aleppo, at one time not only the most important city in Syria but also the third business and financial centre of the Ottoman Empire after Istanbul and Cairo. Believe me, every car, truck, bus and literally every donkey and cart we passed had a poster. Not just one or two, either: sometimes four, five or six. One Land Rover actually had three pictures plastered over the windscreen – and you know how small the windscreen is on a Land Rover.

When I finally reached Aleppo, I discovered that like Damascus it was also one of the oldest continuously inhabited cities in the world. A mere 3,800 years ago it was supposed to be the capital of the Greater Kingdom of Yamhad (and you can bet your life posters of President Yamhad or whoever were holding the place together even then). Today little has changed. The place still looks prehistoric; the buildings still look as though they would collapse at the sight of a dinosaur. The streets and alleys, with one or two dishonourable exceptions, are not wide enough to take one, let alone two, passing pterodactyls. On one visit I got stuck behind a horse-drawn, would you believe, petrol tanker, because there wasn't room for my tiny little Toyota taxi to get past. It's the only place I've been in the world where the inside of the Archaeology Museum looks positively modern compared with what is outside. And that's thanks to Agatha Christie and her archaeologist husband, Max.

In the 1930s Max was busy digging up all kinds of pots and ornaments and bits and pieces all over Syria which, the deal was, had to be shared fifty-fifty with the French. What he did every evening was to divide everything he'd found that day into two piles. Then, being British, he let the French decide which pile they wanted. They, of course, being French, always chose the pile with the best stuff in it: the rubbish was then sent back to Britain. The French, to give them credit, then put all the good stuff in the museum. What happened to the stuff sent back to Britain is a mystery that even Agatha Christie couldn't solve.

Slap-bang in the centre of Aleppo, however, is the Citadel, which is enormous. It dominates everything in sight. It is also in much, much better condition than the Crac. Inside it's just as big, the corridors would take the same size trains and the rooms and chambers are just as huge, but everything is renovated, restored and in its rightful place. The throne room is incredible – huge wooden beams, an elaborately carved and painted ceiling, wooden panelling and a highly polished marble floor. And not one, *not one* poster.

Outside, evidence of restoration is everywhere. The small open air theatre has been restored. A number of the outbuildings have been virtually returned to their former glory. Even a museum has been built to explain the story of the castle and, the one thing that brings joy to any mum's heart on a day out, a *kaftirya* which serves a mean cup of tea. At least, that's what I was told. I was still on arak at the time. What is more there are proper guides, not like the bunch of Ottoman throwbacks running the Crac; there are proper signs; proper lighting and – surprise, surprise – visitors: young, old, families, bunches of soldiers, groups of young people. Why everybody keeps on about the Crac I don't know, because the Citadel is a million times better.

The Souk, on the other hand, is completely different. Why everyone raves about it, I'm totally in the dark – probably because whenever I went there, there were nothing but power cuts. As a result all I can remember is waves of olive oil flooding down the streets from a million ancient olive presses and the roar of motorbikes.

But that doesn't mean to say that Aleppo itself is switched off. If anything it's very switched on as I suppose you would expect of the world's longest continuously inhabited souk of traders and wheeler-dealers. In many respects, it is way ahead of the times. Take the collapse of the old Soviet Union. Who got in there and established themselves as the trading centre for not just Russia but a whole string of the old Soviet republics as well? So much so that today Russian shops and street signs and sales posters are all over the place; charter flights are all the time shuttling backwards and forwards from all points east and, as in Damascus, a whole string of hotels have become either Russian hotels or Uzbeki hotels or Azerbaijani hotels or Armenian hotels or Tajiki hotels or whatever.

One evening, after wandering around the back streets, checking out the churches (where today they still sing the same hymns and chants that St Paul was probably whistling while he was being lowered down the wall in the basket), I stumbled into the daring and imaginatively named Hotel Syria. Not only was it full of Azerbaijanis, but like the hotels in Damascus it was stacked floor to ceiling with boxes, sacks and huge bales of goods waiting to be shipped out. Come Wednesday night, I was told, lorries whip the stuff off to the airport and from there it is all flown direct to Baku.

'People. They make lots of money,' one Syrian wheeler-dealer told me. 'They buy here for one dollar. They sell at home for five dollars. It's big business.'

'So why don't you sell for more than one dollar?' I asked him.

'Why sell for more?' he grimaced. 'One dollar is good price. We are happy. They are happy. It is good business. Yes?'

Well, sure. It's just that somehow or other I got the impression these guys were always out for every penny they could make.

'So how much do these people make per trip?' I went on.

'Anything from US$50,000, $60,000, maybe $100,000. Depends on what they buy. Depends on what they sell.'

Yes, well, that much is obvious, isn't it. I might look stupid but somehow or other I grasped the basics of business just a couple of weeks ago.

'So how often do they come?'

'Maybe once a week. Maybe two, three times a month.'

Which just goes to show how much money some people are making in the new capitalist Eastern Europe. Cash, unofficial, outside the system. It's no wonder the IMF is rushed off its feet.

I'll tell you the other thing that struck me about Aleppo. It is not just a melting-pot for traders and trading, it is also a great mish-mash of religions. Sure, it is predominantly Muslim. But wander around the back streets and alleyways in Al-Jadayda and you'll stumble over a complete roll-call of religions: Syrian Catholics, Catholic Catholics, Roman Catholics, Greek Orthodox, Orthodox Orthodox, Syrian Orthodox, Maronites, Maronite Maronites and so on and so on. What's more, every single religion, I guarantee you, lays claim to the one and only authentic tomb of St George. Not to mention the ones in a couple of monasteries in Iraq, in half a dozen churches in Israel, in another half dozen in Cyprus, the nine on Mount Athos, around twenty in Egypt, twenty-five in Crete and thirty-five in Greece. Oh yes, I nearly forgot, there is of course his one and only official tomb in St George's Chapel in Windsor Castle. Now I'm no expert on St George – my dealings over the years have been more with the dragon – but he must hold the world record for having been buried more times in more places than anyone else in the world. I find this odd, bearing in mind his leader and founder was only buried once, and then for just three days.

What is more, try telling the Syrians he was English and they practically breathe fire and brimstone all over you. Here, St George is the answer to everything. If women want babies, they pray to St George. If farmers want a good harvest, they pray to St George. Orthodox priests even slaughter sheep Muslim-style and claim St George said it was perfectly kosher to do so. I've also lost count of the number of Syrians who told me that they had not only seen him but spoken to him as well, so they know they're right. So there.

If St George is not your hammer then there's the so-called 'famous' Barons Hotel, or rather, barren hotel. When I was there it was barren of snacks in the tiny bar by the front door and barren of food in the restaurant at lunch-time. As for the condition of the place, it was barren of not only a lick of paint but some spit and polish as well. Not surprisingly, it was also practically barren of guests. Outside it looks more like one of those enormous, solid, faceless mausoleums the Russians used to build. Inside it is typically English. The high-beamed ceilings are covered in cobwebs, the brass chandeliers are all dusty, the English coaching prints are all skew-whiff. The bar is ancient while the lounge makes your typical London club look positively modern.

About the only thing the hotel wasn't barren of was memories. I'd hardly got through the door into the tiny reception area before I was hauled off into the sitting-room, which looked more like a doctor's waiting-room, Jarrow, circa 1929, to see the unpaid bill left behind by the great Orance when he dropped in there on 8 June 1914 on his way from Aqaba to Damascus. The bill I assumed was unpaid because the food never arrived. The manager – at least I think he was the manager

because he had less dust and fewer cobwebs on him
than the rest of the staff – asked me if I wanted to see
his room, by which I assumed he meant Orance's room
complete with four-poster bed and presumably his
seven pillows of wisdom. I declined. Somehow or other,
even after all these years, I didn't quite fancy the idea of
being seen coming out of his bedroom.

After that it was 'Agatha Christie, sir. She also stayed
here.'

'Oh really? That's interesting. Can you tell me, please,
does the restaurant actually serve—'

'With Max. Her husband. The archaeologist.'

'Fascinating. Do you think there's the slightest
possibility—'

'Kemal Atatürk. He also…'

'What about the bar? Can I get anything at the…'

'… stayed here. I can show you his room.'

'…bar. No, I don't want to see anyone's bedroom,
thank you.'

'If you would like to come this way.'

'So there's no food. No drink. Nothing.'

'There's Orance's bedroom. There's Kemal Atatürk…'

Now if Damascus, if Homs, if Ebla, if the Crac des
Chevaliers, if Aleppo and if all roads in between
including passing camels were covered with posters,
there could only be one place left worth trying:
Palmyra, The Lost City. Founded, they say, by Solomon.
Ruled by the Arab Queen Zenobia, a great rival of
Cleopatra and in many ways the original superwoman.
She spoke Greek and Egyptian as well as her local
Aramaic. She was a brilliant stateswoman, a fearless
warrior and one of the leading intellectuals of her day.
Under her control, Palmyra conquered Egypt, moved
north through Anatolia to the Bosphorus and threatened
Rome itself. In AD 272, however, she was defeated
outside Antioch by Aurelian who had just been
proclaimed emperor. After that she tried to fight back
but it was downhill all the way until, the final indignity,

she was paraded through the streets of Rome – admittedly wearing, according to the history books, golden handcuffs.

In retaliation, some Palmyrans, determined to the end, slaughtered the Roman garrison in the town. But they, in turn, were crushed. The place was virtually laid waste and eventually abandoned. It disappeared off the face of the map until 1691 when it was discovered again by two English traders based in Aleppo. They had heard strange rumours of a magnificent lost city in the middle of the desert, which was supposed to outstrip any existing Greek or Roman remains, and, like any hardworking, dedicated, English businessmen faced with the choice of waiting for hours on end for a drink at Barrens Hotel or going off into the desert looking for some excitement, they decided to go off into the desert. What they discovered was not, as they first believed, 'Tadur in the Wilderness', the legendary city founded by King Solomon himself, but Palmyra.

Surely, I thought, Palmyra must be a poster-free zone. They wouldn't dare. Forever the optimist, I headed out across the *badiyah*, the part-desert, part-scrub land towards the Lost City. Trouble was, because I couldn't get any lunch at Barrens I gave the driver some money to get some fruit to keep me going. As we headed out of town I checked the bag of fruit: lemons. He'd bought lemons. I spent the journey to Palmyra sucking lemons till my teeth started to melt, deliberately spitting the pips all over the floor of the car and listening to him going on and on about life in the Syrian Army. 'Snake. They make you eat snake. They tell you, Cut. Cut. Eat. Eat. You a soldier now. You eat snake.'

Palmyra, I must tell you, is fantastic. I'm no expert, but a great deal of my life I've been surrounded by ruins: prehistoric, Egyptian, Chinese, Greek, Roman, Inca, Aztec. And a few a bit nearer home. I've done Pompeii, I've dragged myself along the Great Wall of China. I've been up to Macchu Pichu. I've even braved the local guides and done Petra on horseback. But, believe me, Palmyra is different.

First, there is the size of the place. It is a complete Roman city, covering at least ten, maybe twelve, square kilometres.

Secondly, there is its state of preservation. Though by no means intact, there is enough of the city still standing to give you the feel of the place in all its original glory: the narrow, crowded streets, the vast buildings. You can actually see why Hadrian came here in AD 129 for a spot of R and R after all those years building a wall to keep the Scots out. The wonder of it is, he didn't stay here for good.

Thirdly, oh joy of joys, Palmyra is virtually untouched by tourists. The result is that you can wander around at leisure. There are no guides waving their little flags in the air and hustling you to move on before the next air-conditioned coachload arrive, clutching their bottled water, chewing their organic lumps of yuck and doo-wop-wopping to Ladysmith Black Mambazo on their Walkmen. No kids howling and shrieking for whatever it is they want. No pseudo-photographers prancing around snapping inane photographs they'll end up by confusing with the ones they took three years ago in Torremolinos.

When I was there, my teeth still on edge from the lemons, I was practically the only visitor in town. The result was that I got the red carpet treatment. The director of the museum, no less, not only insisted on taking me to see the tombs just outside the town but he also brought along an enormous bunch of keys, some literally over a foot long, so that, a rare privilege, I could actually climb up inside the tombs as well. From the outside they look a bit like a cross between a poor man's pyramid and a Russian-built office block. They are built of giant bricks, about five storeys high, with a single door in the front. Inside, all along the walls, are rack after rack after rack of slabs on which the bodies were laid to rest, a bit like a grown-up's wine cellar.

One tower I went into, the Tomb of Elabl, was amazing. It was four storeys high, with slabs set in the wall all around the first floor. There was a bust of the man himself set in the wall. I then went into an underground tomb built about AD 3 by three brothers, Male, Saadai and Naamain. It had 65 bays with room for six bodies in each bay. No question there about the family being parted by death. At the far end you could still see some of the original decoration as well as some of the original colours. It was quite spectacular. Not in the same league, of course, as some of the tombs you see in Egypt, especially in the Valley of the Kings, but for three brothers somewhere in the north of Syria, it wasn't bad going.

Seeing all the empty racks waiting to be filled, I naturally couldn't help but ask the director if I could reserve the odd space for one or two people I have in mind. He was thrilled at the thought and added some more names of his own. After that I virtually had the freedom of the city as well. I was given a conducted tour of the museum, introduced to all the headless statues rescued during excavations, shown scale models of various temples and encouraged to tap the head of some eagle which is supposed to bring you a long life full of nothing but good luck.

After that I went to Palmyra itself.

I was given a guide, who was supposed to be the best in town. We clambered all over the Temple of Baal, the number one god of the Palmyrans, large sections of which are still intact. We saw where the animals were herded in for slaughter, where they were butchered, where they were sacrificed and where they were eaten. We went into the sanctuary which previously was the sole preserve of the priests. At one end, hidden in the decorations on the ceiling, were the twelve signs of the zodiac. How do I know? Because the best guide in town pointed them out to me with the reflection from a broken bit of mirror he keeps hidden between two steps facing the main altar. But don't tell him I told you otherwise he'll be worried stiff that somebody might steal it. Outside we read the meaning of all the decorations. An egg means life. A spear means death. Grapes mean food and drink. I forget what signified fertility. Apart from sleepless nights and nothing but problems in the years to come.

From the temple, we then walked the length of the high street or rather the Great Colonnade, all 1,300 metres of it, past the official quarters, the theatre, the baths, the forum, right up to the Damascus Gate. First we went through the Monumental Arch, then to the Crossroads, then to the Funerary Temple and finally to the Gate itself. None of the buildings are still standing in their entirety, but there are enough arches and walls and columns and steps to give you a pretty fair idea of what it was actually like. The main street was too narrow, with hardly enough room to swing a toga let alone park your chariot and go off for a drink. And the roundabout? Chock-a-block. Anyone could see that all those streets running into a single, tiny roundabout was going to cause trouble. Wouldn't want to have been there early morning during the rush hour, I can tell you. As for the buildings, they're all at different angles – very pretty to the town planner, but a big, big problem for the people who had to live in them. Not to mention the perfect place for petty crimes and muggings – anyone can see that all those nooks and crannies made ideal hiding places for petty thieves and muggers, as well as drug dealers. Didn't those ancient town planners know anything? It's just as well the modern town planners have got over two thousand years of experience behind them so they don't go on making the same kind of mistakes. And, my God, the sewerage system: just who designed the sewerage system?

Today, it is all very Syrian. Picnicking among the ruins I saw local families. Running around all over everything were hordes of local kids. Munching at the grass were local sheep. Trying to establish the Syrian bicycle long-jump record was a bunch of young local archaeology buffs. (I could tell they were local archaeology buffs because they were trying to leap from one pile of priceless ancient remains across a once-open Roman sewer to another pile of ancient remains on the other side. But then, as I recall, the Koran says that God created man out of 'moist germs' so maybe there was an excuse for their behaviour.)

All the same, if you are planning to go to Palmyra, go soon. There are already plans, I was told, to step up the number of camp sites in the area, to provide more and better hotel rooms and to organise camel racing as well as folklore evenings to keep people amused.

Posters? Oh yes, I nearly forgot. Of course there were posters all over the place. But this time they were for Palmyra's very own 'Queen of the Bedouins' beauty competition. It's no wonder that other great Syrian, St Simeon, finally cracked, climbed a pillar and stayed up there, fifty feet above the ground, for thirty years of his life. Another week in the place and I'd have done the same.

After Palmyra there was only one thing left to see: the famous, historic French restaurant, in the middle of Damascus, owned by a nephew of the guy on all the posters. This restaurant is supposed to be the centre of all power and influence throughout the country but when I got there, it was closed. There in the window, dangling from a hook, was a sign saying it had been closed down by the 'Corruption-Fighting Section, Ministry of Supply' which goes to show how powerful and influential it was. It also goes to prove that in spite of living in a power-crazed country where everything is under the control of the Big Man on the Posters, some free, independent spirits are still prepared to speak out for what is right and just and honourable. All I hope is that the Big Man's nephew lives long enough as a washer-upper in the Syrian Embassy in Mongolia to see the error of his ways.

With the restaurant closed, I went instead to the Grand Mosque in the middle of town. It is, they claim, the third holiest shrine in the Muslim world after Mecca and Medina, which amazed me. I may be no expert but I can tell you I didn't need a blinding flash from anywhere to see immediately that all was not what it seemed. Over the top of the main gateway I spotted, in Greek, the words (oh the joys of a classical education) 'Thy Kingdom, O Christ, will live forever. Thy reign will last for generations.' It was enough to make me drop my shoes and socks in astonishment. Not that I mentioned a word about it to anybody, you understand. One never knows how touchy these guys can be about this kind of thing.

Inside the gateway, the main square is beautiful. In the centre is an octagonal fountain which is supposed to be exactly halfway between Mecca and Istanbul. To the west of it is a pretty little gazebo which is unique. No, not because it hasn't got any posters plastered all over it, but because it is on stilts. Why stilts? Because way back in the old days when Syria had some money, that's where they kept it – and sticking the gazebo on stilts was cheaper than hiring Securicor or whoever.

All around the edge of the courtyard is a fabulous colonnade or ambulacrum, as we used to say at school. Some say the western side is the finest you'll ever see in the Muslim world. Practically the whole length of it is a mosaic, which if it's not in the *Guinness Book of Records* as the longest mosaic in Christendom, or rather Muslimdom, it should be. It is about 120 feet long and 25 feet high. It depicts a wistful, joyous, heavenly landscape of rivers, of waterfalls and even of trees. Look at it, study it, examine it, because it's the only picture of living things you'll ever see in any mosque anywhere – but not, you will notice, a single human being.

Robert Byron, one of the original great luvvies of

travel writing, missed this point altogether. Instead in his book *The Road to Oxiana* he described the mosaics as being 'conceived by Arab fiction to recompense the parched eternities of the desert'. Whatever that means.

Facing this, on the eastern side of the courtyard is another colonnade with another mosaic, although it is nothing like as spectacular as the first.

As for the Grand Mosque itself, all I can say is, it's the Grandest Grand Mosque I've ever been in. Which shows you how objective I can be. In fact, instead of being Grand it should be called the Grandest Mosque. It is huge – about the size of an aircraft hangar. There is a double row of marble-clad pillars running down the length of it. The whole thing is covered in carpets. Everywhere you look people are stretched out on the floor sleeping, or huddled together in little groups gossiping. An old, thin, blind man stumbles in and starts feeling his way along the side of the wall. A group of kids are playing in some far-off corner. Two mullahs walk up and down looking as though they could be discussing some obscure theological point or, I suppose, how are they once and for all going to get Salman Rushdie. A group of old men now crowd in, each carrying his own prayer mat, and furtively make for the far corner. Obviously the local Muslim equivalent of *Opus Dei*. Oh yes, I nearly forgot. One or two people look as though they could actually be praying.

But Grand as it is – said by some to be one of the finest in the whole Muslim world – that wasn't the thing that struck me. Don't whatever you do tell any Muslim, but what struck me was how Christian it was. I mean the Greek inscription is one thing. But what's the first thing I see when I go inside? A marble baptismal font. And the next? Further along, about a quarter of the way down standing all by itself, roughly equidistant between the side walls, the tomb of John the Baptist. Complete with head on a silver coffer. I nearly dropped my prayer beads.

But I'm not the only one who reckons the place. To the south-east of the big, main courtyard is the Tower of Jesus which is not just any old tower. This is where, they say, not St Paul and his basket but Christ Himself is going to make His final Apocalypse Wow appearance on the Last Day. Which, if true, will come as one hell of a shock for the Pope, who, I'm sure, has already drawn up plans for a welcoming committee in Krakow. But I don't reckon He will. Not if He finds out about all those posters first He won't.

Phnom Penh

They might be the most magnificent and extraordinary temples ever built, the biggest concentration of religious buildings and the greatest archaeological site in the world but to me, with apologies to the Lord Buddha, Cambodia is the most fantastic location for one of those fast-moving, action-packed *Raiders of the Lost Ark*-type movies that always send you to sleep – screaming kids permitting – on long-distance flights.

You know the kind of thing I mean. Rider Haggard meets the Evil Empire. John Buchan always wins in the end provided Rudyard Kipling hasn't got there first with the aid of James Bond and done a deal with Miss Marple. And along the way, just to keep the kids amused, close-up after close-up of flaming torches being plunged into people's stomachs, hearts being ripped out of chests and snatches of the latest Spice Girls video.

I can see it now. Speaking, of course, as a Haggard writer of a different kind.

The action would start – okay, sweeties, quiet please. Lights. Action. Camera. Scene one, take one – in Phnom Penh, which everybody says is probably the most beautiful city in South-East Asia. (I must say I prefer Luang Prabang, on the River Mekong, way up in the north of Laos towards the border with China. But that's another story, or rather chapter.) It is boiling hot. The streets are full to overflowing with bicycles, motorcycles, motorbikes, rickshaws, bernardshaws, sandie-shaws and all the other shaws you can think of. And, of course, people. Millions of them, both young and not so young, many of them missing an arm or a leg, or both.

For this heady mix of east and west, which not only suffered carpet bombing by the United States – in one six-month period alone in 1973 more bombs were dropped on poor little Cambodia than were dropped on the whole of Japan throughout the Second World War, including Hiroshima – genocide by the Khmer Rouge, military occupation by the Vietnamese and one coup after another, it is perhaps not surprisingly the most mine-infested country in the world.

It also has more landmine victims than anywhere else on earth including Angola. One out of every 250 people, it is estimated, has lost one limb or more. And it is going to get worse. Those who know about these things reckon that there are anything up to ten million unexploded landmines still out there, strewn across fields and tracks and even entire villages, just waiting to explode. That means there are more bombs than there are people living in Cambodia. Or rather living in Cambodia at the moment, because every hour of every day the damn things are going off, maiming and killing people. Had it been the Russians who had smothered the place with landmines instead of the Americans, things would be much, much better – because apparently less than half the Russian landmines actually go off, whereas the 100-per-cent, super-efficient, top-quality American mines all go off. What is more, they have less of an impact so instead of being blown to smithereens you lose, maybe, a hand or a foot. Which is still terrifying but is at least better than the alternative.

What is even more appalling is that of the ten million unexploded bombs still out there waiting to be destroyed, hundreds of thousands have been found and are being used regularly by people all over the country to protect their houses and farms and property.

One official I talked to at the Ministry of Finance told me that his brother, who lived out in the middle of the country, actually made a point of collecting all the unexploded bombs he could find. Every evening he reburied them in the ground all around his farmhouse. That way he reckoned he was safe from being robbed or attacked during the night. In the morning, he would dig them all up again and store them in the kitchen until he reburied them once more in the evening. Which is why, wherever I go in Cambodia, I can't help but get the impression that people are still nervous, still wary, still uncertain, still trying not only to adjust to life after the unbelievable horrors of the Khmer Rouge but also still trying to cope with the non-stop violence all around them. Shops and offices are being bombed, there are running gun battles in the streets, grenades are thrown into Buddhist temples. People are even being shot dead in their homes, and gunned down in broad daylight. The last time I was in Phnom Penh, even though there were troops and tanks everywhere, some poor guy was still shot dead outside my hotel – for his moped.

Some days, and nights, it can feel like the Alamo, especially when there's a thunderstorm. Then for some reason or other out come all the guns and everybody starts firing like mad at the sky. Believe me, with bullets ricocheting everywhere that is the time to make for your nearest underground *fumerie* for a quick drag. Unless, that is, your friendly, local Triad bosses from Hong Kong have got there first.

After everything they did to their fellow countrymen, the people still have this hatred not only of each other but of foreigners as well, especially of the Vietnamese. Every Cambodian I've met – and I've met millions, especially in California where they seem to monopolise the doughnut business – they're scared stiff that one day they'll wake up and be part of Vietnam again.

Okay. Sorry, dahlings. I got carried away. Now back to the film. The camera, if you would be so kind, now pans oh-so-slowly across the city or maybe I should say reel estate – oops, mind that hand grenade – beginning with the National Museum, which is full of the glories of the past. A thousand or so years ago the Khmer Empire, which in all honesty if it wasn't for Pol Pot would be rated one of the greatest civilisations in the world, then stretched from the Bay of Bengal in the east way into Vietnam in the west and from the tip of the south of present-day Vietnam up to Yunnan in China in the north. One day, while waiting for the restaurants to open for lunch, I popped into the museum to catch up on the classical Funan and Chenla sculptures from the fourth to the ninth centuries. Instead I got a first-hand account of the Khmer Rouge from one of the guides and a lungful of bat droppings.

'It was 17 April 1975,' she told me. Day One of Year Zero in the Khmer Rouge calendar when names were abolished as a bourgeois excess. Instead people were called Brother One, Brother Two or, pity the poor guy, Brother One Million Two Hundred and Seventy-Three Thousand Four Hundred and Fifty-Seven. Money was abolished. Education was banned. Newspapers were shut down. Religion, in other words Buddhism, was outlawed. Stealing, prostitution and drunkenness were forbidden. Nobody was allowed to do any business; marry anybody outside their village; or listen to any radio station apart from the official Khmer Rouge station. As if that wasn't enough, everybody was also forced to wear the same Mao Tse-Tung clothes.

'The soldiers marched into Phnom Penh. We welcomed them. We waved white flags. We thought the war was over. Then the soldiers told us all, the whole city, we must leave. They said the Americans were going to bomb the place. They told us not to take much because we'd be coming back again in three days.' Along with everybody else, they left. But they didn't come back for over three years. Many other people never came back at all.

Plop. A lump of bat dropping fell off the ceiling which was being repaired and disintegrated into the air.

With her family, her husband, her parents, her grandparents and all her brothers and sisters they were marched 50 kilometres to Kompong Spoeu. All along the road were the dead and the dying. In the gutters, in the ditches, just lying there.

Plop. Another lump came floating down, again virtually melting in the air. I was studying this Hindu goddess with four arms, in one of which I swear she is carrying a mobile telephone.

'I have never seen anything like it in my life,' whispered the guide. 'And I never want to ever again.' At Kompong Spoeu, the whole family was split up. She was sent to Battambang, where for the length of the war she was kept in a forced labour camp planting rice. 'I never slept the whole time I was there,' she told me. 'Secret police kept coming and taking people away. Every morning we said, We live another day.'

Plop. Yet another lump. By this time I swear I could taste the stuff. So, as they say, I made my apologies and left.

Now, my dears, if we're being honest and trying to present a true picture of the place, the camera should skim just a teeny-weeny bit faster across some of your typical French colonial buildings – Le Royal Hotel, La Paillote, a string of French mansions and, of course, *les maisons flottantes* where they splash your face with perfumed water and put a banyan leaf behind your left ear, among other things – as a reminder that the place was virtually invented by the French. After all, they arrived in 1863 and no sooner had they popped the first bottle of fizz than they were persuading the King to move from his comfy old wooden palace surrounded by temples at Oudong to a brand new brick palace they were building specially for him in Phnom Penh. That done, they then imported a well-educated, well-trained and thoroughly French civil service to run the place, from Vietnam. They built fancy buildings not to mention a few classy art deco hotels. They discovered all the great temples. Then they set about convincing the Khmer that even though they ate with spoons rather than chopsticks, wore skirts (both men and women) and had a caste system, which at one time consisted of no fewer than fourteen different levels, the height of true civilisation was not only to speak French but to act and behave as much like a Frenchman as it is humanly possible for a poor, deprived, inadequate non-Frenchman to do. Just over forty years later, the task successfully completed, the French at the Great Exhibition in Paris in 1906 in a sea of champagne launched the Khmers on the world as one of the great, graceful, bejewelled, and gentle civilisations in history. Which, of course, was the cause of all the trouble, because the Khmer Rouge then said to themselves if we're one of the great, graceful, bejewelled and gentle civilisations in history, as the French say, who needs anybody else? We should get rid of the lot of them, turn the clock back to zero and do our own thing – after all, as Pol Pot said, 'If we can build Angkor Wat we can do anything.'

But, of course, sweeties, we don't have to be honest and truthful, do we? Especially about the awful French. This is after all a film, not a *livre d'histoire*. Instead I reckon we should stress the fact that Cambodia was the scene of yet another glorious French defeat in a long unbroken line that stretches back as far as 1870 and the Franco-Prussian war, the siege of Paris and the end of the Second Empire. This we do by getting the camera to linger slowly over the Arc de Triomphe in Vientiane. *Oui, oui, mon vieux*. I know it's in a different city in a totally different country, but nobody would know. Apart, that is, from the French. But they would never lower themselves to go and see an Anglo-Saxon film, so we're quite safe. In any case, it would be a perfect shot. It's small. It's grubby. It's unfinished. It's less than half built. The French were able to construct as much as they did only because they lifted all the cement from the nearby US Army base. Such is the glory of France. If, however, I can find anything more embarrassing about the French in Phnom Penh we can use that instead.

Okay, dahlings, we've established we're in Cambodia. We've shown that the Khmers were a great people, we've shown the involvement of the French. Now we've got to show their recent past. This we do by looking at what at first sight seems to be a perfectly ordinary, innocent-looking school building. But what, in fact, was the horrifying prison, S-21, where the Khmer Rouge beat, maimed, tortured, starved and butchered to death over 20,000 people. Of everybody who was arrested and taken there it is said only seven ever came out alive. Overall, out of a total population of maybe ten million, no less than one and a half million, maybe as many as two million, men, women and children were systematically butchered to death in places like this all over the country.

We look in the classrooms, which would make even Tarantino throw up. For there in front of you are row upon row of tiny, cramped cells, one metre by two, still containing the manacles and chains. Some still have the metal boxes that were used as lavatories. We look on the walls where there are thousands of chilling before and after photographs of the victims. Before they were beaten and tortured, and, faces twisted in agony, after they had been beaten, tortured and butchered.

We look on the floor at a pile of clothing, clothing belonging to the thousands of poor innocent men, women and children who never came back. Finally, from a distance, we look at a wall map of Cambodia as a whole. Then the camera slowly comes in closer and closer revealing that the map is made up of the skulls of Khmer Rouge victims. Old people butchered because they were overheard muttering the odd word of 'high' Khmer. Parents murdered because they called their children, children and not young cadres. Children killed because they called their parents such highly inflammatory, anti-revolutionary things as Mum and Dad.

Others, such as teachers, doctors, musicians, artists, monks or just messengers at the British Embassy, because they had soft hands which meant they were not peasants; because they had glasses, so in the eyes of the Khmer Rouge they were intellectuals; or those who wore sandals, let alone shoes, and were thus considered rich, or even more horrifying, if such a thing is possible, because the camp commander wanted to use them as fertiliser for his banyan trees.

Illiterate, brutal, country boys may have done the dirty work but this was no illiterate, brainwashed, uneducated mob-style operation. It was a highly organised, well-regulated professional killing machine. Like the Nazis, it was also backed by a highly organised, well-regulated, professional administrative machine which kept not only photographs of all the victims but also detailed day-to-day records of their operations. Said one entry I saw, 'Also killed 168 children today making a total of 178 enemies exterminated.'

Those who were not killed here were taken just outside the city, past the rice fields, the lotus ponds, the bamboos, the sugar palms and the occasional temple, to the killing fields at Choung Ek. There they had first to dig their own mass grave. Then, because the Khmer Rouge didn't believe in wasting their bullets on their own people (they wanted to keep these for the Vietnamese), the babies and young children were literally smashed against the trees. Adult men and women were battered to death with rifle butts, lumps of wood, shovels, anything they could find.

Go to Choung Ek today and the first thing you see is a three-, maybe four-storey high glass tower in the shape of a cenotaph. Inside, neatly arranged on huge shelves full to overflowing, are piles and piles and piles of skulls and bones. On some of the skulls you can see heavy gashes, cracks, even neatly drilled holes. Wander around the killing fields themselves and here and there you can still see bits of bone sticking up out of the soil. You can even see the pits where the bodies were buried.

The driver who took me there told me he lost his father because one day the Khmer Rouge burst into the village where they had been living since being forced to leave Phnom Penh. One of the soldiers spotted on his father's feet the impression of a pair of sandals he had been wearing just before they arrived. He was shot dead there and then.

A woman stood weeping quietly, looking at the pile of skulls. She told me her grandmother was killed because of her soup. The Khmer Rouge said it was so good it was making the people discontented with their lot.

As I left, an old man sitting by the gate said to me, 'Come back at night time. You can hear them crying and screaming.'

Now past the school the camera zooms in, the way they do, on to an ordinary street, say for instance Rue 166, which is one solid, heaving, teeming mass of sweaty humanity. Frail, painfully thin old men are hobbling along on crutches; others are in rickety old wheelchairs. Tiny, shrivelled-up old women are dragging along behind them. A thousand tiny kids are scrambling around, most of them with festering stumps for arms or legs. Through the middle of this solid, heaving mass, bicycles and rickshaws and even cars are trying to make their way. Bells are ringing. Horns are blaring. Everybody is shouting and haggling over everything in sight.

Finally the camera comes to rest on say, to pick a shop out of the blue, number 47. Hanging on the walls are all kinds of rare animal skins: tiger, bear, leopard. All terribly non-PC. All terribly heart-rending for vegetarians. Not to mention all terribly illegal. Bring one of them back through Heathrow and you'd get more than the rubber glove. In fact, when I went there, purely for research purposes, you understand, I was offered a brand new genuine tiger skin – a rare young Indo-Chinese tiger, it had just been killed – for US$800. The skull was an extra US$100. Fake tiger skins, made of

cleverly dyed hides of, say, deer are much, much
cheaper. Don't ask me how I know, I just know. There
was also a bear skin going for US$1,000. It was not so
impressive to look at but apparently much more
difficult to obtain. Tucked away out at the back they
probably even had a stack of blaubok skins, even
though the last one was supposed to have been shot
dead just east of Cape Town in South Africa in
December 1799 – not to mention an odd assortment of
Chinese alligators, Indonesian Komodo dragons, Timor
pythons, plowshare tortoises from the far north-east of
Madagascar, tuataras, a tiny lizard-like creature from
New Zealand, and a couple of dozen Fijian iguanas,
Indian soft-shelled turtles and Bengal monitor lizards.

All round the skins, taking up practically every square
inch of floor space, are huge sacks full of the strangest-
looking things: tiger bones, bear's brains, lumps of
elephant skin, rolled ganja. Chips of wood which the
Cambodians take home, stew in a saucepan for months
on end, pour the liquid into bottles and keep for
goodness knows how many years and finally drink, to
ward off whatever they think it will protect them from.
Lumps of something called *pueraria mirifica* root,
which is supposed to do for Eastern women what great
bags of silicone do for Western women (although
judging by my admittedly limited experience, I wouldn't
have thought it was worth the paper bag they put it in).
Oh yes, I nearly forgot. Alongside the sacks of ivory at
US$500 a kilo are huge jars of shark bile which – don't
scoff, you might need it one day – reverses liver damage
caused by too much alcohol. Next to them are hundreds
of dirty little plastic bags containing the foulest looking
shapes and mixtures and colours. These, which to me
looked like various forms of bowel scrapings, were, I
was told, the Cambodian equivalent of something for
the weekend.

I asked what else was on offer. Rare baby albino
crocodiles, for a mere US$10,000. Live young spider

monkeys for – can you believe it? – live monkey brain soup. Just jam the head in a special circular vice. Saw the top off. Serve fresh. Nothing like it on earth. You see it in all the best Chinese restaurants. A word of advice: take a big spoon. As if that's not enough to put you off eating for the rest of your life, there were one or two other delicacies you don't normally find even at Fortnums. Tiger steaks, tiger paws, tiger penises. Vital for prolonging your longevity, apparently. Not that I thought longevity was important.

Now, dahlings – are you ready? We've set the scene. This is where the action begins. All of a sudden, from the back of the shop, a man runs out into the open. White, European, three days' stubble. An old, creased, heavily stained, once-white suit. A battered, khaki, Baden-Powell hat pulled down over his face. Scampering after him come three tiny Cambodians. As he races through the shop our hero, showing he's a man of honour and a true respecter of other people's property, starts pulling all the sacks on the ground and tearing the skins off the wall in order to prevent the little guys from following him. He shoots out of the shop and races down the street – big cheer from everybody in the cinema – scattering people in all directions. Women scream, men dodge out of the way, kids get trodden on, little old ladies are trampled underfoot. Cars sound their horns, rickshaws career into each other. Through the chaos, coming straight at our hero and man of honour, is a moped with five people on it, man, woman, grown-up daughter and two young children. (You think I'm kidding? You see them all the time in Phnom Penh.) What does our hero, our man of honour do? He grabs the tiny moped, sending all five crashing to the ground, leaps on it and zooms off into the distance. As he does so, the camera pulls back – pull back, dear, pull back – across to the five unfortunate victims who are picking themselves up out of the dust, back to the three hapless Cambodian pursuers who are running into the distance waving and screaming, back across the mess that was once a shop to the door to the back room. Standing there, taking a mobile telephone out of his pocket is a tall, blond gentleman. Wearing an immaculate white suit, a genuine Panama hat and a monocle. He is munching on a long, thin, tiger-meat sandwich. Exactly which bit of the tiger he is munching, I shudder to think.

The gentleman turns to a frail, painfully thin noodle-seller who everybody says was once a colonel in the Khmer Rouge. He tosses a coin towards him. Everybody now starts to hiss and whistle. No, no. I said hiss and whistle.

The scene – ready when you are Mr de Mille – now shifts to one of the more striking scenes in Phnom Penh, Wat Botum. No. It's not what you think. It's not that kind of film. Wat Botum is the most important pagoda in Phnom Penh. It means, Pagoda of the Lotus Pond. Lots of rich and famous politicians are buried there. It also survived the Khmer Rouge. Most of the other pagodas were either partially or completely destroyed or used as concentration camps or killing centres. This one they left intact. They simply locked the doors and literally threw away the keys.

By the entrance proper, up against one of the green-faced monsters with a dagger in its mouth, is the tiny moped our hero stole from that nice Cambodian family. A long line of monks come ambling by. It is around four o'clock in the afternoon. They have been out collecting alms since maybe six o'clock this morning. They are going into the temple to pray. As they glide past, some wearing vivid orange robes, others darker brown, we see all ages, some as young as nine or ten; others look as though they were the Lord Buddha's original companions. Most are somewhere between the two. All have Buddhist verses tattooed in Pali on their arms, legs and chests. Why? To protect them from bullets. I thought everybody knew that. For some reason or other the last monk in the line still seems to be carrying his begging bowl which, goodness knows why, he is holding up to his face.

(Well, what do you expect, Eisenstein? I told you this was *Raiders of the Lost Ark* Saturday morning pictures country.)

As the last monk steps inside the *vihara* or sanctuary, he puts his bowl on the floor and kneels down; at the far end, from behind one of the very lifelike tigers, appears the man in the immaculate white suit with the Panama hat and the monocle. He is still chewing the long, thin, tiger-meat sandwich. Next to him is the frail, painfully thin noodle-seller who everybody says was once … Remember? Good. That means the plot is simple enough for American audiences.

The monks begin to chant. As they chant, under the cover of clouds of incense. (You don't get incense in Buddhist temples, I know, but that doesn't matter. You won't find 39 steps at Bradgate either. In fact, you'll be lucky even to find Bradgate. This is a film.) Slowly, slowly, imperceptibly almost, a wide space opens up between the man in the white suit and, you've guessed it, our hero, the man of honour, the upholder of justice. As a fully paid-up member of the Establishment – well, I did warn you this was H. Rider Haggard/John Buchan country – and therefore a non-paying member of the Church of England, he has no qualms about other people's religious beliefs. He now starts grabbing the monks and whirling them in turn towards the man in the white suit, sending incense sticks, bowls of food, and those funny trees made of gold leaf flying everywhere. Even the big statue of the Lord Buddha himself begins to rock slowly backwards and forwards. No matter. Our hero is now racing down the steps of the temple, his robe flying in all directions, to the motorcycle. He crashes through a shaky stack of birdcages containing birds which people buy and then release for good luck Within an instant he's on the tiny moped again and roaring away from the temple. But, ha, ha, waiting for him outside the temple gates are our three little Cambodians. This time they are on enormous, souped-up Harley-Davidsons, engines running.

You like that, do you? Who says I fall asleep during all the in-flight Clint Eastwood movies?

Through the late afternoon rush-hour traffic they roar. To try to throw the Harley-Davidsons off his trail, our hero swings suddenly down a side street. The name I can tell you. But it wouldn't mean anything. Because they keep changing them all the time. First, they all had Royalist names. Then Communist names. Now they are gradually changing them back again to Royalist, or if not Royalist to non-Communist, names. Anyhow, the street is full of millions of little shops, great piles of tiger skins and thousands of sacks of even stranger-looking bones etc. He gets through. So do two of the Harley-Davidsons. The third doesn't. He crashes into a post. The post is one of four supporting a tiny, traditional-style Cambodian house. The house, its contents, the family of twelve including grandma who is praying in front of the family shrine, comes crashing down on top of him.

Our man now swings into 182 Street and the Russian market – so called because in the days of the Khmer Rouge everybody would rush in there, buy whatever they wanted, exotic foods, booze, antiques, silver, silk, toiletries, a million counterfeit tapes and CDs from China, all at US$3 each, not to mention a Kalashnikov and a clip of ammunition for US$50, and rush out again.

Through the tiny little alleyways he careers, swinging left one moment, right the next. People are screaming and rushing around all over the place. See what I mean? Rushing around. Oh forget it. He turns down one alleyway. There playing innocently in a filthy puddle of water is a tiny, fragile, maybe only six-months-old baby. He roars towards it. He spots it. He starts to brake. Then in a split-second – you guessed – the mother snatches it out of the way. Big sighs of relief all round. Cheers from everybody, apart from those in the back row who are no doubt going through the preliminaries of having babies of their own.

Soldiers now appear from everywhere waving their AK-47s in the air. One takes aim. Fires. Nothing happens. There's no ammunition in it. Another fires. And misses. Instead he hits the mother who's just rescued the baby. She spins round by a stall piled high with cheap Chinese-made Seagus cameras and crashes back down in the puddle from which she's just snatched her kid. Dead. On top of her fall half-a-million cameras that all start clicking and flashing away like mad. Well, they are Chinese cameras.

Boos from everybody, including those in the back row.

The third soldier now points his gun directly at our hero. He whizzes past. Soldier pulls trigger. Nothing happens. He pulls it again – and hits the second Harley-Davidson roaring up behind.

Now – next scene. Three more even more souped-up Harley-Davidsons appear mysteriously from nowhere and, cue hectic music, the chase is really on. Along crowded pavements they race, where practically everybody is eating chicken soup – which is the best in the world, because in Cambodia they use marijuana as a herb for cooking. So you carry on watching the action while I have another bucketful of the stuff.

In and out of the colonnaded old National Library which under the Khmer Rouge was literally a pigsty, they rocket; in between a long line of Buddhas waiting to be shipped out at the Buddhist Statue Company they swerve; through the middle of a string of market stalls doing a roaring trade (quite by coincidence outside the burnt-out skeleton of a Malaysian garment factory) they veer and roar and skid.

Past a long line of stolen Toyotas and Nissans parked outside government offices where probably most of the civil servants are only there because they or one of their family literally bought the job: US$5,000, the equivalent of twenty-five years' salary, for example, gets you a job as a customs officer … Past the hail of champagne bottles being hurled from the open windows of the bar of the Foreign Correspondents Club which, believe me, makes Rick's Place in Casablanca look like a Girl Guides' tea party. First one to hit the newspaper seller standing by the edge of the river is the winner.

Past the monument to Buddha's finger outside the railway station (what exactly the finger is trying to tell the railway authorities is open to dispute). Into the ticket office they now hurtle. (Because of the number of hold-ups and hijackings and kidnappings that take place once the trains leave Phnom Penh, one-way and return have completely different meanings here. As if that's not enough, everybody is also trying desperately to avoid getting any kind of ticket in the first carriage of any train to anywhere. Why? Because – think about it – in a country littered with so many unexploded bombs, the last thing anybody wants to be is the first in anything. The first to be bombed. The first to be abducted by renegade Khmer Rouge guerrillas. The first to be shot up by the notorious Paet gang who are renowned for their Wild West skills of holding up and robbing trains.)

As they go screaming out of the station again a poor, innocent monk steps right out in front of … but not to worry, our hero, the man of honour, shoots past within inches of his life. This proves not only what a good driver he is but how knowledgeable he is about Buddhist customs and traditions and beliefs: after all, if you mow down a monk he's going to come back again at least thirteen times to scare the hell out of you.

By now, of course, our hero is halfway up 47 Street, where he spots a girl riding side saddle on the back of some guy's motorcycle. Being a man of honour, he does the gentlemanly thing and stops to let them pass. The girl smiles that enigmatic smile and gives him the traditional greeting Cambodian girls learnt as a result of having so many Americans crawling around everywhere during the war.

The Harley-Davidsons are close behind him again –
cue even faster chasing music.

In and out of the traffic they weave. At the top of 47
Street they shoot off to Wat Phnom, where one day, so
the story goes, a woman called Penh noticed, as one
does, a branch floating down the Tonié Sap River;
instead of leaves, it had lots of little golden Buddhas on
it. She immediately rushed off to build a temple on Wat
Phnom hill to commemorate the event.

Round and round Wat Phnom they now hurtle. Past
the statue of a very plump and very happy Mrs Penh
who looks as though she's been drawing royalties on
the use of her name – Phnom Penh, the hill of Penh –
since 1373 when the temple and the city were both
founded. Past the huge footprint of the Buddha. Past the
spot where the draw for the Cambodia National Lottery
takes place at ten o'clock every Thursday morning.

Just as the elephants arrive to begin giving visitors the
usual 'traditional' tours of traditional temples, our hero
dodges between them and is off towards what used to
be Quai Karl Marx and the banks of the river where the
mama-sans run their famous *maisons flottantes*. But
being a man of honour, he's got no time for that kind of
thing.

Now we have another of those – what do they call
them, dahling? – long shots, to add to the ambience, and
remind everybody that we're in, er, Phnom Penh. Look,
there's the deserted car park where a senior executive
of the big floating casino was kidnapped. Over there are
the remains of the burnt-down offices of a cellular
phone company.

Down at the edge of the picture is Caltex's first petrol
station in Cambodia which, in some kind of Cambodian
welcoming ceremony, was shot up by soldiers who first
stole the petrol and then came back for the pumps. Over
there is the big, sprawling military complex. You can tell
it is a military site because of all the 4×4s, chock-a-block
with fancy gadgets: CD-players, stereos, leather seats,

overhead consoles, computers, aluminium sports wheels
and every other luxury option or accessory you can
think of. With one exception. According to an article I
saw in the *Phnom Penh Post* the one option they're not
interested in is a 'wench' even though these were said to
be 'an absolute necessity in the field during the wet
season'.

Now we are back in close-up as our hero and his evil
pursuers flash past all the famous Phnom Penh land-
marks known and loved and recognised throughout the
world. By drug addicts, by mercenaries and by war
correspondents.

Whoosh. That was the No Problem café, once a
famous civil war haunt but now a beautifully manicured precinct for insurance companies.

Whoosh. The Happy Herb, where everything seems
to be laced with, well, the happy herb.

Whoosh. The Heart of Darkness, where the last thing
anybody wants to talk about is Conrad let alone Mr
Kurtz.

Whoosh. Whoosh. Whoosh. There were three of
Cambodia's famous banks, which somehow or other
manage to survive – don't ask me how – by not taking
deposits and not making loans. All I know is their
laundry is always impeccable.

Now suddenly our team are careering through Tuol
Kok, a let's say, traditional part of town. There are piles
of copper wiring all over the place, crates of duty-free
booze piled up on the pavement and a couple of X-ray
machines stacked against a wall, all no doubt lifted from
the airport. Suddenly in front of him the hero sees the
tall, blond guy, in the immaculate white suit, the panama
hat, the monocle. He is munching an enormous long,
thin, tiger-meat sandwich. He is walking up a wooden
plank into a large, rambling, ramshackle house. Hobbling along behind him is the frail, painfully thin noodle-
seller who... You got it.

Our hero roars after him, still on his little moped, and

finds himself inside another traditional Cambodian building providing all kinds of traditional Cambodian services. Suddenly hundreds of men, who have been hitting the powdered unicorn horn, thousands of girls, a couple of dozen *mama-sans* and goodness knows how many pigs are racing up and down yelling and screaming and squealing like mad. For some reason or other they seem to think it's a police raid, even though under the terms of the tough new government crackdown the police had agreed not to raid the place until the following evening. Pigs? Of course. That's how you smuggle drugs in from China – in polythene bags, inside the pigs. I thought everybody knew that. Apart from the customs officials. Nudge. Nudge.

In the midst of all the yelling and screaming and with a stray army jacket over his face, a policeman's trousers around his shoulders, out through the opposite wall hurtles our hero, still on his little moped, and lands on the other side of the street on the balcony of a huge block of tiny, cramped, one-room flats. Along the balcony he roars. Completely oblivious of the chaos, one old man is crouched in a corner smoking a long ivory pipe, with a look of sheer contentment spreading slowly across his face.

Now our man skids to a halt at the top of the stairs. A quick glance over his shoulder. Down the stairs he roars, the Harley-Davidsons still in hot pursuit. Out through the remains of a front door he goes, straight into Lenin Boulevard and towards a passing elephant, which takes no notice of him whatsoever. Harley-Davidson number one, however, tries to avoid the elephant, swings out of control and goes hurtling through a plate-glass window. The camera pulls back to reveal the name of the shop. The Lucky Burger. A nice James Bond touch, that, don't you think?

Leaning against the counter, munching a somewhat smaller tiger-meat sandwich is you-know-who. And next to him ...

None of this, of course, would be possible in real life. All the streets and buildings are spread all over town. But what the hell, it's only a film.

So what does our hero do now? He picks himself up, dusts himself down and hails a passing rickshaw. As he climbs in, the camera drifts up from the elephant as it continues plodding down Lenin Boulevard to the Royal Palace. Then to the fabulous Silver Pagoda, which has more than five thousand silver floor tiles, each weighing one kilogram. Then to the vast Throne Hall, 100 metres long, 30 metres wide, complete with royal bed surrounded by royal mirrors where the king could withdraw, if that's the right word, during long, hot, boring ceremonies, to be fanned and cosseted and no doubt looked after by ladies trained in the ways of royalty. From there the camera rises – not for any symbolic reason – to the 60-metre tower on top because very neatly and, even though I say so myself, very cleverly, this enables us to switch the action to way up in the north, within smoking distance of the Thai border: the tower is exactly the same as one on the famous Bayon Temple at Angkor Wat. Not that the Bayon Temple, with its 49 towers and over 170 huge, smiling, enigmatic Mount Rushmore-type faces standing slap-bang in the centre of the city, is the biggest or most important of them all.

Within just 60 square miles, there are 292 of them, some the size of your average cathedral but most of them bigger, some as much as 20 times bigger. All of them are around 1,000 years old. Many have been literally hacked out of the jungle, so goodness, or rather Buddha, knows how many more temples there might still be out there in that thick tropical forest just waiting to be discovered.

The amazing thing is that nobody knew anything about them until just over a hundred years ago. They were lost and forgotten, literally overgrown and almost destroyed by the rainforest, until one day in the 1860s a

Frenchman, Henri Mouhot, happened across them in what should be considered as important an archaeological discovery as Carter's discovery of the tomb of King Tut.

A number of the temples, like Angkor Wat itself, have since been rescued and restored virtually as good as old, although the Khmer Rouge inevitably got in the way. But some have been only partly cleared. Ta Prohm, for example. If you go there today, you can still see these huge, 300-foot high trees growing literally on top of and all around the walls and buildings of the temple.

I went there just after the Khmer Rouge had retreated. The whole area of Siem Reap, the nearby town, was devastated. People were moving back in again having previously been ordered by the government to evacuate it and leave the place to the mercy of the rebels. Most of them had lost everything: family, friends, possessions. They came back by walking hundreds of miles through the surrounding jungle to find – nothing. The Khmer Rouge had destroyed everything. But these guys, if nothing else, had their sense of priorities: they knew how best to get their town working again, how to start making money. They opened a nightclub. Immediately they were back in business; the big rollers hit town and the owners of what was left of the biggest hotel immediately decided to rebuild it, modernising it in the process.

Oh yes, I forgot: I got carried away. Back to our fast-moving, action-packed movie.

We're on the edge of the jungle. The camera pulls back and back and back to reveal a single, crumbling temple corridor. We see huge stones, some 4 feet long, some as much as 40 feet long. Some weighing half a ton, maybe more. All have crashed to the temple floor. We see gaping holes in the floor. We see huge tree roots deeply embedded in the stones. Some maybe three, four or even five feet in diameter. We also see hundreds of snakes wriggling around, rats busy munching away at something on the floor. In the background parrots are chattering like mad. Cicadas are chirping at the tops of their voices. Rabid dogs are howling. Cue for eerie temple music. This is the great temple of Preahkhan. Two corridors, one north-south, the other east-west, cross in the centre. Standing there we now see munching away on yet another tiger-meat sandwich is the man in the immaculate white suit. With him . . .

Why he is there and how he got there, I have no idea. All I said was Cambodia is one hell of a location for a fast-moving action-packed movie. That's all. I didn't say anything about having a sensible plot. But if you want to buy the rights, I'm always open to offers.

Our hero, meanwhile, is studying the 1,200 metres of bas-reliefs in the Bayon Temple, so called because the Lord Buddha sat under a bayon tree seeking enlightenment. If you look closely, however, you will see that the place is full of Hindu symbolism and Hindu cosmology. But that's a mere detail. Up on the third floor there are no fewer than 54 towers, each side of each one with a beaming face. Walk around it a couple of times and, if you've got a guilty conscience like me, all 216 eyes will be following you. So be careful what you get up to. You have been warned.

But our man of principle is not interested. He only has eyes for the bas-reliefs depicting everyday life in twelfth-century Angkor Thom. Most of them are of war: foot soldiers on foot, officers on elephants, servants, slaves, camp followers, all the usual. Others show more violent and horrific scenes: cock fighting, shopping, at home with the family, kids being sick. You know the kind of thing. There's even one section which must be the first ever picture of a Chinese restaurant. You can see the roof, the guys doing the cooking; kids playing around the cooking pot; people throwing up and complaining about the spring rolls being too soggy, the fact that they don't take credit cards and where the hell's that mini cab. Further along there are guys eating and drinking and enjoying themselves in a bar, or having a quick drag of marijuana.

Suddenly our hero's eye is caught by a picture of two men getting drunk. It is during the war of 1177. The Khmers were being defeated by the Chams. Angkor was under attack. The king had been wounded and was being gently lowered from his elephant. A general who was also wounded was being thrown all over the place in a makeshift hammock slung over a pole. As opposed to a Czech or a Slovakian.

Yet there were these two guys getting bombed out of their minds. Our hero stoops to study it more closely. He steps back, takes his glasses off, wipes them – this is getting good, isn't it? Well, I think it is – puts them back on again and turns and races down the corridor, skids round the corner, tramples over an old lady lighting a candle to her own personal Buddha, tucked away in a hole in the wall, careers past the library and heads for the East Gate. At the East Gate he races down the steps, two ponds either side, and leaps into a waiting rickshaw.

Now we see our man standing facing Angkor Wat, the greatest religious building in the world. It was built around 1150 by a certain Suryavarman II to honour the god Vishnu. Those who know about these things say it is sublime, inspirational, one of the greatest achievements of the human spirit. To me, it is certainly all that and much more. It is in the middle of nowhere. I mean you would have thought, wouldn't you, that if you had to build a temple in the middle of some thick, impenetrable rainforest a million miles from anywhere you'd make life easy and go for something about the size of a garden shed. Not the Cambodians. The moat is practically a mile long and just under a mile wide. The surrounding wall is again about a mile long and just under a mile wide, with gates either side and an enormous main gate. Through the main gate the avenue is about 500 metres long and 10 metres wide. The central temple complex, three storeys high, is a mass of galleries, squares, archways. Then above the temple are huge towers and pointed cupolas. And to crown it all, around the outside of the temple are huge bas-reliefs.

Okay, so now our hero is racing across the bridge to the main entrance. One side is crumbling to pieces and huge chunks of rock are sticking up everywhere. The other side is lined with the poor, the blind, and the crippled, begging from the mass of pilgrims and visitors who come to visit the temple from all over not only South-East Asia and India but also from less civilised countries like Australia and New Zealand. Once across the bridge, does he pause for a moment to look up with awe at the huge temple in front of him? No way. He turns to the right, studies the river bank slipping slowly into the moat and smiles a wry smile. Because he knows that it has just been repaired by the French and that it is already slowly collapsing into the water.

Now he's through the main door, once reserved exclusively for the use of kings but now open to anybody with the courage to fight their way past even more beggars. In front of him is the temple in all its glory. Some say the best time to go is early evening. But I think I prefer the morning when the sun is rising. It is fantastic.

On the face of the inside of the wall of the whole enclosure are more bas-reliefs, depicting the everyday life of simple Khmer folk all those years ago. This time unless I'm mistaken the bad guys have it. I counted 93 demons as opposed to 88 gods.

Now our hero starts running along the avenue which is lined with naga balustrades, the mythical serpents. At the entrance to the temple he keeps running straight up the steps. Now he is on the first level. The Gallery of A Thousand Buddhas. He keeps running. Up more, still steeper, steps: deliberately steeper. The idea is that the higher and the steeper the step, the more you are forced to look up to the Lord Buddha. (In practice, it means the more likely you are to tie your calf-muscles up in knots and be forced to have a traditional Thai massage twice a day for a month. Well, that was my excuse.)

On the second level he shoots into the open court-yard, veers to the right and makes for the giant Buddha, guarded by two bald-headed old ladies up against the far wall. This is the Lottery Buddha. This is where everybody comes to pray they will win the Cambodian National Lottery. One of the old ladies is hobbling across to one of the candles by the feet of the Buddha. She has a tiny, screwed-up piece of paper in her hand. She is about to set light to it when, like the monkey god Hanuman, our hero leaps to her side. He stops her a moment. He smiles. She looks up at him, her shiny, bald head reflecting the candles around the Buddha, her single tooth glinting in the intense sunshine. He grabs the bit of paper off her. Looks at it. It says 024400. In a flash he is running back down the way he came.

02 he reckons stands for two. Smart lad, our hero and man of principle. Two must mean two snakes. What else would it mean in the world's greatest concentration of ancient temples? Two rabbis? Two ices? Too much dashing around all over the place. Where are there two snakes? Why, the Preah Neak Pean Temple, of course, everybody knows that. He hails the nearest putt-putt, graciously helping the occupants clamber out of it even though it's the last thing they want to do. Now he's in the back. He hurtles, hell for leather, along the edge of the moat, across the Siem Reap River. Past Banteay Kdei, a massive Buddhist temple surrounded by no less than four concentric walls. Past a mass grave of hundreds more victims of the Khmer Rouge. Past another temple shaped a bit like a pyramid, which was some kind of up-market crematorium.

There are two temples ahead of him. The one on the left, Ta Som, is in a mess. The one on the right is Preah Neak Pean, which means two snakes twisted together. (Why they are twisted together, what they are doing together, I have no idea. Just stop asking silly questions and watch the goddamn film.) He skids to a halt outside. Our hero rushes in. He sees in front of him an island about the size of a bandstand. Around it are four equal-sized mini-lakes or maxi-ponds, depending on what kind of house you live in. Each lake or pond is dedicated to a different birth sign. Our hero rushes round all four. Nothing. He clambers down from the bank and discovers underneath each lake or pond is a small chapel. Inside each chapel is a statue of the different birth signs: an elephant, a horse, a lion and, yes, a human head. He goes into each chapel. Nothing. He clambers back up again. Of course, of course. Of course. He should have realised the first clue was deliberately meant to throw him off the scent.

He looks at the second set of figures: 44. 44? Why, the Eastern Mebon temple. There are four elephants standing at each corner of the first level and, guess what, four more standing at each corner of the second level. He's off again in the putt-putt. The driver keeps asking for money but the right hand in the right place soon puts a stop to that. They reach the enormous Eastern Baray reservoir with its giant stelae in each corner. On a tiny island in the centre is the Eastern Mebon temple. Supporting it in each corner is a huge stone elephant. Around the temple he races. Nothing. Now he races up to the first floor level. Again four elephants. Nothing. Zero. Nix.

Of course, Ta Prohm. The temple that is still virtually nothing – nothing but jungle, nothing but ruin, nothing but desolation.

The scene now shifts to the jungle. Dark, thick, impenetrable jungle. This is the jungle that protected the Khmer Rouge. This is the jungle that up towards the border with Vietnam is a favourite with drug-smugglers who for some reason or other, I was told, refer to it as a Swiss cheese.

Cue helicopters. You know the kind of shot, dahling. Zooming over treetops, circling over clearings. Then, wait a minute, was that... was that a temple? The camera swings back. It was a temple. Here in the centre of the jungle. A real life temple which has been all but eaten alive by the trees.

Cut to ground shot. Close up of a huge tree. Camera whirls round towards the sky to show its size. Well over 300 feet, maybe more. There are the usual snakes, rats, parrots and rabid dogs. The camera closes in, closer and closer. Wait a minute! The bottom of the tree is not the bottom of the tree at all. It's ... it's roots. Enormous thick sprawling, curling, choking roots the size of a double decker bus. And what's that inside the roots, being squeezed and choked to death? It is part of the Ta Prohm temple itself. A whole massive stone structure maybe 20 to 30 feet high literally overrun and squeezed to death by the jungle.

In fact, the whole area was once like this. But slowly, slowly the trees have been hacked back, destroyed or tamed. Except at Ta Prohm it has been deliberately left to the mercy of the strangler figs and the paler, thicker kapok trees so that it can be used for location shots of corny, fast-moving, action-packed movies like... No. That's not true. It was deliberately left like this so that everybody could see what the whole place was like before restoration work began.

From behind the roots, which like some super giant octopus snake curl and twist in all directions between enormous boulders, we see our hero stepping, slowly, cautiously into the entrance of the temple. A bat screeches overhead. A rat scampers back into its hole. Snakes – it's good this, isn't it? – slither out of sight. He makes his way agonisingly slowly, step by careful step, through corridors choked with vast tree roots and signs saying, Fall Down Danger. He clambers beneath huge slabs and bricks and boulders that are only held in place by prayer, Buddhist prayers. (You can smile, but I tell you it's true. I've been there, I've done it, I know what it's like. What's more I'm still taking the tablets.) He now crawls out into an open courtyard, about the size of a tennis court, completely at the mercy of more of these giant encircling tree roots. He stops. He looks at the lottery ticket. He scratches his head. He kicks a loose stone in frustration, the way they do in all fast-moving, action-packed movies. A snake shoots out from underneath it. A touch of the D.H. Lawrences, that. A dozen rats scamper off in all directions. He drops the bit of paper. The rats go to grab... he suddenly realises. This is the Far East, and in the Far East you read not from left to right but from...

In a second we see him once again at the entrance to the temple: 00, of course, means nothing, the beginning, the entrance. Now he is counting 44. 44 steps? No, too John Buchan. Maybe 44 metres? He gives it a try: 38, 39, 40. A boulder suddenly shakes loose and crashes down from the ceiling just in front of him. He waits for the dust to settle: 41, 42. Whoosh. A snake the size of a cobra darts across his shoes... 43. Ants! A million of them. They're everywhere. He's leaping and jumping and screaming, desperately trying to fight them off... 44. He's at a crossroads. To the left is a corridor. Almost impassable - roots everywhere, boulders balancing precariously on roots, a mass of stones balancing on the boulders. To the right, just 02 statues of Buddha away from him he sees - guess who? The man in the white suit plus the frail, painfully ... Suddenly a whole mass of wild, shrieking, screaming spider monkeys drop down on top of them. Then they seem to disappear into the wall of the temple. He tries to follow. But who's ever heard of anyone walking through walls? Especially two-foot thick solid stone temple walls. But what lies behind the wall? What secrets is the Temple of Ta Prohm trying to hide? Will our hero discover the truth? Sorry, I'm afraid you'll have to wait for Return of Son of Our Hero Meets the Temples of Angkor Wat, Part III.

OK, luvvies. That's it. Cut. Cut. Last one down to the bar buys the champagne. Pink, of course.

Luang Prabang

I don't know about you but I get sick to death of people
going on and on about the peace, the tranquillity, the
enlightenment of Buddhism, not to mention their God-
given right to sit on the floor all day long, spinning their
prayer wheels round and round and round and going
ooooooooooooh. To be honest, it sometimes makes me
feel as if I want to forget the four noble truths
altogether, tear up my picture of the world's leading
Buddhist, Richard Gere, sitting next to some guy from
Tibet, rip my orange robe in half and thump the hell out
of them all. But that only happens now and Zen. Most of
the time, this deep, inner peace comes over me and I
remember the first real Buddhist monk I ever met, a
nice, kind, gentle, friendly little man. He was sitting on
the banks of the Mekong River in Luang Prabang (the r
is silent as in Roy Jenkins), way up in the north of tiny,
mountainous, landlocked Laos, close to the Chinese
border. He taught me how to ignore the trivialities of
this world, to open wide the doors of the Buddhist
kingdom, to concentrate on the vast, eternal realities of
life and then go and get a bottle of champagne. Which
was my kind of spiritual refreshment.

For a moment, I actually thought of turning Buddhist.
But I must admit I didn't fancy the idea of shaving off
what little hair I have left and then picking up an iron
bar almost a centimetre thick and smashing it on the top

237

of my head – although I know there is no shortage of people who would be only too happy to do that for me, notably my wife. The other thing I didn't fancy was this reincarnation business unless, of course, I could choose my next role. I mean it would be great fun, wouldn't it, to spend one whole life, say, wheeling and dealing, and then another moping around like something out of *Brideshead Revisited*, reading poetry all day long and getting bombed out of your mind. Or what about coming back as a rip-roaring, devil-may-care, huntin', shootin' and fishin' type? Or how about choosing something sensible like being a champagne taster, which would last me several lifetimes, or a missionary or a double-glazing salesman? On the other hand, knowing my luck, I'd probably come back as something boring. Like a dung beetle. Or an accountant. Or a lawyer. Or heaven help me, as a Frenchman. Which you've got to admit suddenly gives Dante's eighth concentric circle a certain *je ne sais quoi*.

Actually, come to think of it, the guy in Luang Prabang wasn't the first real Buddhist monk I met. The first was, not surprisingly, in some company in Silicon Valley, just outside Los Angeles. During the day everybody carved everybody up as normal but after work they all went to this chap's special meditation sessions. At the time I can remember doubting the effectiveness of the whole thing. After taking the course for three weeks one hard-bitten vice-president of something or other told me that as he understood it, nirvana was a bit like flying Singapore Airlines.

Most Americans, however, seem to have no problem with Buddhism. Partly because, I guess, most of them idolise themselves so much already that they have no problem idolising a chunk of rock or stone smothered in gold leaf. Also because most of them, particularly the middle-aged flakes, don't know what to do next. Bio-food? Fast cars? A yacht? Another wife? Good heavens, no. But I tell you what. I'll become a Buddhist, like

Richard Gere. Provided, of course, that I can have a Porsche and pick up somebody like Julia Roberts. In a deeply meaningful, Buddhist way, of course.

Then what happens? When these up-scale Buddy Buddhists are not standing on their heads on a parquet floor, hyperventilating and spouting a whole load of mumbo-jumbo, they spend all day driving around the trendy, trendy West Side of Los Angeles or wherever with their rubber mats no longer in the front but instead in the back of their 4×4s, dropping in at their local New Age Spiritual Renaissance Yoga Studio for a nut crunch and dodging off to special yoga weeks in luxury, five-star, vaas-tu-approved hotels in Rishikesh or Hardwav in the foothills of the Himalayas. Of course, these hotels offer full air conditioning; room service; a private helicopter pad and a spot of river-rafting on the Ganges. All for the non-dukkha price of US$600 per pair of bare feet per week.

One guy I met in Boston went even further. He wasn't just a Buddhist. He was a Buddhist gong therapist. He travelled the world studying the vibrations of Buddhist gongs. Certain gongs, he reckoned, gave out not only certain sounds but different auras and spectrums as well. Some, he said, could cure bad colds and even pneumonia. Some he used as sound mantras. Some he used to create what he called gong baths. I said the only thing I thought they could create was deafness, which I think upset him.

Now I don't know much about anything, as my wife keeps telling me, but believe me I've done the Buddha bit. I've seen big Buddhas, small Buddhas and medium-size Buddhas. I've seen standing-up Buddhas, sitting-down Buddhas and the reclining and dead Buddhas. I've been to temples in tiny villages in the middle of nowhere with barely two grains of rice to rub together and I've been to massive temples in all the big towns and cities from practically this side of nirvana to the other side and back again. In Laos, once known as The

Land of a Million Elephants, tucked away in the central highlands of South-East Asia (the least developed country in the region, they have virtually no roads, no railway and no industry, apart that is from a toothpick factory which is their biggest export earner), I even went to a Buddhist Theme Park. All your conventional Buddhas were there but they also had some pretty unconventional ones as well: huge reclining Buddhas; slightly camp Buddhas; and Buddhas with ten arms, which are obviously brother-in-law Buddhas. My favourite, though, was a huge octopus-like Buddha with three hideous faces, six massive grasping hands stretched out like tentacles, a man being crushed to death in each hand, and seven terrified skulls who obviously met their fate during some kind of Buddhist away-day in the Himalayas: which can be nothing else but a mother-in-law Buddha.

I also went way up north to Pack Ou where, almost on the Chinese border where the dark muddy Mekong meets the clear blue Nam Ou, there is a whole string of enormous limestone caves literally full to overflowing with thousands upon thousands upon thousands of Buddhas, of all shapes and sizes. All the serious, totally dedicated, committed Buddhists, vegetarians and environmental freaks go there, crash helmets on their heads, knees tucked up tight under their chins, by means of a 50mph hi-speed speedboat, which screams like a jet engine. Being a non-Buddhist, non-vegetarian, non-environmentally obsessed kind of guy I went there by a slow, traditional Laotian long-tail boat, which was a million times better. There are mountains on either side of the river in which it is said there are still many animals unknown to man; bamboo forests cling to the banks; white and black buffaloes, taking a break from the day's ploughing, graze by the edge of the water. You see fishermen forever mending their nets; the odd sand bank; and even monks doing their laundry, waving their robes in the breeze to dry. Now and then I popped into tiny villages, where I very quickly learnt that even to decline as politely as possible the headman's offer of a quick puff on his opium pipe, meant having to force down yet another plate of fried buffalo strips, assorted lumps of fish and pork as well as a mountain of green beans and a huge dollop of sticky rice.

In one tiny village, Xang Hai, on the Plain of Jars, however, the problem wasn't the pipe of peace, but the wine. Rice wine, fermented in huge jars. Ideal for getting completely bombed out of your tiny little Buddhist mind on. Most of the ones I saw – jars not minds – were about three feet high and must have weighed half-a-ton, maybe even a ton. Others can be ten feet high and weigh five or six tons. Hence the name Plain of Jars. Some people say – though how they say it I do not understand – that the jars are not meant for boozing but for burials. According to them the whole area is some kind of enormous Bronze Age cemetery.

My own view, after a couple of sticky glasses of rice wine, is that it's both. You get so plastered on the wine you end up, as we Buddhists say, *sivasana*. In other words, in the Duke of Clarence totally prone corpse position. The following morning, or whenever they finish drinking the rest of the wine in the jar, whichever is the first, they then roll you to your final resting place where you gently ferment for a couple of hundred years until some way-out archaeologist with lots of degrees and no common sense discovers you and comes up with another crazy theory for people to start chasing for a few years. I'm not joking. I've seen similar jars being used for the same thing all around Cochabamba in Bolivia.

But that's not all. I've also done my desk research on Buddhism. I've read everything from *Mr Easter Humphreys at Christmas* – or was it *Mr Christmas Humphreys at Easter* – to *Zen and the Mysteries of Wallpaper Hanging* let alone *The Art of Motorcycle Maintenance*. I've burnt the odd joss stick. But not, I

hasten to add, in goody-goody, squeaky-clean Singapore.
Because there burning joss sticks and even your giant
24-inch candle are banned because, would you believe
it, it is claimed that they create air pollution and can thus
damage the environment. I've spent hours on end
playing with my Tibetan prayer cymbals. I have even
learnt to tell the difference between my *tanha* and my
dukkha which I can assure you has brought me a great
sense of relief over the years and helped me no end of
times to avoid an embarrassing moment. So if you put
down that damn prayer wheel for a minute, I'll tell you
what I like about Buddhism, like about Buddhism, like
about Buddhism, like about Buddhism...

I like its genuine, honest, back to basics simplicity. I
know in Thailand, for example, you sometimes see the
occasional monk going around collecting his alms for
the day in a chauffeur-driven car. You also hear all kinds
of strange stories; for example, in Myanmar I was told
that in some temples would-be monks are forced to take
a lie-detector test to see how serious they are about
being celibate for the rest of their lives. In Taiwan I came
across the opposite. Parents were going on hunger-strike
to stop their children from becoming Buddhist monks
and nuns. In Japan, of course, they tell you the reason
the temples are so full is because most of the monks are
on the run from either the police, their friends, their
local Yakuza gang, particularly the Sokaiyas who
specialise in extortion, or the worst extortioners of all,
their wives and families. But overall I reckon they're
pretty genuine.

I also like the Buddhist idea of *dharmakaya*, the
concept of complete and utter emptiness in a total, all-
encompassing silence. After all, as I see it, it's better for
me to discover oblivion than for oblivion to discover
me.

But best of all, I just love Luang Prabang which to
those who know, champagne or no champagne, is heaven
on earth. A Buddhist heaven that is. Old Asia hands

claim it is the most beautiful town in Indo-China, Asia, or indeed the whole world, depending on how many jars they can remember emptying on the plains. One, a hard-bitten Dutch trader, even told me that whenever he went to Luang Prabang he felt as if the gates of heaven had opened, the whole heavenly array had descended before his eyes and he was being swept up to the clouds. But then he had probably hit the ten-foot jars.

Squeezed on to a tiny peninsula between the Mekong and the Nam Khan – outside a tiny temple on top of the hill where the two rivers actually meet, there is still an old Russian anti-aircraft gun – Luang Prabang is the kind of town that makes cynical, bitter, twisted visitors go all soppy and dewy-eyed.

'The spires,' they say, with tears welling in their eyes. 'The temples. The setting sun.'

And with good reason. The town is small. It's quiet. It's practically untouched by the outside world, apart from the odd invasion by the Khmers of ancient Cambodia, the Chinese, the Burmese, the Vietnamese, the Thai and finally in 1893 the French – Bad karma! Bad karma! Bad karma! – although the French being the French they didn't call it an invasion. They said it was part of their divinely ordained '*mission civilisatrice*'. But no sooner had they got their *pieds au-dessous de la table* than they shipped in a whole load of Vietnamese labourers from next door to make it French. First, they built a school to teach everybody to be civilised. Then a post office, so they could write and tell the world how civilised they now were. Finally, a hospital so they could make certain all their new little French citizens had the best possible chance of surviving and becoming proud members of the greatest people that have ever deigned to grace the face of the world with their illustrious presence.

Despite the fact that average annual earnings are just US$250 a year; life expectancy at 50 years is the lowest in the whole of Asia; that it has the highest infant mortality rate in the world – one child dies for every ten that are born; and that health care, including drugs, works out at an unbelievable 25 cents per person, per annum; despite all this, the place is full to overflowing with *wats*, or Buddhist monasteries and temples. Wherever you look, wherever you turn there's a Buddhist *wat* staring sedately back at you. In fact, with so many *wats* at its disposal it must be one of the brightest lights in the Buddhist world. If not it soon will be. For any day now it will also be home – or in this case a rather rich, gold-decorated palace – to the famous Pha Bang Buddha, which contains ashes of the Lord Buddha himself. Presented by the Khmers to King Fa Ngum way back in the late 1300s, it also gave the town its name: Pha Bang, large sacred image, Luang, great or royal. Why it had taken so long to build a palace for the Buddha nobody could tell me. Neither could they tell me why it took a Communist government to do it after they had originally started in power by virtually trying to ban Buddhism.

It is also the only town I've been to anywhere in the world where there is nothing but one traffic jam after another – of Buddhist monks. Monks in the usual saffron robes. Monks in bright saffron. Monks in dark saffron. Monks in clean saffron. Monks in dirty saffron. Monks in stained saffron. There are so many of them attached to so many different *wats* all over town that when they hit the streets at dawn to begin their daily round of begging for rice and fish, traffic comes to a complete standstill. And when I say traffic I mean both ox-carts, all three rickshaws and that decrepit Peugeot.

Surrounding heavenly Luang Prabang on practically all sides is purgatory, if not hell itself. When I went there – Luang Prabang that is, not heaven; that would be expecting far too much – the road from Laos's capital, Vientiane, especially the final stretch from Vang Vieng, was practically under siege. Individual travellers were being picked off. Single cars were being showered with bullets. Groups of about twenty men would suddenly leap out of the bushes and spray a minibus with automatic gunfire. Some said it was bandits. Others that it was Hmong tribesmen which, if true, is ironic to say the least, because it was the Hmong who not only refused to fight alongside the Americans, but also against the Communists during the civil war in the 1960s and 1970s. In other words, if it was the Hmong they must have been doing it because they were just out for a bit of looting and pillaging; or they wanted to show that whoever was the government they were anti-government or, more likely still, they were protecting their drug routes from Phu Bia, high in the mountains, into Thailand.

As I had no strong Thais one way or the other, I did what the Americans did. I flew in. The difference was that I landed, toured the area, met lots of marvellous people and had a great time, while the Americans just tried to bomb the place to kingdom come. From 1964 to 1973 the whole area, the Plain of Jars, the Eastern Provinces right up to the Vietnamese border was, against all the rules and regulations you can imagine, subjected to the most intensive bombardment in history. In a secret war run by the CIA and denied a million times by the Americans, more bombs were dropped on poor, little, mountainous, landlocked Laos than by both sides during the whole of the Second World War. Which must make it probably the most bombed nation on earth and this part of the country the most bombed region on earth. The cost: US$7 billion. Which means that for every single day of the war-that-never-was the Americans were spending over US$2 million a day. Why? Because they wanted to cut the Ho Chi Minh trail, which wasn't even in Laos but next door in Vietnam.

I say bombs. They didn't just drop your conventional bombs. They dropped a whole range of bombs with countless different ways of inflicting the harshest and cruellest injuries and the most agonising of deaths. For example, the spray dart bomb, which didn't just kill you but it shot your guts out of your body first. Not to mention the deadly, green-painted cluster bombs, the size of tennis balls, which each contained enough explosive and ball-bearings to kill everything within a 150-metre circle. Then, of course, there were the extras, such as napalm and Agent Orange.

The big problem today is to know how many are still out there waiting to go off. Go for a stroll across the fields anywhere in the Eastern Province and you will see virtually nothing but bomb casings: bomb casings being used as fences, as scarecrows, as animal feed trays, huts, and to build huts, sheds and pig-sties and even people's homes.

If you can stop thinking about the bombing raids for a moment, to prove to you what a good non-Buddhist I am, I will now give you my own guide to visiting the Buddhist temples of Luang Prabang.

Are you sitting comfortably? Lotus-flower position, of course.

First, kick off your shoes. I once saw a sign outside a temple in Hanoi which said, 'Get your trousers on. Keep your shoes off.' What on earth the monks thought you were doing wandering around Hanoi with your trousers off I have no idea. And in Burma I came across another sign outside a temple which was even worse. 'Foot wearing,' it said, 'is not allowed.' Which could present all kinds of problems. So, trousers on, shoes off, amble inside. Bill and coo about how pretty it is and my, just think how many people could have a Mercedes of their own if they melted down all that gold and gave it to the not-so-poor. Okay, that out of the way, now to the basics. Is it a temple temple? Or is it a temple complex? Is there a stupa? Are there any chapels? Where is the library? Is there a drum tower? What time do they start banging the damn thing in the morning? Well, that could be important, especially if you have spent the previous evening hitting the Lao Lao, the local fire water. One evening I had three, which was a wonderful intro- duction to the timelessness of the East. I was ten minutes late for breakfast the following morning and everything was cleared away. No, they couldn't get me anything to eat or drink. I would have to wait till lunchtime.

Okay, back to the temple itself. Wat Xien Thon, the Golden City Temple, is all this – and more. In fact, it is probably the most complex complex in town. The *wat* itself, a colossal mass of a temple, a giant exuberant psychedelic hodge-podge of a building, which your purist would sneer at and say it gives kitsch a bad name, is reckoned to be the oldest and most beautiful in the whole city. The roof sweeps low to the ground. Inside there are massive columns and a luscious 'tree of life' mosaic on the far wall. Outside there are stupas, a chapel containing a rare reclining Buddha, a library, a drum tower and even a special building containing the old royal funeral carriage as well as an impressive collection of old royal funeral urns for any amount of old royal ashes. The interesting thing is that they can't get the funeral carriage out of the door. Whether this is an implicit admission that they've stopped killing kings or whether they used the same builder I use I couldn't find out.

Now for the temple building itself. Look at the roof. Not all temple roofs are the same just as, I suppose, not all church roofs are the same. Is it a single roof or is it split? If it is split, is it split horizontally, vertically or in all directions? Does it have one tier or even five? Each region has its own style. Luang Prabang, incidentally, goes for five tiers. Why, I don't know.

What about the things on the roof? Hey. Is that incense I can smell? Or am I just imagining things? Is there a crown or *naga* (serpent) on top? If so it's better than an insurance policy. How about flowers? Flowers on the roof show the temple is either a Thai-built or a Thai-influenced temple.

Outside panels? Wat Mai has probably the best outside decorations of all. The verandah is all ornate columns and walls dripping with gold. Probably because the Pha Bang Buddha comes here for the Laotian new year celebrations.

Cloisters? Some have. Some haven't. The best set of cloisters I think I've come across were not in Luang Prabang (hope this doesn't mean I'm really going to come back again as, *mon Dieu*, a Frenchman) but in the Wat Si Saket in Vientiane. The whole thing was lined with Buddhas, hundreds of them.

Now the fun bit. Buddhas are not just plain Buddhas. There are different types. For example, there's a Khmer Buddha, which looks like a Buddha on a diet. Then there's the Vishnu Buddha, which looks as though he's never heard of such a thing as a diet. And there's what I call the pointed-nose Buddha, which together with those arched eyebrows and flat, Mr Spock, slablike ears is very, very Laos.

Then there are the different positions of the Buddha.

Standing up, hands by his side: he's calling for rain. A favourite of farmers, you usually find these all over country districts.

Standing up, one hand up in the air: he wants the rain to stop. Obviously the townies' Buddha. The last thing they want is rain, especially at weekends.

Standing up, hands crossed in front of him: he's analysing the future. Probably trying to decide whether he should have his hands by his side or not.

Standing up, both hands palms forward like a traffic cop: 'Please, please stop fighting. Let's have some peace and quiet around here. It's not my fault it's raining/not raining.'

Standing up, giving the weak wrist wave: 'Best of luck, sunshine.'

Sitting down, lotus position, right hand touching the ground: 'Listen to me, you guys. It's true. As the earth is my witness.'

Sitting down, lotus position, right hand on top of left hand: 'For heaven's sake, can we have some peace around here? I want to do my meditation.'

Sitting down, lotus position, hands together: he's praying. 'Please don't let there be any more visitors.'

Then there is – wait a minute, I can hear monks chanting in the background – what I like to think of as the Jewish Buddha: sitting down, lotus position, both hands open as if to say, 'My life, my life.' (It is supposed to mean that the Buddha is ready to receive our gifts. But I don't believe it. I still think my explanation is the right one.)

Only once have I ever seen the complete set of sitting and standing Buddhas. That was in a temple in Georgetown, Penang, far up in the north-west of Malaysia which also happens to be the disk drive capital of the world. They had the full thirteen Buddhas, each in its own glass case. Seeing them all together was like winning some great Buddhist lottery.

Finally, of course, there are the stretched-out reclining Buddhas. I can't think of any reclining Christ statues or paintings: funny that. Propped languidly on an elbow. The Buddha is resting. Head right down in his hand. He's dead!

But whether the Buddha is resting or just plain dead, have a look at his feet, because here you will find the soul of Buddhism. I'm being serious. All those squiggly lines and circles mean something. Not just something, they mean everything to a Buddhist. Some Buddhists spend their lives doing nothing but studying the soles of the feet of the Buddha.

What about all the stuff around the base of the Buddha? The fancy paper trees, as well as the candle trees, represent the bodi or banyan tree under which the Lord Buddha sat when he was searching for enlightenment. Fruit, gifts, money. Well, we all know what they are, don't we?

Sometimes you also see, if there are not too many tiny, cross-legged figures sitting on the floor blocking your view, photographs or even statues of benign old abbots as there are in the Wat Sen *soukharam*. I think this is a nice touch: maybe we should have photographs of all our old parish priests in our churches at home. On the other hand, maybe not.

Now for the rest of the inside of the temple. Sometimes if can be plain and simple. Sometimes it can be rich and luxurious as in the Red Chapel at Xieng Thong or in Wat Mai, close to the post office: dark, wine red ceilings and gold leaf all over the place. As if it had been designed by William Morris when he was high on candy floss. If you go to Wat Xien Muan you will find gold dragons all over the ceiling and also probably the fanciest set of candle rails in town. Wat Paa Huak, on the hill facing the museum, has a string of murals and mosaics showing the Lord Buddha charging around all over the place on Erawan, the three-headed elephant, as well as all the usual stuff such as Chinese diplomats and Chinese warriors and the Mekong River. Wat Si Mahathat, on the other hand, goes in for bells. Temple bells – millions of them. It also has some pretty elaborate pillars. The Aham Temple is nothing but paintings of the life of the Lord Buddha. When he lived in the palace, ignorant of sickness and poverty, the old, the sick and the dying. When he went outside with his bodyguards and for the first time came face to face with reality. His decision to devote himself to meditation. (Which always, incidentally, strikes me as odd. I would have thought if he was so shocked by what he saw in the real world outside the palace he would have devoted himself to a life of actually helping and caring for the poor. But maybe I haven't yet reached a high enough plane to appreciate the reasons for his sense of detachment.) On the way out, by the way, whatever you do take a look at the two big bodhi or banyan trees outside. Ignore them at your peril. They represent the most important spirit shrine in town. Don't say I didn't warn you.

Now if you really want to score on the I-want-to-be-a-

Buddy-Buddhist scale, see if you can spot a Buddha shower. That's right, a Buddha shower. Come the Buddhist new year, everybody wants to wash the Buddha for good luck. So what did our clever, unworldly monks do? Instead of having long, long queues of people all waiting in line with a bucket and a sponge they rigged up their own Heath Robinson, instant shower-a-Buddha system. Pull the rope at this end of the temple, a chute opens in the roof, water rushes along an intricate network of overhead wooden pipes and channels until – whoosh – it all pours straight down on top of the head of the Buddha himself. Buddhist technology strikes again. Give that monk a Nobel prize.

But sometimes there's something even more important than any temple or temple complex or fancy decoration or bodhi or banyan tree. That's a footprint. Not just an ordinary footprint, but the Lord Buddha's very own footprint. Believe me, you can't go to Luang Prabang without visiting the Wat Pha Phutthabat on the hill facing the museum. This, according to my spiritual adviser, is what Buddhism is all about.

So now, having hobbled around all the temples in Luang Prabang, I was ready for the real thing. The flap of sandal on bare feet. The lotus position. Eyes closed. Everything quiet on the eastern front. Meditation.

Now I will admit that I am not your usual meditation groupie or religious junkie. I know I'm old-fashioned but I haven't pierced my nose let alone got round to getting my own personal prayer wheel and heap of rose petals. But I can assure you that doesn't mean I haven't had one or two ecstatic experiences in my life and with a bit of luck I'll have a few more before the old prayer wheel stops spinning. I have, however, done my bit. I've read and studied enough of St John of the Cross and all the other mystics to at least realise meditation is not just a matter of sitting on the floor, crossing your legs and doing nothing. Well, not if you're attached to the concept of doing nothing, as good old St John of the

Cross would say. You genuinely have to search deeper and deeper into your own interior. And you have to work at it, provided of course that you're not attached to the concept of working at it, as good old St John of the Cross would say.

Yet the problem I have with the Buddhists is all their Mickey Mouse talk.

'The past has gone. The future is yet to be. The present moment is the most wonderful moment of our life.'

I mean, do me a favour.

'The simplest way to internalise is by breathing in and out and saying, Mother Earth I am here.'

Eh? Say that again?

And finally – are you ready?

'When you drink a cup of tea, drink it mindfully. You then drink all your worries and problems as well. Drinking mindfully is like walking, talking and thinking mindfully.'

Yuk.

I much prefer simple, practical sayings like, for example, 'Oh, all right. Make it a large one', or 'What time did you say he'd be back?' or even William Blake's, 'The road of excess leads to the path of wisdom'. Now they're the kind of statements I can relate to. Unfortunately, the monk I met, who was as charming and civilised a man as you could expect to meet on a day's march through the jungle surrounded by the Vietcong and being bombed by the Americans, didn't seem to be at all interested in any of that kind of thing.

He came up to me as I was about to go into Wat Xieng Thon. For some reason, he must have thought I was not from their part of the world, because straight away he said he wanted to practise what he called his British. I told him I did too. But it didn't make any difference to him. He was already telling me about the Mekong River.

Mekong, he said, is short for Mae Nam Khong, the Mother of Waters. The river is 2,700 miles long. It starts way up in the Qinglai Province in China and flows through the infamous Golden Triangle, where Laos, Burma and Thailand meet, the biggest opium-growing area in the world. If you have teenage children you may be interested to know that they have now also started manufacturing morphine and heroin as well as Ecstasy in the Wa Hills up close to the Burma border. From there it flows – the river not the drugs, although, come to think of it, probably the drugs as well – down through Laos into Vietnam, through Ho Chi Minh City and out through the sprawling Mekong Delta made famous the world over by too many CNN news bulletins. In terms of volume it is the tenth largest river in the world; in terms of length, the twelfth. In terms of pollution, probably the first. There is not a factory or a large town or a city the whole length of it.

Just as I was beginning to wonder what happened to the Buddhist sense of *dharmakaya*, he told me that, what's more, come the rainy season the river level where we were actually standing could easily rise a staggering five metres in a single day. But he warned me not to drink any of it, which was the last thing I had in mind – especially as from where I was standing, in spite of all the business about the river being pollution-free, it looked like one huge, dirty, muddy, reddy-brown splodge.

I sat down on the steps which ran down from the temple to the edge of the river. On the bank opposite was the tiny Wat Long Khun Royal Temple where the kings used to spend three days deep in prayer before being crowned. Presumably praying that they would survive.

The monk joined me. Having found somebody who spoke British, he was obviously determined not to let me go. He told me his name was Phone which was much better than some of the other Laotian names I came across. A girl in one of the offices I visited in Vientiane was called Manyphone, which seemed appropriate. Another girl in one of the ministries I couldn't help but notice was called Bang-on. Whether that was also appropriate or not, I didn't get a chance to find out.

When he was young, my friendly monk went on, his father was something or other to do with the king. As a result they were fairly well-to-do. They were one of the first families outside the royal palace to have an old-fashioned wind-up record player. As a child he remembered charging other children an egg to hear one of the records playing. Then in the evenings the family would sit around it listening to music and drinking champagne. But all that was a long, long time ago. When the king was overthrown and the Pathet Lao took over, back in 1975, the monk was a teacher. In addition to his British, he could speak French, so along with goodness knows how many others he was packed off to a *samana*, a re-education camp.

'Where?'

'Nearby. North of here.'

'How many of you?'

'There were around three thousand in our camp.'

'So how long were you there for?'

'Three years. Some were only there a few months. Others never came back.'

The Pathet Lao, he told me, also packed off old King Savang Vatthana, together with members of his family, to a re-education camp, but they were never seen again. Or at least never seen again alive, although a pile of bones were found in a big limestone cave at Sam Neua in the far north-east.

To look at the monk now you would never guess he had been in a re-education camp for as long as three years. He looked more like, say, a football referee or one of the guys with a bucket and sponge who rush into the boxing ring at the end of every round or even a personnel manager. He was small, about five feet tall, but stocky and well-built. For all his three years' re-education he was still, between you and me, a royalist. Because he had come from a well-to-do family and because they had had connections with the royal palace he said he had experienced all the good things of life: good food, good drink, good company, good conversation, good clothes, good music. Did he miss any of it? 'No,' he said. He was very happy as a monk.

'Nothing. You mean you miss nothing at all?'

'Well,' he hesitated. 'Perhaps a glass of champagne.'

He hadn't drunk champagne since the Pathet Lao took over. First, because even before he became a monk he didn't have the money. Second, because anyone buying champagne now would attract attention and the last thing he wanted was to attract attention. Three years in a re-education camp when he was thirty was bad enough. Three years now he was fifty would probably kill him.

Well, what could I do? I promptly reincarnated myself into a good guy and set off for Dala Market, close to the hospital, in search of spiritual refreshment. Went past all the stacks of colourful vegetables. Past all the slabs of meat. Past all the strangest-looking shapes and sizes you can imagine. Until... until... buried deep in the recesses of a filthy old shack on the edge of the market, where some old guy looked like he was doing a roaring trade in vampire bats (a string of ten for under a pound) I found, would you believe it, a bottle of Moët. How old it was I couldn't tell you. All I know is it didn't look as though the grapes had been picked that morning. The price: all of US$10. Including two paper cups. Somehow I thought crystal might in the circumstances be a touch ostentatious.

Back I went to Buddha's answer to Dom Perignon. He was still sitting on the steps facing the Royal Temple. I broke opened the bottle, filled the plastic cups and together we drank first to the Dalai Lama and to the Pope. Then the Pope and the Dalai Lama. I don't know whether the Buddhist monks' secret hand movements include knocking back glass after glass, or rather plastic cup after plastic cup, of champagne but this one was certainly good at it. Within minutes, it was gone.

Thus fortified, he continued to practise his British. It was his third time as a monk. (Hic.) The first time was while he was (hic) still at school. He stayed for three (hic) weeks. He came in again when he had qualified as a teacher. He had had enough of schools and school-children and just (hic) wanted to get away. He stayed for practically (hic) three months. This time he said it was for real. (Hic.) His wife had died. His daughter had just got married. His two sons were working. One of them was also (hic) thinking of becoming a monk but had not decided definitely one way or the other. Whatever he (hic) decided was up to him. He was not going to try and persuade him one way or the other. His own mind, however, was made up. He was going to remain a monk. Burp. He was also, he said, going to make me the first British Buddhist monk in Luang Prabang. But, a minor detail, first I had to know something about Buddhism. Which in the circumstances seemed to be fair enough. After all, of all the religions I've come across, it's only the Church of England which seems to let people believe or not believe whatever they like, whenever they like and for as long as they like. In any case I thought being a Buddhist would always come in handy for receptions or dinner parties or the next time I bumped into a famous Hollywood star who was not a Scientologist. So as we staggered from one temple to another, my education as a Buddhist monk began.

Siddhartha Gautama or, to give him his full name, Buddha, was born in Lumbini, Nepal in either 563 or 623 BC, depending on who you ask. Funny that. Even the Buddhists date everything in terms of the birth of Christ. His mother, Queen Maya Devi, was on her way to visit her parents in Rangram, as good daughters do, when she walked into a wood and zonk, out came Prince Siddhartha. Who, perhaps significantly, perhaps not significantly, promptly jumped up and walked seven steps, away from his mother.

By now we had left Wat Xing Thon behind us, ambled

past a collection of French colonial buildings, past five or six other temples and were heading towards the Royal Palace on Thanon Phothisalat or rather, seeing as the royals were no more, the Royal Palace Museum.

Okay, so broadly speaking there are two kinds of Buddhists: the Theravadas and the Mahayanas.

The Theravadas are, as I see it, the Roman Catholics of Buddhism. They stick strictly to whatever Buddha said. They follow the lunar calendar and believe all the important things in Buddha's life happened on the day of the full moon in the sixth lunar month. His birth. His conversion under the bodhi tree from a life of delicious, diligent indolence to the search for enlightenment. His death at the age of eighty.

The other guys, the Mahayanas, are I suppose the Protestants. Founded a hundred years after the death of Buddha, their sect has expanded and developed his teaching in order to make it, they say, more relevant to the present day. They also follow the solar calendar and celebrate his birthday on 8 April.

The Theravadas call themselves the Southern School of Buddhism because Myanmar, Thailand, Laos and Cambodia who are all Theravada are in the south, whereas the Northern School includes Nepal, Tibet, China, Mongolia, Korea, Vietnam and Japan which are all in the north. Damned clever, what?

Another point to remember. The Theravadas are also the guys who've done more than anybody else to preserve that monastic way of silence in Buddhism. But I wouldn't worry about that too much, especially if you're ever in California. The buddy-buddy-Buddhists I've met over there never stop talking about their karmas long enough to let you get a word in about the importance of silence in Buddhist culture.

When we got to the Palace Museum, my spiritual counsellor decided he didn't want to visit it after all. It would bring back too many memories, he said. So I went in alone.

Built at the turn of the century by the French, it was pretty much what you would expect: huge open reception rooms; royal portraits; Laotian and French motifs everywhere. Not to mention the usual collection of elephant tusks, silk screens and friendship flags. To me the most interesting exhibit was a fragment of moon rock which was actually presented to Laos by Richard Nixon with the left hand while with the right hand he was actually bombing them to bits. After trying to find out whether the fragment of moon rock was delivered by DHL or by B52s at a height of 30,000 feet (nobody seemed to know or if they did, being inscrutable Buddhists, they didn't want to tell me), I returned to my spiritual counsellor for a session on the what's *wat* of Buddhist meditation.

'You want to meditate?' he slurred, as we staggered back to Wat Xien Thon.

I nodded.

'You see the temple over there,' he said, speaking oh-so-deliberately and pointing across the river. 'That's where the old king went to meditate. You concentrate on the temple. You see the steps leading from the temple down to the river. You concentrate on the steps. Now you concentrate on the river. Now on the steps leading up from the river on this side of the bank. Now to where we are.'

'That's it?'

'That's it.'

'So how long does it take?'

'About an hour. Maybe two hours.'

'No, I mean to learn to meditate.'

'Maybe a week. Maybe two. It's not difficult, it depends on the individual.'

No years of wearing hair shirts! No agonies of self-detachment! Poor St John of the Cross would turn in his grave.

'Could I do it?'

'Anybody can do it.'

'Can women learn to—'

For some reason, don't ask me why, maybe it was the champagne, he started giggling away like mad. Try as I might, I couldn't get another word of British out of him.

Now if you'll excuse me, I feel *ooooooooooooh* a meditation coming on. Or is it the craving for more champagne? Either way, with a bit of luck it will transport me either to nirvana or to Rheims. So if you would be so kind as to close the door on your way out . . .

Maputo

French Africa I know inside out. British Africa outside in. Belgian Africa I could waffle on about for ages. German Africa, *mein Gott*, just order me to tell you whatever you want to know. As for Dutch Africa, I could Boer you to tears. Maputo, however, was my introduction to Portuguese Africa. It was a revelation.

I thought it was going to be far more Portuguese than it was. After all, Mozambique put up with them for over five hundred years. Or rather, survived them. Because by all accounts the Portuguese were the roughest and toughest of all the colonialists who at some time or other trampled all over Africa. But the country wasn't very Portuguese at all. If anything it looked and felt, how shall I say, international – with a strong dash of South Africa, which, I suppose, is not surprising as it is just down the road. For years Maputo was the play-ground of rich, strait-laced, sober-suited, serious-minded Boers who every weekend used to escape the rigours of South Africa to drop the occasional *obrigado* and then get paralytic in the city's fun spots. Not, of course, that they told their wives or families or the local kirke what they were up to.

Obviously the Portuguese influence is still there. Maputo has a bull ring although it's no longer used. They drink Mateus Rosé. They speak Portuguese. Or, at least, the educated élite do which is reckoned to be 10 to

20 per cent of the population. In fact, more is said to have been done to encourage people to speak the language since Mozambique became independent from the Portuguese than the Portuguese did in the whole of the previous five hundred years. But then I suppose few people wanted to know the Portuguese for, 'Faster. If you don't stop snivelling and complaining I'll beat the living daylights out of you', or words to that effect.

They maintain links with the old country, although the old country is not so keen to return the compliment – even though at one time the Portuguese were convinced that King Solomon's Mines were actually in Mozambique. The occasional escudo, however, still finds its way into the local economy, usually via investment in local construction companies or builders' merchants or bars or hotels. But, at least, it's there. The people are also very punctual and very creative. They always, precisely five minutes before a meeting is scheduled to begin, decide to cancel it. Now you can't say that's not being organised and efficient. The reasons they give are very creative. The manager has a meeting with the director. The director has a meeting with the minister. The minister has a meeting with... Forget it. I'll go and find that bar that South African was telling me about.

But even though the Portuguese have just formed their own Lusaphone Community of Portuguese-speaking countries – it's called Lusaphone because nowhere else in the world are people looser than when they go to Portuguese-speaking countries – the contact and the relationship is nowhere near as overpowering as, for example, the French influence in French Africa. If you carve open a guy from Mozambique, as plenty of them did to each other during their disastrous fifteen-year civil war, there is no way you will see Lisbon, or even Lisboa, engraved on his heart as you would Paris on a French African's. It is more likely to be J'burg. On the other hand, if you've got anything whatsoever to do with the government, it's more likely to be Zürich. At least that's what they say in the *baixa* in Maputo.

Neither are there as many two-way contacts between Maputo and Lisbon as, say, there are between Lomé or Ouagadougou and Paris where ministers and officials seem to be jumping in and out of bed with each other all the time. Chambers of commerce and business associations have exchange visits but rarely, unlike top French businessmen, who seem to be in Africa all the time. As for visits by local mayors, dance groups, orchestras, writers, artists, dancers and, God help us, intellectuals, there are none. In fact, it's probably not insignificant that the smart blue and white French Cultural Centre in Maputo is a vastly bigger, better, more modern and equipped with far more services and facilities than the Portuguese Centre. As for a British cultural presence, now and then you find a week-old copy of the overseas edition of the *Daily Telegraph* lying around some hotel lobby somewhere.

Although to be fair, which is something I don't like being, this probably has something to do with the fact that the Portuguese can't even dominate their own association of Portuguese-speaking countries: Cape Verde, Guinea-Bissau, São Tomé. Even Angola. They're not the problem. Neither is Mozambique. The problem is Brazil. It's just too big, too huge, too dominant. Who wants to talk about the importance of promoting the Portuguese language, Portuguese culture and the role of sixteenth-century Portuguese philosophers in the development of the nation state when the only thing anybody wants is a trade, technology and economic co-operation agreement with Brazil?

Not that Mozambique (or rather Mozambique, Portugal, as two American secret service men I met once at Johannesburg Airport kept calling it) seems too worried. Practically everybody I came across, from diplomats wrestling with the complexities of Southern African economic development and co-operation to businessmen hoping to grab a slice of the action, all the way up to barmen and drivers, were busy learning English. They obviously see their future linked more closely with South Africa, which has already ridden in and seized most of their prize assets ranging from the now truly magnificent Polana Hotel to Graça Machel, the former President's widow, now wife of ex-President Mandela. Naturally they want to know what's next on the list. The port? The big farms in the highlands? Game reserves, especially the one bordering Kruger National Park?

Undaunted, Mozambique has also decided to join that glorious post-colonial talking shop, the Commonwealth. But hang on a bit, before you start leaping to attention, playing the National Anthem and going on about the old Empire, the Mozambicans are going around joining practically any organisation that will have them purely and simply because they reckon the more organisations they're in the more aid money they will get. It's only because the eastern bloc hasn't got any money that they haven't put their names down to become members of the Commonwealth of Independent States as well. If they did, however, they'd have no problems getting in. They'd be instantly accepted. They are, after all, the only country in the world actually to feature on their national flag what the Russians claim is one of their major contributions to world peace: a Kalashnikov AK-47.

Talking of the peaceful purposes for which the Kalashnikov was invented and manufactured and distributed on such a huge scale, the other thing I expected to see in Mozambique was complete and utter devastation. The country has been at war with itself for practically twenty years since FRELIMO, the victorious Liberation movement against the Portuguese, decided to swing the country from crazy, way-out right to crazy way-out left and build a Cuban-style paradise in Africa. This completely devastated the country, shattered the economy and killed and maimed millions. Some people estimate that between 5 and 10 per cent of the population were killed, between 250,000 and 500,000 children orphaned and anything between three and five million people uprooted, their homes destroyed, and forced to flee to either safer areas or to any one of the surrounding countries. Then suddenly in October 1992, thanks to the UN, which acted as peace-broker, peace-keeper and source of untold aid, the fighting stopped and everyone was friends again.

Sure, there are still huge problems. The country's debts are enormous. The war alone is said to have cost US$15 billion, maybe more. What industries there were have been completely destroyed. At one time Mozambique was the world's biggest exporter of cashew nuts. They also shipped out massive quantities of cotton, coconuts and prawns. Now that's all gone. Exports of cashew nuts barely reach 10 per cent of the original quota, and next to no cotton or coconuts. As for the prawns, they can't spear enough for their own requirements let alone supply a world market.

Maputo, like capital cities often do, seems to have escaped the worst of the devastation. One day, though, I took a swing through the surrounding countryside, just to see what it was like outside the towns and cities. It was a mess. The bush seemed to be full of nothing but Soviet tanks crumbling into the dust. Where once there were homes or villages there was nothing, not even ant hills. And the roads – they were virtually non-existent. Practically every truck I saw was shattered to pieces. Most of them looked somehow twisted, as if the chassis had thrown a wobbly. I even saw one being driven along on three wheels. A whole pile of rocks were stacked up in the corner opposite the missing wheel to balance the truck and keep the axle off the road. It was terrifying. One's first reaction was to overtake and get as far away from it as quickly as possible. But hang on a moment. This is Mozambique. Swing off the road? Overtake? It could be the last thing you do, because like

Angola the place is still littered with mines. Instead we stuck behind it. It was less dangerous.

And things are getting even worse. All the people who fled to surrounding countries are now coming back. More than a million from Malawi, thousands more from Zimbabwe, Zambia, South Africa and Swaziland. Each of them is clutching a welcome-home present from the United Nations: a sheet of blue plastic for a home, a hoe, a bucket, a few sacks of maize and beans and some cooking oil. Their homes and villages are destroyed. Their fields are overgrown. With tractors and massive earth-moving equipment they would face a daunting, back-breaking task. With a hoe and a bucket, God help them.

Much as the IMF trumpets Mozambique as a success story, all the key economic indicators, such as inflation, exchange rates, unemployment, the price of a Big Mac must all be somewhat academic. Except for one thing: the time it takes to shift a single container through the port in Maputo. In Rotterdam, Singapore and all the other super-efficient ports of the world, it takes a matter of minutes. In Maputo, it takes 114. Not minutes. Not hours. But days. You don't believe me? Well, that's what the World Bank says. If you disagree, write and tell them. But whatever you do send the letter airmail: if it goes by sea it'll never get there.

On the other hand, there are rich people. Very rich people, making money. A lot of money. And I don't just mean the gold run. One guy told me Maputo was the centre of a vast, illegal gold-smuggling operation. Every year over US$350 million worth of gold was smuggled out of South Africa into Maputo, most of it from a small suburban airport near Johannesburg. This was then broken up and flown from Maputo to small provincial airports in the UK.

Then, of course, there are the drugs. Outside the container terminal I met driver after driver on the Johannesburg run who told me openly about the money they had been offered to smuggle in drugs.

'Half a million. That's how much I was offered once,' one driver with a Rasta hairstyle told me. 'At first, I said yes. But then I changed my mind. It's too risky. You don't know if you're going to get caught. You don't know if you're going to get your money. And if you don't get your money, what are you going to do? Go to the police?'

'So did you do it?'

'No.'

Is it all the fault of the Portuguese? Hardly. You've only got to be in Maputo ten minutes and you can see why it's got problems. Practically every *avenida* or street you come across is named after a loser. Kenneth Kaunda Street, Julius Nyerere Street, Patrice Lumumba Street, Ho Chi Minh Street, Mao Tse-Tung Street, Kwame Nkrumah Street. Bang in the centre of town there's even a Vladimir Lenin Street. And there in the middle of it, set among beautiful rolling lawns, is a gloriously elegant country mansion which for all the world looks as though it has been shipped lock, stock and a couple of dozen port barrels from some quinto overlooking the Douro. What is it? The British Embassy, no less. Some time back I was told the Ambassador lobbied hard to have the street renamed Winston Churchill Street. Maputo was, after all, where he came when he escaped from the Boers. But the Mozambicans said no. Instead, they suggested Harold Wilson Street. The Ambassador, I gather, dropped the whole idea immediately and has not mentioned it since.

Everything else, by comparison, is somewhat run of the mill apart from some smart, long, tree-lined avenues and some wonderful, elegant, obviously Portuguese-style houses which seem to be nothing but iron balconies. There are also some exciting skyscrapers. Exciting because they turn the electricity off at five pm. If you're still inside when the time comes you could have as many as twenty-two storeys to walk down. One of the office blocks is, in fact, the National Assembly, which I was told is hardly used. At first I thought it was because people were frightened of being trapped in there when they cut the electricity off. But then I discovered it was because people can't find it. It looks so much like an ordinary office block they walk straight past it.

One building you can't miss is the cathedral, which is one of the most beautiful I've seen anywhere in the world – It was built by child labour. Apparently, the Portuguese had a very strict approach to sex. Any young girl rounded up by one of their so-called morality squads who was found not to be a virgin was sent to help build the cathedral. Which is nothing to be proud of, because it means that today Maputo has a cathedral only because so many of their young girls were not virgins. In other parts of the world, people have their cathedrals as evidence of the sanctity of the local population. But then I'm not Portuguese, so maybe I don't understand their logic. Similarly I don't understand why way back in 1892 despite their tropical climate they commissioned a three-storey metal building to be the official residence of the governor-general. The world's first prefabricated building it may have been but even I could have told them it wasn't going to work. It didn't seem to do the architect any harm though. He went on to build a whole string of world-famous, practical buildings all over the world. His name: Alexandre Gustave Eiffel.

Surprisingly, there are two art galleries. One is the National Art Museum in the centre of town. The other is the Ungumi, which also happens to contain, according to many people I know who work for a big bank in Washington, the best restaurant in the whole of southern Africa. Well, not being one to shirk my cultural responsibilities, I decided to go to the Ungumi. Now, not being a member of the international aid and development circus I'm no expert on luxury five-star

restaurants, I mean, art galleries. All I can say is it's
certainly one of the best I've come across. And that
includes the Mount Nelson or Nellie, as we regulars say,
in Cape Town.

The Ungumi offers unbridled luxury, in the most
restrained, dignified and respectable way, of course.
Which is what you would expect as, according to the
gossip, it is owned by the wife of someone terribly
important. But I didn't tell you that.

First there is the setting. It's in a splendid villa or
mansion of a house set back in an elegant courtyard
with a huge flight of stone steps leading up to the front
door. Once through the front door you're in heaven.
Gastronomically speaking. Before you can say, 'What is
the average income per head of population in Mozam—
?' a glass of exquisitely chilled champagne is in your
hand. To the left and right are two beautiful dining-
rooms. Different styles, different colours, different
settings. Upstairs, leading off the balcony, still more
rooms – Chinese, Japanese. All beautifully furnished,
and all in fantastic condition.

Normally I don't have any problem taking the first
big decision when it comes to dining out: a glass or a full
bottle. In this case, it was different. Even though I was in
a restaurant, I had first to choose my restaurant. I chose
the one downstairs on the right, which was all light
pastel colours and the tables were covered with glasses.
After that it was Wow, wow, wow. The food; the service;
the wines; the whole style of the place. How much did it
cost? Probably enough to keep a whole village in rice
for a month. But talk to the aid organisations – they say
it's vital to stimulate every sector of the economy. I
stimulated it all right.

Oh yes, I nearly forgot. The paintings. They were
amazing. They were everywhere: crammed on to the
walls, squeezed on to the landings, all along the balcony.
Wherever you looked there was another painting. Some
of them I can still vaguely remember. I can also

remember the name of the two greats of Mozambican art: Malagatana and Chissano.

To me, Malagatana is Hieronymous Bosch meets Picasso. His paintings, or at least the ones I've seen, tend to be a mass of tiny, often horrid, gruesome figures, crammed one on top of another like a scene from hell or an annual general meeting gone wrong. As for colours, he doesn't restrict himself. He uses everything from light red to medium red to violent blood reds. Sometimes even violent, violent blood reds. The titles of his paintings tend to be bland: like Tomorrow, The Sacred Well, Prelude, Transcendencies. In my view they should have titles like Hiroshima, Nagasaki, Belsen, Angola, Zaire, Rwanda. Perhaps even one or two from Mozambique. They would be a far more accurate description of his work.

Born just outside Maputo, he followed the traditional route for a painter: house boy, cleaner, political prisoner. Today he is world famous, or rather internationally recognised as they say in art-speak. He exhibits everywhere and has retrospectives wherever you can think of. Awards and honours and medals he wins practically every day of the week. He is certainly the best painter in Mozambique if not in the whole of Africa. Or, at least, I think so. And it's not just because I had an excellent meal.

Chissano, on the other hand, is a wood sculptor. Think of weird, twisted, anguished shapes. Polish them so they shine like mad. Say they represent all the brutal realities of modern life like Colonialisation, Civil War, Structural Adjustment Programmes imposed by the World Bank, and you've got him.

To me, I'm afraid, most African wood sculpture is what you keep getting thrust up your nose all the time you're in Dakar and what you try to avoid by racing from your car to the door of your hotel. But Chissano is different. He somehow goes a stage further. His ideas are always a little bit more surreal, the grasp on reality a touch more tenuous. They are also invariably cheaper, especially compared to the ones they are hustling in Dakar. What's more I like the way most of his sculptures are called Untitled. It makes it so much easier to remember them.

Like Malagatana, Chissano also followed the traditional career pattern for an artist: servant, cook, miner. He only stumbled across sculpture at the age of 29 when he was working as a cleaner for some local Mozambican art association. Within a couple of years he was having his own one-man exhibitions. Today he exhibits and wins prizes all over the world.

After the Ungumi, the National Art Museum was, by comparison, full of hang-ups. There was nowhere to eat. The guy on the front desk wouldn't make me a cup of coffee either.

Now, I'm not the greatest enthusiast when it comes to paintings but I've had a brush with most of the world's galleries and it seems to me that unless there's a change of art, galleries will continue to be somewhere to go once you've done everything else. I mean, after a hard day in the office, who wants to spend a few hours relaxing by looking at life-size cows made out of dung, fridges of jellied blood, sixty-foot submarines made of car tyres, seven-foot high sculptures of men made out of wire coathangers, empty black skips or even, dare I say, dead sheep in huge tanks of formaldehyde.

Now, don't think I don't like paintings. You can give me a Stubbs or a Munnings or a Mark Wallingford any day. I've even got Susan Crawford's print of *We Three Kings* on the wall of my study at home. As for Italian baroque, I don't mind admitting it makes me go all dreamy. Once I even plucked up courage and ventured into the Chelsea Arts Club. (Only because I didn't believe it when I was told that there they call the toilets the Lautrec Rooms. Because there are two loos.)

The National Art Museum, however, was hard work. I don't mean the style of the paintings. Everything was sharp and vivid and, in most cases, as colourful as anything you can imagine. The problem was the subject matter. Everything was so depressing. I know there has been almost twenty years of civil war, that the whole place has been destroyed, that Mozambique is now one of the poorest countries in the world – but there must be some hope somewhere, mustn't there? If nothing else, why don't they try and cheer the place up a bit by say, getting the Natural History Museum down the road to lend them their complete collection of elephant foetuses – the most comprehensive collection in the whole world – that have been preserved for practically a hundred years. All they would have to do is line them up one after the other and people would be bound to think they're the latest Damien Hirst masterpiece.

On the other hand, a visit to the National Art Museum does get you in the mood for a tour of Maputo's bars and clubs and cafés. After all that misery, you're just desperate for a drink. Luckily there are hundreds of them. Well, don't forget it's got all the necessary ingredients. It is the capital of one of the poorest countries in the world. Its economy is in ruins and people are scrambling for their next slice of bread. It's also full of aid workers and delegations from the World Bank. All day long, therefore, you can sit in one open-air café after another sampling, among other things, the delights of its pseudo-Mediterranean Casablanca type tropical climate.

Malcolm Muggeridge, who spent practically the whole of the last war spying for MI6 in Maputo, or Laurenço Marques, as it then was – he was recruited by Graham Greene – reckoned the Costa do Sol, a Greek-run restaurant way out of town on the beach, was the best. He'd breakfast at the Polana with, sitting at separate tables, his German and Italian counterparts, Herr Wertz and Signor Campini. Then off he would go to lunch at the Costa do Sol. Tough life some of these guys had trying to protect our freedom.

Today the Costa do Sol is scruffy, dusty and shabby. The beach is covered with broken-down cars, broken-down vans, broken-down practically everything. As for spies, I didn't see one. Instead the place seemed to be full of guys talking about mining and construction equipment. Which is not exactly a bundle of intrigue. The strange thing is the café is still run by the same Greek family. Whether this was because old Muggers ruined any chances they ever had of selling the place I couldn't find out.

If, however, you're a Lord Lucan hunter, head for the Piri Piri restaurant in the centre of town instead. There, on the day he was officially declared dead, he was spotted by a Welsh doctor called Brian Hill. The two of them had dinner together, in the course of which Lucan is supposed to have told the good doctor he was on the run, wanted for murder and could never go home again. After that try the Hotel Les Ambassadeurs. He is supposed to have stayed there as well. I don't believe it myself. He's in Montevideo in Uruguay. I know. I saw him there one night at the casino.

But if you really want to experience all the fun of the Fereira, South Africa-style, make for the seedy grown-ups' funfair virtually – maybe that's not the right word – in the middle of town. Forget the hot dog stands. Try to ignore the guys selling all kinds of cigarettes. Instead head for the top right-hand corner to what looks like a single-storey, prefabricated scout hut or church hall by an open-air stage. This is Madam Zo-Zo's. This is what kept all those strait-laced, serious-minded, sober-suited Boers coming back to Maputo weekend after weekend after weekend for all those years. This is what helped sustain everyone during the long years of the civil war. This is what is now bringing in the tourists and helping to build up those shattered reserves.

But a word of advice. Try to avoid the Russians. Whenever they turn up they put a damper on the whole place. Apparently when they finally decided to quit Mozambique they naturally did it the Russian way. All the thousands of Soviet aid workers, special advisers and special special advisers were given free tickets back home on Aeroflot. But only two planes arrived to take them and it was every comrade for himself. Those that made it are now living miserably in Russia. Those that didn't are living equally miserably in Mozambique. Most of them don't have passports, money or even a job. They just struggle by hustling drinks and one or two other things.

Why did I go to Zo-Zo's? In pursuit of Portuguese culture, naturally. I wanted to find out how the hell she made those tassels do that.

Luanda

Somehow or other, from the moment I dragged myself into the Angolan Embassy in London to try to get a visa, I just knew I wasn't going to like the place.

Some countries make it easy for you. The best ones, whose names I can't quite recall at the moment, give you a visa there and then. It might involve an additional, how shall I say, service charge, but I'm not complaining. After all, we're always being told to do everything we can to help sub-Saharan Africa.

Others say, come back in four hours when the attaché gets back from lunch or tomorrow morning when the Ambassador is not here or, at worst, the day after tomorrow when we'll have a new government and we'll know to which bank account in Switzerland we have to send the visa money. Unless, of course, they're Russian and it's a Wednesday, because for some reason or other the visa section at the Russian Embassy in London closes on Wednesdays. At first I thought it had something to do with getting their own back because Lenin was delayed at the Finland Station on his way back from Switzerland in March 1917. Then I realised it's because they are so far behind on issuing visas but because they're Russian they think they're so up-to-date, efficient and far ahead of everybody else, they deliberately take the day off so the rest of the world can try to catch up. The Japanese, however, are different again. They insist you collect your visa in person. Which is one hell of a sweat if you live in Land's End or John O'Groats or anywhere in the area covered by Virgin trains. For me it's no problem, as their place is just down the road from my office. Other countries give you a visa at the airport when you arrive. The really sensible ones don't bother with them at all.

The Angolans, though, are in a class of their own. Not only must you fill in a three-page, intensive, in-depth, third-degree interrogation of a form, which demands to know everything about you including your inside leg measurement, but they also want proof that you are who you say you are. In addition you must provide a letter from your boss or whoever also saying you are who you say you are, that you are going to Angola, that you have enough money for your trip, that you have a return ticket and that if anything goes wrong they will immediately pay for anything and everything. As if that's not enough they also want about a thousand passport photographs.

All this information, including a letter from me saying I was who I said I was – at least, I thought I was – that I was going to Angola, that I had enough money for my trip, a return ticket and that if anything went wrong I would immediately pay anything and everything for myself, I piled on to the enormous counter in the visa department just below their friendly little sign telling me in no uncertain terms to turn my mobile telephone off or else.

'Don't put them there,' barked this bureaucratic harpy of all bureaucratic harpies in a Hermès scarf as she swept them on to the floor. 'I need this space for my documents.'

For a moment I did think of mounting a counter-attack but in the end, swallowing hard and switching into my best what's-the-point-in-arguing-this-is-Africa mood, I gathered everything together as best I could.

'Where's your itinerary?' the friendly harpy behind the counter snapped at me.

'What do you mean itinerary? Nobody said anything about—'

'You must have itinerary. If you don't have itinerary, you don't have visa. Those are the regulations.'

'But where does it say anything about—?'

'Those are our regulations. If you want visa you must give us…'

I take out my little pad of paper. I put it on the enormous counter. I start to write.

'Don't put your book on the counter,' she barks again. 'I need space for papers. You must take your book off counter.'

Well. It's not the first time and it obviously won't be the last time I experience the joys of dealing with petty little officials of foreign governments. I take my little pad of paper off their enormous counter which is still bare, bereft, empty of even the tiniest piece of official Angolan paper.

'Come back when you have papers. Don't bother me now.'

The following day, I'm back at the visa department. I hand in my passport, my three-page, intensive, in-depth interrogation form, my letter from myself, my collection of passport photographs. And my itinerary.

'This itinerary is no good!' snaps the harpy.

'What d'you mean, no good?' Somehow I restrain myself from leaping across the counter and throttling her with today's Hermès scarf.

'You said you wanted my itinerary. That's my itinerary.'

'But how do I know it's your itinerary?'

'Because it's mine. It ties in with the dates on the forms. And I'm telling you it's—'

'But it doesn't have your name on.' The harpy grins at me.

'But why does it need my name on, if it's mine?'

'It must have name on. Those are our rules.'

'But' – a gentle sigh – 'you never said the itinerary had

to have my name on. You said you had to have my itinerary. That's my itinerary. You didn't say anything about—'

'Those are the rules. If you don't obey the rules, you won't get visa.'

'Okay,' I say, trying to keep calm. 'Give me back the itinerary and I'll write my name on it.'

'That's not allowed.'

'Why not? You said the itinerary must have my name on it. If I write my name on it, then it's got my name on it, hasn't it?'

'But how do I know it is you?'

'How do you...!!' Keep calm. Keep calm. Deep breath. 'Because it *is* me. You have my passport. You have my photographs. You have a letter from me saying I am who I say I am. You have everything else. How can it not be me?'

'Those are our rules. If you want visa, itinerary must have your name on.'

So back to the office I go again. I type my name on the top of my itinerary. The following day I'm back at the visa department.

'Itinerary,' I say slowly. Taking a deep breath between each word, I continue, 'with my name on. For visa, okay?'

The harpy takes it. Doesn't look at me. Doesn't say a word.

'Okay?' I say again. 'For visa. Itinerary. With name on.' No acknowledgement, nothing.

'So how long does it take,' deep breath, 'to get the visa?' She looks at me.

'Three weeks.'

'Three weeks! How can it take three weeks?' I can't help exploding. 'That's crazy. I can't leave my passport here for three weeks. It's a nonsense. Is there an express service?'

'Yes.'

'How quick is the express service?'

'Ten days.'

'Ten days?' Now I'm going bananas. 'How can it take ten days? All you've got to do is stamp . . .'

'Ten *working* days.'

'Ten working days. That's two weeks! That's absurd.'

'Those are the rules. If you don't follow the rules, you don't get visa.'

What can I do? Precisely n-o-t-h-i-n-g. Zilch. Zero. I say goodbye to my passport, hand over a staggering £35 for the privilege of having them thump a rubber stamp on a piece of paper and storm back to the office, steam coming out of my ears. I mean here we have one of the poorest, most desolate, most godforsaken countries in the world, where even the mosquitoes have AIDS. So where is their embassy based? Park Lane. One of the most expensive streets in the world. Instead of taking money off me, why don't they sell the building and give everything to the poor and hungry and destitute back home? Then there is all the staff: the Ambassador, a couple of diplomats, clerks, secretaries, the old harpy who runs the visa office and all her Hermès scarves. All they need is a tiny office or, better still, a consul, who would do the job as well if not better. Which, let's face it, would not be difficult. It would also make a lot of children very happy, not to mention a couple of dozen aid organisations who are desperately scratching around trying to raise money for the Angolans when all along they must be sitting on a fair chunk of expensive real estate – not only in the UK but probably throughout the world as well.

Ten days – ten *working* days – later, I'm back at the embassy.

'See,' says the harpy, flaunting yet another Hermès scarf. 'If you follow the rules, you get your visa.'

Follow the rules, nonsense. When I filled in their intensive, in-depth, three-page interrogation form and came to the bit asking me for my profession, I put Housewife. So much for their rules.

'Thank you,' I said. And deliberately switched on my mobile phone there and then, just to spite her.

Angola visa service rating: minus 6,752, ten days and a shredded Hermès scarf.

I go to check in at the Sabena desk at Heathrow. All the Belgians have left. Instead it's being run by Aer Lingus. The Irish managing a Belgian operation. Oh well, it could be worse. It could be the Belgians running an Aer Lingus operation.

I'm queuing to go through passport control. This guy behind me asks me where I'm going. I tell him.

'And you're going by Sabena?' He's laughing away to himself. 'What, direct to Luanda?'

'Sure. Via Kinshasa.'

By now he's howling like a hyena.

'And how much did it cost you?'

I tell him. It's part of a package. This travel agent who knows Africa inside out told me it was the best possible route.

Now he's practically rolling around on the floor.

'You're crazy!' He begins to sob, tears running down his face. 'I'm going to Luanda also. But I'm flying direct to Johannesburg. Then back up to Luanda. It's South African Airlines. It's quicker. And,' he draws a deep breath, 'it's £700 cheaper.'

Does that cheer me up? Like hell it does. It's yet another minus, but this time a big £700 minus against Angola.

The flight out was okay, but try as I might there was no way I could put away an extra £700 worth of food and drink. In fact, it was touch and go whether I'd be able to put away £7 worth of food and drink. Sabena is not the most generous of airlines at the best of times, but on this occasion they were positively, well, Belgian.

Angola flight rating: minus a whopping £700 for starters.

*

We land. The health check is as strict and as thorough and as effective as any health check anywhere in the world. Some scruffy guy in a white coat stamps the back of my disembarkation card without even looking at it, let alone at my British Airways health passport which is positively festering with details of every tetanus, polio, typhoid, hepatitis and yellow fever jab I've had over the last fifty years. As if that's not bad enough, he is not only wearing a white coat that would be the dream of every bacteriologist and microbiologist in the world, but he has got it on back to front.

Angola health check rating: minus ten rounds of dysentery and a touch of bubonic plague, plus a greasy white coat.

We land. I queue up for three days to get through passport control. There's no way it needs to take so long. Hasn't Angola got millions of people without jobs, living desperate lives, struggling even to survive? Why don't they recruit some of them and make them immigration officers?

Angola hasn't got any money even to pay the wages and salaries of their present full-time immigration officers, so not paying the wages and salaries of a few more is neither here nor there. Anyway, with over 40 per cent of the country outside government control, with private armies roaming around at will, with a totally unprotected frontier of thousands of miles, and with government reserves being looted left, right and centre, what possible point is there in subjecting anyone to a long, boring, totally useless security check at the airport? If anybody wants to do anything illegal anywhere in Angola, are they going to fly in on a scheduled flight?

And what penetrating, searching, in-depth questions do they finally subject me to, in order to try to make me admit I'm an undercover agent intent on trying to destroy in a couple of weeks the country which they themselves have been tearing apart for practically thirty years? I look at my disembarkation card. They want to know my 'Organism of Contact'.

Angola passport control rating: minus two containers of AK-47s and a cup of coffee for Carlos the Jackal.

I collect my suitcase. I amble up to the customs desk, expecting things to get even worse. Are they going to make me unpack everything? Are they going to take me apart? But I needn't have worried. I sailed straight through without the slightest delay. Not even a single question. Partly because the place was empty. As soon as I started to walk towards them, suddenly all the customs officials turned as one and rushed out of the building.

When I got outside, I realised it was nothing personal. They had completely surrounded this poor woman and were literally kicking and beating her to the ground. I asked some guy standing by watching if this was a traditional Angolan welcome home. No, he said, it was very unusual. They usually shoot people. A few weeks earlier a guard with an AK-47 had pumped the entire twenty-seven bullets in the magazine into some colonel who was slow at producing his identity card.

It was, I discovered later, Women's Day and a public holiday throughout the sixty per cent of the country controlled by the government. All I can assume, therefore, is that it was all part of their traditional way of celebrating the role of women in Angolan society.

Angolan beating up women rating: plus 12 army boots, a couple of rifle butts and a string of broken ribs.

Angola should be one of the richest and most success-ful countries in Africa if not the world. It has everything: enormous oil reserves, the second largest in the whole of Africa. Massive diamond deposits, the fourth largest in the world. It also has gold, copper, platinum, quartz, phosphates, manganese, marble and a long list of industrial minerals. Not to mention beautiful, lush, green countryside, especially in the east, which at one time made it the third largest coffee producer in the world. But the Angolans have blown it all in the longest, cruellest, most savage and senseless civil war in the whole of Africa. For more than 35 years they've inflicted on each other an unbelievable wave of murder, mayhem and out-and-out destruction which for sheer horror and brutality can only be compared to that waged by the Khmer Rouge in Cambodia.

People, probably half a million of them, have died not only from their injuries and wounds but from mutilation and starvation as well. The result is the country is littered with burial places. Many people were buried where they died: in backyards, in alleyways, in open ground. Hundreds of thousands of innocent people, trapped helplessly in the war between the two sides, were forced to eat dogs, cockroaches, even rats, to survive. And as if that is not more than enough for any country to suffer, it now has the most horribly mutilated population, the *mutilados*, the world has ever seen. At least 40 per cent of the population have lost one limb or another. That is the highest percentage of amputees in any country anywhere in the world, and it is going to get worse because there are supposed to be more than 20 million explosives or landmines still left buried in the country. These range from the smallest, an Elsie, which weighs two kilos and can take your foot off, up to the big daddy of them all, the Bar mine, which weighs 300 kilos and can destroy practically a whole town. That's more than enough to kill every Angolan at least twice over.

Against such an appalling background it hardly seems worth mentioning that the whole country is still suffering from almost total annihilation as well as almost complete economic and administrative collapse.

The currency is worthless. A university professor earns
£15.70 a month, a teacher, £1.70, and a nurse just 70p.
Schools and universities are crumbling into the dust.
What health service there was collapsed years ago.
Maternal mortality has nearly doubled since the late
1980s. Under-five-year-olds die at the rate of a hundred a
day. Angola has also seen the most unbelievable displace-
ment of people the continent has ever experienced.

But not all is doom and gloom. Inflation is now a
manageable 1,000 per cent. Well, fair's fair, it was 12,000
per cent.

The whole problem began way back in the 1960s. A
whole bunch of insane Angolan initials, MPLA, UPNA
and FNLA, not only started fighting the Portuguese but
they also started fighting each other. Some initials
disappeared. Other new initials, particularly UNITA, the
National Union for the Total Independence of Angola,
appeared. The result, to put it simply, is that between the
lot of them they destroyed the country.

Some people blame the Portuguese. They say that
they didn't prepare the Angolans for independence,
they just quit. Although, to be fair, they did turn the bath
taps off before leaving unlike next door in Zaire where
the Belgians just left them running.

Others blame the Angolans for fighting amongst
themselves. They say that they should have solved their
differences at the start, formed a united front, stuck with
it and turned the country into what it should be today,
one of the leading economic powers in Africa, if not the
world.

The majority, however, although frightened to say so
in public, blame one man: Jonas Savimbi. The son of a
station master from the north of the country, he trained
as a medical man in Lisbon and later Lausanne, and over
the last thirty years has done nothing but keep his old
profession more than fully occupied. First he claimed
most of the other initials were Communists and in the
pay of Moscow, which of course they were. In order to

protect his country, he didn't just go right wing, he went as right wing as anyone could possibly go. A transitional government was established, made up of all three nationalist sets of initials together with Portugal. But the whole thing fell apart and the country was plunged into what has turned out to be the longest civil war in African history.

Why people huddle into their bullet-proof jackets and claim, or rather whisper, that Savimbi is responsible, is because not only did he seize 40 per cent of the country for himself, grab all the valuable diamond mines which are supposed to yield over US$500 million a year, and wage one of the most ruthless wars the world has ever had the misfortune to experience, but because he never accepts defeat. Again and again he's been defeated. Again and again he's refused to accept it. Once he stood for election as president of not only his 40 per cent of the country but the remaining 60 per cent as well. He was defeated. But he refused to accept the vote. Again and again he is invited to peace conferences. Again and again he accepts. But again and again he refuses to turn up. Savimbi even agreed to join a power-sharing government of national unity. But then he refused to attend the swearing-in of the new government.

The result is that today Angola's capital, Luanda, is Dodge City, Chicago, New York, Belfast at the height of the troubles and Manchester Moss Side all rolled into one. The old, once graceful city of ochre-painted villas, wrought-iron balconies, violets, jacaranda trees, huge trellises of bougainvillaea and streets paved with mosaics – once it was known as the Rio de Janeiro of Africa – is no more. It is a complete and utter disaster area. The streets are like those of any poor, desperate, struggling Third World country: full of rubbish and chock-a-block with big, shiny, gleaming brand new Mercedes and every 4x4 you can think of. With one big difference: the piles of rubbish are not just piles but huge mountains.

Many buildings are falling to pieces. Apart, that is, from the Central Bank, which is beautifully painted, beautifully furnished and in beautiful condition: yet another sign of a poor, desperate, struggling Third World country. Offices have no floors, no wall coverings, no facilities. Ministries are the same, if not worse. One civil servant's office I visited looked like the inside of a freezer – after a week-long power cut.

Roads are nothing but potholes, huge stretches of sand and enormous black, slimy puddles that even Vasco da Gama would have thought twice about crossing. The electricity is about as reliable as a politician's promise. My razor went on and off so frequently one morning I now know where designer stubble was invented. I was told the power was off completely for two whole weeks once because somebody ran into one of the pylons on the outskirts of town and it took that long for it to be repaired.

The water, when it's working, which is about twice a week, is so contaminated that even a drop of it in your mouth while you're taking a shower will give you the runs for a fortnight. Take in two drops and you might just as well donate your body to science: it would make a lot of bacteriologists very happy. Even supposing you could find an undertaker to handle it.

As for telephones, they don't even think of working. Everyone spends all day long hollering 'Papa, Papa. Come in Papa,' into their two-way radios. Things are so bad it's difficult to tell where the city comes to an end and the *musseques*, the vast shanty towns surrounding the place, actually begin.

And if all that is not enough to contend with, violence and corruption are everywhere. Believe me, a knock on the door of your hotel room at five o'clock in the morning is definitely not room service. Poke your head outside the main door of your hotel and you're likely to get it shot off. Even think of racing down the steps to your car and you'll be cut up into little bits and fed to the crocodiles. There are so many guns every-where that Angola is like one huge, living, breathing weapons dump. And I don't just mean small stuff, I mean the big stuff.

Go out at night and you risk the joys of an AK-47 barrel being pushed by some armed *bandido* through the window of your car, whether it's open or not. Alternatively you could find yourself riveted to the spot unable to intervene as gangs of kids actually stone old people to death in full view of police and passers-by who stand and watch, doing nothing. Try to do something about it and you'll end up on television looking as though you've either accidentally fallen downstairs in some police headquarters or had the once over from Kate Adie. Only one thing is worse: bumping into your local neighbourhood death squad.

In the countryside it's even worse, if that is possible. Gangs of armed men can suddenly swoop down on schools, houses, even hospitals, killing everyone and everything in sight. The worst attack I heard about was in Benguela Province down in the south-west when over six hundred armed men attacked a Catholic mission taking six nuns hostage, killing thirty people and forcing more than two thousand others to flee their homes in the surrounding area.

Corruption is everywhere. Which is probably not surprising when you realise a policeman earns or rather gets US$5 a month, yes a month – if they're paid, that is – and hotel maids come sneaking into your room begging not for money but for a can of Coke from the mini-bar for the family to share (I'm not kidding, to share) for their one and only meal of the day. With the average wage around US$50 to $100 a month and managers earning maybe US$500 to $1,000 I'm convinced that without corruption the place wouldn't function at all.

First, there's the big one: the oil revenues which total over US$3.5 billion a year, practically 95 per cent of their exports. Somewhere between the oil company, the

Central Bank and the Ministry of Finance there is an enormous black hole that even the International Monetary fund has been unable to detect. Nobody knows how much has disappeared, or if they do they're not saying. All I know is that the governor of the Central Bank has been changed four times in three years and still it's going on.

If, however, you prefer your corruption on a smaller scale I can recommend nothing better than sitting in the sixth-floor restaurant of the Meridien Hotel, paying practically US$100 for a cold buffet lunch with a can of Coca-Cola (a bottle of wine would make it US$200) watching gangs swarming all over the port below, looting container after container, loading everything on to the backs of open-top lorries, driving through the port gates waving at the police and then throwing the boxes off one by one to the women lining the streets outside.

'What are they taking?' I asked one of the waiters.

'You'll soon know,' he grinned. 'They'll be selling it outside when you leave.'

Sure enough they were. But as I didn't need any car polish or sprays or fillers I didn't bother.

The problem is that you can get used to anything. When you first arrive you're too scared even to think of going round the corner from the hotel to Pintos, the most expensive restaurant in town – what am I saying, in town? It's the most expensive restaurant in the whole country. There everything is lush, lush, lush and the shock of the bill at the end of the evening is like a bullet through the heart. Yet after a few days, the gunfire, the rattle of AK-47s, even the armed guards at the door of the hotel counting everybody out and everybody back in again, don't seem to make any difference. At least, not to me.

By the morning of the second day I was happily wandering around town on foot, mooching up and down the back streets checking out the cathedral, willingly paying the police whatever they wanted and, on the basis that you can't help everyone, dropping one or two of my favourite *mutilados* the occasional US$5 bill. Then at night I was off having drinks in the Ponta Final, at the top of the Ihla peninsula, where during the war everyone used to complain that they couldn't hear themselves complaining about the champagne not being properly chilled for all the MIGs flying backwards and forwards on bombing raids into the interior; having dinner at Number 8, a Vietnamese restaurant in a garage once owned by a Brit with a reputation for smoking cigarettes under water at embassy parties; and, God help me, ending up by climbing six flights of stairs in the pitch black to the Mira Mortis, the only bar in town with a view. The drawback was the view was of the local cemetery. Now I've been forced to go to one or two bars in my time but this place was unbelievable. First of all because of where it was: as I said, on the top of a six-storey building overlooking a cemetery. Second, because we were in a country wracked by thirty years of civil war, crippled by unbelievable destitution and poverty and where forty per cent of the population are missing one limb or another. Inside it was a cross between Studio 54 and, I suppose, the Hungry Duck in Moscow. It was packed. In fact, it was so packed many people couldn't help but be on top of one another. It was expensive, so expensive you didn't dare think of what even the empties could pay for. It was also unbelievably hot. Like being inside some hot, sticky, throbbing stew. It was also the kind of place where nobody goes home alone. A South African guy who said he was working with Savimbi drove me back to my hotel. He insisted. He said the streets weren't safe at that time of night. Which I assumed he should know something about.

It turned out that he was one of Savimbi's bomb disposal experts. He was taking home US$250,000 a year. In cash.

'So how dangerous is being a bomb disposal expert?' I

slurred, as he swung his 4×4 down the hill back towards town.

'Not as dangerous as being in the infantry,' he grinned. 'With bomb disposals you know where the danger is, you can concentrate on it. With the infantry, the danger is everywhere. There's also no way you can control the risk.'

'So why do bomb disposal guys have this reputation?'

'Image. It's also a much better life than the infantry. No uniforms, no ranks, no square-bashing. If something looks dangerous, we just send in the robots.'

'But there must be some danger, otherwise—'

He swung along the waterfront.

'Sure, but only where the bomb is inaccessible.'

'Like hidden somewhere in a building?'

'No, like in a plane. We once had to get on board a plane, find the bomb, retrieve it, then take it away and dispose of it. That was terrifying, I can tell you.'

'So how do you actually defuse a bomb?'

'Water. It's the best disabling agent there is.'

'So how do you get the water inside the bomb?'

'There are ways. You can force a jet of water through most things. You can force it into a bomb.'

'Without it going off?'

'Without it going off.' He paused. 'Hopefully.'

He went on to tell me that after he quit the army he couldn't adjust to life without bombs. They were in his blood.

'I kept setting fire crackers off everywhere. On the drawer of my desk. On the door to the office. On the boss's desk. In the end I had to leave. I couldn't live without it. It gets you. It's also a good life. Providing you survive.'

The doorman counted me back in again. I was safe.

But please don't feel sorry for me. Search hard enough and even Luanda has its little luxuries. Like sugar and oil and soap, which only the very rich can afford. For believe it or not, with people spending their lives doing nothing but picking over piles of rubbish that have been picked over a thousand times before, Luanda is one of the most expensive cities in the world in which to live or, I suppose, die. And I'm not talking about going to the Mira Mortis once a week.

Go mad. Treat yourself to a simple steak and chips and a can of cola in a not too terribly expensive restaurant and it'll cost you US$50. Force yourself to have an ordinary cheap bottle of Portuguese vinho verde, nothing extravagant, and it will cost you another US$15 to $20.

But if that was a shock, day one of my trip produced the greatest shock of all. Just as it is getting light I come to with a start. There are either dustbins being rolled down the stairs of the hotel or there's a raging gunfight outside. I prefer to think it's dustbins. By eight o'clock I'm downstairs outside the hotel. I'm rarin' to go. I've got a string of people to see. Then I discover the startling, unbelievable, shocking truth. No taxis. Luanda is the only capital city in the world without a taxi service.

Angola welcome mat for visitors rating: shot full of holes.

Day two. I've got myself organised. I've got a car and a driver and an interpreter, a young guy who wants nothing whatsoever to do with politics. Politicians, he says, you can't trust. They twist words. They say things they don't mean. They are not interested in people. All they are interested in is making money. Instead, would you believe, he wants to be a lawyer.

So I begin my calls. Very quickly, I'm pleased to say, I feel at home. Companies I was told to visit do not exist. Factories that are supposed to be in full production closed down years ago. People are not in their offices when they said they were going to be. Meetings are cancelled. Interviews are postponed. Reports and documents that should be waiting to be collected are not there.

I go to one office off a side street off a side street

round the back of the National Bank building. You must know it. It's the one with the two wrecked cars and the pile of rubbish outside. No, wait a minute, that could be any one of a thousand buildings in Luanda. Okay, it's the one opposite the video shop which doesn't have any electricity. The guy said to be there at nine o'clock sharp. In spite of all the dead bodies blocking the door of the hotel, the driver being late because of three new roadblocks on the way in from Viana and the interpreter having to visit the French Embassy to collect some more work, I'm there at nine o'clock. On the dot. But nobody else is there. I wait and wait and wait and wait. At eleven o'clock I have to go. But because the guy said it was important I call in again three or four times during the day. Still nobody. No message. Nothing. Two days later I get a note from him saying that as I wasn't interested in meeting him he would now contact somebody else.

Because of all the running around and the cost of running practically a private office, I run out of money quicker than usual. No. It's got nothing to do with buying all those drinks at the Mira Mortis. Wash your mouth out with Pisco Sours. As a result, all I've got left are a couple of credit cards, about £17.53 in cash, a Malaysian one ringgit note, 100 colónes from Costa Rica and 50 Czech korunas. I go to the hotel reception. The girl changes US$100 travellers' cheques for US$100 cash. No problem. She can't change any more she says because she doesn't have any more dollars. If I want to change any more money I should go to the bank, any bank. Fantastic, I thought. Maybe I've misjudged it, maybe this place isn't so bad after all. So that's precisely what I did, except it took me four banks to do it. First they didn't want to know. Then they wouldn't accept travellers' cheques. Then they wouldn't accept dollars. Then they thought the travellers' cheques were forged. Then they wanted to see my passport. Then they couldn't read my visa. Then there was something wrong with my disembarkation card. Then I had to see a sub, sub, sub manager. Then a sub, sub manager. Then a sub manager. Then the big boss, Mr Luis George, himself. Mr George invited me into his office, checked and re-checked everything all over again: the travellers' cheques, my passport, my visa, my disembarkation card, my collar size, the size of my shoes, my pulse. Eventually the big decision came. *Sí.* But hang on. That wasn't the end of it. He then called his sub manager who passed everything on to the sub, sub manager who passed everything on to the sub, sub, sub manager who dumped the whole lot on some girl's desk in the general office and disappeared into thin air. The girl, of course, ignored the whole thing and carried on chatting to the girl at the desk next to her about, no doubt, the relative merits of the finalists in the forthcoming Mr Luanda competition.

I waited. She carried on chatting.

I waited. Still she carried on chatting.

I coughed. Only quietly. Long experience of Africa and all that. Still she carried on chatting.

A louder cough. A still louder cough. A touch of the bronchitis and double pneumonia. Only when I was rolling around the floor in an advanced state of triple pneumonia did she look up and even notice my presence. But credit where credit is due, once she saw how desperate I was to be paid, she immediately leapt up and disappeared out of the door at the back of the general office. Three days later she ambled back in with another girl who proceeded to fill out masses more forms, laboriously shaping each letter with the precision of someone dismantling a landmine and taking a good, I'm not kidding, ten to fifteen minutes in the process. When I finally collected my money I noticed good ole Mr Luis George had deducted practically ten per cent in commission. For service.

Did I complain? What do you think?

Angolan travellers' cheque interest rating: stratospheric.

*

During the night there is a full-scale gun battle outside the hotel. One of the guards tells me there are a lot of dead bodies lying around. I hadn't heard a thing. I'd been reading a DTI briefing on the place and had obviously fallen into a deep coma. Over breakfast – cognacs and coffee – a group of French businessmen told me they were keeping a count of the number of dead bodies they had spotted since they arrived. After just a week, they were already up to 13. Which I must admit surprised me. I'd have thought it would have been at least 113.

All the time squads of police are driving round and round the streets in open trucks, guns at the ready. Security guards are everywhere with their guns, pistols and even the occasional Israeli-made Uzi at the ready. Practically everybody I met had a gun, an AK-47, the more modern, more advanced AK-74, or even a machine-gun either on them or tucked away in the car.

'So how often do you use it?' I asked this civilised, Portuguese-looking guy with thick glasses, a bundle of files under his arm and some kind of Spanish- or Brazilian-made pistol stuck into his belt.

'Quite often.'

'How often is quite often? Once a week? Once a fortnight?'

'Oh no,' he said. 'More like once an evening. I use it to shoot at the trouble going on in the street.'

'What, you mean people being attacked?'

'Just trouble.'

'What kind of trouble?'

'Just trouble.'

If you go to a reception, or meet someone for a drink, the talk is always about who's been shot, how badly and God, the odds are shortening all the time, maybe I should take a spot of leave.

'Watch out between six-thirty and nine o'clock in the evening,' one security guard, an ex-Gurkha from Hong

Kong told me. 'That's when you tend to get the car-jackings, just as people are going home.'

'So what about muggings, shootings, hi-jacking. Is there a special time of day for them as well?'

'No,' he grinned. 'That goes on all the time. By the way, have you heard a security guard at the Swedish Embassy got shot in the back the other day? Also one of the Irish aid workers got badly attacked last night. He was on his way home from the Mira Mortis. He was lucky to escape with his life.'

Angolan marksmanship rating: bullseye.

Outside Luanda, with maybe the possible exception of Lubango, which I'm told somehow miraculously escaped the ravages of the war and is today still a beautifully preserved, untouched, unspoilt throw-back to the days of the Portuguese in Africa, there is nothing. But nothing. Roads are nothing but potholes overgrown with bush and elephant grass. What towns there are, are smashed to pieces. Street names, signs and the occasional war memorial are riddled with bullets and machine-gunfire. There are no schools. What hospitals there are don't even have the diesel to operate their generators. If they need the generators for an operation, the patient or the patient's family have to find the diesel or it's no go. Similarly, I was told, with blood. If a patient needs blood, the family must provide it or find somebody to provide it or that's it. In some parts of the country people who survived the ravages of war now face raging epidemics of such things as leprosy, sleeping sickness, tuberculosis and every other horror you can think of. It's no wonder they say the dead are the lucky ones.

I tried to get up to Kuito, which for two years stood between the two opposing sides. It was, I was told, the end of the world. The whole place had been practically levelled. More than thirty thousand people had died there. Nowhere on earth had so many people been maimed and mutilated first by the siege itself then by the thousands upon thousands of mines both sides left behind as they retreated. But nobody would take me. I even tried to hitch a lift with some diamond guy who had his own private plane. But no go.

Instead, in between meetings, I made do with forays outside Luanda. All I can say is, if the rest of the country is worse than the conditions I saw around Luanda they've got even bigger problems than anyone could possibly imagine.

There is no housing, or at least no decent housing. No roads, or at least nothing without a pothole the size of a swimming pool every hundred metres. Markets are few and far between. What markets there are, are pathetic: hundreds of people just sitting around trying to sell almost nothing to people who have less than nothing to spend. Factory after factory after factory has closed down, is falling down, or rotting into the ground. The two local breweries are, of course, still working. So too is the cigarette plant, the milk plant and the cement works, a factory making ice for the hotels and the oil refinery. Practically everything else, a paint factory, an engineering works, a textile plant and warehouse after warehouse after warehouse all closed long ago.

'When did they close?' I asked one guy sitting outside what used to be the big Lada plant overlooking the bay.

'Before I was born,' he replied. 'For me they have always been like this.'

But that doesn't mean there's no industrial activity. Judging by what I saw, the Angolans are the best, most efficient, most sophisticated industrial vultures in the world. A car or a van or better still a coach or a truck has only got to break down and - zap - they're all over it immediately, stripping the thing literally to bits. Here the Angolans are in a class of their own. The country may be littered with wrecks, but they are the cleanest wrecks you can imagine. First, go tyres. Then the wheels. Next, it's the whole of the interior: radios, seats, steering wheel. Even the ashtray. Finally, everything else: the doors, the windows, the battery, even tiny clips and springs and bits of wire. How do I know? Because as they pick the thing clean they display everything out by the side of the road in order to sell on whatever they can to passing motorists who are desperate for cheap spare parts. And people buy everything, even the bumpers, which they use for fencing posts around their shacks and huts and houses.

They are, I am sorry to say, experts at first creating huge mountains of rubbish and then constantly picking over them for anything that might be of value. They are also good, I noticed, at waiting for the next load to arrive so they can have first refusal of other people's throw-outs. Just outside Viana, which was once a thriving industrial sector, I saw a whole gang of guys busy dismantling a complete electricity pylon. Not that it was complete for long. I tried to ask one guy where they had got it from. I was particularly interested because the previous evening the lights in the hotel were flickering on and off like a Christmas tree. I wondered if somehow the two events could be linked. But by the time I'd got him to understand what I was talking about, the thing had disappeared and everybody else as well. He didn't seem to want to hang around chatting either so I never did find out.

The police and the military are everywhere. All along the so-called main streets, in the villages, even way out in the bush. Sometimes they are just wandering up and down doing their duty: stopping people and demanding money. Other times, they are huddled up fast asleep under a tree. On two or three occasions I stumbled across enormous barracks completely surrounded by a solid wall of huge, 40-foot containers piled one on top of another all round the edge.

'For protection,' one policeman told me.

'Whose?' I asked.

But he didn't say a word. Just as well, I discovered

later, because there was a big prison just down the road.

I also saw *mutilados* everywhere, although there are not supposed to be anywhere near as many landmines in and around Luanda as there are in other parts of the country, particularly up in the north. Most of them were teenagers and young people, hobbling across roads, begging or just sitting there doing nothing. I did see one kid, maybe about five or six, rummaging around on a rubbish dump, with a pair of rough and ready obviously home-made crutches. So maybe the statistics are even worse than we think.

Yet the crazy thing is, deep in the soil below the piles of rubbish, are not only the world's richest diamond reserves but probably, according to the experts, some of the best diamonds the world has ever seen. Catoca, for example, is the biggest diamond-producing area in the world. Estimates vary but some people say that every year Angola ships out, or rather flies out, diamonds worth more than US$300 million in tiny little bags in large Russian cargo planes across the border into Zaire and then on to the dungeons and cellars round the back of the railway station in Antwerp, the diamond trading capital of the world, before the stones end up goodness knows where. Others say that the Cuango Valley alone is capable of producing diamonds worth maybe US$20 million a month. And that's only half the country's production. The trouble is, it's all outside the government's control, in the hands of the rebels.

The Angolans also had to deal with something equally sparkling, equally attractive and equally tough: Lady Di, who, of course, dragged herself out of purdah in Kensington Palace to launch her anti-landmine campaign in Luanda. I was there shortly after what was known as her 'charidee visit'. It was interesting to hear the comments, to say the least.

Nobody denied it was the most heavily mined country in the world. There are mines in every hedgerow. By the side of the road. In the middle of a path. Underneath a clump of green corn. In the corner of any building. Underneath that stone over there. Everybody, it seems, who has had anything to do with Angola has littered the place with them. The Portuguese used them to suppress the early wars of independence. After independence the MPLA, backed by the Cubans, as well as troops from Guinea and Guinea-Bissau, used them against the FNLA. UNITA used them against the MPLA and the MPLA against UNITA. And not just Russian or American mines, either: apparently so far mines from over thirty different countries including Portugal, France, the Czech Republic and South Africa have been discovered. But not so far from Britain, which has caused a great deal of, how shall I say, interest in the Ministry of Defence as well as in the arms industry itself.

Nobody denies the plight of the *mutilados*, especially the children who have been horribly maimed, mutilated and crippled by the mines. Talk to anybody, a guy at the bar in the hotel, a driver, a local businessman, somebody in the queue at the bank, a civil servant, even hard-working heavily sunburnt officials at the British Embassy, and they all know somebody who has been blown up by a mine, both in areas that have been cleared as well as areas that have not been cleared.

'It's unbelievable. They are everywhere. Just yester-day a relative of one of the women who works in the office, a young boy, was blown up in an area that was supposed to have been cleared. Lost both legs. Only ten,' one official in the Ministry of Finance told me.

'But if they've cleared the area…'

'The trouble is you never know whether an area has been really cleared until it's too late.'

Because there are so many mines over such a vast area, inevitably everybody is looking for faster and faster ways of clearing them.

'Look, some people are using so-called electronic systems. Others are using dogs. The only way of making one hundred per cent certain that there are no mines under the ground is to keep prodding the whole area with little sticks. That takes time. Time is something we don't have. Inevitably there are going to be accidents,' the official added.

Driving around Luanda, you can see people are cautious. Nobody swings too far off the road. Out in the bush you always travel in the centre of the road; overtaking is something everybody avoids if it means going anywhere near the edge. Coming up to junctions and crossroads everybody stops talking and practically crosses their fingers. And the problem is not going to go away: most people I spoke to agree that at the present rate of progress, it's going to take a hundred, maybe even a hundred and fifty years before the place is totally clear of mines – apart from the odd one or two which are inevitably going to slip through. In the meantime the poor, sick and destitute continue to be maimed and die horrible, agonising deaths while the rich buy all the big 4×4s they can. Why are they so big? Because they're not only bullet-proof they've got bomb-proof protection underneath as well.

'So what about Lady Di and her walk through the minefield?' I asked one official at the British Embassy. 'Did it help? Did it make matters worse?'

'It helped. It highlighted the problem,' he said, very quickly adding, 'but it was a private visit. It was nothing to do with us. It was all organised by the Red Cross.'

'But I thought she stayed at the British Embassy.'

'Did I tell you that David Livingstone stayed at the Embassy once? He walked all the way here from South Africa. See that jasmine tree in the corner there? That's where he used to sit and write up his notes. Then afterwards he went on to discover the Victoria Falls.'

'But Lady Di … Private visit … why should the tax-payer … not that I mind myself.'

'Another drink, old chap? I'm going to have a gin and tonic myself.'

To me, I'm afraid, the Royal visit smacked too much of a publicity stunt. If you or I went to Angola for the Red Cross, and if we were really serious about helping these poor kids who had their arms or legs blown off, and we had £18 million stashed away in the bank, what would we do? We'd either stay and help; bring some of the kids back with us to at least try to give them a decent life, or, better still, give them a straight £1 million to help the Red Cross do things properly. After all, with £18 million in the bank earning at least 30 per cent a year, the minimum you should get with a decent fund manager, £1 million, is neither here nor there. Then why stick to Luanda? Why not go up to Cuito? I know I couldn't, but I'm sure had Princess Di wanted to, she could. She did, after all, have a reputation for getting her own way.

Then why just landmines? What about the anti-personnel cluster bombs that were dropped by the million all over Vietnam and Laos by the Americans? Shouldn't they be banned as well? These, like landmines, can stay hidden for twenty or thirty years until somebody steps on them or drives over them, horribly maiming and killing still more people. I'm sure if you or I were genuinely trying to draw worldwide attention to such horrors we'd be off to Vietnam and Laos launching an equally worldwide campaign against cluster bombs.

The other thing that makes me ever so slightly suspicious is the fact that during the whole time Princess Di was on her 'charidee' visit in Luanda, apart from the couple of hours she spent in front of the cameras, she was holed up in her room at the embassy. Finally, of course, the most telling point of all: landmine clearance has received not a penny from the £85 million Princess of Wales Memorial Fund.

For long-term services to the armaments industry: a used landmine.

Being one of the poorest countries in the world – in fact, Angola is so poor, it has practically fallen off the list of statistics for poor countries – you would have thought it would be desperate for every penny it could get. So where do they put their foreign investment office? Where do staid, sober, cautious, invariably elderly potential investors have to go if they want to discuss investing their money in the country? To the Office of Foreign Investment, of course. In the Ministry of Industry. On the ninth floor. Where there's no lift. Honestly, it makes you wonder if they are doing it on purpose. Would *you* expect these investors to risk life, limb and heart attack by making them huff and puff their way up nine storeys in the broiling heat to discuss the matter? Then when they finally – puff, puff – got there, would you tell them – puff, puff – that you only had one copy of the law on foreign investment and that no, they couldn't have it? Well, that's what happened to me. So could I see the director? Perhaps if I could explain ... 'No.' Could they possibly photocopy it for me? 'No.'

Eventually, however, I managed to persuade the sub, sub, sub director's secretary to let me have their one and only copy so I could go and photocopy it myself and take her back the original copy. Which is what I did, or rather what I tried to do. Bright and early, having resisted the temptation to spend another night drinking at the Mira Mortis, I'm back at the Ministry of Industry with the original copy of the Investment Code. This time they won't even let me in.

A very tall, very thin, security man in a greasy blue uniform with 'Segind' all over it wants to know who do I want to see? Why? Who am I? Who do I represent? Why do I want a meeting? What do I want to discuss? Can I discuss the matter with someone else? Does the meeting have to be today? Could I have the meeting another time?

So what the hell has it got to do with you? I'm

thinking. But all the time I'm the model of politeness. If the security guard would be so kind I would favour a meeting with the lowest possible minion in the whole of the Ministry of Industry. Even the Minister himself. I'm not proud. If he agrees, I would like to discuss the somewhat inconsequential matter of investing in the region of, say, US$100 million in his beautiful, polite and wonderfully considerate country. I, of course, am a nobody. So are the people I represent. The meeting doesn't have to be today. I have all the time in the world. If he would like me to stay until the week after Christmas next year I would be more than pleased to do so if it meets with his wishes. And certainly if it is more convenient for him I would be thrilled to discuss the whole matter with his brother who I am sure could arrange the most flexible package possible for my clients.

His reply: No, push off. We don't want the likes of you in here. So, never one to outstay my welcome, I pushed off. Yet my Calvinist conscience kept nagging at me. I still had the original copy of their Investment Code. I had promised to return it. So return it I must.

The following morning, bright and early, I'm back at the Ministry of Industry. Bright and early because the previous afternoon back at the hotel I actually started reading the Investment Code and I fell into such a deep sleep I didn't come to until around dawn.

This time, there is a short, fat security guard with an expensive watch who keeps coughing and sneezing and spitting all over the place. So security conscious is he that he won't even let me through the door of the Ministry or rather where the door of the Ministry used to be some years ago. Instead, I have to stand on the top of the steps outside.

Again he gives me the traditional Angolan welcome. Who the hell are you? What the hell do you want? No. Nobody's here. Nobody wants to have anything to do with you. Push off.

Again I respond in the traditional oh-so-polite, snivelling, grovelling manner that by now long experience tells me you have to adopt if you want to get anywhere in Angola. I go through the usual rigmarole. If the all-seeing all-gracious all-powerful security guard would be so kind I would favour blah, blah, blah.

'No.'

Never one to shirk a challenge, I now open my briefcase, drag all my files out and launch into my set two-hour presentation on Foreign Investment: Its Role in Helping Developing Countries.

'No.'

I'm just about to pack up and head for the airport when some guy with a tie and a briefcase says something to the security guard and – hey presto – I'm suddenly over the magic boundary. I head for the stairs and the nine-storey climb. But no. Suddenly there is another security man. He wants me to empty my briefcase all over his greasy desk. He wants me to open all my files. He even wants to see the label on the back of my shirt.

I show him everything. But still he's not satisfied. He wants my passport. He wants to keep it in case I'm a dangerous, international criminal intent on forcing money on a poor, defenceless, starving country like Angola. In return he gives me a filthy yellow badge to stick on my jacket pocket. I go to put it on but it's so rusty that the clip falls to pieces. Instead I stuff it in my pocket, turn and begin the nine-storey slog. Now I'm not saying it's a struggle in the boiling eighty-degree heat but halfway up I swear I saw Sherpa Tensing. Come to think of it, it was a bit like climbing Everest: the staircase was about as rubbish-strewn.

On the ninth floor it begins all over again. The girl at reception wants to know, blah blah. I tell her blah, blah, blah which I know impressed her because twice she looked up from cleaning her nails and watching two flies having the time of each other's lives on top of her desk.

'Wait,' she grunted, and wait I did. For practically an hour. Eventually I was ushered into what looked like a store-room with tables and chairs piled haphazardly all over the place. What seemed like three days later, this guy arrives with an open necked shirt and a camera.

I explain blah, blah. I tell him blah, blah. I give him the copy of their absolutely riveting and exciting Investment Code. Yawn. I ask him when they are going to sign their agreement with the International Monetary Fund. He plays with his camera. I ask him if they are going to sign an investment protection agreement with the UK. He is now looking through the viewfinder. I ask him how many companies have invested already in Angola. He thanks me very much for coming and says he has to go to another meeting.

I race back down the stairs, all nine flights of them, grab my passport, wave goodbye to the security guards, leap into my car and head for the nearest bar to celebrate my triumph. I've managed to keep their damned security badge which means they'll be in big trouble when they come to do their security check at the end of the day. If in such a security-conscious country they bother to do such an obvious thing as a security check at the end of the day.

Even more important, I'm the only person alive today with not only one of their precious security badges but also a copy of the Angolan law on foreign investment. If you would like a copy please send a cheque for US$100 made out to the Mira Mortis and I will send you a smudgy photocopy by return.

For doing everything in their power to encourage foreign investors rating: a copy of the 'Invest in Northern Ireland' brochure.

The only part of the country that knows anything about hard work, management, buying and selling, wheeling and dealing and making money is not the government, nor the central bank, nor the state-owned industries, nor even the occasional private company. It is Roque Santeiro, the biggest, filthiest, richest and most dangerous open-air market in the whole of Africa.

Imagine over 200 hectares on a hillside swooping down to the sea, packed literally every single square inch with the most decrepit sheds and shacks and stalls and benches and rickety old tables you can imagine, full to overflowing with people – maybe quarter of a million, maybe even half a million – and you begin to have an idea of what Roque Santeiro is all about. But only an idea. Add in suffocating heat, a stench so foul it makes your eyes water, women offering to provide you with all kinds of services on stained, sweaty blankets for a couple of dollars and the threat of violence, not just punch-up violence but bombs, grenades, guns and machine-gun violence and you're still only part way there.

The day I went there, against I must say the advice of practically the whole of Angola, I'd no sooner arrived than I saw a woman stretched out motionless on the ground. Was she dead? I couldn't tell you. All I know is she was surrounded by a mass of police and a huge crowd shouting and screaming and yelling at each other. The guy I was with, an Angolan, wanted to leave immediately.

'It is dangerous,' he kept saying, practically from the moment we left the hotel.

'We go now. Yes?'

'No,' I kept saying. 'I want to look around.'

After all, this was the real Angola. Hundreds and thousands of desperately poor people buying and selling everything under the sun: shirts, shorts, shoes, dresses, hats, empty plastic bottles, dirty, greasy tins, single lumps of charcoal, rolled-up maps of Angola, strips of useless lengths of metal, lumps of wood, the inside of a cat's stomach. Even diamonds.

Deep in the centre of the market, far away from the

eyes of the police, I was told you could buy not only
every drug you can think of but every type of weapon
as well: guns, grenades, rifles, even machine-guns.
During just my brief visit I saw guns made in Spain and
Brazil; grenades made in America; AK-47s made in
Russia and different parts of Eastern Europe; the equally
famous Israeli-made Uzi machine-guns; and a whole
collection of M-16s, Belgian FNs, Lugers, not so poetic
Brownings, and a whole stack of rocket-propelled
grenades.

'Come. We go now. It is dangerous.'

'No. I want to have a look around.'

As for the people, there were old men and women
who looked as though they had barely five minutes left
to live; hundreds of people with legs and arms and great
chunks of their bodies either missing or swathed in
filthy, fly-covered bandages; kids as thin as nothing at all,
not a stitch of clothing on them, eating, actually eating,
lumps of polystyrene. There was a man, maybe six feet
six inches tall, as thin as a beanpole, his hair sticking out
all over the place, wearing the blackest, slimiest clothes
you can imagine, walking up and down shouting and
screaming at everything in sight. Kids were rolling bits
of tin in the dust and actually fighting over scraps of
cardboard. Dogs as thin and as mangy as they could
possibly be were sniffing around everywhere, including
the stalls selling food. I even saw one man washing a live
lobster in the filthiest puddle of water you can imagine
before throwing it straight into an enormous pot of
boiling water.

'Okay. You see everything. We go now.'

'No. Five minutes. Another five minutes. Then we go.'

Of course it's filthy. Of course it's dangerous. Of
course nobody should be expected to put up with such
conditions. But think for a moment what Roque Santeiro
means. It means that left to themselves, people will
survive. It means that somehow a whole lot of people in
Angola know about buying and selling and collecting

and delivering and re-ordering and restocking. It also means that there is a whole lot of money outside the system. Say quarter of a million people go to the market every day. Say they only spend one or two dollars each. That's still a quarter or half a million dollars a day. Multiply that by seven days a week, fifty-two weeks of the year and we're talking big business for a filthy, God-forsaken patch of dust in the middle of nowhere. Now doesn't that give you hope? It does me. Or at least more hope than I have for the shopkeeper in town I met who was, I kid you not, in temperatures of over 95 degrees and climbing, selling anti-freeze. Suitable for use, the label said, in temperatures down to –38 degrees centigrade.

For offering the best hope to the people of Angola: You decide. Princess Di, the guy selling anti-freeze or the harpy in the Hermès scarf at the embassy?

Victoria Falls

'Dr Livingstone. Missionary. Explorer. Liberator.' That's what it says – honest! – on the plinth of the big bronze statue overlooking Victoria Falls, or to give them their real name, Mosi-oa-Tunya, The Smoke that Thunders.

Well, all I can say is, somebody is kidding somebody, because to me, he was nothing but a three-faced old fraud. And Scottish to boot.

Missionary? He was no more a missionary than I am. Just think about it. If he had really been determined to be a missionary, he would have stayed in South Africa, where he originally went in 1840 as a medical missionary, instead of dropping everything and racing off at a moment's notice across the Kalahari in search of some large lake he had heard people talking about. Or, better still, stayed behind in Blantyre in Lanarkshire, where, it seems to me, even today there are still plenty of people who could do with a little bit of Christian charity. St Paul may have spent his life travelling the world, but at least he stuck to being a missionary. He didn't suddenly rush off to try to find the source of the Dead Sea. But, okay, let's give the good doctor the enormous benefit of a huge doubt. The fact remains that even when he tried to be a missionary he was a complete and utter failure. In the whole of his life he made only one convert – who lapsed after six months. Maybe it had something to do with the fact that learning Latin, Greek and Hebrew is not necessarily the ideal preparation for converting Africans to Christianity.

An explorer? No way. He got everything wrong, including the source of the Nile. John Hanning Speke, a young army officer, said it was Lake Victoria, while Livingstone said it was further south. Speke was right. What Livingstone was talking about was the source of the Upper Congo. Livingstone then said that the Zambezi was navigable. It wasn't. He had completely overlooked the Cabora Bassa gorge, which is not, I am assured, an easy thing to do. Next door in Botswana while he was surveying Lake Ngami in 1849, he even lost the whole range of four Tsodilo Hills, which stretch for practically ten square miles, rise to about a thousand feet in height and contain more than three thousand individual rock paintings. Not one word about them is mentioned in his diaries. It was left to a German geologist to come along fifty years later and discover what our great explorer had missed.

I reckon the only reason Sir Robert Murchison, then President of the Royal Geographical Society, hailed Livingstone as the great explorer and encouraged him so much was to get rid of him. Why else would he have gone out of his way to persuade the government to back him if he didn't want him out of the way? I mean nobody praises anyone the way Murchison praised Livingstone if he actually *likes* him and wants him to stick around. You know what I mean. Compare it with the way the whole board will suddenly turn and start heaping praise on some poor innocent guy just because nobody else wants to go and open a branch office in Mongolia. I would go a stage further. I reckon it was Murchison who arranged for Speke to be shot accidentally on purpose on the grouse moor the day before he was going to present to the British Association for the Advancement of Science his evidence that Lake Victoria was the source of the Nile. Because – you know office politics as well as I do – with Speke out of the way, Murchison calculated that Livingstone, the stubborn Scot, would feel he just had to go back to Africa to find out for himself one way or another. Whereas if he was English and sensible he would have just sat back, saved himself all the fuss and bother and waited for a Norwegian to get there first. Then he would have gone out there and claimed all the glory, not to mention the television rights.

The big irony is that many people now say Livingstone wasn't the first outsider to see the Falls anyway. Some say it was a Portuguese explorer, Antonio da Silvo Porto. Others say it was a Hungarian, Lazlo Magyar. A few even claim an Englishman, James Chapman, got there first – which would be a turn-up for the books.

As for being a liberator, of what? Africa? You're kidding. There's no way Livingstone liberated Africa, let alone a single banana. If anything Africa is worse off today than it was when he arrived and started stomping around. Stories about Livingstone exploring the area simply because he wanted to find an east-west route across Africa in order to kill off the slave trade is nothing but a lot of stuff and nonsense. His objective from the start, he said, was to open up Africa to 'commerce, Christianity and civilisation'. In that order. Not to free Africans from the yoke of slavery. That was the last thing he had on his mind – he depended, especially towards the end of his travels, on Arab slave dealers to provide him with all the poor, struggling, desperate African porters his warm, human, under-standing, Christian charity needed to carry his gear for him.

As for this story about two of his, how shall I say, servants, James Chuma and Abdulla Susi, being so grateful to him that they devoted nine months of their lives to carrying his preserved body back from Chitembo, where he died in 1873, over two thousand miles to the coast so it could be brought back to Britain being a selfless act of true devotion to a great man, forget it. The only reason they did it, I'd say, was first to prove that if you can carry a coffin two thousand miles through the African jungle, all these African expeditions to the great heart of darkness can't be anywhere near as dangerous as those Europeans make out, and second, from experience, they probably knew it was quicker than queuing up day after day outside some British Embassy in the middle of nowhere trying to get an entry visa, let alone permission to take a body back to the UK. James was, after all, a Nigerian. As soon as the body was tucked up in Westminster Abbey, some clever chap at the Home Office checked the Africans out, found they didn't have visas after all and packed them off on the next boat home. So much for British gratitude and hospitality.

To me – I'm sorry but I don't care how strongly you disagree – Livingstone was nothing but a sweaty, toothless, khaki-clad disaster area who insisted on having his cheap, rough-and-ready caps made specially for him by none other than Starkey's of Bond Street. As naturally any poor, God-fearing Christian missionary would do.

Just look at the way he treated his poor wife, Mary. There she was, the young, innocent daughter of a proper missionary, living on the edge of the glorious Kalahari Desert. The great so-called missionary, explorer and liberator drops down on one knee and proposes to her under an almond tree. He's a young man, Scottish, a doctor and a missionary. What kind of life does she expect to lead? Respectable, hard-working, a life dedicated to feeding the hungry, giving drink to the thirsty, clothing the naked, harbouring the harbourless, visiting the sick, visiting the imprisoned and burying the dead. How does she end up? Dragging herself and her children backwards and forwards across Africa. Which, incidentally, means that travelling across Africa was not as rough and tough as Livingstone made out, or if it was, he was out of his mind to insist on taking his wife and children with him. Either way, poor old Mary, who seems to have been pregnant practically the whole of her life, ends up a lonely, pathetic, dishevelled old drunk. And when she died Livingstone didn't even try to send her body home. Instead he had her buried at Shupanga on the banks of the Zambezi. And from that day to this nobody has bothered to see whether a place could be found for her alongside her impossible husband in Westminster Abbey. Not even under his left foot.

Then there were the men who risked their lives, either willingly or unwillingly, to follow him in the wrong direction to the wrong places at the wrong time. Ignore for a moment the incidental fact that all his missions ended in tragedy, and you have to admit he was a lousy leader of men. He was supposed to be against slavery. But if he didn't exactly hire slaves, he treated everyone virtually like slaves and paid them slave wages. Then, like any born leader, if there was any glory going he grabbed it for himself with both hands. What about George Rae, the engineer? When did you ever hear him get any praise? How about Tom Baines, the artist? Did he ever get any glory? And, of course, there was John Kirk (which was about the nearest our great missionary came to a church in years) who, to me, was a marvellous man. He was the expedition's medical officer. He collected all the ethnographic and natural history specimens. He kept the official journal. He painted water colours. He took the photographs. He came to love Africa so much that he even stayed on afterwards finally ending up as the first British vice-consul and then consul-general in Zanzibar. Finally, because Livingstone lacked the power of 'vivid, verbal, description', he had two ghost writers: Horace Waller and his brother, Charles. It was Waller, don't forget, who wrote, oops I mean edited, all Livingstone's journals, threw in quotes from various people and created the image of the saintly explorer. It was brother Charles who wrote the book that made Livingstone a legend,

Narrative of an Expedition to the Zambezi and its Tributaries.

If that's not bad enough, look at what he did to the environment. It is 16 November 1855. Our great missionary, explorer and liberator is in a *kololo* canoe. They are paddling down the mighty Zambezi. They come to an island. They beach the canoes and push forward on foot.

'No one could perceive where the vast body of water went,' he wrote in his diary. (Or Horace Waller or his brother Charles did.) 'It seemed to lose itself in the earth.'

Then there's this enormous roar like thunder. Spray is pouring down on top of them and they are soaked to the skin. Suddenly he drops to his knees. No, not to pray. He is no longer a missionary. Now he's an explorer. He crawls right up to the edge. There it is in front of him.

'The most awesome sight I had witnessed in Africa ... dense white cloud ... two bright rainbows ... myriads of small currents rushing in one direction,' added Horace or brother Charles in his diary.

What did our great missionary, explorer and liberator immediately do to commemorate such an awesome historic sight? He did what anyone would do in the circumstances. He leapt up and promptly carved his initials on the nearest tree. Unless, of course, Horace or brother Charles did that for him as well. The tree has long since disappeared. Or rather, has been liberated.

But it is not just the trees that suffered at the hands of the great man. The animals suffered as well: zebra, giraffe, buffalo, wildebeest, antelope. They've all been turned over by Livingstone. Snakes, especially the large poisonous ones, no longer roam the forests. Instead they've all been recruited by local security companies and used to protect people's homes while they go off on holiday to escape the tourists. Worst hit of all are the elephants. Thanks to the good doctor, one of their traditional routes has been destroyed forever. Before Livingstone arrived on the scene they could wander around at leisure munching practically half a rainforest a day and making snide remarks about David Attenborough. Now, because of all the tourists and tourist buses, they risk crashing into barriers or falling into ditches designed to stop them from crossing the roads. If they do cross the roads they risk being knocked down by a passing truck or tourist bus or a fate worse than anything else they've experienced so far: being surrounded by cameras and shot to death. Even under the famous 'viewing tree', from where you can see nothing but trees and which has been a favourite elephant meeting-place for generations, they can't escape the click of those damn cameras. No wonder they all end up trunk and disorderly.

The greatest criticism of all has to be of Livingstone's absolute, total failure to come up with a reply to one of the greatest soundbites of all time. Whatever it was that Stanley said to him when, preceded by an African carrying the Stars and Stripes, he stumbled across him in Ujiji on that fateful day in November 1871, his reply could have lived in quiz shows and dictionaries of quotations for all time. But he blew it. He said nothing memorable, nothing exciting, nothing even mildly newsworthy. Not even a merry quip like, 'This is a hell of a mess you've come to get me out of, Stanley.' Instead, no doubt like any self-respecting God-fearing missionary would do, he doffed his expensive hand-made hat and said lamely, 'I feel thankful that I am here to welcome you.' How wet and limp-wristed can you get? This guy, a journalist mark you, not an explorer, so you can guess how unfit he was, has just dragged himself halfway across Africa to find you and all the thrill and excitement you can muster is to mumble, 'I feel thankful that I am here to welcome you.' When you think about it, it's a pretty stupid thing to say at all. It was obvious he was there. If he wasn't there, he could hardly welcome him, could he? As a result, all the books of quotations I've seen jump from Litvinoff, Maxim, 'Peace is indivisible', straight to Livy, '*Vae victis*'. Which serves Livingstone right.

Other, less responsible people will, of course, say the most damning criticism of our great missionary, explorer and liberator is the damage he inflicted on the locals. Before he arrived on the scene they were happy worshipping their ancestors at their so-called sacred spots around the Falls and spending all their time searching for green and yellow mopane caterpillars which feed, appropriately enough, off the mopane tree (it makes you wonder what a Red Admiral does). These are something of a delicacy in the area, especially when roasted, dried and left to mature over a couple of weeks. Today the whole place is overrun by backpackers who spend all their time arguing about whether or not they can drink a whole crate of Mosi beer in an hour.

Depending on your point of view, Livingstone, the town closest to the Falls, is either a glorious wonder full of exciting, old, historic buildings or it's a bit of a dump. Either way it's definitely not worth dragging yourself all over Africa to the wrong places in the wrong direction at the wrong times just to get it named after you. Many of the buildings date back to the early days: the Northwestern Hotel, the oldest surviving hotel in Zambia; Nanoos, which started off as a bar and is now a supermarket; St Andrew's Church; the Zambezi Bar; and any dagga-walled hut that looks in an acute state of collapse. The mayor, Edwin Hatemba, goes on and on about deliberately leaving 'the historic fabric of the town intact', which is Zambian local-politician-speak for we haven't got two pennies to rub together let alone buy a pot of paint, so to hell with it.

Livingstone doesn't seem to have done Zambia any favours either. Either that or the reason KK, Kenneth Kaunda, kept waving that damned white handkerchief of his around all the time was because he was weeping with shame at the fact that even after 27 years of virtual dictatorship and with his reputation as one of the so-called big men of post-independence Africa, he still didn't know how the hell to run the place. Humanism, he called it, which as far as I can understand it is Christianity in theory, Communism in practice and if it still doesn't work wave a big, white handkerchief at it. The result is that today what should be one of sub-Saharan Africa's most prosperous countries is one of the most debt-ridden nations on earth – with sky-high inflation, a currency so weak it can hardly stand up, an economy in ruins, manufacturing companies that can't whistle let alone manufacture anything, farms which can hardly grow weeds and in every road you come across potholes the size of Lake Victoria. On paper, the country has everything. It is the world's largest producer of cobalt, the world's fourth largest producer of copper. It's got amethyst, feldspar, fluorite, gypsum, lead, tin, zinc and even some gold. But everything is run-down, dilapidated, decaying and operating way, way below its proper capacity. Far from KK waving his handkerchief about, every single Zambian should be weeping into his own handkerchief. The problem is that he left the place in such a mess they can't afford to buy them, especially not the big expensive humanist ones like his.

I've been to millions of African towns and cities in my time and Lusaka, I can tell you, is not a pretty sight. Especially if you turn up in the middle of some kind of pro-Kenneth Kaunda rally. First because you can hardly believe your ears. Some people actually want him back. Second because you can hardly believe your eyes. All the old women in town are practically stark naked. Zambian traditionalists hail it as their own special unique form of political demonstration. They call it *umulapo* and trace its modern origins back to one Julia Chikamoneka, Zambia's answer to Lady Godiva. She apparently stripped off in front of the British Foreign Secretary, Iain Macleod, when he arrived at Lusaka Airport in the 1960s during pre-independence days. African feminists say it demonstrates nothing more nor less than an 'insatiable appetite for women's naked bodies'. If the demonstrators were young, maybe. But old women? All I can say is, I hope it doesn't catch on.

As far as I was concerned, I had excitement enough dodging the potholes. Everyone goes on about driving through the arid, rocky, scarred and pitted bush. They should try driving through the arid, rocky, scarred and pitted so-called streets of Lusaka. Cornering and braking in sand, even driving through their famous 'black-cotton' soil which, take it from me, is totally impossible when it is wet, is nothing compared to dodging the potholes that literally cover Lusaka from end to end. There are so many, I promise you, it's practically the only topic of conversation. Everyone you meet tells you he's got a PhD: a degree in pothole driving.

Go into a bar, and sooner or later somebody will warn you, 'If you see someone and they are driving along the road in a straight line you know they are not from Zambia.'

People even reminisce about them: 'That pothole along the Musonda Ngosa road. I remember it in 1951. I'd just got a new car. I got stuck in it. Never forget it. And it's still there today.'

And, Africa being Africa, there are a million pothole dodges.

Drive through a puddle, no matter how slowly, and some guy will immediately appear from nowhere, bang on your window, claim you've splashed his clothes and demand compensation – while somebody else opens the passenger door and grabs whatever they can get.

But that's not the worst pothole danger you have to face. Because the roads are so bad it's not unusual to come across lorries and vans and trucks which have literally had the brakes shaken out of them.

When I first got to Zambia, I noticed all these guys hanging around street corners with great piles of stones and rocks and tree trunks. Uh-uh, I thought, here we go again. The Livingstone syndrome: I'm in the wrong place at the wrong time. But I wasn't. It was another traditional Zambian custom: their sophisticated method for stopping lorries, vans and trucks which are driving around without brakes. The lorry comes hurtling down the street, the horn blaring like mad. The driver swings it sharp right which is supposed to slow it up – in theory. The street corner gangs then go to work throwing all the bricks and stones and tree trunks they can muster under the back wheels to bring the vehicle to a halt. It is, I can assure you, terrifying. Especially if you happen to be in a car anywhere near the lorry while all this is going on.

Other health risks are just as deadly although maybe not as dramatic. The whole place is so filthy and the drinking water so lethal that diarrhoea or diarrhoeal epidemics, as the medics say, are commonplace, especially during and immediately after the monsoons. Cholera and typhoid are also growing in popularity to such an extent that Lusaka city council has banned the digging of water wells and latrines. Except, of course, that this is Africa and the city council can only ban the digging of water wells and latrines on official planned sites. Most of the problems, inevitably, are in the shanty towns which are all unofficial sites so the council says there's nothing they can do about what is dug there. Similarly, the council has banned the digging of deep water wells. Except they haven't said exactly how deep a deep water well is. But don't worry, the government is not totally powerless. When I was last there the Home Affairs Minister had just summoned up all the full panoply and authority of his office and instructed the Zambian police service not to hesitate for a second but to take immediate, strong and decisive action against anyone they come across who is – are you ready? –. pompous, disobedient or careless in talk. And, if necessary, to use force.

If, however, this is all too much for you, you could try to ease the tension by looking out for the old Saddam

Hussein Boulevard signs which, until the Gulf War, graced the tree-lined, over-grown potholed road outside the President's mansion and private game reserve. Now it has been renamed Los Angeles Boulevard – although I would have thought Colin Powell Highway or even Norman Schwarzkopf Main Road would have been more appropriate.

Alternatively, you could wander down the main street, Cairo Road. It's called Cairo Road to commemorate the last visit of a Pharaoh to Lusaka, which naturally was the last time the place was swept let alone saw a lick of paint. Today it is full of dilapidated office buildings, that look as though they were thrown together with a lethal mix of straw and cow dung, one or two crumbling stores and a mass of pathetic, collapsing shops and holes in the wall – which is crazy, because given Zambia's enormous mineral resources it should really be full of huge office blocks, giant shopping malls and masses of boutiques.

Freedom Way is just as bad. Except there's no freedom for anyone, pedestrian or driver, with one obstacle after another blocking one's progress: abandoned cars, piles of rubbish and rickety old stalls covering practically every square inch of the pavement as well as most of the road. Not only that but the street sellers are the most persistent in town. I was followed the whole length of the street by a guy in a scruffy coat and hat who kept asking me if I was interested in buying African guns. When I got to the end, in sheer desperation, I said yes. His African guns turned out to be giant catapults.

The huge, sprawling Kamwa Market, on the other hand, is quite different; it is a heaving, thriving, hot, sweaty, exciting, money-making machine. Everywhere there are hastily assembled stalls selling everything from T-shirts to packets of rice to sacks of cement to cheap pairs of shoes to anything else you can think of.

For culture, you could get quite a thrill reading the

government posters stuck up all over town. My favourite says, 'A government without women is like a pot sitting on one stone'. Then there is the Kabwata traditional African village which is about as traditional as you can get: the whole place is a mess. The thatched roofs are rotting and caving in. The huts themselves are falling down. There is rubbish everywhere. Luckily the traditional little African open theatre where they perform their traditional African dances is so overgrown with traditional African elephant grass that I was spared another traditional African evening *folklorique*.

If, however, you prefer a laugh, go to Chilenje on the outskirts of town. This is where the great man with the white handkerchief was supposed to have been born. To the old man who showed me round, this was more than a national shrine, this was heaven on earth. Look, here is where the great Weepie slept. Here is where he ate. Here is where he drank. And over there by the tree is where he, well, never mind. I saw the table he worked at, the letters and pamphlets he wrote, even the Land Rover he used.

'When was the last time the great man came back here to visit?' I asked him.

'In 1990,' the old man told me, 'to look at the Land Rover. But he came in the middle of the night. He didn't want to attract any attention.'

You bet your life he didn't.

As for the most important thing of all, restaurants, they are few and far between. Whichever one you go into, the speciality of the house seems to be warm bread – which means either that they are in the forefront of another revolution in the food industry or they're having trouble shifting yesterday's supplies. All the menus carry a heavily underlined warning that Tipping Is Against The Law, although I noticed nobody ran after me whenever I accidentally dropped a couple of US$10 bills on the table after finishing my meal.

To be honest, the only reason anyone would go to

Zambia today is to see Mosi-oa-Tunya, as Victoria Falls where called by the Kololos, the South African tribe who colonised the place in the 1830s – although strictly speaking the Falls should be called Shungu na Miutitima, the name given to them originally by the Leya people who first inhabited the area a million years before that. Everybody tends to forget that Zambia also has the Kalambo Falls, which are double the length of the Victoria Falls but nowhere near as wide or spectacular. Nor does anybody know much about them because they weren't discovered by the Missionary, Explorer and Liberator.

There is no doubt, though, that the Victoria Falls are truly spectacular and well worth every hyperbole and exaggeration people have rained down on them for years.

First, you see the Zambezi, which is certainly wide and fast-flowing. As you walk along the bank you see islands and rocks and inlets. In the background you hear the thunder which gradually gets louder and louder and louder. Then suddenly there it is: more than 1,700 metres long and around 100 metres deep. An incredible one million gallons of water a second – *one million gallons of water a second* – crashing over the top down into the gorge below. The Falls are so huge, so dramatic, so spectacular that as you walk along the banks of the river you cannot possibly imagine that you're going to see such a thing.

Livingstone was so stunned by the Falls that in that flip, catchy way of his he scribbled in his diary – or one of his ghost writers did – 'Scenes so lovely must have been gazed upon by angels in their flights.'

Everyone says it's noisy. And, believe me, it is. The guys who called it The Smoke that Thunders knew what they were on about. You really have to holler and shout to make yourself heard above the never-ending roar.

The other thing that amazed me was the spray. All the

guide books keep on about the spray; at the hotel near the Falls they warned me about the spray; the driver taking me there told me about the spray.

Spray? It's not spray. Spray is what you get ambling along the coast in, say, Brighton or Eastbourne, with the waves lapping gently along the beach. Not this – this is full scale, whirling, swirling, churning heavy tropical downpour stuff. I went there wearing my usual gear. No, I tell a lie, I did loosen my tie and, if you promise not to tell my wife, I also undid the top button of my shirt. Within three seconds – what am I talking about? In a nanosecond – I was wringing wet. My jacket, my shirt, my trousers, my shoes. Everything. Not just surface wet, either, but right-the-way-through-and-out-the-other-side wet.

After that, of course, there's no point in turning back. As a result I squelched along the Knife Edge Walk, facing the huge Eastern Cataract, and across this long, narrow, slippery bridge. At least, I think that's where I went: I was so soaked and battered by the 'spray' I could hardly see. Back on to soaking wet, sodden ground again I slipped and slid and skidded my way right up to the very edge of the huge cliff facing the Falls. It was absolutely breathtaking. Such a huge area, such massive amounts of water, and it goes on like this, hour after hour, day after day. Non-stop. Forever. There are no barriers or fences or handrails. Just you, and over there the Falls.

Once, following the death of a tourist who skidded and slipped off the edge, the Swedes offered to build a proper walkway along here with handrails. But the Zambians said no, it would ruin the natural view of the Falls. Which is one of the few things they have ever done that makes any sense.

The wettest I've ever been in my life, I slop and slush my way along to the Rainbow Falls where, funnily enough, there are masses of rainbows. Not your scrappy Sunday afternoon rainbows though – these are the real thing. Huge. Massive. Full. Complete. One hundred per cent 180-degree rainbows with a crock of gold tied at the end of each one. There are so many you are walking in and out of them all the time.

At Danger Point, you can see why it's called that; the water is somehow louder, wilder, more furious, even more thunderous. Somebody once called it an apocalyptic symphony. I don't think I'd go that far even if I knew what it meant but you get the idea. It is also, obviously, extremely dangerous, as slippery as hell, and there's nothing to grab on to. I was told that the local Leya people often go there to offer sacrifices to the spirits of their ancestors who, they believe, live in the Falls. Which means that you can be clambering all over – Oops. Quick. Where's he gone? He was here a moment ago.

Turn round now – if you dare – and you can see the railway bridge which crosses the mighty Zambezi. It is spectacular. Part of Cecil Rhodes's grand design to build a railway all the way from Cape Town to Cairo, the track couldn't get any closer to the Falls if it wanted to. Rhodes is supposed to have said that he wanted it as close as possible to the Falls because he wanted the spray 'to fall upon the carriages'. Well that's what they say. My guess is that Rhodes decided it had to be as close to the Falls as possible because he knew in Africa that was the only way he could guarantee to keep the carriages clean.

Not everyone agreed. Many people, including Rhodes's own brother, Frank, thought the bridge should never have been built. Frank, the good, kind, under-standing, considerate brother that he was even prayed for an earthquake apparently to stop it being built. But the bridge was built – twice, in fact. First in England where it was made. Then it was shipped out and moved bit by bit, all 1,500 tons of it, by train up to the Falls where at seven o'clock on 1 April 1905 the final piece was dropped into place. Rhodes had painted a little bit more of the map red. Trouble was, the red was inevitably African blood.

There always used to be great excitement when the famous Blue Train arrived from Cape Town and trundled across the bridge, but not any more because it has become such a regular event. Today the excitement is bungee jumping into the Falls.

As I splodged further along the path, I found myself opposite Livingstone Island from where the great missionary, explorer and liberator first saw the Falls. A bit further along, a few more squelchy steps, and I'm at the Main Falls. This is it. This is the business. A real, total, slam-down, massive explosion of water. The spray flies a thousand feet into the air, while below is just a huge, heaving, churning, boiling mass of water.

Finally, all by itself, is the Devil's Cataract, an almost self-contained waterfall.

The main part of the Falls is in Zambia while the rest of it, some say the best part, is in Zimbabwe – or Zim as we old Africa hands say. This means that you see one bit of the Falls, then you have to come all the way back, get in your car, drive to the border post, queue up get your spray-sodden passport stamped, queue up again, and get your by this time slightly less spray-sodden passport stamped again to go and tackle the other bit. The fun is in trying to decide which side has the best quality spray: Zim or Zam. My judgement is Zim has the quality, but Zam has the quantity. I'm afraid, as in most things, I go for the quantity.

The other thing you can compare, if you can ever get the spray out of your eyes, is what's on offer on the two sides.

The Zam side is rough and ready, run down, a bit tatty round the edges. It has just one decent hotel, which is funnily enough the best hotel from which to visit the Falls, because it's the closest, because it's surrounded by bush and because there's nothing like the thrill of waking up in the middle of the night to the sound of grunting coming from the bushes outside your window. Those hippos. They never stop.

On the Zim side, the amount of spray continually raining down on it seems to have produced a fertile climate for virtually non-stop growth. There's a sign proclaiming to the world 'Coca-Cola welcomes you to Victoria Falls' – a fancy little designer town of around twenty thousand people with a clutch of fabulous hotels including, get this, the hotel with the longest thatched roof in the whole of Africa. I just knew that would impress you. There is a baobab tree which is supposed to be a thousand years old, the oldest tree in Africa. There is also a thriving business which hires out yellow plastic macs and hats – an idea that doesn't seem to have occurred to anyone on the other side.

The trump card is the famous Victoria Falls Hotel which, believe me, has everything. It has the Falls, which it overlooks. It has the railway bridge: from the terrace, with a glass of champagne in your hand, you can count the copper ore wagons going over it. Turn round and look out of the front door of the hotel and there is the railway station – a genuine Edwardian one, just like our local station back home. The platform has a pond and a row of palm trees. (In our case the pond is somewhat more informal and the trees tend to grow out of the middle of the platform).

The hotel might once have been a wood and corrugated-iron hut and the dining-room a locomotive shed but not any more. This is not an hotel for your ordinary explorer, let alone your common or garden missionary and liberator, although Laurens van der Post, when he was supposed to be having a rough time of it exploring the Lost World of the Kalahari, somehow or other managed to keep popping in there for a hot bath. Then he would slip on his dinner jacket and treat himself to what he called a civilised dinner. As I'm sure we all would, given half a chance. Although what he did with the stick of scarlet sealing wax he carried with him all the time on his adventures I have never been able to find out.

Today, if your shorts don't have razor-sharp creases, if your socks have not been properly blancoed, if your pith helmet is not properly polished and if you're not dashing off to lake-hop by seaplane down the Rift Valley all the way to Cape Town, then back to London for the season, Ascot, Wimbledon and all that, don't even bother to ask for a reservation.

The decor is all very colonial-chic, if you know what I mean: over-lush, over-ornate, over-elegant. Vast rooms. Enormous paintings. Sumptuous furniture. Unbelievable service. About three doormen per suitcase.

The one thing that puzzles me in the Livingstone restaurant, though, is the way they all speak. I go in and slump down in the corner. The maître d' comes up to me. He asks me how I am. I tell him all my problems. Well he did ask, didn't he? I then ask him how he is. 'I am handsome well,' he replies.

For the rest of the evening he keeps telling me everything is 'gloriously well'.

'How's the elephant's feet stew?'

'Gloriously well.'

'How's the hippopotamus steak?'

'Gloriously well.'

'How's the boiled egg and toast?'

'Gloriously well.'

At the end of the evening I'm staggering towards the door. He waves at me.

'I hope you will have a heavenly journey,' he says.

I can only assume it's got something to do with all the starch they put in their uniforms. Too much starch in my collar and I'll probably start speaking like that too.

Gaborone

Botswana is virtually a single street surrounded by not
much else. The street in question is The Mall in the
capital, Gaborone, which is about a thousand metres
long – the average length of the queue of people waiting
in front of me whenever I go to check in for any flight
to anywhere in the world. At one end of The Mall is the
swish, modern National Assembly. At the other is the
more cost-conscious, slightly down-at-heel Civic Centre.
Sure, there are a couple of other streets and a few other
buildings in town as well, but not many, because Gaborone (or Gabs, as we locals say) is tiny. The population is
only around 150,000.

But that doesn't mean to say it's not big in other
things: like success. Tiny little landlocked Botswana (or
Bots, as we locals also say) is one of the most successful
countries in the whole of Africa. In fact, you could say
Bots is the tops. It's also big in security. You can stroll
down The Mall, or any other street in the country come
to think of it, at virtually any time of the day or night
without being grabbed or hassled or even jumped on.
You can look at your watch without fear of your hand
being chopped off. You can even take your wallet out in
broad daylight, count your credit cards and look at your
diary to make certain you still remember your own
address.

What is more, there are no corrugated-iron shacks

stretching as far as the eye can see. No rivers of thick black slime flowing between them. No heaps of abandoned cars. No vast mountains of garbage. No kids with enormous pot bellies playing in the middle of heaps of putrid, stinking rubbish. No dust. No sand. No potholes. No roadblocks. No marauding soldiers sticking their guns in your face and demanding money. No old men and women, thin as a wire, sitting on filthy wooden boxes just staring, staring, staring, at nothing. Which, I am afraid, unnerves me. Because this is not the Africa I've come to know and love. As a result, whenever I go to Gabs I must admit I feel unsettled and slightly ill at ease.

As for the rest of Botswana, it really is nothing. Nothing but desert, salt, scrub and miles and miles and miles of emptiness.

Down in the south-west is the Kalahari. Now normally if you show me a desert I have to cross it. Not, however, the Kalahari. Whenever I think about it I can't help but think of Laurens van der Post, which puts me off the whole thing completely. It's not so much his books on the bushmen of the Kalahari, which are not exactly the most exciting books in the world, it's the man himself and all his woolly, wishy-washy, pseudo-mystic, Jungian tosh. I mean, what the hell are 'intuitive intimations of reality', 'god-given intuition of natural rhythms', 'mindless, pre-human hymns', 'cosmic schisms of light'? Then, of course, there was his deep, intimate knowledge of Africa and his unique ability to assess people, their ability, their character and their leadership qualities, which is why he dismissed Nelson Mandela as worthless and second-rate and instead heaped unstinting praise on Chief Buthelezi and the Zulus. But the worst thing of all was the shocking story that came out after his death. Our great egomanical Jungian mystic, a spiritual guru to Prince Charles, godfather to Prince William, confidant to the mighty and fierce upholder of every principle, moral and standard you can think of, had, at the age of forty-seven, seduced a fourteen-year-old girl entrusted to his care, later denied he was the father of her baby and then dumped both the teenage mother and the child. So much for his intuitive intimations of reality, let alone his god-given intuition of natural rhythms.

Up in the north-west is the Okavango delta which, I reckon, is the biggest oasis in the world, all 20,000 square kilometres of it. Or at least it used to be because it is now drying up. Water levels are the lowest they have been for fifty years. In the old days the place was a mass of rivers and streams and Mokoro canoes leisurely drifting into the sunset. Every species of wildlife you could think of was there – hundreds of animals, birds and insects, enough to keep David Attenborough churning out new programmes until the return of the dinosaurs.

Today, however, the Okavango basin is nothing but sweltering heat, dried-up river beds, dust and rubbish. What is more it's going to get worse, much worse, because in addition to the natural drainage caused by climatic changes, Namibia next door (which is facing even worse drought conditions – their rainfall is about forty per cent below normal levels) has started unofficially tapping into the delta and drawing off twenty million cubic metres of water a year. Unofficially, because the Namibians say if they do it officially, by the time they've completed all the obligatory environmental impact studies and negotiatied all the official agreements, it will be too late. They'll all be lying in the sand with their legs sticking up in the air. Not that everything has stopped flowing through the delta: what is flowing through there now is blood. Animal blood. When I was last there, the government were busy slaughtering over a quarter of a million cattle that had caught some kind of lung disease. There were even spotter planes flying everywhere with sharpshooters on board, to make certain none of them got away. In my view they should have gone around slaughtering all the backpackers and pseudo-safari hunters and wannabe explorers who are clogging it up as much if not more than the papyrus is clogging up what's left of the delta.

Maun - probably the biggest town in the area, with only about four streets and a couple of hundred people - is being overrun by a different kind of pest: donkeys. There are at least sixteen thousand of them, probably nearer twenty thousand by now. As a result, somebody's come up with the idea of rounding them up and slaughtering them as well; except they want to slaughter them for food. You know the kind of thing: donkey neck-muscle stew, donkey mince, donkey salami. There are plenty of airlines I can think of who would probably welcome the idea as a way of livening up their lunch and dinner menus. Donkey-meat is, after all, healthier than horse-meat. It's leaner and less greasy.

In the north-east of Botswana is Chobe, which could probably do a parallel deal with donkey-meat exports. It consists of nothing but salt, vast pans of the stuff. If everybody who ever lived came to Chobe and just pinched some of the salt instead of throwing it over their shoulders there would still be masses of it left over. If you insist on going there, go to Nxai Pan because there you don't just see salt you also see the seven famous giant baobab trees painted by the explorer, Thomas Baines, on 22 May 1862. They are exactly the same today as they were then. After that try Makgadikgadi. Not because it has more grass than Nxai Pan but because you'll never be able to pronounce it properly. Best time to go? During the dry season; our summer and autumn. Actually it isn't. I only said that to try to protect the environment, or what's left of it. The best time to go - I cannot tell a lie - is during the wet season, our winter and spring. I think.

Back in the south-east is the Gabs of a gift of the British. Originally Bots, or the Bechuanaland Protectorate as it then was, was going to be part of South Africa. Then suddenly in 1964 everything changed. It

was decided to make the country independent in its
own right. The rush was then on to find and create a
capital and Gabs got the vote. As a result, today it has a
long, long history stretching back all of thirty-five years
– in fact it was only in 1986 that it became a city. Which
is what, I'm afraid, unnerves me. Because in that short
space of time from being nothing but a desperately
poor patch of dust in one of the world's harshest and
most inhospitable climates, tiny little Bots has turned
itself, as I said, into one of the richest and most
prosperous and most successful countries in the whole
of Africa.

In 1964 its GDP per capita was a couple of shields and
a handful of spears. By 1980 it was an unbelievable
US$3,460. Today it's a staggering US$28,950, which in
African terms is unbelievable. Guess how much it has
got in the bank? Over US$5 billion. Which means that
while the rest of Africa is clamouring to borrow still
more money from the IMF, these guys are busy lending
it to them and making still more money as well. It's no
wonder they have the highest per capita foreign
exchange reserves in sub-Saharan Africa. On top of that
it has built up its agricultural sector so successfully that
give or take the odd slaughter programme there are
twice as many cattle in the country as there are people.
Which means that it is not only more than self-sufficient
in meat, it is one of the few African countries that is also
a major food exporter. As if that's not more than
enough, Botswana has also developed its industrial base.
It has done everything it can to bring in foreign investors: it has liberalised exchange controls, and offered
fantastic incentives to companies to do whatever they
want to do. There are also posters all over the place
proclaiming, 'Productivity for enhanced quality of life',
which I don't quite follow. But who cares, it obviously
works. They even sweep up the leaves in The Mall every
morning.

According to the World Bank, little old Bots has been

the world's fastest-growing economy over the last thirty years, beating the once-powerful Asian tiger economies, not to mention China. The trouble is, they're about to make their one big mistake. They want to attract more tourists, who will inevitably spend fortunes buying themselves designer camouflage safari suits, the better to merge into the landscape, and then promptly leap into huge 4×4s and roar all over the place destroying what little environment is left and scaring the hell out of any living being south of the equator.

So why do I never feel relaxed and happy in Bots? Because all the time I'm there I keep asking myself, how come these guys can do it while the rest of Africa can't? Is it because they pursued what Britain's Chancellor of the Exchequer, Gordon Brown, once famously referred to as a 'post-neo-classical endogenous growth theory' (not that anyone understood what on earth he was talking about)? Plenty of other African countries are larger, have far more people and far, far more natural resources, yet they are absolute, complete, total disasters. People are hungry, if not actually starving to death. There are hardly any schools, no jobs and no hospitals. It's unsafe to walk the streets in the daytime, let alone at night. Their natural resources – far, far, far larger than those of Botswana – are either still in the ground or being smuggled out of the country lump by lump.

When you think about it, which is something I try not to do because it depresses me, why is Africa, with its vast mineral resources, its huge agricultural potential, its unlimited supply of human resources, in such a mess? How come only around 35 per cent of their food is processed in Africa compared to 90, 95, even 100 per cent in other countries? How come they process less than 10 per cent of their timber? And what about their coffee, cocoa, cotton? The whole thing is a nonsense.

Take, say, Ghana and Togo, two countries I know very well. In 1957, when they got their independence, they had about the same GNP as Japan, South Korea and all the other Asian countries. Today they are still struggling to survive while Japan, South Korea and the rest of Asia, who have had their own problems recently, are still a million times better off than they were.

So what is Botswana's secret?

First, it could be something to do with its size. It must be easier to organise smaller countries and populations than huge, sprawling countries and huge, fast-growing populations. Though that doesn't always follow. Huge countries can be split up and run as virtually a collection of regions under a strong central authority. Look at China, for example. It's much better run and organised and managed than, say, India. Similarly, not all small countries are successful. Look at ... No. I haven't got time to list all the small countries in Africa where more than 50 per cent of the population are struggling to survive on less than US$1 a day, the World Bank's minimum poverty level.

Second, people: for a country to succeed it needs decent, honest, sensible people, especially at the top. People who are prepared to struggle and do everything they can to see if it's possible to survive without necessarily having huge mansions in Switzerland, several homes in Belgium, two in France, a collection of limos and a Concorde parked in the backyard. But also decency and honesty must run through society as a whole. Hence the problem is twofold: how do you get decent, honest, sensible people to go into politics? And how do you make sure they remain so? The answer is: I don't know. Some people are born crooks and will remain crooks throughout their lives, while others have crookedness thrust upon them. But there must be a way of controlling corruption – controlling not eliminating, because we're never going to eliminate it altogether.

Third, there has to be some form of democracy. Now, I know democracy doesn't automatically solve everything and there are many variations of it. But I'm afraid we're stuck with it as a system; it's the best one we've got so far.

Fourth, to be successful a country has to have some kind of legal system, some kind of political stability, a bureaucracy that more or less works and minimum controls, especially exchange controls. And, finally, luck: lots of it.

But you don't want to listen to me going on about Africa. There's nothing particular going on in Gabs at the moment, so let's wander down The Mall. I'll tell you what Gabs is up to. Then you can then tell me why, in spite of receiving God knows how much financial assistance over the years, Africa is not only still in such a mess but on top of that owes a staggering US$320 billion.

Okay. This is the National Assembly. Yes, I know there are no tanks or soldiers hanging around outside and neither is it shot to pieces. There are no rotting corpses, no stacks of arms and legs around the back, no piles of skulls. That doesn't mean to say it's not a National Assembly. In fact, sorry to disappoint you further, but it's also a pretty dull National Assembly: no coups, no military takeovers. Just the usual, boring democratic process, year in, year out, for thirty years since their independence from Britain. Their elections are also pretty boring, unlike those in some other parts of Africa where people vote because they need the money. Here if you want to vote for a guy, you put a cross alongside his name – but not in the same way as you do in some African countries I know, where politicians openly go around telling people, 'If you like me, put a large cross against my name. If you don't like me, put a small one.'

In Botswana they've also got the crazy habit of not just passing laws but keeping them. And, by the way, when Gabs first became the capital of Bots it only had 15,000 people. So the jump in population to 150,000 is further proof of how little there is to do in the place. Oh, the other thing I forgot to tell you: Bots is a united country. There are no alternative power centres, no no-go areas, no barons with their own slice of the country. What's more, the army actually stays in the barracks.

The second biggest city is Francistown, up in the north, on the way to Zimbabwe. It was founded by Daniel Francis about a hundred years ago. A bunch of Europeans discovered there was still some gold left in the original prehistoric mines in the area and all hell broke loose. Francis negotiated mining and other land rights with the local King Lobengula and before you could say lumps of coloured glass, there was a hotel, three banks and a couple of dozen shops and offices there. Today it's a nice little town, with a bit of industry - shoes, ceramics, clothing, knitwear and chemicals - population around 65,000. It's also full of Zimbabweans, who pour across the border to do their shopping.

Next comes Selibe Phikwe, which is virtually the industrial capital, also in the north. Turn right before you get to Francistown. If Francistown is gold, Selibe Phikwe is copper and nickel and foreign investment. Copper and nickel because the mines are nearby and employ about ten per cent of the 40,000 population; foreign investment because this is where the Mauritians, the Hong Kong Chinese, the Japanese, mysterious South Africans and everybody else comes to build their factories and processing plants. It is small, pleasant, and cheap. There is plenty of labour around too, and the town is in an ideal position: 400 kilometres away from Jo'burg, 200 from Bulawayo. And best of all, there are good roads all the way, especially on the Botswana side. But you guessed that already.

Finally, down in the south, there is Lobatse, which is cattle country. Animals are driven there from all over the country to be sold and slaughtered. There's a big meat canning plant and also a tannery. At one time, like Francistown, it was in the running to be the capital. It's higher than Gabs (the Otse Mountain, the highest peak in the country, is a few miles away) and it's cooler, but the water supply is limited so Gabs got the vote. In any other country, of course, Lobatse would have got the vote. Who's ever heard of a capital city, especially in Africa, being interested in water? Champagne, yes. But water, never.

Now come along here, past all the fancy fountains. Don't you think the National Assembly looks more like a mosque than a National Assembly? All those neat little paths. Those arches. The tall doors and high ceilings and marble floors. I really like the hollow globe of the world hanging over the front door: to me it signifies how the world had been drained of all its natural resources. Although to the artist I suppose it meant something more profound, like three months' work and a cheque at the end of it.

Across the car park, out of the gate and we're in Whitehall, or rather ministry-land. This is where some of the big ministries are located. In Bots they actually pay their civil servants, and regularly too. What they say they are going to pay them. Unlike in some countries, where the only way civil servants can live is to charge people for everything they do, or rather don't do. To us it's corruption; to them it's survival. Over there is the Ministry of Finance and Development. No, don't look at the front door, it's the back door you look at. Don't you know anything about Africa? More than US$1 billion a year is regularly shuffled out of back doors all over the continent every year: but see here, no brown envelopes or empty sacks waiting to be filled, no mysterious unmarked cars with their engines running, no sound of presses running day and night printing more and more worthless currency.

Now, you see that small red brick building that looks a bit like a supermarket going for a heritage award? That's the Botswana National Archive. I keep meaning to go in there and ask them complicated questions about the Bakalanga, the Bayei and the Mbukushu, three tiny tribes who live in and around Francistown, but I haven't had a chance yet. Maybe next time.

That funny-looking tower? The one with the satellite dish? Well now, it's either the headquarters of the Botswana Secret Service or the Telecom HQ. Which do you think? Across there, on the other side – you can hardly see it for that giant skip with 'Daisy Loo' written all over it and the pile of rubbish on top, but that's the Ministry of Health.

Okay. Through this little bit of park to the war memorial. These are the guys I feel sorry for. They fought and died for us in the last war. And see that separate plate there – that's for Jonas Messenger, who was with the Bechuanaland Protectorate Police. He died for us during the First World War. Which, incidentally, always makes me wonder why we haven't got any proper memorials in London to the African soldiers who sacrificed their lives for us in two world wars. Over there, standing on top of that giant boulder, doing up the buttons of his jacket, is Botswana's first President, Sir Seretse Khama, so called not because he did more than anyone to make Bots one of the Khama countries in a volatile continent but because he was one of the Khamas from Serowe, which is supposed to be the biggest traditional village in Bots and one of the largest in Africa.

Just outside town is the burial place of Khama III. He was one of the three chiefs who kept Botswana Botswana. When Cecil Rhodes wanted to lump it in with his Cape Colony, Khama persuaded the British to stop him. As for the man on the boulder, I've always thought he was probably the most radical and the most revolutionary of all African leaders. From the beginning he not only preached democracy and complete political, economic, social and racial equality, he also practised it. Can you imagine how difficult that must have been for him? No milking the country dry. No shuffling IMF loans worth millions of dollars into his foreign bank accounts in Paris, London, Brussels, Zurich or wherever. He also, as old Africa hands will recall, married an

Englishwoman, which caused no end of fuss at the time.

As for today's President, Sir Ketumile Masire, he doesn't seem to get anywhere near the recognition, let alone glory, for running a pretty good ship from African, let alone world, leaders that, say, Laurent Kabila got from the Organisation of African Unity all the way up to the Secretary-General of the United Nations when he shot his way to power in Zaire, or that Nigeria's military dictator, General Abacha, got when, in total violation of international law, he sent his troops into Sierra Leone to try to restore his old buddy Tejan Kabbah to power.

Across the road is Khama Crescent. Which it most definitely isn't, especially during the rush hour. Now we're in The Mall. It might not look much to you, just a pedestrian walkway and a collection of shops and offices, but every square inch of it is engraved on the heart and soul of every man, woman and child in the country. The next time you meet someone from Bots, ask them to tell you the names of the shops, one by one, all the way down one side of it, and I bet you they'll do it straight off. This place is so deeply ingrained in their national consciousness that they even write poems about it. Poems about a shopping mall. Can you imagine that?

That big six-storey thing over there on the right is, appropriately enough, Debswana House, the head-quarters of all Botswana's diamond mining operations. Appropriately, because diamond mining is by far and away the number one industry in the country. In fact, they are the largest producer of rough diamonds in the world. Check out the jewellery you've been buying your secretary all these years. If it's any good, the diamonds will have come from Botswana. Although I've always thought that how they discovered them was a bit, how shall I say, suspicious. After all, they've been living in the place for, say, 30,000 years. The British arrive in 1885 and declare the whole area the British Protectorate of Bechuanaland. On 30 September 1996 the British finally quit, and the last pair of khaki shorts is hardly out of the country before, surprise, surprise, what do they discover out near Orapa? Diamonds. Not just handfuls, but armfuls, some as big not as the Ritz but as the President Hotel, Gaborone.

But credit where credit is due. Diamonds are not necessarily a country's best friend. They don't automatically mean riches. Look at Angola and Zaire, or Congo, as we are supposed to call it nowadays. They've got all the diamonds in the world, yet they've barely got two halfpennies to rub together. Making money out of them – and keeping the money in the country – is something else. There are plenty of countries in Africa that have enormous natural resources, like diamonds or oil or gold, but for one reason or another, they haven't been able to develop them, even though mining is about the only thing that makes money in Africa. The International Finance Corporation, the private sector part of the World Bank, for instance, has nearly US$1 billion invested in projects all over Africa. What makes the money? Cement plants, textile factories, steel mills, even exporting cut flowers. But the big stuff, the only thing that is anywhere near successful, is mining. All praise, therefore, to Botswana for showing that you can do other things with diamonds apart from flying them across the border, selling them to all kinds of shady dealers and stashing away the proceeds in bank accounts all over the world.

Next to Debswana House is Barclays Bank, which looks just like a Barclays Bank back home. But there the similarity ends. Here the staff are friendly and chatty. They actually seem to want to help. They are even eager to help small companies. Apparently, they, along with all the commercial banks in Botswana, have been criticised for not helping small and medium-sized businesses. Back home, of course, they would have ignored all that. Here they've actually done something about it. I go in there to catch up on their names. They're fantastic. So far I've seen a Chapson, a Moffat, a Drops, a Fabian, a Freedman, a Size and a very fat man called Worm. I once met a manager called Only and a lady called Beauty, which I'm sure she was at one time or another.

On the ground floor is the local firm of stockbrokers. I am, don't forget, the world's leading expert on African stock exchanges. I've been to every single one of them. The Botswana Stock Exchange is quite a star among African exchanges. Even though, as at all the others, nobody wants to let go of their shares. About 60 per cent of the market is controlled by overseas parents of local companies; about 20 per cent held by overseas investors. But they still manage to trade a higher percentage of their total market capitalisation than they do in Jo'burg.

Next to Barclays is Standard and Chartered, which I've never been in. But I've come across various Standard Chartered people at various receptions and get-togethers all over Africa. They've always struck me as solid, reliable, terribly Rotary Club types: the kind of people you would never imagine giving up the cosy life in Virginia Water to go and work and live in the middle of nowhere in Africa. John Major, don't forget, was also a Standard and Chartered man. How he managed to survive not only Africa but in Lagos, goodness only knows.

My favourite shop in the whole of The Mall, if not in the whole country, is the Botswana Book Centre. Okay, compared to Hatchards, say, or your local Waterstone's, it might look a bit scruffy and a bit disorganised - especially with all those piles of last week's newspapers stacked up near the door. But it's a proper bookshop. It's got all the Jeffrey Archers and Jilly Coopers you could want. I should know: I got stuck in there once during a heavy storm. It was terrible. The choice was between flicking through masses of educational self-help books (Getting to Know This, The Management of That or

How to Finance the Other – there was even one on How to be Headhunted) or reading the blurb on all these Jeffrey Archers and Jilly Coopers. I went for the self-help section, and spent the whole thunderstorm flicking through a book I thought I'd never see anywhere in the whole of Africa: *The Index of Criminal Procedure and Evidence Act.* Criminal Procedure? Evidence? An act making the whole thing legal? See what I mean about Botswana? In most other African countries criminal procedure is arranging car crashes; evidence is what you get rid of before the guy falls out of the top-floor window and 'act' is what you do, all innocent, when the guys arrive from Amnesty.

The Central Post Office delivers letters. You may think that's obvious, but I know plenty of post offices in Africa which would never dream of delivering a letter. All they do is strip the stamps off the envelope, re-sell the ones that have not been franked then rip open the envelope and grab any notes or cash or valuables inside.

Now we're in the main square: Gabs's Piccadilly Circus, Times Square and Red Square all rolled into one. You see that platform over there? Many's the time I've stood and watched the various shows and concerts they put on there at lunchtime. Some of them are performed by local schools and groups; sometimes they get guys from South Africa. There's a great atmosphere, not only on the stage, but in the crowd as well. Everybody is talking and laughing and joking with each other. It's also quite exciting afterwards when you realise you've been in the centre of a crowd of a million Africans and you've still got your wallet.

Behind the stage and up the stairs is the President's Hotel, the first hotel built in Gabs. It is nothing like your typical African hotel. It's not plastered in marble, the carpets are not six foot deep and there is not one single giant 100-ton crystal chandelier in the place. There are no presidential suites, no back staircases, no caviar or foie gras on the menu. Dom Perignon is definitely not the house wine. The reception area is not full of big, heavy men in dark glasses. And you don't see a never-ending stream of younger sisters and younger nieces and younger cousins going in and out of the lifts all day long on their way to visit their older brothers, uncles or cousins who are ministers and ambassadors and good friends of the President.

This, you'll be pleased to hear, is where I stay whenever I'm in Gabs. It's not the greatest hotel in the world; it's not even the best in town. The 'gooder' one, as they say, is the Gaborone Sun, which to me is a Holiday Inn with pretentions: a bit flash, one of those hotels that could be anywhere in the world. The President suits me. It's in the centre of everything, unlike the Gabarone Sun, which is way outside town virtually in the middle of nowhere. It's close to the ministries and everything, there's a cab rank outside and it's got everything I need. They also do a mean 300-gramme prime Botswana beef steak for next to nothing, which is a big big bonus for someone married to a vegetarian. I can feel my white corpuscles do a little skip whenever I go there.

Now we're into supermarket territory. There are two, and I've never been inside either of them. I have no intention of doing so, either. I have my share of supermarkets at Christmas, when I dash into Fortnum's in Piccadilly about ten minutes before they close for the holiday to do all my shopping. But I do know that there are no lumps of rotting meat on the floor, no sacks of rice spilling all over the show, and no flies.

Now for the final stretch. Across this little open square – mind the old lady selling corn on the cob. Oops, and careful, there's a kid sitting inside that cardboard box. Okay, so maybe he shouldn't be sitting in a cardboard box, but at least he's got two arms and two legs and has made it so far. There are plenty of kids in the rest of Africa who'd give anything for two arms, two legs and the luxury of a cardboard box.

Over there is the National Development Bank which, as far as I can tell, is one of the best development banks in Africa, if for no other reason than that development is pouring into little old Bots: knitwear, footwear, textiles, soft drinks, concentrates, healthcare products. You name it, they've either got it already or it's on its way. At first they were promoting themselves just as little old Bots, but now they're saying they are the investment centre for the whole of southern Africa. And still the investment is coming. Some people believe the country is now so powerful that it even controls the world movement of the pound and the dollar. In fact, so many people believed this that one of Botswana's top officials had to issue a special public statement saying it was all a myth. But believe me, the power behind the world's currency markets is here in Gaborone. Don't forget the first Biddlecombe law of communications: nothing is true until it's denied.

Next to the Development Bank is another Standard Chartered, then Botswana Insurance Corporation. Now, what on earth can you say that's interesting about insurance? So passing quickly on, on the other side of the road is Jet Stores, which looks like some kind of upmarket fashion shop. It must be upmarket, because they're selling autumn fashions and it is still only spring. Who says you have to go to Paris for the latest fashions? That'll come as a shock to a good few African presidents' wives and whatever.

All that's left now is to go through the archway. The other end of The Mall, remember, is national government. This end is local government. The perfect balance. Quite often in the Civic Centre here they have parties and receptions. I came to a reception here once during a big conference on democracy in Africa, where everybody was discussing the usual boring things. Secret ballots, one man, one vote, no intimidation, equal access to the media, that kind of thing. None of the delegates were interested. All they wanted to do was to get back to the Gaborone Sun and hit the casino.

On the left is the Catholic church, and on the right the Dutch Reformed church. Again, balance. Just as Botswana's common law is based on Dutch Roman law, and their criminal law on the English legal system. These churches, you'll be surprised to hear, have no electronic keyboards belting out hard rock music, no electric guitars, not even an electronic set of bells. Nobody shrieks and screams during the services; nobody dances up and down the aisle during the sermon. Nobody throws themselves on the floor rolling around hysterically, sticking strange things into themselves in all kinds of uncomfortable places. Especially halfway up the nave. The ministers don't bawl and holler and rant and rave down half a dozen microphones all going at full blast. Instead it's terribly boring, but typically Bots.

Across the road from the Catholic church, a bit further along – I don't know if you can see it – is the National Museum and Art Gallery and, hidden away in the centre of it all, the Little Theatre. The National Museum is a glorious example of the oh-so-politically-correct Swedes putting their foot right in it. The pre-history section, which they designed and laid out, goes on and on about evolution. Pretty safe, non-controversial stuff, you would have thought. Not in Bots. Here they reckon that man was created in a hole in a rock in Matsieng, way up in the north of the country. What's more they say they've got the footprints to prove it. The poor Swedes don't know what to do: stick with the evolutionists and upset half of Botswana, or go for the Matsieng version and upset everybody else. It's wonderful.

But my real favourite is the Little theatre, tucked away at the back. This is where I catch up on the latest shows in town. It's pretty basic. It seats around 150 people, costs all of 6 pula – a couple of dollars – to get in, which is far, far less than even a glass of water at the Old

Vic. But it's worth every penny. If you're interested in African theatre, try to get to Gabs March-time, when they hold their annual Maitisong Festival. It's a bit like the Edinburgh Festival comes to Botswana. For ten days there are non-stop plays and concerts and musicals and even workshops in flamenco dancing all over town – in the Little Theatre, in the Cathedral, even on the Bonnington Farm picnic area.

Okay. So that's the famous Mall. Now, what's the one thing that strikes you about the place more than anything? That's right, it's khama, I mean, calm. It's quiet. It's peaceful. It's hardworking. What's more we didn't see one policeman the whole length of it. Wasn't that fantastic?

During the time it took us to stroll down The Mall, the rest of Africa has fallen still further behind the rest of the world. In food production, in healthcare, in education. In GDP per head of population. Take Nigeria, for example – the biggest and potentially the richest country in Africa. Twenty-five years ago Nigeria had a higher GDP per head of population than Indonesia. Today, for all it's current problems, Indonesia's is three times that of Nigeria's, and increasing.

Or look at it another way. The difference between, say, Switzerland, one of the world's richest countries, and, say, Mozambique, one of the poorest, is already an unbelievable 400:1. Now tell me, how on earth can countries like Mozambique ever hope to catch up? The answer is, of course, they can't.

I don't think I'll go to Gabs again. It's not good for me. It makes me think unkind thoughts about the rest of Africa.

Ponce

Well, I just had to go to Ponce, didn't I? How could I miss the opportunity to add it to my collection of silly place-name stories? Like the time I tackled the two Virgins, one British and one American, and found I was far more moved by the British one than by the American one. Which was not what I was expecting. Like the time I tried to experience the delights of Intercourse in Pennsylvania. Like the guy who told me he was going to Tampa with his children. Like the number of times my wife tells me to go to Hell, which I know is somewhere in Michigan, but I can never find it on the map.

So, after another swing through the States, instead of heading straight back home from Miami I took a detour to Puerto Rico, famous I was told by a guy on the plane, for the Camuy, the world's third largest underground river. Wow. I knew you'd be impressed. When I got there, though, I discovered far, far more exciting things about Puerto Rico. That it is also home to the world's largest dog show followed very quickly by the world's largest clean-up operation. That they get American movies at the same time as they are released in the rest of the States. Lucky things. At least it means they can get them over and done with straight away and not have to sit for months on end dreading the release of the next Arnold Schwarzenegger. And that in 1963 they witnessed the invention of one of the greatest-ever benefits

to mankind – the *piña colada* – at 104 Fortalzo in Old
San Juan, by one of their greatest national heroes, a
certain Don Ramón Portas Mingot. Cheers, Donny baby.
To what extent, however, Donny baby's *piña coladas*
have been responsible for making Puerto Rico one of
the richest countries in Latin America and one of the
poorest states in the US, I couldn't find out. All I know is
it has certainly made them one of the happiest. Every
night of the week they knock them back and rave it up
until dawn.

As for me, the days I spent racing around the capital,
San Juan. With its huge hotels and gallerías and
shopping malls it is more a US beach resort grafted on to
a Spanish theme park than a Spanish theme park
grafted on to a US beach resort. The nights I spent racing
around looking for peace and quiet.

The oldest city in the whole for the US (it was
founded in 1521, just 24 years after the arrival of
Christopher Columbus) San Juan is also the best
preserved. At least, the old part is. From the top of the
hill overlooking the Atlantic running down to the ocean
the whole place consists of wall-to-wall traditional
Spanish architecture laid out Spanish-style. Narrow
cobblestone streets radiate out in straight lines north–
south, east–west from the Plaza de Armas in the centre.
There are elaborate balconies everywhere, and tiny
houses with thick walls, high ceilings and huge, lush
inner courtyards crammed tight together like Spanish
fishing boats in the North Sea. There are masses of
churches, not to mention churches for the masses: and
huge, rock-solid, four-square monasteries and convents,
most of which are now small luxury hotels famous
around the world.

Wandering around San Juan is like wandering
through an elegant, beautifully preserved Spanish
military town full of classical or, I suppose, the experts
would say, neo-classical Spanish wedding-cake architecture. The massive six-storey fortress built by the

Spanish to guard the entrance of San Juan Bay, which withstood the bombardment of Sir Francis Drake, is 140 feet high with walls 18 feet thick. The church, San José, is the second oldest in the whole of North and South America. Opposite, the barracks is the largest built by the Spanish in the whole of the Americas. If you think City Hall, with its plaza and statues of the four seasons, looks like the City Hall in Madrid, it does. It's a copy. La Princesa, the old jail, is still destroying people's lives and condemning them to unimaginable horrors: it is now the local tourist board.

Lean up against the wall of virtually any bar in the old city and across the Bay you can see what to many people is the most important cathedral in the world: the Cathedral of Rum, as it is called. It consists of twenty giant 50,000-gallon tanks of Bacardi, making it also the largest rum distillery in the world. When I called in there, for research purposes only, you understand, I remember seeing a sign outside saying 'Caution: swans crossing'. After that things got a bit hazy.

The old buildings are not just confined to the old city. They're all over town. There's the Caribe Hilton, which the Puerto Ricans boast is one of the oldest hotels on the island. It was built in 1949. There's the Performing Arts Centre which, like performing arts centres the world over, looks like some nuclear bunker. No, I shouldn't say that, especially as there I experienced one of the most memorable evenings I think I've ever spent at the opera. Halfway through *Don Giovanni* the statue is supposed to come to life, step down from its pedestal and start having a go at the Old Charmer. Except in this case, it fell off, crashed to the floor with a resounding thunk and then stood up to thunderous applause. It was wonderful. It almost made me drop the notebook in which I was frantically scribbling down all the tricks and dodges that obviously made the old boy such a success but which have so far eluded me.

Whether I was racing around town or squeezing

myself into my seat at the opera, I hardly had room to breathe. The pavements were crowded, the bars packed, the restaurants full to overflowing. Partly this was because the Puerto Ricans themselves are so huge. I'm not kidding - they're like barrels. I don't think I've been anywhere in the world where practically everyone you come across is as wide as they are tall. If these guys ever take up sumo wrestling they'll be world champions in a fortnight. As a result, put two Puerto Ricans on a pavement and nobody can get past; stick them in a bar, nobody stands a chance of getting a drink; sit them down in a restaurant - any restaurant, especially in Hato Rey, the financial district - and you can kiss goodbye to seeing any sunshine, let alone catching the waiter's eye.

Faced with the prospect of a dry weekend in San Juan sitting in the dark unable to get anywhere near the bar to get a drink, I decided to head out of town. I was up early Saturday morning to do all my paperwork. As conscientious as ever, I wrote up all my reports, did all my proposals, draw up a thousand ideas for feasibility studies and fired off a million faxes and by 7.15 I was ready to leave. Instead of following the sign of the parrot to the rainforests or the sign of the tree to the fishing village, I decided to follow the sign of Puerto Rico's famous *paso fino* horse to Ponce. Who on earth was responsible for this pictorial signpost system I cannot imagine, unless it is some kind of subtle plea for greater understanding for dyslexics.

Out of San Juan we swung, on to this enormous six-lane highway, which was packed solid with traffic crawling along at about three or four miles an hour. Rush hour? Accident? Traffic jam? No way. It's just that the Puerto Ricans are so huge there's no way any cars or vans or trucks can do 13, let alone 30, mph. Four Puerto Ricans in a car - let alone, say, one of those, what do they call them, people carriers - and the springs are popping out all over the place, the chassis is straining like mad, the tyres are bursting and the whole thing is scraping along on its metal rims. Or what's left of them.

Gradually, however, once we got out into open country, things speeded up. We hit 17 mph. This was marvellous, because it meant that I could at least see the scenery. As a result, I'm very pleased to be able to report that the island is actually two islands. The first consists of beautiful, sweeping fields, green grass, sugar cane, bananas and rainforests. The second is practically nothing but arid desert, dust, sand. The change is very sudden. One second you're in beautiful green fields, the next you're straining to make the top of a hill and you coast down the other side practically into the middle of the Sahara Desert.

I went to Ponce around, er, what I mean is, I got to Ponce, their second largest and, they say, most distinguished city, around mid-morning when it was in full swing. It was hilarious. Well worth the trip. Or at least, I thought it was. There were Ponce buses and Ponce taxis, Ponce police looking after Ponce banks, Ponce ambulances taking Ponce victims to the Ponce hospital. There was even a Ponce High School, whose professional qualifications, I was assured, were of the highest order. I would have thought they would have been of the lowest order, but then I know nothing about these things. For the first time in my life I discovered something suitable to take home for my brother-in-law. A T-shirt proclaiming 'Ponce 1997'.

I met a Ponce accountant, a Ponce auditor, who I was sure wasn't the only Juan in town, and a Ponce management consultant, although apparently there are plenty of them around the world. But the biggest Ponce I came across – well, apart from the one years ago in Barclays Bank in Piccadilly – must have thought I was a Labour Member of Parliament. He ambled up to me in a black leather suit, looking like an out-of-work flamenco dancer, while I was having a drink in one of the back-street bars. There was something odd about him. I couldn't put my finger on it and I wasn't going to, either.

Then he told me he wanted to get one thing straight: he wasn't. Which didn't surprise me. But the last thing I was going to do was bend over backwards to be grateful to him for telling me.

As for the city itself – or Historic Ponce as it proclaims itself – it's full of balconies and balustrades, ornate ironwork and horse-drawn carriages. You can tell how historic it is: they even keep their gas lamps on during the day. Towards the end of the 1800s Ponce was a wealthy port in its own right. It provided essential support services to the island's coffee, sugar cane, rum and shipping industries. The island's first governor was a Ponce, Juan Ponce to be precise. Although I know that is not in itself unusual. Two other Ponces have also been governors.

The centre of town, the tree-lined Plaza Las Delicias is, well, Delicias. At one end is the striking red-and-black striped Parques de Bombas. No, not a park where bombers can meet and compare notes on the merits of different types of fertiliser. It started out as an agricultural exhibition stand in 1883. It was then used as a fire station. In 1990 it became the distinguished home of the famous Ponce fire engine exhibition. Today, everybody kept telling me it is the oldest, most distinguished fire station in the Spanish-speaking world, run by a group of dedicated Ponces who, if I understood them correctly, are all called José. Which I suppose couldn't be more appropriate in the circumstances.

At the other end of the square, more concerned with combating the fires not of today but of eternity, is the cathedral, which is not as lush and Delicias as I expected. If anything it is practical and workmanlike. More concerned, perhaps, with putting out fires than with kindling the mystic flames of passion or desire for the next world.

All around are people, people, people. Families sitting on benches. Kids playing and getting under everybody's feet. Old men in hats and coats reliving old memories.

Around them is non-stop traffic, cars, buses, trucks. Facing into the square are all the wonderful, traditional Ponce stores and shops: Ponce Burger King, Ponce McDonald's and Ponce Taco Bells.

What struck me more than anything, whether I was in San Juan or Ponce or in the middle of nowhere looking for offices or factories or warehouses, was the fact that, over 450 years after Puerto Rico was discovered, everyone is still trying to make up their minds whether they want to be Spanish or American. Or, I suppose, Spanish American. Or Spanish Puerto Rican American. Or Puerto Rican Spanish American. Or even American Puerto Rican Spanish.

Take food, for example. Like Americans, Puerto Ricans have to have a Danish for breakfast, a lite lunch for lunch, or rather, for their Happy Champagne Brunch, and half a dozen Chateaubriands for dinner. Then they'll suddenly feel guilty and come over Spanish and drown the lot in sour cream or hot sauce or, if they really want to be American, both. They then eat the lot with a fork.

Similarly drinks. They don't know whether to be Spanish and drink wine or be American and drink cocktails. So what do they do? They complain non-stop that their AT & T chargecards are not working and drink cocktails in big glasses with tiny straws. All the way through their meal, as if they were drinking wine.

With music, their big dilemma is whether to salsa or to rock'n'roll. So they do both. At max, max, maximum decibels. One Saturday night I drove practically the length of San Juan and, I tell you, my eardrums went into meltdown. Especially when we got stuck in this enormous Puerto Rican-American-Spanish traffic jam down by the port caused by everybody driving clapped-out American bangers the Spanish way. Three times my taxi driver swung this huge age-old Chevy across the strip of grass running down the centre of the road and into the face of the oncoming traffic only to get stuck again in another jam up another side street, next to yet another set of speakers the size of the Empire State Building.

But the biggest comedy of all is the language. Do they speak Spanish? Or English? Or American? Or what? The answer is, you'll have to shout louder. I can't hear. Sometimes I think it's Spanish. Sometimes I think it's English. Sometimes I don't know what the hell it is. Whatever it is, they do it their own way.

One morning I had this big session at the university. The meeting was supposed to be about the economy, economic development and all that blah, blah, blah. They wanted me, they said, to be up-front and share with them the space I was in and where I was coming from. 'Certainly. I will do my best,' I mumbled. Which threw them. I don't think they knew what I meant.

I then had to shake hands with practically the whole faculty, with each one telling me, 'I appreciate your co-operation. Have a nice day.' By the time I had finished there wasn't much time for me to be up-front and share anything with them. All the time I was speaking they kept murmuring things like 'Go with it', 'I understand where you're coming from', 'You're on my case', 'I acknowledge you'. For a moment, I thought I'd strayed into one of those charismatic church services. When it came to the discussion afterwards – sorry, I mean the sharing continuum – they kept on about 'lone dependencies' and 'positive reinforcements' and 'intimacies', whatever they are. Then all of a sudden someone jumps up and starts rambling on about 'mind games' and 'low esteem levels' and that it has been his life's ambition to see the sale of cannabis legalised. It was then that I noticed the pencils all the students were using. Originally the slogan printed down the side had obviously read 'Too Cool to Do Drugs'. But after a few weeks of sharpening they were saying 'Cool to Do Drugs'. You can bet your life that before long they were simply going to say, 'Do Drugs'.

Afterwards I wanted to use the phone. Because of all the handshaking and have-a-nice-day business I was running late, and I wanted to tell the next guy I was going to see that I was on my way. I go back to this guy's office. Can I use his phone? No way. Every time I pick it up his goddamn daughter is there.

'Will you tell my Daddy it's a lovely day and I love him very much?'

Will I hell. I'm not passing on that sort of slushy, yucky nonsense to anyone

'Did you tell my Daddy I love him? Did you? It's important to me.'

It's also important to me that I make this call. Now get off the line.

'Please. Did you tell my Daddy the sun is shining and I am thinking of him all the time?'

Now look. I don't care whose daughter you are. Will you get off the phone! How can I call this guy if you're always on the flippin' phone? Clear off!

The biggest laugh of all is when they mix everything up together and you get what I call Spanglish or rather Spanamerican, which is a glorious misho-macho between taking the Miguel out of English and putting the Michael into Español or whatever.

One morning, I kid you not, I had two *crimanales* or rather taxi drivers fighting over me outside the hotel.

'Silencio, you big gorillos,' one was screaming at the otro. 'I'll punch you on your patio.'

'Oh, Santo Cristo,' the other one sighed. 'You're loco. You like bandito outta a Spaghetti westerno.'

Wow, I thought. All those years learning Latin and Greek. This is the language for me: a bit of English, a bit of Spanish, or if you don't know any Spanish just make it up. Nobody's going to notice the difference. And if they do, what the *diablo*. By the end of my trip, therefore, I was as goodo or as baddo, I suppose, as the rest of them.

I go to see this biggo cheeso running this industrio

pipeline operatione. All the participationes in the projectos, he tells me, are going to make voluminous dollares. It was going to be a big bonanza for todo persones. But at the moment he had 'muchos massos problemos'. He was 'takingos all the flakos from the cuatro corners of the mundo'. He said he wanted to make a requesto of me. Would I make an 'heroico sacrificio' and over the weekend visit the projectos, he was sure, I would find one of the most extraordinario under the luna.

Pushing my Spanglish, or rather Spanamerican to the limits, I said with mucho lamentatione that it wasn't necessario. If I could have a copia, por favor, and a catalogo, I would take it back with me to Inglaterra. That would be sufficiemente por el momento. In casa of any problemos I could then come back to him or call him on the telefono.

Would he agree? No wayo. He kept saying no, no, no. To actualamente see the projectos would make a big impressione on me. I would see why. The potentia was enorme.

In the end, though, he got the message. I just said I wanted to have a 'Placido Domingo', and that was that.

He just stared at me. 'Clara,' he grunted.

Now I'm stuck. Who the hell is Clara? And what has she got to do with pipelines? Or is that what they call Placido Domingo in Spanglish or Spanamerican? Or even Spanish.

Sometimes Spanglish or Spanamerican doesn't quite work out the way you expected. Or, at least, mine doesn't.

One evening I got back to the hotel. There was this very independiente Juanita waiting for me who said she wanted to tell me about her servicios particularios. She had a great deal of experiencia. She was totalemnte interested in experimentas. But no electricos. Mechanismos, sí. But electricos, definitely no. She thought we could have a co-operatione together. She was confidente that my performance would be more than satisfactoria, if not exuberanta.

Oh sí, sí, sí, I thought.

I wouldn't have to shello outta my back pocketo, she went on. She wasn't looking for a grande totale from me, or anything like that.

Oh sí, sí, sí, I thought. I've heard that before.

Instead she said all she wanted me to do was primo the pumo. She would do the rest.

Oh sí, sí, sí, I thought. I know your ultimo objetivo. So I wished her hasta la vista, made a grande exito and headed back to the rancho.

It was only later, of course, that I discovered she worked for a firm of accountants. They were interested, as an experiment, in setting up an investment operation that would concentrate initially on small and medium-sized engineering companies. If it was successful they would expand the whole operation, in terms of both size and geographic spread. They wanted to talk about ways in which we could work together. By the time I finalmente got back to her it was, not surprisingly, mucho too late. They'd found an otro hombre to work with who presumably spoke their kind of lingo. Well, that's my versione of eventos and I'm sticking to it.

All this, however, is supposed to be coming to an end. The Puerto Ricans have to decide whether to stay independent or whether to become really American, the 51st state. At the moment they are neither one thing nor the other. They are wholly independent but they are part of the so-called Commonwealth of the United States. They have their own currency, but everybody uses US dollars anyway. They are US citizens. They can be drafted into the US Army. They can drive you mad with tales of Ben Franklin's cherry tree, George Washington's axe and Paul Bunyan's kite. Or is it Ben Franklin's axe, George Washington's kite and Paul Bunyan's cherry tree? I can never remember. But they still can't vote for the US President. They have a representative in the US Congress, but he can't vote either - or at least he can vote, but nobody takes any notice of him.

Puerto Ricans can do business with whoever they want - apart from the countries the US doesn't want them to do business with. On top of that, whatever they import has to be shipped in, regardless of all the free trading agreements in the world, by the US Navy at, again regardless of all the fair trade agreements in the world, whatever price the US Navy wants to charge them.

Some people are happy with things the way they are. They don't want any changes. They like going retailing instead of shopping. They prefer check-in lines to queues. They like nothing better than to verbalise instead of have a chat. And they have nothing against being knocked down by joggers at five o'clock in the morning. They are also worried about what would happen, if they broke with the US, the next time they were hit by earthquakes, floods or hurricanes. Would the Americans turn away and not bother to come and help them? These people belong to the Leave Things Alone School of Politics. If you change anything, life will obviously get worse.

On the other hand some Puerto Ricans actually want to become Americans. They can remember the day the Americans arrived in 1898 with the end of the Spanish American War. They can remember how, in the 1950s, with US help, Operation Bootstrap transformed the economy. Before that their country was known as the poorhouse of the Caribbean. They had nothing but agriculture and mostly subsistence agriculture at that. Today, they can see, they are hailed the world over not only for giving the US the hammock, the maraca and slow-roasting chicken but also Iris Chacon, the original Latin bombshell. Come on. You don't mean to say you've never heard of the original Latin bombshell, as opposed to the second: the collapse of the Mexican peso on 20

December 1994. A few twisted cynics from the Che Guevara School of Latin American Diplomacy also want to become American. They know Puerto Rico costs the US billions. Being part of the States is, they reckon, the quickest way to bring down the mighty America.

The sensible majority, including the whole of the West Side of New York City, say, 'Mucho here and nowo wanto draw the line in these extremos circumstanciones and fundamentale stando firme passionamente, blacko and blanco, importante reasone, interna and externa, excessione regulationes, keepa takinga the tablettos, amigo. Non, non, non. Which, from my acute in-depth knowledge of Spanglish or Spanamerican, roughly translated, means yes.

Since Columbus stumbled across the island on 19 November 1493 it has only been allowed to run its own show for all of twelve months, from 1897 to 1898. Spain granted them their independence in 1897 while Uncle Sam arrived in 1898. It's about time, the Puerto Ricans feel, that they had the chance to ruin their own country the way so many other people have ruined theirs. In any case they say, look at Vietnam. America has done far more damage to Vietnam since the guns stopped and they started being friends.

Without the Americans, they say, there is no reason why Puerto Rico couldn't be more successful. They are smart. Already they're big in electronics, in pharmaceuticals, in insurance, in bananas and in a string of hi-tech industries. Already many of the world's biggest, most dynamic, most aggressive companies have investments there. They would have to engineer something pretty cataclysmic for them to jump ship, and I can't see them doing that.

Having tried to find out what people think in San Juan, I also tried to find out what people thought in Ponce. But nobody was interested. In discussing politics, that is. All people seemed to want to do in Las Delicias was to sit, gaze up at the sun or eat ice cream. The guy in charge of the Bombas only wanted to talk about fire engines. Isabel and Cristina were concerned only with shops. Isabel Street and Cristina Street that is. I tried the Juan Morel Camps Music Institute but I got nothing noteworthy there. Similarly La Perla theatre. No perlas of wisdom there, either.

Just up the street I tried the Ponce History Museum which, I reckon, deserves some kind of getting-blood-out-of-a-stone award. I don't think I've been in a museum anywhere in the world which has squeezed every last drop of information from a place. 'Few cities can boast a history as varied and significant as Ponce's,' they bragged. Well, I don't know about that, but certainly few museums can boast as much history and gossip and this and that. The best bit, though, was out the back, down a corridor and into an art gallery which had the most amazing collection of paintings of horses by a local artist. It was incredible.

My appetite whetted by the paintings of horses, I decided I was ready to take on the Ponce Museum of Art, which modestly proclaims itself 'the Parthenon of the Antilles'. Would this introduce me to the real Ponce? Would I see row after row of famous Ponces staring down at me? Would I finally learn what made the Ponces what they are today? From the outside, the building looked impressive – no way was this another converted church hall job. It was sleek and modern, designed by the same hombre who designed the Museum of Modern Art in New York, Edward Durrell Stone. Inside, I was right. There were the Ponces in their powdered faces, wigs, stockings and buckled shoes, striking elaborate poses. In elegant settings with dreamy faraway looks in their eyes.

But they weren't Puerto Rican Ponces. They were all fey, dreamy chocolate-boxy, otherworldly English Ponces. The place was practically full of Reynolds and Gainsboroughs and Rossettis and Burne-Joneses. Leighton's *Flaming June* was there (I've always thought

'Flaming' was not quite the right word. She's more curled up fast asleep November as far as I'm concerned). There were also a whole bundle of Millais and Ford Maddox Browns and Tilly Kettles. Tilly Kettle? Come on, don't say you've never heard of Tilly Kettle. The wife will go bananas, especially if she's one of those liberated types. Tilly Kettle is about the only halfway decent woman painter we've got. Pre-Raphaelite or otherwise. She's like a Reynolds or a Gainsborough, but without the powder and the wig and the fancy shoes, if you see what I mean. Either way, I came to Ponce around ten o'clock, and by three o'clock I had ended up with an English mistress – or rather master – of art.

In the circumstances, I thought the least I could do was to go back to the cathedral and say a prayer to help me stop making silly remarks about towns and cities. Which I did.

How far is the White Nile from Haifa?
Hanoi be thy Nice
Thy Kazakhstan
Thy Williamsburg in Iran as it is in Harlem
Give us this Dallas our Dominica
And Fort Worth our Tajikistans as we
　　Fort Worth those who Tajikistan against us
Liechtenstein into Tennessee
For thine is the Kingston
The Prague and the Ghana
For India and India
Yemen.

St John's

'The chairman.' I could hear this plummy secretary who looked as though she came straight out of *Country Life* declaiming to the telephone. 'He is not here. He is in Antigua. On holiday. Not,' she spat the words out one by one, 'To. Be. Disturbed.' A pause. 'Who is it, may I ask, who wishes to speak to him?'

I shuffled up and down the corridor outside waiting to be granted an audience. God knows some chairmen are bad enough. But in my experience chairmen's secretaries are a million times worse.

'Oh! The Palace!' I could now hear her shrieking. 'Why didn't you tell me they were from the Palace? Yes, of course, send them up, send them up. Straight away. Straight away. I'll meet them at the lift.'

She slammed down the phone, burst out of her office and was down the corridor to the lift in the time it takes to say, three's a crowd, shrieking all the time like a demented banshee, 'The Palace! The Palace! They're from the Palace!'

Time to go, I thought. I'm not going to get any sense out of anyone today. Try again tomorrow.

Later I heard that the two visitors looked like retired colonels or major-generals or whatever. What is more, they had arrived bearing a large brown envelope. The envelope, everyone told me, had express instructions written on it: 'To be delivered to the chairman. Personally.'

By hand.' Her Royal Supreme Highness the secretary apparently told them that she was the chairman's personal, private and highly confidential secretary, had been for a million years and was quite capable, thank you so much, of opening such a thing as a large brown envelope. Even from the Palace.

Apparently the two old buffers went red, white and blue. For the chairman's eyes only, they spluttered. They had their instructions and they were duty-bound to abide by them. HRH. The Palace, you know.

But the chairman was not there. He was in Antigua. She had his express permission ...

'The chairman,' said the two men.

They could stand there while she opened ...

'The chairman,' said the two men once more, bowler hats at the ready. *Only* the chairman could open the envelope. It was their sacred, sworn and solemn duty to ensure that the Palace's instructions were carried out to the letter. Heels click. Eyes to the front. Attention.

But, said the secretary, if she rang the chairman now this instant, this very instant, in Antigua and they spoke to him and he gave his permission would they then allow her to open the ...

'But I thought you said the chairman was not to be disturbed,' said the first bowler hat.

'And that you didn't have his number,' said the second.

'Oh yes. But in this case,' trilled the secretary. 'The *Palace*. I know the chairman has been expecting ... for many years ... after everything he's ... I'm sure he won't ... be delighted.'

Antigua. The playground for holidaying chairmen. An island paradise? Beautiful hotels? Luxury developments? Wide boulevards? Palm trees? Sophisticated shops? No way. It's a dump. It looks as though it's gone to the birds. Vere Cornwall Bird, Lester Bird and Vere Bird Junior, who have virtually been running the place for the last sixty years. In fact, it's pretty near the top of my list of places I never want to visit again. Ever. Which has probably ruined my chances of getting one of their fancy honours, such as the Knight Companion Most Distinguished Grand Collar Most Exalted Order of National Hero, or even, I suppose, the Dame Grand Collar of the Most Precious Order of Princely Heritage.

Antigua is like one of those James Bond islands. Millions of peasants slaving away living off nothing at all. Hidden somewhere halfway up a mountain, or in the bottom of some volcano, there is this bird brain whooping it up, killing everyone who crosses his path, while all the time drawing up plans to destroy the island. Here and there, to fool MI6, the CIA, the KGB and all the rest of them into thinking it's just another one of your common-or-garden millionaire playgrounds, he throws up the odd one or two luxury hotels. Then the real stroke of genius which proves I'm right. Once a year, in late April and early May, he organises what's known as Antigua Sailing Week, when the whole island is not only pretty well blockaded by luxury yachts so that nobody can get in or out, it is also invaded by the most awful people imaginable.

People will tell you that during that week the seas around Antigua are what Monte Carlo is to tennis, St Andrews to snooker or Wimbledon to the end of the District Line. Or something like that. Have you heard the noise a single yacht makes with a load of Hooray Henrys and Henriettas on board? Imagine that multiplied a million times over. It's like Royal Ascot goes to the seaside. Those voices, those accents. 'Keep the sea on your right-hand side, old chap, and you won't go far wrong. What?'

I don't know about you but I couldn't care less if they did go far wrong. I'm with Nelson, who no doubt knew more about sailing than probably the whole of the local Sea Scouts and the Royal Antigua Yacht Squadron combined when he put his telescope up to his ear and called the place 'this infernal hell'.

Either way, Sailing Week is the perfect cover for Mr Big to ship into his underground headquarters all kinds of secret weapons to destroy mankind's ability to think, act or function properly: inter-continental nerve gas bombs from Libya, that awful cheap champagne from Spain or copies of Bill Bryson's book – what's it called? – about all those boring small towns in America which, not surprisingly, everybody begins but nobody ever finishes.

The whole of the rest of the world could blow itself to bits before any radar station covering Antigua would pick up any unusual movements. In any case, knowing the loyalty and life-long dedication of most CIA or MI6 or even KGB officers, they're probably all working for Mr Big already.

But if Sailing Week is bad, Carnival Week is a million times worse. First, because it's not a week. It's ten days. Second, because – *can you hear me?* – it's non-stop blaring, high octane, ultra-pulsating, hip-swishing, foot-tapping, ear-splitting ra-ra-ra. So if everybody's happy, I hear you screaming, what's the problem? The problem is that that's not why they have the carnival. It is organised, I was told again and again, because that's the time all the big guys smuggle in their goodies while everybody, including the customs officers, are looking the other way. One year someone actually tried to smuggle in, would you believe, a real live Rolls Royce and got caught. Had he slipped in a tiny little plastic bag instead he might have got away with it.

Now, of course, the message is, carnival or not, everyone must be on full alert at all times – until, that is, they hear the sound of that oh-so-familiar rhythm: the rhythm of 100-dollar bills being dropped carelessly into brown paper bags.

'Hello. Hello... Hello, hello. Can you hear me? It's

London here. No, not Londonair. London *here*. Look, is there anybody in charge? Oh, you're in charge. Good. Now I want to talk to ... Hello, hello! Oh, no. Would you believe it, they've put the phone down. These colonials. We never had these problems in ... Oh, you are still there. Why didn't you say so? I haven't got all day. Now, my good ... Hello. Hello. Oh this is too much ... *Hello.* Hello ... you're still ... No, I have an important job I want you to do for me. You understand? Yes ... Good ... Now have you got a pencil and paper? ... Hello. Hello.'

Of all the places in the world to visit, Antigua is definitely not one of them. To tell you the truth, one of the reasons I didn't set out to become a company chairman (well, apart from all the lying and cheating and back-stabbing involved) was because I didn't want to have to spend 36 weeks of the year on holiday in Antigua.

Oh paper, however – especially on thick, glossy, holiday brochure paper – it looks fantastic. Sunshine? It's dripping with the stuff. When it's not being lashed by monsoon-like rains, howling winds and, of course, the occasional hurricane. Take a bow, Hurricane Hugo, from which the islanders are still recovering five years later. Then there are the tanorexics, people who throw up if they spend a week in the place and don't go home with the most amazing all-over tan. Stay there two weeks and they throw up if they don't end up looking like some giant walking raisin.

I myself suffer from thermalpsychosis. Which means I can't stand being anywhere hot where people go on and on about the joys of being cool. Which, I admit, rules out about half the world at a stroke. I'm also allergic to water, although I can do a perfect crawl on dry land. So I'm worried.

Beaches? There are 365 of them. Trouble is, you can't enjoy a single one of them in peace, because no sooner have you settled down in your deckchair, taken your braces off and tied your little red handkerchief over the top of your head than some *nouveau riche* lottery millionaire will come prancing over to you, half out of his Ralph Lauren Factory Outlet shorts, to tell you that there are 364 other beaches just like the one you're on. Tell him to push off, kick sand in his face or do whatever you like, because he's wrong. Dickenson Bay, the main beach on the island, has something to hide. The fact that it is fast disappearing. On Hawksbill Beach, however, they have nothing to hide. Absolutely nothing. Which reminds me: there are these two huge swells of which to be wary. They might look wonderfully attractive but take my word for it, they can be highly dangerous. Wouldn't want to go scraping the bottom of our hired self-catering yacht, would we? Especially the prices they charge: US$7,000 a week for a 44-foot ketch; US$15,000 for a Swan-65 and US$30,000 for the custom maxi. Plus, of course, all the extras, if you know what I mean. The worst swell I'm told is around Indian Town Cove when the wind is up. The other one is the small hurricane hole just south-east of Parham Harbour.

For the nautical adventurer or should I say, yachtie, who wants, as they say, to swing his anchor in a different watering hole every night, it's perhaps not as easy around Antigua as it is in so many other places around the world. Take Crab Hill Bay, for example. There's a rocky patch about 500 metres off shore, just west of the church. Five Island Bay can also be a problem: the eastern part is plagued with mosquitoes. Definitely not nice, especially if you've stopped taking the tablets. Then there is English Harbour. First you must head for Berkeley Point or Barclay Point depending on whether your map is a sponsored map or not. See the hotel high on the hill way behind Freeman's Point. That's a good guide. Line up with that big beachhouse to the west of – *waaaagh.* Watch out for Charlotte Point. That's one hell of a reef. Don't want to hit that – Now where was I? Oh yes. The big beach house to the west of Freeman's Bay. Four knots only in the inner harbour. All right now, chaps?

But the real killer is Falmouth Harbour. Now I tell you what you do. Get out your British Admiralty Charts, numbers 2064 and 2065. See the red and green channel markers? Now watch out for Bishop Shoal. It's usually marked by a large buoy but if for one reason or another it's not there you can easily see the shoal. Unless, of course, it's calm weather. Then all you can do is pray. Anyway, you've got to keep her to starboard. All right then? You must keep her to your right. Now you see Falmouth Harbour ahead of you. Head for the eastern end. Mind the first buoy to starboard. I mean, right. That's the way to the Catamaran Club Marina. Oh well, never mind. Now we're in the middle of the bar we might as well have a drink. Mine's a large one, please, skipper

As for history, the refuge of the anti-tanorexic, Antigua's got more than its fair share of that as well. Nelson's Dockyard, on the far side of the island, was once the headquarters of the British Navy. How about that then? The trouble was that Nelson hated the place. When he was just twenty-six he was appointed second-in-command to Sir Richard Hughes, a man far older and far more experienced in naval matters, as well as in the ways of the world. He had just demonstrated the in-born superiority of a British officer by blinding himself in one eye while trying to stab a cockroach with a fork. Now I ask you. How on earth can you lose the sight of an eye trying to stab a cockroach with a fork? It's crazy. Although you can tell he was an English gentleman, in that he was using a fork. A French gentleman would have just picked it up with his fingers and swallowed it whole.

When Nelson took over he did three things for which he will forever be remembered.

He closed the port to all but British ships. Which made him none too popular with the local members of the Chamber of Commerce who were doing a roaring trade wheeling and dealing with America.

He built up the dockyard, making it one of the biggest and most efficient in the British Navy. Hence the headquarters status.

Most important of all, he brought in the booze: a hogshead of port, a hogshead of wine, twelve dozen bottles of porter. *A day.* To keep all the jolly jack tars happy.

Nelson himself, however, was far from happy. In spite of dousing himself every day in six buckets of salt water, drinking a quart of goat's milk, walking a mile and smothering himself with nets at night, he was bitten to death by mosquitoes. 'An infernal hole' he called the place - in official histories, that is. What he called it unofficially I think I can imagine.

Talking of infernal holes, Antigua has also got the odd hotel. What am I saying? It's got many an odd hotel. I once went to one which was charging US$750 a night which was crazy. Admittedly it was surrounded by lush, beautifully manicured gardens and long, empty, pristine beaches but the rooms were basic. Really basic. What's more there was no bath, no phone, no air conditioning, not even a proper door. As if that wasn't bad enough, there on the table in the centre of the room was a can of fly-spray and a note telling me if I wanted the room sprayed then I should do it myself. Oh yes, I nearly forgot. The food was extra.

Another so-called upmarket hotel, I was told, was a series of low concrete bunkers cleverly concealed on the edge of the beach in order to blend in with the local environment. I set out one afternoon on a golf cart to visit it, but I couldn't find it. Honest. But, praise be, the English Harbour Hotel still serves afternoon tea. Be warned though - whatever you do don't mention Gilbert and Sullivan. All the old sailors who hang out there still think *HMS Pinafore* is a touch subversive.

*

'Hello. Hello. Can you hear me? Yes, hello, hello… Well, there's no need to take that attitude. I couldn't hear… Hello. Hello. My God. What is she saying? Why can't they speak English? Hello. Hello… golf club? Golf club? Hello. Is that the…? Oh yes, I wonder if you could. I'm looking for our chairman. Yes, the chairman of our company. It's very important, very urgent that I speak to him. Do you understand? Very important. Is he there? Hello. Hello. Can you… Yes, yes, is he there? It's very… What do you mean, you don't know? You must know. He is a member. He is one of your most important… what do you mean, you can't tell me? Oh, this is not good enough. Put me through to somebody in… his name? What do you mean you don't know his name? Everybody knows…'

Psst. In case you're interested. Academically speaking, of course. What I forgot to mention was that Antigua is also one of the world's largest and most successful tax havens, where literally everything is taken on trust: offshore trusts. You've got cash, bundles, even sacks of the stuff, like the guys on Heritage Quay selling T-shirts and cleaned-up sea shells to the poor suckers who tumble off the cruise ships three days a week. No problem. You can put it on deposit, stick it into a string of trusts, even set up a whole web of secret interlocking accounts. No questions asked, no answers expected. In Switzerland. In Liechtenstein. In Luxembourg. In the Canaries. In Trieste. God bless us and save us, even in Dublin Docks itself. It's becoming more and more difficult to make a dishonest living. Those who know say it's going to get more and more difficult. Not in Antigua, it isn't. Here it's gee whizz. They will even let you open your own bank. All you need is a phone, a computer and a brass plate, preferably a big brass plate as a guarantee of your size, your strength and your stability, and a single room, say, above a coffee bar or opposite a dentist's surgery. Oh yes, and an innocent

English lord to sit on the board, or even better to be chairman, and you're in business. Not that they don't have rules and regulations. Goodness me, they're not completely stupid. Of course they have rules and regulations. Some of the strictest rules and regulations in the world. It's just that they don't bother to implement them.

One morning I went to see the department at the Ministry of Finance responsible for regulating the financial sector and ensuring that without fear or favour their rules and regulations were strictly adhered to. It was in a Nissen hut. And they were both out. In fact, everybody in the whole Ministry was out. The girl at reception told me that the guy I had an appointment to see was at home. He had more important things to do there, she said, than regulate the banking sector.

Instead I strolled down to the Commissioner's Grill, which I reckon is the one good thing about Antigua. It's the only place in the world where I've had lobster not only for dinner but for breakfast and lunch as well. Over a couple of dozen rums I got the lowdown on banking Antigua-style from this guy with a fancy shirt, dark glasses and a big cigar – in other words, a corporate lawyer.

To set up an ICB (sorry, I mean a bank. That's just the way we international corporate lawyers speak) is, he said, as easy as ordering another round of rum punches. Licences? Charters? Forget it. The Antiguan government was eager to attract as many offshore banks as they could. Already they had 58. They were going for 100. With that kind of growth they didn't have time to get bogged down in detail. Total privacy? Strict confidentiality? No problem. Under Antiguan law 'no person shall disclose any information relating to the business affairs of a customer, that he/she acquired as an officer, employee, director, share holder, agent, auditor or solicitor except pursuant to an order of a court in Antigua', he said in his best US$5,000-an-hour lawyer's voice.

So how many court orders have there been ordering people to spill the beans? You got it. Not a single one. How many will there be? Right again. None.

My final question: costs. How much does it cost to set up your own international bank? Prepare yourself for a shock. Around US$1,200, yes US$1,200. Plus US$750 a year to maintain it. Plus anything between US$5,000 and US $10,000 to handle all the paperwork.

Agreed? We open a bank of our own. The lawyer said he could let me have all the necessary documents early next week.

But whatever you do, don't run away with the idea that wheeling and dealing and setting up banks is simple. It isn't. There are some big obstacles to over-come. Such as, if you get that upstairs office in Church Street almost opposite the police station – a perfect site for a bank – will the coffee bar downstairs keep you supplied with coffee and will the dentist on the top floor keep the screaming to a minimum? Don't want to frighten the clients away, do we ...

'I thought you said you knew where the chairman was?'

'I did.'

'And you had his personal, private telephone number?'

'I do.'

'But you haven't been able to reach him?'

'No.'

'Isn't that a bit strange?'

'Well, it's the first time I've had to try and reach him.'

'You mean it might not even be his number?'

'No. I mean, yes. He gave it to me twenty-three years ago when he first started going there. I just assumed it was ...'

'I think we'd better leave it for now, thank you so much. We'll come back again ...'

'No, no, let me just try three more numbers where he might be. As it's the Palace ...'

*

Skyscrapers. Immaculate lawns. Sweeping six-lane highways. Exotic nightclubs. Fabulous bars and restaurants. Casinos the size of aircraft hangars. Never-ending plantations of bananas, pineapples, mangoes...

You have to be kidding.

If anything, Antigua is the exact opposite. It is an island rich in more than 400 years history and culture of the Caribbean, where it is still possible to catch a glimpse of the quaint ways and traditions of the islanders all those years ago: not because they have been lovingly restored and recreated in some kind of Caribbean heritage theme park, but because that's the way they still live today.

Antigua, the real Antigua, is nothing but 168 square miles of poor, pathetic undeveloped coral limestone and volcanic ash which has remained virtually unchanged for generations and where the only unmistakeable, authentic, idyllic Caribbean sounds you're likely to hear are the stirring rhythms of a smashed gearbox, the tropical screeching of long worn-out brake linings and the unmistakable, non-stop rap, guaranteed to melt your eardrums at several inches' distance. What am I saying, inches? I mean paces. If you're lucky you might also hear the rare sound of a small plane landing in the middle of a long, broad, flat field and then rapidly taking off again. Rarer still is the sound of small trucks and 4×4s creeping in and out of the edge of strips of woodland and forest. A word of advice. If you do see them, don't get out your camera and twitcher's notebook. They are very temperamental and are easily frightened by the slightest sound.

As for your ordinary Antiguan, most of them are not just in the land of their fathers, they are also still in the same tiny, pathetic, tumbledown wooden huts and sheds or simple brick buildings that their fathers lived in and probably their fathers before them. The only tropical punch they're ever likely to get is between the eyes if they stop and watch a 4×4 creeping down a country lane in the middle of the night.

The roads are no more than pot-holes linked together by rough tracks. I went all over the island and I think I only saw about ten miles of decent tarmac. Most of that was driveways and private roads leading up to big houses or hotels: it was difficult to tell the difference.

Running water is about as common as bank enquiries while electricity, especially out in the countryside, is as common as bank audits and inspections. Surprisingly, though, bearing in mind the state of the rest of the island, it does have an airport capable of handling any number of 747s.

It doesn't take a financial genius, let alone a banking regulator, to see that even though Antiguans play cricket – they are one of the many teams that we have allowed to grind us into the dust – the place has gone to pot or to the birds or to both, depending on your view of the local political situation.

To be honest, the capital, St John's, does not look 400 years old. One of the oldest trading ports in the Caribbean, it is rich in history, it is quaint and it is natural. Just to stroll through its streets is to catch a rare glimpse of Caribbean history. In other words, it's a dump. Half the place is falling down. The other half has fallen down.

The buildings are mainly clapboard. Government House – do I detect some Italianate influence? – looks as though it's been subject to too many compromises and is now unable to accommodate anyone. A guardhouse built in 1754 which served as Antigua's first jail is now the charge room of the local police station which shows you how far justice on the island has travelled in less than 250 years. The old Court House which suffered so many setbacks is now a museum and what looks like a warehouse for contraband cigarettes is now the new Court House. As I was standing revelling in its magisterial glory an old lady hustled past me. 'Move over, white man,' she barked. Which I must admit upset me no end. What with waiting ages for a cab outside the King's Casino with a nice lady called Nora, who seemed to spend her life hanging around there, I was convinced I had turned a delicate shade of pink, but there you go.

Then there is the cathedral, whose outside public face is nothing like its inside private faith. A bit like the Church of England, I suppose. Outside it looks big and impressive. Well, big and impressive for Bath. It was designed in fact by one of Bath's finest, a certain Mr J. Fuller. With its free stone blocks and its twin baroque-style towers, it has been dismissed as a 'pagan temple with two dumpy pepperpots'. Inside, however, it is all wood and pitchpine, like one of those upmarket pseudo wine bars you find nowadays all over the Home Counties. The reason apparently is to protect it from hurricanes and earthquakes, which frankly I can no more accept than the Bishop of Durham could accept the Virgin birth. Surely if the outside is going to be blown apart by a hurricane then the inside is bound to be at the least, shall we say, mildly affected. Everybody I spoke to naturally said I was wrong. But they still wanted me to contribute to their US$2 million fund to restore it to its former glory after it had, in fact, been battered by half a dozen hurricanes and an earthquake.

The occasional modern building is small, nondescript, pretty undistinguished, which is crazy when you think of the amount of money that must be stashed away in the place. The famous shopping mall is not a shopping mall. It's a collection of tiny, slightly upmarket shops designed to catch the cruise liner punters. The bit near Redcliffe Street close to the quay is supposed to be being restored but it looks just like the rest of the place. Even the banks, which all seem to have funny names, are no big deal. They all look as though they haven't got two roubles to rub together. That includes the Swiss American Bank, the first offshore operation to open in the country as far back as 1983. To look at it you would think it was down to its last few million. Which might be deliberate. You never know with off shore bankers. In fact, one of the swishest buildings in town is the beautifully painted, well-appointed, well-kept, two-storey Antigua Workers Union Headquarters which is almost opposite a scruffy, single-storey, unpainted wooden hut which houses the Antiguan Industrial Development Board. Which you must admit is a different approach. But for me the most interesting building of all is at the end of Church Street down by the port: not a supermarket, but a Food Emporium called Bryson's. Which is obviously where Bill gets all his money from when he's not at home relaxing while walking the full length of the Appalachian Trail.

As for hotels, the only halfway decent hotel (and that's bargain-basement-Holiday-Inn decent, not your luxury-The Peninsula-George V decent) in the capital of an island which is host to nearly sixty banks and one of the most successful tax havens in the world, is the Heritage Hotel. Which doesn't even serve meals and almost doesn't serve snacks either. The day I checked in I practically had to fight to get even a Coke – a Coca-Cola – and a slice of bread. The following morning when I asked to check out at six pm instead of two pm they insisted on charging me for two full nights' stay, even though the place was practically empty. Definitely a hotel to recommend to one's friends and colleagues.

As far as the rest of the island is concerned, the expats, who all look like upmarket lager louts, slur on and on about panoramic views, sweeping coastlines, beautiful sunsets. All I can say is, it might look that way through the bottom of a glass. All the maps I saw of the place are so desperate to list as many interesting and exciting things as they can that they even feature all the traffic lights on the island.

So how to while away a couple of hours? Shirley Heights, I kept being told. An hour, two hours on top of Shirley Heights, your typical blue-blazered expat told me one evening, would be an impressive, unforgettable, exhausting experience. I should give it a go. Everybody else did. Shirley Valentine I've heard of, and Shirley Williams. Even Shirley Temple. But never Shirley Heights. It turned out to have been originally Fort Shirley, built by Major-General Sir Thomas Shirley as a naval look-out point (why, what did you think I meant?) where for over 200 years during the Caribbean Wars the British could spot a French, Spanish or even Dutch group of would-be visitors as easily as they could moan about the weather.

Go there today and you can see why all the English expats rave about the place. It reminds them so much of home. In other words, it's a dump. Imagine the scruffy top of a scruffy hill. No paths. No gardens. No paving. Just a scruffy patch of earth. A scruffy old pub. A rough old bar. A tiny makeshift stage about the size of a billiard table with a greasy awning splitting in two. A couple of rickety old wooden benches. Empty cans and bottles of beer all over the place. Piles of plastic beakers and cardboard plates and cigarette packets. The occasional black plastic sack. And the final clincher: once I was so desperate for a drink I turned up there on a brilliant, hot, sunny Bank Holiday afternoon. It was closed.

Having done the traffic lights and Shirley Heights there's only one other place to go: Nelson's Harbour, the only surviving complete Georgian naval dockyard in the world. If you have a thing about complete Georgian naval dockyards, that is.

There is an old Georgian ship's bell mounted at the top of the old Georgian gates. It was presented to the dockyards by HMS *Tartar* which, according to Lady Hamilton, was named after Lord Nelson's wife. On the left is the Georgian porters lodge. On the right, the friendly old Georgian guard house. After that it's Georgian sick bays, Georgian boat repair shops, Georgian wooden pillars with lumps of concrete on top, a Georgian boat house made of brick actually shipped all the way from England (which was quicker than teaching the locals how to make them), a Georgian shipwright's house, the tiny, insignificant Georgian admiral's house and a mass of other extremely important, extremely historic Georgian buildings which I can't remember. The one thing that was missing was a typical Georgian tribute to Nelson like the ones they pay on board HMS *Victory* in Portsmouth Dockyard. 'And now,' whenever I go there say the sailors conducting the tour, as they take their hats off and hold them in front of them, 'this is where England's greatest sea captain died. To give you an idea of what it was like in his day, I'll turn the light off for a moment.' The light goes off. Everything is pitch black. But suddenly there is the chink of coins in the sailor's hat. He puts the lights back on again. Everybody thinks everybody else has dropped a couple of coins in his hat and promptly does the same thing. All in the best possible Georgian taste, of course.

One thing, though, I will give Antigua: it is full of glorious romantic names such as Deep Bay, Long Bay, Half Moon Bay, Old Road, Goat Hill and Rat Island.

As for the locals, I'm sorry to say they're as miserable as sin. They have none of the Jamaicans' razzle-dazzle; none of the more serious Barbadian chatter; none of the Trinnies' cricketing gossip; none of the non-stop, US-style banter that you get in Puerto Rico or the Virgin Islands. Instead, poor dears, they are like the quiet, withdrawn, cold-blooded English who will only speak or rather mumble when they are mumbled at. Maybe this is because, deep down in the Antiguan psyche, they are still feeling sore even after all these years that unlike practically everything else in the area Columbus didn't even bother to try to discover them. Instead he is supposed to have sighted the island, seen a bunch of natives jumping up and down on the beach waving prospectuses for offshore banks, and passed very quickly by on the other side. As a result, the first to actually destroy, oops, I mean civilise Antigua was, would you believe, a bunch of English sailors in 1632. The guy who finished this process off was Sir Christopher Codrington, who arrived in 1674. He practically cleared the place in order to grow sugar. By the time he had finished there were over 150 sugar mills on the island. And so it remained until modern-day tourism arrived on the scene. Then, as far as the locals were concerned, it was off the sugar plantations and into the bars, the clubs and the taxis to devote themselves to a lifetime of ignoring the tourists.

But if the locals are bad, the expats are even worse. After a couple of miserable evenings spent roaming the bars, which seemed to be full of nothing but bankers with black leather jackets and names like Mikhail or Sergei or Alexander or Vitali, I got dragged off to something called the Tot Club, which meets every evening at nine bells or whatever (in other words six o'clock) in some back room in the dockyard, where a whole bunch of jolly expats are dedicated to carrying on the good old naval tradition of having a tot of rum, proposing a loyal toast to the Queen, making silly jokes about what's brown and steams and comes out of Cowes backwards and generally getting bombed out of their tiny minds. You think I'm exaggerating? Okay, so what do they make you do if you turn up late for the loyal toast? Walk the plank into English Harbour dressed only in your wife's underwear. So am I right, or am I right?

'So he's got it at long last?'
   'Got what?'
   'A gong. A knighthood.'
   'How do you know?'
   'Well, that's what all this letter business is about, isn't it? I mean what else could it be about?'
   'I dunno.'

'Well, I suppose he deserves it. Dragging himself round the country. All those speeches. All those lectures. Government working parties. Lunches. Dinners. School prize-givings. Meetings with Ministers. Royal openings.'

'So what makes you so sure?'

'Queen's Birthday coming up. Probably the preliminary announcement. Asking them if they're given it will they accept. That kind of thing.'

'Suppose you're right.'

'What else can it be?'

Now, don't get me wrong. Not for one moment am I saying I don't like Antigua: I love it. Because from Antigua I can get to practically all the other places in the Caribbean I can't stand, especially all those secret hideaways that everybody insists on telling you about in such exhausting detail.

I might not be a finance director or an international lawyer or, God help us, an accountant, but I can tell you I've been forced to do more than my unfair share of island hopping. All that leaping in and out of boats with grown men in jaunty little sailorboy suits and getting drenched in spray and waving and shouting across yacht-infested waters at complete strangers in even bigger boats and even jauntier little sailorboys suits. And what about the years of my life I've wasted in some of the world's richest, most beautifully manicured and most boring eco-groovy countryside battling my way through life size fruit salads just for the privilege of – oh joys of joys – actually picking a real live mango off a real live tree? And not just a mango, either. I reckon I've done the full bananarama. I've picked everything in sight: bananas, papaya, avocado, coconut, breadfruit, even empty beer bottles off the beach. What's more, I've had it up to here with crystal clear turquoise waters; azure coloured skies and pristine, powdery, white, sun-bleached beaches with throbbing wall-to-wall melanoma and everyone knocking back genuine, authentic,

Caribbean cocktails that look like liquefied parrot juice and going on and on about how their particular patch of dust is the best anyone has ever seen in the whole history of the universe.

Stand on top of Shirley Heights, if she doesn't object – she doesn't normally object to anything – and you can practically see all the usual run-of-the-mill Caribbean islands I've been forced to visit, and why it's not worth your while bothering with them.

Just south of you are Guadeloupe, Dominica and Martinique.

Martinique and Guadeloupe are not the Caribbean at all. They're French. Which means more or less everything you see has been financed not by the French but by the European Fund for Regional Development. Even the brick walls plastered with anti-European slogans and posters calling for independence. The French traded in vast chunks of India as well as the whole of Canada in order to hang on to Martinique because of all its truly fabulous hotels, bars, clubs and restaurants. But it's not the Caribbean. It's Paris: the buildings, the roads, the bars, the shops, the offices, the *boulangeries. Mon Dieu*, every restaurant even has its own cat mooching around hoping for a quick nibble. They should be so lucky. The prices are as high as the Eiffel Tower.

Gaudeloupe, on the other hand, especially the capital, Point à Pitre, is a touch more Marseilles, even though all the French there behave as if they've come from Paris – especially the *vieille carcasse* in the Lebanese restaurant down by the port. *Mon Dieu*, you should have seen the look on her face when I told her I'd have the set menu for two on the basis that one Englishman was worth two Frenchmen any day. After I'd finished, and her husband broke open his secret bottle of absinthe, which he kept hidden under the cupboard by the freezer, *zut alors*, you could see she was determined that if they had to fight the last war all over again, the last thing the

French would do was come to the help of the British.

Between the two of them is Dominica, which is an old Spanish word for Hell, it's raining again. When the King and Queen of Spain asked Columbus to describe Dominica to them he is supposed to have taken a bit of paper, screwed it up and thrown it down on the table in front of them. What he should have done is soaked it first. The place is virtually non-stop rain, although the Dominicans will have none of this. They go on instead about eco-tourism, rugged beauty, high steep mountains covered in rich forest, swift cool streams, craggy coastlines and being the nature island of the Caribbean. You bet they do. It's the only way they can avoid mentioning the fact that the sun hardly gets a chance to break through the rain clouds. Believe me, whenever I've been there it has made me feel as if I was having a bath at eleven o'clock in the morning. It is also the place for catching crabs. At least, so I was told. There are about 200 different varieties, more than enough for everyone. Big bright yellow ones, little brown ones, and every colour in between. I asked one of the fishermen in the capital, Roseau, what was the best time to catch crabs. 'Night time,' he said.

Next come St Vincent and Grenada. St Vincent is really thirty islands, many of them lumps of sand, where the rich can get away from us all, thank God, including what's-the-one-Princess-Thingy-used-to-holiday-on. Somebody told me it's the only Caribbean island which carries a health warning: nothing but cigarette smoke, empty gin bottles and slurred voices saying that Fergie has been a complete disgrace to the Royal Family. If in spite of all this you still want to go there, whatever you do don't ask for a non-smoking room: they haven't got any. I prefer the capital, Kingstown. It's a nice, quiet hideaway type of a town. The Botanical Gardens also boast a breadfruit tree grown from the original plant that Captain Bligh gave them together with lots of other, perhaps, unhealthy things when he landed there in 1793.

Now isn't that more exciting than coughing your lungs up in all that smoke?

As for Grenada, that was another big disappointment. Everybody told me that I should stay at the No Problem Hotel, just outside the capital, St George's, which definitely sounded like my kind of hotel. Except it was only no problem provided that you knew you had to book in advance for dinner even before you knew you were going to stay there; no problem so long as all you wanted was an egg sandwich; no problem so long as you didn't mind people screaming their heads off outside your room all night; no problem so long as you didn't mind being continuously blasted by radios blaring out some religious broadcasting station in California appealing for just another US$20,000 so they could hit their weekly target of US$1 million in order to continue the Lord's work. There was one redeeming factor. One morning I got a cab into St George's. How far is it? I asked the driver, a lady. 'If it wasn't for the traffic we'd be there by now,' she said.

Barbados, out to the left, has slipped a bit over the years since I first went there. Today it seems to attract nothing but millionaires. In fact, there are so many of them the only way to get any space on the beach, let alone a table in the restaurant, is to say you're expecting Michael Winner to join you shortly. The place, I'm told, just empties.

At the end of the line going south is Trinni, or rather Trinidad and Tobago. I must admit I go to Trinidad quite a bit. I find that after a hard-working trip to Venezuela where night after night one is forced to sample the delights of Caracas, there is nothing better to bring you back down to earth again than a greasy English breakfast of sausage, bacon, egg and tomato. Then there are those steel drums. Once they get going you can't think of anything else even if you want to. Tobago, on the other hand, is Trinidad ten, maybe twenty years ago. Relaxed, slow, dozy. No fast cars, no fast lanes, no fast food. It's so slow that even Trinnies go there for a rest. Two hundred years ago, however, everybody wanted to go there: the Dutch, the French, the Brits, even the Latvians. The sea, it is said, in Bloody Bay was flowing with so much blood that it was decided to call a truce and head for Eleven Degrees North for some spicy Cajun cooking.

Okay. Those are the islands, or rather the main places you don't want to visit, running virtually south of Antigua. Now turn a little, say, south-west, and there is Montserrat. Or rather there was Montserrat. Most of it is now buried under tons of volcanic ash. But in spite of that I've always wanted to go there because it's supposed to be the Emerald Isle of the Caribbean. Its passports are stamped with a shamrock. Not even the Irish Irish do that. One of the main towns is called St Patrick's, and they reckon they speak with an Irish, well, an Irish-Caribbean, accent. And all because the Irish landed there in 1667, couldn't find a bar open and left immediately for O'Caseys down the lane.

Unfortunately, I can never get near it. Whenever I try to get a helicopter to Montserrat out of Antigua the thing is full of wheeler-dealers from Bermuda off to buy up US$600,000 houses from the poor, destitute islanders for US$60,000 and then re-sell them to rich, innocent Germans for US$260,000. As for the boat, the sea is always so rough they either cancel the thing or there's some story about not being able to guarantee it can get to the island, or if it can, not being abl to guarantee a landing. If you do actually get there, you can't just take a swing around the place and get the next boat home. You've got to stay maybe one night, maybe two, until the boat is able to get in to pick you up.

Now move a bit more to the west. Facing you now are St Kitts and Nevis – or rather St Christopher, to give it its proper name, which nobody ever does – Sint Maarten, or St Martin, depending on where your loyalties lie; the two Virgin Islands; and way behind them the Dominican Republic.

St Kitts I like, especially the tiny capital, Basseterre. It is what a Caribbean town should be: on the coast, with lots of fancy buildings, a village green, two churches and lots of bars you can sit in all day long, getting gently plastered and thanking God you're not some punter on a cruise ship wandering around lost, wondering for the life of you which country you're in and what the hell are you going to do until bingo at six pm. Once I got trapped in a bar round the back of the main square by a p-p-pig farmer from P-P-Plymouth who had a st-st-stutter. He'd just r-r-retired he told me and now he spent his life going on c-c-cruise after c-c-cruise. He didn't care which c-c-country he was in so long as he d-d-didn't have to m-m-muck out his b-b-bloody pigs any more.

Nevis is okay. At least, I can understand far more of what the people are saying in the capital, Newcastle, than I can in Newcastle back home. And they don't keep calling me Hinny, either. It's also home to the World Investors Stock Exchange. Which tells you how flexible they are.

Sint Maarten, or St Martin, on the other hand, is hilarious. Especially for anyone who believes in European harmonisation. Come out of the airport, turn right and you're heading for Philipsburg, the capital of the Dutch half of the island which is, how shall I say, typically Dutch. There are two main roads, well, one road, Front Street, and one track, Back Street, which faces on to the beach. The shops are okay. The hotels are okay. The casinos are okay. The Indonesian restaurants are okay. In that typical Dutch kind of way.

Turn left out of the airport, however, and you're heading for Marigot, the capital of the French half of the island, which is so typically French it's unbelievable. The whole of the centre of the town is clean, smart and just packed with exclusive upmarket shops selling all the usual basics without which no Frenchman or woman can survive: clothes, still more clothes, perfume, still more perfume. There are also masses of bars and restaurants, a couple of swish, upmarket hotels and a big, sprawling, luxury marina.

Even though both sides of the island say they are great friends, they still insist on having their own flags, their own currencies and their own official languages. To phone one side from the other is also not a domestic but an international call. Oh well, *C'est la vie.*

Sheltering behind Sint Maarten or St Martin, perhaps not surprisingly, are the Virgins of the Caribbean. All two of them. The US Virgins are, as you would imagine, not for virgins. They are brash, raucous, in your face and have absolutely no idea when to stop. There's a Blackbeard's Castle; a Bluebeard's Castle tucked away, as you would imagine, on Frenchman's Bay; hundreds of bars; thousands of restaurants and enough shopping malls to keep you out of the sun for a month so that when you go home you're more wan and pale than when you arrived. Traffic, especially on St Thomas, the second largest of the three US islands, is horrendous – both on land and at sea. On land, the roads are chock-a-block with limos, especially in Charlotte Amalie, the capital, named after some seventeenth-century Queen of Denmark. At sea, there are nothing but cruise ships offloading practically non-stop more and more happy-dappy punters who don't know where the hell they are.

Everywhere you look there are uprooted trees, twisted girders, huge containers dumped precariously by the side of the road, half-finished houses and half-finished bungalows. Whether they're half-finished because they were half-destroyed by one hurricane or another, or half-destroyed and half-rebuilt before they half ran out of half of the money I have no idea. Even the palm trees are half-supported by half-posts and half-lumps of wood. But to be honest you hardly ever see any of this for all the signs all over the place proclaiming, 'It's nice to tip for service. It's the American way.'

British Virgins, as everybody knows, are in a class of their own. They are quieter, more restrained, less confident, less sure of themselves and virtually unspoilt if such a thing is possible. But it's still US dollars; 'Hi. Howyadointoday?'; rest-rooms; and half a gallon of honey poured over anything that doesn't move. Believe me, it's definitely the place to go for an orgy. Of eating. Of drinking. Of whatever else takes your fancy. Contrary to what you might think, not everything labelled Virgin is owned by Richard Branson. He's only got one of them: Necker Island, which surprisingly he is forced to rent out in its entirety for parties of ten or twenty people at a time in order to help pay the rent. But that's all right. There are enough Virgins left over for me. At least another fifty as far as I can recall.

Tortola, the main island, is fantastic. I shall never forget the first thing they offered me the moment I arrived there: an Island Woman. I felt positively unbuttoned. After that it was one Island Woman after another – in the bars around Cane Garden Bay, in Bomba's Shack, which looks like you imagine, or worse. All junk and rubbish and stuff you wouldn't be seen dead with. But it's one of the best bars I've been to in the Caribbean and that's not including one of their Full Moon Madness nights which I'm told is something else. As for what they offered me across the Sir Francis Drake Channel on Cooper Island: wow. To the uninitiated perhaps I should explain that an Island Woman is two shots of rum, the local Pussers rum, of course; one shot of cherry brandy; one ounce each of lemon, pineapple and orange juice. All mixed with crushed ice. Shaken and served. Fantastic.

The Dominican Republic is El Dumpo. Probably because for goodness knows how many years the place was run by a President who was blind, so even though everybody says he was a good guy, he obviously couldn't see anything that was going on, let alone being dumped, around him. I'm not exaggerating. I wanted to stay in the capital, Santo Domingo, and good old Freddy, my travel agent, booked me into a hotel practically the other side of the island, so I reckon I've seen it all. I also, incidentally, spent more on cabs than I would have done if I had stayed in the most expensive pad in town for a whole month.

It's also pretty faceless to boot. Literally. Take the wooden statues and models in the shops. If they've got faces they're from the other half of the island, Haiti. If they haven't, they're from the Dominican Republic. Why, nobody could tell me. Maybe because I was English. Wherever I went people kept reminding me that on 26 January 1586 Sir Francis Drake, accompanied by no fewer than 1,500 men, sacked the place and made off with all the gold and silver he could get his hands on. 'He might have been the Queen's friend, but to us he is a big thief,' people told me.

Right behind the Dominican Republic are the Turks and Caicos Islands, Christopher Columbus's first landing place in the so-called New World. Definitely not somewhere for hard-line Protestants from Northern Ireland. Land at Providenciales and all you see are Provo signs and Provo displays. Mr Paisley would only have to be there two minutes and he would have a heart attack. On the other hand, there are enough salt flats to make a million Mrs Lots and mud flats and mangrove swamps so choked with silt and sludge that even he could walk on them.

Okay, nearly finished our Caribbean tour of places not to visit. A touch north-west is Anguilla, which is a laugh. Here, in a world that was turning against us and everything we stagger for, is a country that wanted to remain British. And what did we do to reward them for their undying loyalty, admiration and life-long dedication to all things British? We crept in in the middle of the night, anchored our ships offshore and, at the crack of dawn, sent in the troops, for all the world as if the place was run by a bunch of Nazi hotheads.

Today, of course, the story can be told. As a slow, dozy country completely out of touch with reality, Anguilla realised that the only way it was going to survive in this world was by associating itself with whoever would make it look like a red-hot professional. Hence its wish, while the rest of the world was desperately trying to go independent, to remain British. Did it pay off? I reckon so.

The Anguillan immigration operation is certainly as efficient as that at Heathrow. I was sixth in line and it took me just 27.35 minutes to get to the desk. To be checked out took another 4.72 minutes. The taxis are a tribute to London cabs. The first one I got just disappeared and left me stranded in the middle of nowhere. The second drove so slowly that even old ladies with wooden legs were not just overtaking us, they were lapping us as well. The third one charged me so much money I reckon I bought half the island. As for the hotels, well, at the one where I stayed, first they couldn't find my reservation; second they tried to hustle me into a suite at US$1,500 a night instead of the broom cupboard I had booked, and third, even though they billed me in Eastern Caribbean dollars they made out they were US dollars.

As for the countryside, it's dull and flat and boring, like Norfolk. Which, I suppose, proves my point. And everybody I met had just got back home after a stint in the UK with the Jehovah's Witnesses, going around banging on doors and – scoff as much as you like – helping many people not only to discover God, but to realise for the first time in their lives the immense power of prayer by making them stand silently for hours on end behind the curtains, saying again and again, 'Please God, please let them go away.'

The true Caribbean experts will notice that I've left out one place that is really, really not worth a visit: St Lucia. Now, I know I go there as often as I can. I even fly in there sometimes just to have lunch at the fantastic Green

Parrot overlooking the capital, Castries, and the bay and everything else. But it's not because I enjoy it. It's out of a sense of duty. Having to knock back all those rums. Having to eat their lobsters. Drink that wine, that cognac. No, you wouldn't enjoy it, I promise you. You would be depresso bongo every second you were there.

I mean, there's no way you'd like landing at Charles Wheeler Airport and not being able to get a cab because the Prime Minister is out the back with all the taxi drivers playing dominoes. You wouldn't want to meet Harry the Banana Man, who from a shack by the side of the road presides over the best view of the Roso Valley, the biggest banana plantation on the island. You would just hate the way he treats you like a geest of honour and insists you munch one banana after another while he gives you the life story of the St Lucia banana: the juiciest, sweetest, most fantastic banana in the world; how they replaced sugar cane; how they grow them in blue polythene bags to get them in perfect condition; how they harvest them three times a week and how in 1999 all the farmers will finally own the land on which they have been growing them for so long.

As for Steve McQueen, who has appeared in a string of Hollywood movies, you would just do everything you could to avoid him. 'I'm not really Steve McQueen,' he says. 'It's just that I call myself Steve McQueen.' You'd just hate stopping and chatting to him on your way down into Soufrière on the far side of the island. A tiny, wiry old man, he would regale you if you're not careful with stories about how he's appeared alongside such minor stars as Christopher Reeve, Michael Douglas and Michael Caine in such run-of-the-mill hits as *Superman, Romancing the Stone, Water,* and *The Creature* along with, it must be admitted, half the island when the films were being made on location there.

And then there is Margaret. You would just hate her, the only lady in the world who can make me forsake the heavy stuff for one of her mean fruit cocktails. Today she presides over this terrible little bar in the Hummingbird Beach Resort on the edge of Soufrière. Where was she before? In Sutton in Surrey. When she got married she brought her husband back home for a quick visit. They've been there ever since. Not that *you* would enjoy it, of course.

Then there is the atmosphere and the scenery and the relaxed way of doing things. Even the clocks unwind on St Lucia. Not only is there a volcano, it's the world's only drive-in volcano. That's how casual it is. But most of all you would just hate the people, who are all so friendly and chatty and approachable. In fact, promise me that whatever you do you won't go there. Go to Antigua instead.

'You wanted me.'

'Yes. Thank you very…'

'What is it? I'm very—'

'There are two gentlemen here, sir. They…'

'Two gentlemen. You ring me all the way here in Antigua to tell me there are two—'

'They're from the Palace, sir.'

'The Palace? You mean…?'

'Yes, sir.'

'My God, girl. Why didn't you ring me?'

'I tried to, sir. I rang the—'

'Yes, yes. that's enough about that. What do they want?'

'They have an envelope for you, sir.'

'An envelope? What kind of envelope?'

'Well. It's brown, sir. It's…'

'Yes, yes. But what kind of envelope? What's in it?'

'I don't know, sir. They won't let me open it. They say it's private and, um, very confidential.'

'Private? Confidential? Well, tell them I said you could open it.'

Poor Miss Smith turns to the two gentlemen from the Palace. 'He says to tell you I can open it for him.'

They look at each other. The first bowler hat gives her the letter.

'Hello, sir. You still—'

'Yes, yes, I'm still here. Get on with it. What does it say?'

Miss Smith tears open the envelope. The two bowler hats from the Palace stiffen to attention. She takes out a single sheet of paper. As she begins to read she instinctively stands up.

'Come along! Come along!' I can hear the chairman's voice barking down the phone. 'What does it say? What does it say? Good God, how long does it take?'

'Hello, sir. You still . . .' Miss Smith's voice is trembling.

'Yes, yes. Read it.'

'It says . . .' she pauses, draws a deep breath. 'It says, Thank you for sending me a copy of your latest speech. I found it very interesting. Charles. Hello? Hello? Are you there? Hello, sir. Hello . . . ?'

Caracas

In the director's office in Chacao, the swish upmarket end of Caracas, the talk, as in directors' offices all over the world, is of the bottom line. Improving and even massaging figures: an addition here, a subtraction there, an overall adjustment in this direction, a slight, ever-so-slight amendment in that direction. Cross fingers, nobody will notice the difference. Then, with a bit of luck, they'll have another big success on their hands.

But this is a factory with a difference. This factory mass-produces non-stop beauty queens: Miss Venezuelas, Miss Latin Americas, Miss Worlds, Miss Universes and presumably in the not too distant future Miss Inter-Galactic Inter-Stellar Spaces as well. The director is Osmel Sousa. The factory – a tiny, rambling, scruffy pink building, with iron bars not only on the windows but on the doors as well – is the Miss Venezuela Foundation. It is the most successful beauty queen operation in the world with, to date, five Miss Latin Americas, five Miss Worlds and four Miss Universe titles to its credit not to mention goodness knows how many others.

As for the figures in question, they're only too pleased to be revealed in all their glory. Massaged even, if that is thought necessary.

Past the Parque Central. Past the ever-so-slightly camp statue of the grande Simon Bolivar, the only statue of him in the world where he's not wearing a uniform. Past the 72-storey Central Park Tower which is full of civil servants.

In the director's office in 23 de Enero at the other end of town the talk is also of massaging figures. But this is no beauty queen operation. This is the Los Magallenos Hospital in the centre of the roughest, toughest and most dangerous part of Caracas. They say it is called 23 de Enero or 23 January district because that was the only day of the year when there was no violence – twenty years ago. Since then it's been non-stop. Here gang fights and drug wars and poverty and destitution are as common as silicone implants in Chacao. Twenty to sixty people killed on a Saturday night is neither here nor there. As for vital statistics, the only one that interests them is how much money they've got left in the bank and how much longer they can stay open.

One hospital nearby, the biggest public hospital in Caracas if not in the whole of Venezuela, with over 1,800 beds, has just been forced to close for want of US$20,000. They didn't have the money, so they went to the government. The government, would you believe, didn't have it either. Out of twenty-two public hospitals in Caracas, this means four are closed. Now the director of the Los Magallenos is desperately trying to avoid the same thing happening to his.

As if that is not bad enough, he is also facing a revolt by patients. All over the hospital, which reeks of urine and is smeared with dirt, are plastered enormous posters complaining about what the patients say he is doing to them. One doctor, a tiny guy with a thick shock of hair who looked no more than sixteen or seventeen, told me they wanted to rename the hospital Magallenos Hope after Chicago Hope, the hospital in the television series. I said that sounded like a good idea. He said it was a joke: it should really be renamed Magallenos Despair.

The waiting-room in the Miss Venezuela Foundation is

the size of a doctor's waiting-room. The floor is covered in a thick pile carpet. Around the walls are rows and rows and rows of Miss Venezuelas, Miss Latin Americas, Miss Worlds, Miss Universes. Not one of them with what the Americans call a negative self-image. In the centre on a low table is, for some reason I couldn't fathom, a statue of Buddha and a collection of cups of coffee, every one of them full to overflowing. Come to think of it, every cup I saw there was full to overflowing. In one of the chairs sits another would-be cracker from Caracas, displaying for all the world to see both the qualities she is confident will propel her to the dizzy heights, plus a dazzling smile that would light up a million casting couches throughout the world – although whether she could butter a slice of bread let alone bake a cherry pie is another matter. Comes the summons and off she struts for her consultation.

Mr Sousa sits in air-conditioned luxury in a mock Regency chair by a desk piled high with papers. On the wall to one side of him is an enormous gilt mirror. In the corner opposite, a giant vase of flowers. In front of his chair is the viewing platform. This is where he studies the raw material he has to work on. Or rather with. Yes. Yes. No. Too big. Too small. Not enough. Maybe. Next one, please. Yes. Yes. Possible. On the other hand. Perhaps. Next one, please. Yes. This is more like it. Needs a bit of adjustment though. A snip here. A bit of a tuck there. He swings his golf club in the air, hooks it gently behind the subject's left knee and pulls it ever so slightly forward.

'Mmm,' he murmurs. 'Mmm.'

'Is beauty born or made?' I wonder.

'We create beautiful women,' he says. 'We don't make them.'

Creating in his terms doesn't just mean reshaping the candidates, it also means teaching them how to apply their make-up, how to style their hair (which should always be shoulder length at least), to lose weight in all the right places, vital for looking good on camera, and, of course, to keep out of the sun. The sun can cause a massive amount of damage to fragile, delicate, young skin. Don't I know it.

So how much does all this cost?

Nobody wants to say. But the guess is anything up to US$250,000 per girl, maybe even more, although somehow or other, whatever the budget, I noticed there always seemed to be very little left at the end of the day to spend on clothes for the would-be Miss Venzuelas, Miss Latin Americas or Miss Whatevers so that they couldn't help but reveal the full extent of their charms. Not that Mr Sousa has to worry about mundane figures when he spends his life surrounded by so many heavenly ones. The Miss Venezuela operation is backed by the Cisneros family, one of Venezuela's wealthiest and most controversial business groups which is in everything from Burger King and Pizza Hut to television and telecommunications.

The waiting-room in Los Magallenos isn't. It's one long, greasy, smelly corridor lined with collapsing metal chairs. In the old days it was bursting with people. That's when the hospital had enough doctors to look after them. Now it's empty, save for one old lady who looks as though she has big problems with her feet. They seem to have ballooned up over her shoes. She obviously has difficulty in walking. She is weeping into a filthy rag.

The consulting-room is tiny, about the size of a telephone box. A window is part open but it is hot and stuffy. The walls are running with condensation which is gathering in tiny puddles of grease on the floor. The doctor, who looks too young to be a doctor, has a white coat on that has obviously seen better days, or even years. The top pocket is stuffed full of papers and biros. He leans up against a table barely the size of a chess board. There are no cups of coffee or anything else anywhere. If there were I'm sure they would also be full to overflowing. With anger, bitterness, grief, frustration. You name it. They are suffering it.

The old lady hobbles in and collapses on yet another broken metal chair. The doctor seems brisk and to the point. A quick question. A slow, agonised reply. He seems to say something reassuring. The old lady starts crying. Again he tries to be reassuring, but in vain. The tears continue. The doctor takes a pen and some paper from his top pocket. He scribbles on it, puts them back in his pocket again. He stands up and motions the old lady to leave. The consultation is over. She staggers to her feet and hobbles slowly down the empty corridor. No medicines. No potions. Nothing. The doctor hasn't even got time to murmur after her. He's out of the room and up the corridor. He's got a million other things to worry about.

The amazing thing is that at one time, with oil revenues pouring in of well over US$1 billion a month, Venezuela had not only the fourth largest economy in Latin America, it was also the wealthiest and most developed country in the whole region. For more than fifty years the place was booming. The Venezuelans had more petro-dollars than they knew what to do with. Everybody who knew a politician and many who didn't were building office blocks, factories, shopping malls all over the place. Everybody, but everybody, went shopping in Miami at least once a month where they were known as the *damedos*, the give me twos. They bought all the big, flashy American cars they could get hold of while the Americans themselves were trading down and going Japanese. 'I love Miami' stickers were slapped on everything that moved. Venezuela was the Saudi Arabia of South America. Super-rich. Super-confident. Super-secure.

Then everything went wrong.

Come the late 1980s, the whole thing crashed. Inflation went bananas. The currency was devalued again and again. Military coup followed military coup. One president was impeached. Corruption became a way of life. One judge, Rosa Natasha Fernandez, was actually caught with nearly US$1,000 stuffed into her underwear. By a policeman who put his hand down her knickers, in front of, it must be stressed, forty witnesses. Another woman judge was caught with US$12,000 in an even more embarrassing place: her flat. But however much you deride her, her neighbours will not have a word said against her. For when the police arrived, she threw all the money out of the window. Who says even judges don't love their neighbours as themselves?

The only way to solve the problem they decided was to print their way out of it. Then in 1994, inevitably, the banks started to cave in. One after another like a pack of cards they crashed to the ground starting with Banco Latino, the second largest bank in the country. By the time the mayhem was over no less than sixteen banks had to be either nationalised or closed and a further 47 bailed out by the state.

Prices started to rise. First by 57 per cent in one year. Then by 103 per cent the next. Inflation started to soar. Reserves plummeted. Devaluation followed devaluation. Capital fled the country not in buckets but in huge container lorries.

Today, all talk of a gradualist Venezuelan solution to their problem is out of the window. The government instead is taking all the necessary tough decisions to bring everything, especially inflation, under control once again. Interest rates have been freed. Exchange rates have been freed. And the toughest decision of all: they have actually grasped the nettle, broken every promise in the book and increased the price of petrol no less than six times to the unheard-of, unbelievable price of 31 cents a gallon for 95-octane and 11.5 cents a gallon for 87-octane. The result is, you'll be pleased to hear, that petrol is still cheaper than mineral water and to fill your tank, even if it is one of those American gas-guzzling dinosaurs, will still cost you less than a glass of Johnny Walker.

Don't you just feel sorry for them, having to tighten their belts like that?

Chacao is one hundred per cent pure adrenalin. It's New York, Los Angeles, Paris, Madrid and Miami all rolled into one. It's the world of big business, skyscrapers, statues, banks, limousines, Baskin-Robbins and McDonald's. Wheeling and dealing. International telephone calls. A line of credit here. A contract there. Another day, another million. Everybody you see is rich, tanned and immaculately groomed. Everywhere you go is the best and most expensive whatever it is. Except for the cinemas. On Mondays they charge half price. Something to do with families that don't stay at home and talk and instead go to the movies together, stay together.

The streets are full of BMWs and Porsches and Mercedes. The pavements are full of people – real-life, friendly, non-aggressive, non-knife-carrying, non-murder-committing people. In fact, it is quite possible to wander aimlessly around the streets. If you really want to live dangerously you could go up to one of the guys lolling around a stall at the edge of the pavement and get yourself a freshly squeezed watermelon, passion fruit, orange or pineapple juice. If you really want to cast all caution to the winds you could even try one of their killer hot-dogs.

The shops are the best and most expensive there are. Versace, Armani, Gucci – all the designer labels are there and a million others as well. Shopping malls are not just big, they're the biggest in South America. Go back there in five years' time and the mall that is currently the biggest in South America will, I bet you, be the biggest in the whole of North and South America. Because they're building another one virtually the same size – five floors up, five floors down – practically opposite and they're going to link the two together.

Bars. I've spent years of my life being dragged from bar to bar to bar. Chacao has got the lot: the swish up-market ones, the tiny, cramped, popular, packed-to-overflowing ones and the downmarket, seedy ones. They're all fantastic – the style, the atmosphere, the people. Oh yes, of course, and the booze. Anyone fancy another glass of champers?

Restaurants. Again they've got the lot: Spanish, Basque (where you can sample a thousand different types of fish soup, tuck into marinated fish with slices of hot, crisp toast, or just have a whole baby goat to yourself), Italian, French, Indian and Chinese. But search though I might, I couldn't find an English restaurant, which must mean something or other.

As for nightclubs, I must tell you I never, ever go to nightclubs. They are everything I detest: extravagant, expensive, outrageous. Full of all the wrong kind of people. When I'm travelling I much prefer to spend my evenings alone locked in my room studying my Ukrainian irregular verbs or getting the hang of Andrew Rublev and his influence on the development of the Russian icon.

So this Venezuelan guy (who looked just like Moshe Dayan, complete with black eyepatch) only had to mention there was some, er, nightclub round the corner and zap, I was there. Purely in the interests of research, you understand. He said it was the place to study the Macarena, which was supposed to have been invented by the mother of some famous Venezuelan flamenco dancer. All I can say is it was that as well. To tell you the truth, I found it impossible to have any kind of conversation about the Macarena with anyone that was long enough to cover the essentials but short enough to be interesting. Come to think of it, nothing there was long enough to cover the essentials but short enough to be interesting. One who was obviously an expert seemed to outstrip everyone in her enthusiasm. Moshe

Dayan didn't do so badly, either. At first he didn't seem to know where to put himself but then he obviously worked things out. Although at one stage he did look as though he was going to fall from grace. Or whatever her name was.

I, naturally, sat at the bar all evening. All around me the French and the Italians and the Spanish were having the time of their lives. At the end of the bar was another poor, hardworking, underpaid, pathetic English business-man sipping half a glass of beer. He said he was waiting for someone to come in who was old, fat, covered in spots and did nothing but moan and complain all the time.

'What on earth for?' I asked.

'I'm homesick,' he said.

I can't for the life of me remember what I was drinking that night. All I know is it was reaching parts no other drinks had ever reached. At one point I can vaguely remember Moshe Dayan coming up to me, flicking his eyepatch up and down and telling me that Venezuela had 'a wealth of natural resources which have hardly been touched'. Which came as a big surprise to me, I can tell you. Because by then my distinct impression was that practically everything in Venezuela had been touched if not pawed over a million times.

Incidentally, Moshe baby, thanks for the present. It certainly made a change from the usual company tie or keyring.

Los Magallenos is the Bronx, Naples, Chicago South Side and the big Castellane estate in Marseilles - where even the Grand Mufti himself, the head of the city's Muslim community, can't park his car without it being stolen - all rolled into one. It's the world of the *barrios*, the slum-dwellers: bits of rags, cardboard boxes, tin shacks, rickety old brick huts built on top of rickety old brick huts built on top of rickety old brick huts that go on for mile after mile after mile. Move just one brick - move just half a brick - and the whole place will come crashing down.

A few years ago it rained so much that part of the hillside gave way, sending God knows how many precarious shacks and huts and cardboard boxes crashing into the valley below. Nobody knows how many people were killed. I was told they didn't even bother to look for them because by the time the rains stopped another million shacks and huts and cardboard boxes had replaced the ones that had just been swept away.

Wander around the *barrios* (everybody told me I shouldn't, but what the hell) and what you see is unbelievable.

First, the great mass of people: you can literally hardly move for them. Once one person gets in, whether into a rickety old brick hut or a cardboard box, he brings another, then another, then the family, then the wife's family, then the wife's uncle's aunt's family. But the space they have to live in is exactly the same: nothing. Yet somehow, don't ask me how, they manage it. The electricity they get from pylons, electricity cables, other people's electricity supply, anything. Some streets are so overhung with cables going in every direction into everybody else's electricity supply that you can hardly see the sky. Water comes the same way, from somebody else's water main.

The lucky ones are the squatters. Years ago, before the *barrios* smothered the whole area, there was still the odd house or shop or office or even garage. But gradually as the *barrios* spread and spread, people just upped and walked away unable to bear the conditions any longer. The doors were barely closed before the squatters moved in. Stay there two years and under Venezuelan law it's yours. Stay there five years and if the government takes it away from you, they've got to pay you compensation. It might not be much. It might not be in the best part of town. But it's a darn sight better than nothing. Most *barrios* I saw were pretty rough but some were not quite what I had imagined. They had tables and chairs and carpets and, of course, television sets and music centres and refrigerators and even video players.

One guy I met told me his family were one of the first to take over a squatter's house. They had all worked hard and could now afford to move out. (He himself was a qualified engineer; he'd been sent to the United States on a government grant, qualified and then returned home.) But they had decided against it. The *barrios* were their home. They had all the space they wanted. They had no electricity bills, no water bills, no other kind of bills. They could buy whatever they wanted. They knew everybody. If they moved out into a middle-class area, they would have less space, they would have to pay for everything and they would also know nobody. The only problem was the violence.

Over the past few years, more and more Colombians had moved in. First, they came because they had nothing: the Colombian economy was in ruins, the currency was worthless and there were no jobs. The Venezuelan economy at the time was booming: the currency was going through the roof and there were more than enough jobs for everybody. Now things had changed. The Colombian economy was in still ruins, the currency was still worthless and still there were no jobs for anybody. But Venezuela was now in trouble too: heap big trouble. Still it was better than Colombia. The result was brawls, fights and killings, night after night after night. For drugs, for money, for a pair of designer shoes. For the sheer hell of it.

A normal weekday tally especially in the desperately poor El Junquito area, I was told, produced anything from pierced noses and scratched chests and slashed tongues to cheeks pierced with daggers. Sometimes there would even be signs of black magic or voodoo beatings. Saturday nights produced anything from crucifixions, slayings and lighted candles stabbed in the eyes to straightforward killings with *chuzos*, knives and daggers made out of water pipes or strips of metal, or just a common old iron bar.

Having survived Los Magallenos with only two knives between my shoulder blades, but then I'm used to being stabbed in the back, I headed downhill to Cataeia, a tiny huddle of rough old shops which seemed to be selling nothing but cheap clothes, cheap shoes and cheap booze. Again it was packed with people. The guys on drugs – crack and something called *basuco*, the cheap local coca paste – dripped with sweat, their eyes on fire.

Everybody else was desperately struggling just to survive. I even came across one old woman in a shack by the side of the road who was busy hiring out not particularly new pairs of shoes at around US50 cents an hour.

The operating theatre had all the latest technology. Lippos, as we say in the trade, for sucking up the fat. Bundles of tiny three-by-seven centimetre strips of some kind of filler made from human skin taken from skeletons which can be packed into lips, cheeks, noses or wherever it is felt an extra bit of padding or rather augmentation is needed. They even had buckets of facial plastic, not to mention the best range of fashionable white coats this side of the Orinoco.

I was in one of the best private hospitals in Caracas where in a world of privacy the most private thing is how much money the doctors and surgeons make for cutting up their victims. The betting is about the same as the handful of doctors left in Los Magallenos. Except here the doctors make it in an hour. In Los Magallenos, they make it in a year. And there is not just one hospital like this in Caracas. There are masses of them. Small specialist ones for ears, eyes, nose, throat or whatever. Medium-sized ones for medium-sized problems like women's things and births. And vast empires for all the heavy stuff like plastic surgery, or 'giving them the cut' as it is known in polite circles.

An upper eyelid tuck? An under-eye dermabrasion? A lower neck lift? No problem. If you don't fancy any of that perhaps we can interest you in a course of collagen injections or maybe a spot of chin or neck liposuction. We could, if you prefer, go for the full forehead peel. That means we lift the brow a full two inches from the top of your head and pull it back into the hair line.

Hello. Hello. Are you all right? Well, I told you not to look in that black plastic sack. Would you like a glass of ... Well, in that case I'll continue.

You might be interested in the full body sculpting. That involves a whole series of peels. In order to reposition the tissue what we do is ...

Oops. Mind what you're doing with that knife.

To think, all those years ago when I was young and innocent and believed everything was genuine and every woman I met was self-made. Not any more. In fact, I don't reckon there's a woman in Chacao who is wholly self-made. At some time or other I reckon they've all followed the three-point plan to guaranteed beauty: keep quiet; keep out of sight for six weeks after; and pray to goodness nobody ever finds out how much it all cost.

How much plastic surgery it takes to make a Miss Venezuela or a Miss Latin América or a Miss World or even a Miss Universe nobody knows. Neither does anybody know how much it all costs, although you can bet your life they're not talking rock-bottom prices or rock-bottom anything come to think of it. All Mr Sousman admits is that it's done. It's paid for. And it's one hell of an investment. A nip here. A tuck there. The very slightest adjustment to the ... But implants, never, although a friend of a friend did assure me on condition I told nobody, not even my own mother, that from time to time they have been known deliberately to crack and reset the odd rib or three in order to perfect what is already close to perfection. But you won't tell anyone will you? Because if you do I might need some pretty heavy plastic surgery myself.

The operating theatre has nothing. No sheets, no swabs, hardly any instruments. No anaesthetic. A wobbly-looking table. But most of all, no staff.

The young doctor with all the pens and papers in his pocket told me they'd stopped doing operations ages ago. If anyone needed an operation they either had to go to one of the private hospitals and pay for it like everybody else, or hope they could find a private doctor who makes a killing out of the private sector but who eases his own conscience by either doing operations for nothing or next to nothing in the public sector.

'So how do people find these doctors?' I asked.

'Luck,' he said.

But if the operating theatres are empty and not working so too, thanks to the efficiencies and planning of the Venezuelan government, is everything else. In the so-called emergency admission ward, none of the cardio-electric machines and none of the cardio-vascular monitors were working. The only things that were working were a machine for treating asthmatics, a blood pressure gauge and an X-ray machine. Then only on certain days, provided you kicked it properly. The only things that were working and working overtime were the use-once-only disposable gloves: there was a whole sink full of them. They were being washed to be re-used, again and again and again.

At Los Magallenos they had virtually no blood, at least not where it should be in the blood bank. The blood bank was down to less than a quarter of its so-called official quota. Two types had completely run out. On the other hand, there was plenty of blood seeping into filthy bandages, running all over twisted legs and arms and misshapen bodies and dripping slowly on to the floor. If anyone needed any blood – proper blood – all they had to do was hope that one of their family turned up in time who had the same blood group. Failing that, they had to somehow get someone to rush them from hospital to hospital until they found one that was open and one with not only the right blood group but also a sufficiently flexible blood-bank manager. If you get my drift.

The young doctor now took me down to the store-room on the ground floor. There was a long line of people, staff, patients and relatives, queuing up outside for medicines and even painkillers that weren't there.

'So what will they do?'

'Nothing. There's nothing they can do.'

'Unless they go and steal the money.'

'Plenty of them do that.'

As for common-or-garden run-of-the-mill hospital items such as towels and bedlinen, a patient either had to bring them themselves or get their family to go and get them. Which conjures up a bizarre world where in Caracas anyone going out on a Saturday night is best advised to take with them a set of clean bedlinen. Just in case.

Clean linen or no clean linen, if you ended up in the morgue, they couldn't even guarantee you a proper ice-box because not even the refrigeration machines were working.

'So what do you do with the – er – hm?' I asked.

He shrugged his shoulders.

'We cope,' he said.

To us, maybe, the beauty queen business is a laugh: nothing but stick insects on high heels tottering across the stage wearing over-polished toenails and a big smile saying they all want to be brain surgeons or nuclear scientists. Not to the Venezuelans, however. Venezuela is the world's last totally unreconstructed pre-women's lib country. Here men are most definitely macho men and women most definitely women. What is more, they unashamedly rejoice and glorify in it. In fact, for both men and women the whole beauty queen business is more important than religion, or even football. It is as much a part of their culture as bad service, late deliveries and smashing up foreign football supporters is part of ours.

Beauty queens are literally everywhere. Pick up a newspaper, and they're all over it promoting one product or another: cars, booze, cigarettes, electronic connectors. Switch on the television, and they're on practically every programme, decorating the set, introducing somebody to somebody, even hosting the show.

Go to a mundane event like a factory opening: it will not be boring in Venezuela. The factory's very own beauty queen will be prancing and pouting and pirouetting around all over the place, not to mention all over the company president, the company vice-president and anyone else that has to work for a living. And if Juanita in the machine shop is not reckoned to be good enough to be their beauty queen, they'll go out and hire one for the day. What am I saying? If Juanita is not good enough, indeed. Most companies when they advertise jobs for women insist on *buena aparencia*, only potential brain surgeons or nuclear scientists need apply.

During one trip I was out visiting a company up on the Orinoco. All the companies in the area were getting together for some kind of month-long sports competition. For the Olympic-style opening ceremony, each company's team was going to be led by their very own beauty queen. Trouble was they didn't feel they had the right kind of beauty queen, so they were going to go out and hire the best they could find.

'But didn't, ah, hm,' I muttered to the company president 'the, ah, hm, ladies in the company mind being, ah, hm, being passed over for, ah, hm, an outsider?'

'Not at all,' he said. 'They were thrilled. The better the beauty queen, the more favourably it reflects on the company. The men,' he grinned, 'they like it too. The old bulls, we say, they like tender greens.'

I asked his secretary what she thought. She said it was good for the company. It kept the men happy. But as far as she was concerned, she didn't have time for that kind of thing. She had to cope with $7\frac{1}{2}$ inches of mail every morning.

'So how much is the beauty queen going to cost?' I asked the president.

He wouldn't tell me. But it was obviously going to be a lot of money. Later one of the other managers whispered something about US$10,000. Which was probably right. Especially as he was the vice-president.

The other thing I noticed is that the beauty queen culture has seeped into their language. Buildings are always tall, slim and elegant. Cars always range from the small and compact to the big and bouncy. Computers are nothing but hardware and software and Servicio Rapido. Everything, whether it's an ice-cream or a dust cart is soft, gentle, luscious, gorgeous, unstoppable, unquenchable and wide-open. In Venezuela, believe me, nothing but nothing is plump, homely, or even comely.

If a spell under the knife and a couple of months in hiding waiting for the bruises to heal is the price girls have to pay to be beauty queens, then so be it. There's no shortage of volunteers. Hope springs eternal in the siliconed breast of every Venezuelan brain surgeon or nuclear scientist.

Inevitably, being completely surrounded by nothing but beautiful women has a profound effect on the poor guys. Their eyes begin to go pop. They start having hallucinations. Eventually, of course, the worst affected become so addicted that wherever they turn, whatever they look at, they see nothing but these gorgeous shapes.

But not all beauty queens end up being displayed all over an advertising slogan or under a new factory sign or whatever. Many of them go on to assume such important jobs in society as lawyers and accountants and estate agents. Actually, believe it or not, Venezuela has more than its fair share of women on top. There are women judges. (Most of them, one assumes, without a policeman's hand in their knickers.) Women lawyers. Women doctors. Women directors.

Mr Ousman's biggest success, at least in political terms, is Irena Saez who, in 1981, for the first time in her life, put on a swimsuit and, no doubt because of her full-blown charms, sashayed away with not only the Miss Venezuela but also the Miss Universe title as well. Other girls who won either the Miss World or the Miss Universe title went off and did the usual. Not our Miss Saez, or Irena as she is now known throughout Venezuela and practically the whole of Latin America. She strutted her stuff, she kissed the babies, then off she went to walk the political catwalk. She went to university to study politics. Within five years she was in New York as Venezuela's very own cultural representative at the United Nations where she no doubt made a big impression.

In 1992 she made an even bigger impression on even more people and at 29, without being a member of any political party or group, she got herself elected mayor of Chacao. Before she took over, the place was a disaster area, a truly Venezuelan disaster area. The streets were filthy. The pavements were clogged with beggars. Crime was rampant. Gangs would not just rob people; they would burst into expensive restaurants and rob everybody there at the same time. As a result, people had started moving out: businesses were moving out and what little industry there was left was moving out. The tax take, therefore, was getting lower and lower. With less and less money to spend on trying to keep the place up to scratch, it was heading even further downhill. And fast.

Today, it has all changed. The place is unbelievably

squeaky-clean and tidy. Almost Seattle or Tokyo clean
and tidy. Everything has been given a spring clean. The
squares and plazas are the cleanest they've ever been.
All the previous no-go areas have been opened up for
cultural and musical events. Buildings have been newly
painted and decorated. In fact, it's the Sousa philosophy
applied to bricks and mortar. On the crime front, our
Irena brought in a whole educated, even university-
educated, bunch of new policemen. She put them in
smart uniforms which she designed herself, gave them
cars and motorbikes as well as fancy-looking golf carts
and sent them out to do their stuff. Now crime is a
staggering 60 per cent down on what it used to be.

As a result, people are now moving back in. So too are
businesses and banks and huge international corpor-
ations, many of them from other parts of Caracas.
People have even started going to restaurants again,
confident that if they are going to be robbed at least it
won't be by a bunch of gangsters bursting in on them
during their meal.

What is more, as a sign of her success, the area is now
known the length and breadth of Venezuela not as
Chacao but as Irenaland, the funny-looking golf carts as
Irenavans and the police as Irenapolice. As if that's not
enough a new word, *irenizar*, to improve, has entered
the Venezuelan vocabulary. Not even Mrs Thatcher
achieved such adulation and she was at least twice
Irena's age and certainly did more than keep the streets
clean. Although come to think of it she didn't actually
keep the streets clean: not even Richard Branson could
do that.

The big question now is: today, Chacao. Tomorrow,
Venezuela? Will she ever be President? Never one for
parties when she was a beauty queen, she is today. She is
busy putting together one of her own. Don't ask me
what it's called. All I know is, its initials spell out – you
got it – I.R.E.N.A.

The even more important question is whether with a

track record like that anyone will stand against her. My guess is that nobody would dare. She's untouchable. I did hear, however, that if she does decide to stand there are growing demands that this time people are allowed to vote by braille.

You might not believe it but Los Magallenos Hospital also has its own success story.

He is Doctor José Gregorio Hernandez.

His statue stands in the centre of a patch of grass just outside the front door.

It is a centre of pilgrimage for people from all over Latin America. They come and place flowers at the foot of the statue. They pray. Even the Pope has been to Los Magallenos Hospital and prayed at the statue. For by many Dr Hernandez is considered to be a saint, almost the Mother Teresa of Latin America. Some say he has miraculous powers, that his image often appears on X-ray plates and that people are cured as a result.

During his life he devoted himself to the poor. Other doctors would turn them away from their surgeries and hospitals, but not Dr Hernandez. He would always care for them first. Then, the irony of ironies. When there were only two cars in the whole of the city of Caracas he had to be knocked down and killed by one of them. It was the one he didn't own himself.

Paramaribo

I've got news for the Dutch: you blew it.

Call yourselves big wheeler-dealers, the Chinese of Europe, the clever clogs of international trading. You practically ran the world. Your traders out-traded everyone in sight. Your ships dominated the seas. You shipped more goods to more places than anybody else. Not only that, but you were far and away one of the richest countries in the world.

There in your hands you had the deal of a lifetime and what did you do? You blew it. You swapped New York, or rather Nieuw Amsterdam, for Suriname, a God-forsaken, never-ending tropical rainforest stuck down there between Venezuela and Brazil on the shoulder of South America. On a disastrous-decision scale it doesn't just rank above Western Union's decision to reject Alexander Graham Bell's telephone ('an electrical toy'): Remington Arms' decision to reject the typewriter ('no mere machine will ever replace a reliable and honest clerk'); Warner Brothers' decision to reject the talkies ('who the hell wants to hear actors talk?') and Krug's decision to reject me as a champagne taster ('Ze fool. He would trink ze stuff'). It is all of them combined and multiplied a million times over. Squared.

What on earth possessed you? How could you possibly have thought you could make more money out of Suriname than out of Nieuw Amsterdam? You must have been out of your minds. Either that or the Genever and the herrings finally got to you. One old boy I met years ago in a bar in Eindhoven told me it wasn't really your fault. He said you had nobody around at the time to advise you. Because you had melted down all the lawyers to make advocaat.

Now New York, I know, is not the Big Apple of everybody's eye. The noise. The traffic. The crazy, hectic, non-stop, 24-hours-a-day shoutin' and bawlin' and screamin'. But it has got a certain pzazz, if not speed, of its own. The Pierre, The Plaza, The Waldorf, even the coffee shop down Lexington. Then there's Times Square, Broadway, the Empire State Building, the World Trade Centre and the New York Stock Exchange. Squeegee merchants on every street corner. Central Park, the Lincoln Center, the Rockefeller Center, Greenwich Village, Chinatown, SoHo. Rollerblades. Even the Statue of Liberty.

Not that the Dutch, a nation rich in culture and history, didn't leave behind them one or two major contributions to so-called American civilisation. For example, chilled water. What's more, free chilled water. To Americans, of course, it's just chilled water. To the Dutch, however, it's much, much more. It means they can go into a bar, a café or a restaurant without being scared out of their lives they might actually have to buy something extravagant, like a Coca-Cola or even a Pepsi.

Then there are salads. Have you ever wondered why the Americans are obsessed with salad? It was the Dutch way of making certain that their farmers would not only continue to enjoy a high standard of living for all time but that KLM would make millions refrigerating the stuff and flying it across the Atlantic.

But the one thing the Dutch did more than anything else was to bequeath to the Americans their very own unique way of butchering the English language. You've seen advertisements and posters and shop signs all over the States, not to mention the English lessons given by

American vice-presidents. Come on. You didn't think they came up with that all by themselves, did you? It's the Dutch effect.

Markt, for example. How many times have you seen Markt in the ads in the *New York Times*? The word is everywhere: Spring Markt, Summer Markt, Xmas Markt, Lower East Side 57th Street Precinct Markt. Exottca is another one – and I don't just mean around the back of Times Square. Karaat you see all over the jewellery stores. Similarly Goud and Zilversmids. Then there's kalm and cultureel and favoriete and relaxen and sportieve and garantie and speciaal and compleet and inclusief and plastiek. They're the ones I've seen just this morning in a fax from the New York Public Library. If I get another one like it this afternoon – Hulp. Hulp. Hulp – I'm going to be on to the telphoniste to fix me therapie for my haart conditionen.

But whatever you do, don't think the Americans are not grateful to the Dutch for being dumped in favour of Suriname. AT & T, the huge telecommunications giant, for example, regularly runs advertisements – 'Travel in a world without borders, time zones or language barriers' – which puts Suriname slap-bang in the middle of Africa.

But why Suriname of all places? It's nothing. It had nothing then, give or take the odd sandy beach and a couple of million trees. It's still got nothing now. Except aggro, heartache, a million birds that don't exist because they've yet to be identified and a bunch of footballers like Patrick Kluivert, Winston Bogarde and Ruud Gullit, who I'm told have played for all the big European teams such as AC Milan, Ajax and even Chelsea FC.

But that's not all. After extensive research throughout the Dutch Caribbean, often at great personal risk to my health (do you know how many daiquiris I had to drink?) I am finally able to reveal that the New York-Suriname deal was only part of an even bigger package put together by the Dutch. Thrilled with what they obviously thought was the bargain of all time, the clever clogs of international wheeler-dealing then went on to swap Paris for Aruba, Sankt Pieter Burkh, or rather St Petersburg, for Bonaire – admittedly just before the Italians arrived and kicked them out – and the Orange Free State or rather the Oranje Vrijstaat, for Curaçao, where they obviously thought they'd get even more oranges.

You don't believe me? Listen, on the basis that nobody could possibly want to swap New York for Suriname in the first place, why shouldn't they also have gone ahead and swapped Paris, Sankt Pieter Burkh, I mean St Petersburg, and the Orange Free State (or rather the Oranje Vrijstaat) for Aruba, Bonaire and Curaçao – or the ABC countries, as the Dutch call them today? Except that in this case ABC doesn't stand for Another Bloody Chardonnay, as it does in the sophisticated circles I stagger around in, but Another Bloody Cock-up. You've only got to visit them to see why.

Aruba is great fun – if you're a cactus. Particularly one of those big, Wild West ones with yellow flowers. Apart from that, it has got some big US-style hotels, a handful of casinos and – how could I possibly forget? – a big red typically Dutch windmill. After they did the swap with Paris, the Dutch were obviously planning to take back with them to Aruba what to them was the most precious thing in the whole city, the Moulin Rouge. But even though it had been agreed a million times over and written into all the contracts, when it finally came to it, the French being the French said they had changed their minds. They wanted to hold on to it themselves. The Dutch, who even then would do nothing to upset European harmonisation, gave in as they've done so many times since and will no doubt do so many times again in the future. Instead they decided to build another one of their own in Holland, dismantle it, ship it out to Aruba and reassemble it again.

As for the locals, they're your normal, average,

hardworking, practical Dutch. They are all trying to put together impossible property deals. Like one woman I met who told me she owned half of London. What's more, she said, they had some kind of document in their family to prove it.

'My brother, he says Buckingham Palace is built on our land. When we get it back, The Queen, she's goin' to owe us a lot of money for rent,' she told me. And she was serious.

Bonaire, on the other hand, is completely deserted. I went all over it, from Bachelor's Beach, where there were no bachelors (this was at one time going to be Harry Belafonte's Island in the Sun, but he got fed up with it and sold it), first to Willemstoren in the south, where there was no beach at all because the Dutch had literally sold it to Curaçao, and then on to Hilma Hooker Beach where there was nothing, either. Not even a Hilma. Which shows you how deserted it was.

In fact, the whole time I was there I met only one man. He told me he was in a business where the pleasure lasted just a few minutes and the cost was anything between US$4 and US$25. As he was Dutch I knew it could be only one thing: the ice-cream business. When I asked him where everybody had gone, he tried to tell me all the locals had gone off to Aruba and Curaçao for jobs and, Bonaire being one of the best places in the world for snorkelling and underwater swimming, all the tourists were under the water. As soon as anyone arrived on the island, he said, they immediately leapt into their rubber gear and couldn't bear to take it off again until the moment they left. Which I took with a pinch of salt. The Dutch say so many things about their ABC countries and Suriname that you have to take with a pinch of salt that luckily there's no shortage of the stuff on Bonaire. If anything the salt flats cover practically half the island and they ship the stuff out all over the world. Wherever you go, the chances are that if you hear any Dutchman or woman going on about them being a nation of wheeler-dealers and you look for a pinch of salt, it will be Dutch salt.

As for the third island in the pack, things get Curaçao and Curaçao. Did the Dutch really swap the Orange Free State for Curaçao for the oranges? Or, was it, as some people say, because they liked all the tall, narrow buildings with fancy gables all along the waterfront in the capital, Willemstad, wanted to copy them, and decided that a swap was cheaper than paying an architect's fees? Well, all I can say is, if they did it was worth it. The houses they built in exactly the same style all along the canals in Amsterdam certainly look fantastic.

Then there's the port. My first day there, I thought there was an eclipse of the sun every few minutes or else the sudden black-outs my wife has been threatening me with for years because of my dedication to supporting the French wine industry had finally arrived. There I was working, what else, in my hotel in Otrobanda, the wrong side of the bay, when suddenly – whoosh – the room went practically pitch black. Then light again. Then – whoosh – dark again. What was it? It was these enormous 500-storey liners coming up and down St Anna Bay and into the enormous Schottegat Bay, which they say is the second busiest harbour in the world. The liners were so huge and the hotel was so small and so close to the water that they literally blocked out the light as they went backwards and forwards. Which I can tell you was a relief. For a while I thought I'd be on Diet Coke for the rest of my life.

Now I know that Rotterdam is today the biggest harbour in the world but did the Dutch really have to swap the Oranje Vrijstaat for Curaçao just to find out everything they were doing in Schottegat Bay so they could copy it? I mean they could have just turned up, said they were doing an MBA in port development or whatever and they would have been given all the information they wanted. It would have been much cheaper and much simpler. The only explanation I can think of – and I've studied a good few daiquiris in the process, unlike Stephen Jay Gould, the famous American scientist who came all the way to Curaçao and only studied his beloved land snail, the Cerion uva – is Papiamentu, the local language.

I say language, but the little I know about it, it seems to me to be both everything and nothing. Everything, because it's a mixture of Spanish, Portuguese, Dutch, English, German and probably a dash of Mongol as well. Nothing, because there's practically no grammar, no verbs, no nothing. *Buki*, for example, means either book or a thousand books. *Mucha* is either boy or girl, son or daughter, one or a hundred. *Bai* means go, going, has gone, will go, will have gone and all the rest of it. So what I reckon happened was that the Dutch, who also, of course, consider themselves fantastic linguists, suddenly arrived out of the blue. The locals started chatting them up. The Dutch, who can all speak Spanish, Portuguese, English, German and probably Mongol as well, thought they understood what was being said, agreed, nodded their heads and the deal was done. The problem was that, while the Dutch can speak Spanish, Portuguese and all the others, they can only speak each language separately whereas the Curaçao guys speak them all at the same time. So – whateco bunchi offao Willemses, as they say in Papiamentu – the Dutch suddenly found that without even realising it they had blown Paris and Sankt Pieter Burkh as well as the Orange Free State.

Obviously, with what's known as heijnsight, the Dutch realise this and are now so ashamed of what they have done and want as few people as possible to see the mistake they made that they have made it as difficult as possible for people to visit the place.

Take the biggest mistake of all, Suriname, for example. Try getting into it. It's practically impossible.

Like getting a Dutchman to put his hand in his pocket. I landed at Paramaribo, pronounced not as you would expect Para-mari-boo but Para-mareeboo. At first we weren't allowed into the Immigration Hall so we all had to huddle up outside like a bunch of would-be immigrants on Staten Island, which is obviously a trick they brought with them from the old days. Then they let us in. But where to go? Which queue to join? There were no signs. Nothing. Just a mass of people pressing forward like a solid phalanx towards these three desks where I was certain some guy was going to insist on giving me a new name like Potverdriedubbeltjes Nog Eens An Toe Zeg because Biddlecombe was too difficult to pronounce. Then they started playing what must be the immigration officers' form of Dutch roulette. They kept closing down different desks at a moment's notice so we all had to rush across from one to another. The number of *Godverdommes* and *verdullemes* and *gat-dakkies* that were hurtling backwards and forwards was nobody's business.

I'm not saying it took a long time. All I'm saying is by the time I got to the head of the queue my visa had expired and I had to go to the grubby little office at the back and get another one.

After that, it was baggage reclaim. Imagine the smallest regional airport you've been to anywhere in the world. Imagine the whole floor completely covered in suitcases and giant multi-coloured plastic sacks and shattered cardboard boxes. Imagine it packed with people stepping all over the suitcases and giant plastic sacks and shattered cardboard boxes. Well, that's what it was like before they even started unloading our luggage. It's no wonder the Surinamese go bananas over football. They are obviously never more at home than when they are in the middle of a football crowd. Not me. I had to wait, I'm not kidding, well over an hour in this heaving, sweating, pulsating mass before I finally got my suitcase. And because it was taking so long all the locals were handing round cups and beakers and glasses and bottles of drinks. Which means that - 'Hey! *godsamme*, mind that bag' - you not only had to avoid the suitcases being swung all over the place - 'No. That's okay. Don't worry. I've got another *potverdorie* foot' - you also had to avoid great splashes of tea and Coke and milk and horrible chocolatey things being slopped all over you. 'No, please don't apologise. I've always wanted great red stains all down the front of my trousers.'

When my suitcase finally arrived, was that the end of it? No way. We then had to go through customs. All I can say is their most popular custom seems to involve doing everything they possibly can to keep people out of the place altogether. We've all been bounced by customs. But this one I can tell you is pretty near the top - or should it be the bottom? - of my list. It was back to the phalanx again: another solid, heaving, sweating, throbbing mass inching towards three guys who were opening everything. Believe me, if Suriname was the most volatile, most dangerous, most security-conscious country in the world they could not have been taking us apart more thoroughly. Russia, China, Saudi Arabia, Nigeria, Heathrow - you know what I mean. But these guys! They were in a class of their own. All I can say is that you'll never catch me rooting for AC Milan, Ajax or even Chelsea FC. Ever.

Okay, so I'm out. Straight into a cab. Straight into the hotel and a couple of swift... You've got to be kidding. Paramaribo is miles from the airport. Along rough, winding, twisting, potholed tracks with the occasional stretch of tarmac. A left-hand drive car driving on the left-hand side of the road made overtaking even more interesting than usual, especially with a seat belt which didn't work. I can't tell you how long it took before I got to the hotel. I'd left my diary behind. But I can tell you the name of the taxi company: it was Dippo Taxis.

If they really want to encourage more visitors, my advice is simple. Apart from sorting out the airport, lay on another plane to fly people from the airport to Paramaribo. It would make more sense.

Candide, of course, had none of these problems. But then the French never do. They just land and are immediately whisked through customs to a waiting car. When he arrived with good old Cacambo they were so pleased and relaxed and at one with the world they were convinced they were at the end of their sufferings and the beginning of their happiness. But it didn't last long. It never does. First the one-armed one-legged negro slave put them right about living conditions. Then wicked Mr Vanderdendur pushed the cost of a ticket to Venice up from ten thousand piastres to thirty thousand before scarpering without even taking poor old innocent, trusting Candide and his friend the Amsterdam bookseller on board.

Was I glad, that in spite of everything, I made it? You bet. Paramaribo, or rather Para as we locals say, is an object lesson to anyone who wants to do deals: don't. Thanks to the reckless habit the Dutch have of flinging their money around – there's no beginning to their generosity – you can actually still see today the very city, or rather town, virtually untouched, unchanged and unaltered, that they were so convinced was going to outgun the Big Apple.

The National Assembly building, with its fly-up-in-the-air roof like one of those old Dutch hats, looks out on one side on the river and on the other side on the biggest patch of green in town. Immediately outside facing the entrance is a simple white column. Inscribed on it are the words 'In Memoriam' , which I can only assume are there to commemorate the untimely death of their fragile democracy.

The poor Surinamese only really got their genuine independence in 1975. The Dutch hung on to the place so long no doubt because they didn't want anyone raking through the press clippings and reminding the world of why they were there in the first place. Since then, with politicians with names like Frank Playfair, it's probably not surprising the place has been under the thumb of one dictator after another practically ever since.

Today, of course, I would guess that the members of the National Assembly are grateful that the building is where it is. If ever anyone tries to round them up again it means they can escape either across the river or across the green. Sensible people.

Facing the National Assembly is the old town itself, which to me has what I can only describe as the feel of an over-rich *rijstrafel.* The kind you get in Jakarta, not in Amsterdam. Either that or everybody was smoking marijuana cigarettes laced with cocaine. It's a glorious mish-mash of everything: buildings, people, cultures, languages, clothes, histories, religions, the lot. A bit like a taxi rank in Toronto, but with the heat turned up. Most striking of all are the seventeenth- and eighteenth-century Dutch colonial wooden mansions and merchants' houses, because this is obviously what Dutch architecture was about before they started stealing ideas from Curaçao. Some are in amazing condition, but most of them look as though they are living on borrowed time. Similarly the government offices, where I was told they are so strapped for cash they have to send their faxes in plain brown envelopes.

Public squalor apart, there are also some pretty affluent private offices, especially lawyers' offices, shops and banks, not to mention thirty churches, a glittering new mosque, a synagogue and a cathedral, the tallest wooden building in the whole of South America, which, surprise, surprise, is closed for repairs.

So authentic, so historic, so accurate is the whole ambience of Para that every street I crossed I kept expecting to be run down by a horse and carriage; every bar I went into to be assaulted by an outbreak of yellow fever; and at every meeting to be greeted by Voltaire himself notebook in one hand, plume in the other.

What I didn't see, however, which was a great surprise bearing in mind the Dutch connection, were any bicycles. Given the environment, obviously a case of fin de cycle.

If Candide was to drop by again he'd have no problems finding his way around. The old negro slave has certainly gone. As soon as he heard the Dutch were taking over he was off to south-east Amsterdam, where he's been living like a king on Dutch social security ever since. The wicked, two-faced, double-dealing, lying, cheating Mr Vanderdendur, on the other hand, is still there. He is now one of the local bank managers, a pillar of Para society and a regular at all the expat get-togethers at the Torarica Hotel, the only halfway decent hotel in town, which some evenings is so packed that it boasts more Dutchmen than even the Barcelona football team.

But what about Suriname's real history? One morning between meetings I grabbed a cab and went to the Suriname Museum way out in Zorg-en-Hoop, miles from the centre of Para. See what I mean about doing everything to avoid telling people the truth? Here I thought they would tell the story of the deal – after all, a history museum is a history museum is a history museum. There's no way they can avoid mentioning their own history. Oh yes there is. The Suriname Museum consists of nothing but junk: decrepit old gas cookers, one of those old-fashioned cash registers, and piles and piles of unopened cardboard boxes from museums all over Holland no doubt offering them treasured exhibits to put on display. Of their history, of how they came to be Dutch, there is nothing. Not a broken display panel, not a half mouldy leaflet. Nothing.

I then tried the Old Fort along the waterfront just past the National Assembly. Built about the same time as the deal was done, I thought there must be some mention of how they came to be, who built it, where they... But there wasn't. Not a word, I promise you, about the deal.

Not a display cabinet. Not even a cheap leaflet. The fort is being restored at the moment by - you got it - the Dutch.

Not that it's unusual for the Dutch either to rewrite or conveniently forget whole chunks of their history. Even today Queen Beatrix, for example, goes around claiming that the constitution of 1848 laid the foundation for Dutch parliamentary democracy when we all know it was actually in 1798 that the foundations were laid, three years before the Dutch, using their newly won freedom, drove her illustrious predecessor King Willem V and his family into exile in England. But who am I to quibble, a mere subject of the Dutch conquest of Britain in 1688.

Stuck in the middle of all this official amnesia are, of course, the locals, the poor people who for the whole of their lives have to live with the fact that they're the losing end of a gamble that went disastrously wrong - like a wife who discovers her husband only proposed to her for a bet, he was really after the blonde with the big bank account. It is no wonder that the locals are a crazy mixed-up bunch.

First there are the Creoles, the Africans, descendants of the ex-slaves or what they call the Bushnegroes. Next come the Amerindians, the guys who live mainly in the bush but who stray into town from time to time. Finally there is practically every other nationality under the sun: Indians (Hindustanis, who make up around a third of the population), Indonesians, Chinese, Chinese Creoles, Hong Kong Chinese who got out before 1997, Portuguese Jews from Brazil, the odd Canadian, a couple of French guys and a girl - *toujours la même histoire* - oh yes, and a collection of Dutchmen, who have all successfully avoided buying each other a drink since the deal was done. Neither must we forget a bunch of solitary Stone Age tribes up in the rainforest who are regularly being ambushed by television producers eager to preserve their integrity, guard them from evil influences and protect them from the outside world.

Communicating with the Creoles, the Bushnegroes and the Amerindians is simple, according to some graduate of Florida State University. Having during three years made over fifteen different trips, lasting anything from three days to three months, visited over sixty villages in the bush, spoken to anything that moved as well as the US Ambassador and his wife, this researcher, obviously the world's greatest living expert on what she grandly calls 'inter-cultural communication', has just come up with the definitive guide. When visiting natives in the bush, whether you are looking for toothache plants or a couple of iguanas for a pot roast, you must, she insists as all graduates tend to do, especially women, 'Immediately introduce yourself giving the reason and purpose of your visit'.

Wowee. That I would never have guessed. Doesn't it just make you feel humble to be the recipient of such awesome brain power? And Florida brain power at that. But wait. There's more to come.

'Do not sit until you are invited to sit.'

Please. You must excuse me. This is too, too much for me. I need a moment to collect myself. I don't think even Einstein came up with a more original, penetrating and perceptive comment. And the amazing thing is it only took fifteen different trips to over sixty different villages (not forgetting the meeting with the US Ambassador and, of course, his charming wife) to come up with such a revolutionary inter-cultural communication breakthrough. But, hang on, there are still more world-shattering revelations to come.

'Do not go alone on village visits as a woman.'

Well, lady, you might be a graduate of Florida State University and the world's greatest living expert on inter-cultural communication, but I've got news for you. I ain't going nowhere, not even the throne room of Buckingham Palace, let alone into a Bushnegro village, as a woman. And I don't care how many of your precious rules of protocol I upset. It's just not my hammer.

As for taking with me an autographed picture of the President of the United States to present to the Big Chief, you must think I'm a couple of dishes short of a *rijsttafel.* A picture of the President of the United States? Of Bill Clinton? Autographed? Presumably framed in genuine American hardwood and decorated in gold leaf? If you honestly expect me to believe that that is what every jungle chief in Suriname is praying for every day of his life, you must think I've just fallen out of a tree or something.

I'll tell you what every jungle chief wants and I haven't been anywhere near their villages. Booze. And thanks to President Bill Clinton, cigars. That's all they're interested in. Well, strictly speaking, not all they're interested in. But the only thing they're likely to get from any visitors in a bottle that's likely to blow their minds.

Communicating with the rest of the population is, by comparison, as simple as hell. At first I thought it would be in Dutch. Although how the Dutch manage to communicate in Dutch still baffles me. All those thick gutturals sound like a bad attack of pneumonia. Well you try saying Scheveningen, let alone *achtentachtig kacheltjes,* the two test phrases the Dutch used in order to try to recognise German spies during the last war, without sounding as if you're going to have a relapse. Then there's the way they communicate in English, which is even more hilarious.

Like the way signs saying 'Free Parking' don't mean, you can park here for free but this place is to be kept free of parking.

Or the way, if you've got a lot of work to be done very quickly, Dutch secretaries always say, 'Okay, I'll strip off and we can get started.' At least they do to me.

My favourites, however, are newspaper headlines. I once saw an article put out by the Dutch news agency,

ANP, proclaiming 'Kok pees furthest in foreign papers'.
Which I must admit caught me short for a moment until
I realised what it meant was that the prime minister,
Wim Kok, had made a bigger splash in the foreign press
than anyone else. I think.

I discovered the best way to communicate in
Paramaribo is in *taki-taki*, which at first I thought was
some kind of comment on what they thought of the
Dutch and all the imports they keep shipping in.

'So what do you think of the Dutch?' I would ask.

'*Taki-taki*,' they would reply, waving their hands in
the air. '*Taki-taki*.'

But this wasn't what they thought of the Dutch at all:
they were trying to tell me to speak in *taki-taki*, their
local language.

If you wander around town for just five minutes,
though, you get the impression they speak every
language under the sun. There are stores and winkels
and meilleur delicatessens and Bargain Busters and Luo
supermarkets and Green Leaf fast-food outlets and
super and magna plazas which are about the size of a
garage. There are pork butchers next to halal butchers
and halal butchers next to Obsessions. There's Johnny's
Autoshop and Kong Autoparts, Stylissimo Gussanti
fashions and Rainbow Shoe shops and Jerusalem
Bazaars and Nazareth Stores and a Madjoe Furniture
shop, and Integrated Computer Services and the elegant
Combe Bazaar which must be run by some long lost
half-brother of mine. There are also Low Heng Fat and
Karaat and Goodness and the gloriously named We Kon
Yu juweliers. On the food and drinks front there's
everything from Orlandos' Coffee Shop to Jogja
Cafeteria Restaurant; from Hung Kee's Kentucky – 'For
all your snacks. We are the best' – to a million Indisch
restaurants. Which means for practically next to nothing
you can live like a Sun Kong. But I'm afraid there's only
one Fook-on bar and, thank goodness, only one Shi Tin
Win.

The result is that with all the different people and all the different languages, racing around town going from meeting to meeting, your head begins to buzz and you don't quite know where you are or what to expect. Currie, I thought, was bound to be an Indian restaurant. But it wasn't, it was a firm of lawyers. Aladdin I felt sure sold lamps. It didn't, it sold clothes. So too did a shop called Frits. On the other hand, Lie-in, which I was convinced just had to be another bunch of lawyers, turned out to be a Chinese restaurant. And as for Woodstock, backwoodsman that I am, even I would have been prepared to bet my last Dutch ten-bob note on it being a music store. But, it wasn't. It was – are you ready? – a yard where they stocked wood.

But the real shock was the Krasnapolsky Hotel on Domineestraat, the main business street. I thought it was going to be like the swish, elegant, expensive Krasnapolskys you come across in Amsterdam and other parts of Europe. No way. Although, to be fair, if you close your eyes and think of *rijsttafel*, it could be like the annexe of the Krasnapolsky in Amsterdam where I was once forced to stay when I got bounced off a plane at Schipol in the middle of the night because of fog and all the other rooms in town were taken. Even the ones round the corner from the Krasnapolsky that you can usually rent by the hour.

On the other hand, a Dutch colony Suriname may have been for over three hundred years, but don't for a moment imagine it has slavishly copied the Dutch in everything. Their coffee shops still sell only coffee. Their soldiers walk around with short hair. The officers don't wear lipstick. Shops and offices around the back of the church have not been converted wholesale to the service industry. And a speed crackdown is a speed crackdown not a speed crackdown, if you see what I mean.

I cannot deny, however, that some Dutch influence has rubbed off. Locals desperately try to avoid giving taxi drivers a tip and do everything they can to be last at the bar. Under no circumstances will they ever, ever buy you lunch or good heavens, certainly not dinner.

One Surinamese businessman I met insisted we had a meal together. Armadillo with spicy peanut sauce, he suggested. We ended up at some hotel for what they called a business happy hour, from 9.30 to 10.30. In the morning. We had two coffees. I paid for both.

Another guy in one of the ministries invited me to dinner one evening. He said he wanted to discuss a book he'd just read called *Privatisering: Praktish Landmeten, Waterpassen en Uitzetten* which sounded a bundle of laughs. The special attraction at the dinner I thought I heard him say was something that sounded like *tjapeer* but when I got there it was: tap beer. Which we paid for ourselves. No food. Just beer. Tap beer.

So where do they eat? Obviously in the strict privacy of their homes or, if they're travelling, in their hotel rooms. Of all the hotels I've ever stayed in all over the world, the one in Para was the only one to have signs literally plastered all over it telling me that in no circumstances should I do any cooking in my room. Cook in my room? I couldn't cook in any of the rooms if I wanted to. There was nothing there to cook *on*. Even I could tell that. Which can only mean the Dutch travel the world with little primus stoves tucked away in their suitcases so that wherever they go they don't have to pay any exorbitant restaurant bills let alone buy anyone a beer. Instead they cook their own food themselves, in their rooms. Well, if that's not true, how come the rooms were plastered with all those signs?

But I'll tell you what I did do to get my own back. In the bathroom was another typical Dutch sign proclaiming that not only was the water healthy and rich in calcium but in addition 'you can drink it freely from the tap'. Gee whizz. Freely. Just to spite them I drank practically a gallon of the stuff even though I know water never agrees with me. I felt as though I'd won their *grote goederen loterij.*

On the other hand, maybe the Dutch did the right thing. Maybe it was the sand that appealed to them. After all, Para has got plenty of it, unlike New York, which has plenty of white powder that looks like sand but which isn't the same thing at all.

Dykes? Maybe they had enough of the dykes in New York and just wanted out.

Plants in the window? Who knows, maybe they thought Suriname could be a big market for putting plants in the window. The Dutch are fond of putting all kinds of exotic things in their windows. Maybe they thought they could teach the Surinamese to do the same thing.

Then there's the effect the deal had on New York. Can you imagine what New York would be like today if it was still being run by the Netherlanders? Central Park would, of course, be Centraal Park. Manhattan would still have masses of tall buildings, but Dutch tall buildings, with decorative gables, all lined up facing the sea, and it would be called Manhoedop. Broadway would be Breederstraat, which is probably not so far off the mark. Times Square would be Tijd Plein. The Empire State Building would be Koninklijk Staatsgebouw. Greenwich Village would be Groenig Dorp. The Lincoln Center would probably be something like the Van Agt Centre.

Forget Michael Jackson and Madonna and Bing Crosby. The music scene would be dominated by the likes of Willie Alberti, Ramses Shaffy and Feek de Jong, who seems to live at the top of the Dutch hit parade whopping it up with 'Neuwe Amsterdam, Neuwe Amsterdam', tracks from Westerkant Verhaal with the girls dressed in their traditional Vrouw Antje Dutch milkmaid outfits, or even Twee-en-veertigste Straat.

Instead of gorging themselves on Big Macs and huge rib-eye steaks everybody would be munching *broodjeswinkels, eethuisjes* and *pannekoekhuisjes* and gagging it up on *spiegeleieren met ontbijtspek, hutspot met kapstuk* and *rolpens met rode kool* followed by a slice of *taai-taai*. Plus, of course, a lump of Edam and a glass of freely water. But nobody would dare even to think of waving at a waiter or a barman.

As for flip, everyday catchphrases like yup, nope, howyadoin, yourplaceormine, they'd all be screaming at each other *scheeipbiscuit lijn niet beschikbaar op schiermonnik*oog or *zesenzestig flessen bessensap alstublief*.

Then what about names: instead of sensible, practical American names such as Starr, Clinton and Lewinsky, people would have sensible Dutch names such as Winkle, Pryk and Kok. While on the subject of names, second-generation immigrant children would all be known as *allochtonen* or aliens.

Other things would be different as well.

People could leave their bicycles unlocked when they went shopping. Nobody would own cars. Instead, because it's cheaper, they'd hire them from companies with typical Dutch names like Hertz van Rental.

Businessmen would go around making the maximum use of the Dutch language by saying things like, 'We willen gebruikmaken van een hogere gearing en een lagere interest coverage op onze balance sheet. Dat heeft een positieve invloed op onze earnings per share.'

Drug addicts would form themselves into junkiebond associations and set up their own grading system to ensure that if their members bought good quality heroin and paid good or rather bad money for it they got what they paid for.

Gay civil servants would be entitled to five days' 'marriage leave' if they changed partners and moved in with somebody else. This would give them both time to attend either lectures at their local zoo on Homosexuality Among Animals, or pop round the corner to the Bible Museum for an exhibition on same-sex biblical friendships: Moses and Aaron, David and Jonathan, Ruth and Naomi, Martha and Mary.

Hospitals would officially arrange for long-stay patients to use the local brothels at specially negotiated cut-price rates and if they got too exhausted and couldn't take any more all they would have to do is write a letter requesting the final pleasure of euthanasia – which of course gives a whole new meaning to e-mail.

The disadvantages? It's difficult to think of any apart from, maybe, there being a Dutch master in every living room and a Dutch wife in every bed. A Dutch wife is, of course, one of those long, old-fashioned bolsters which the Dutch are supposed to clutch tightly to themselves to absorb the sweat. Which I think tells us a lot about the Dutch. Oh yes, and people would be terrified to drink Moët et Chandon. Apart that is from the cost. Because in Dutch *moet* sounds like something nasty and *chandon* sounds like something even worse.

Other countries have apologised for the mistakes they have made in the past. I think the wheeler-dealing Dutch should apologise to Suriname for the mistake they made in trading New York for them. After all, who knows, maybe without the Dutch Suriname would today be the greatest, richest, most powerful nation on earth – just as the United States without the Dutch is today the greatest, richest, most powerful nation on earth.

Cayenne

I don't care what you say, *mon vieux*. You've got to hand it to the French. Wherever they go in the world, it's the dreaded F-word, France. Or if not, they very quickly make it France. Croissants, *képis, vespasiennes, cabinets à la Turque. Maisons closées.* Kickbacks on public contracts. Grand-sounding titles but no jobs, free luxury flats for top officials. Total confidence that if something is not American it must be good. But what really gets me, bless their little cotton *chaussettes*, is the shy, modest, unassuming way they automatically believe, sorry, *know*, that whatever they do is a million times better than anybody else could ever have hoped to do. Their croissants are more buttery and flaky, their *képis* crisper. Their *vespasiennes* colder. Their *cabinets à la Turque* filthier, their *maisons closées*, more - how do you say? - efficient. The kickbacks bigger, the grand titles longer, the luxury flats more sumptuous. And the total confidence... Hey - d'yawannaBigMac?

Take French Guiana. It might be stuck over there on the top right-hand corner of South America between Suriname and Brazil, but actually it's France. It is a full-size, full-scale, 100-per-cent department in its own right. Just like Lyons, Marseilles or, I suppose, Paris. What is more, it's the biggest of the lot. Its *deputé* sits in the great French Parliament in Paris alongside *deputés* from parts of France that probably have fewer French residents than there are in French Guiana. It has the same overbearing bureaucracy; the same guaranteed French minimum wage of 5,000 francs a month, which is wildly out of proportion to the surrounding countries; the same French free education system; the same French subsidised healthcare and the same French freedom to ensure they'll need it. As for the businessmen, they have exactly the same freedom to rig tender procedures, issue false invoices, put their hands in the till, funnel money illegally to Switzerland and wheel and deal away on the Stock Exchange to their hearts' content, making use of all the insider information they can get hold of.

What is more, *mon ami*, Guiana *feels* like France. The real France *de nos jours*. Potholed pavements, cats and dogs and kids running around everywhere. And nothing but *coiffeurs* and *parfumiers* and *pâtisseries*, and signs saying, '*Défense de jêter des ordures sur peine d'amendes*'.

Cayenne, the capital, is I swear as French as a day-old Camembert. And as smelly. Either that, or it was the combination of the heat and the fact that being French nobody had had a bath or a shower for six months. All the same, parts of it look as though they haven't changed since the birth of the Second let alone the Third Republic. The whole town looks as though it came as a job lot from any one of a thousand little towns or villages in the South of France which had decided to close down, sell up and disappear rather than put up with any more *rosbifs* driving around moaning about it not being as good as the book. In desperation, I reckon, they then threw everything in a box marked, '*Grandeur de la France*' and sent it off to Ouaga-dougou. Instead it ended up in Cayenne. Well, have you ever known the French Post Office deliver anything to the correct address first time round?

When I say job lot, I mean job lot. The road signs are French, the telephone boxes are French. *Mon Dieu*, not only are the toilets French, but so is the rusty nail on which they hang the sheets of newspaper. And all the fat men you see also have French trumpets.

The main square, the Place des Palmistes, could be the main square of any little French town or village. Trees. Grass. Dogs. Fast-food vans. Taxis. It's got the lot. I wouldn't be surprised if there's a guillotine tucked away round the corner somewhere just waiting to be used.

Across the way the Hôtel de la Ville looks as though it could have come direct from anywhere south of Paris. It is rock solid, impregnable, built to last a thousand generations, as if 1789, 1830, 1848, 1871, 1968 were just a string of unlucky numbers in some local lottery. Well, let's be honest, democracy has never really been popular in France – especially among the rulers, who've always had far more important things on their mind. Like the latest delivery of Grandes Horizontales at the local *maison closée*.

Similarly, the court house, which is so pristine and innocent, it looks as if it has never heard of the phrase *mis en examen* – French legal jargon for 'We're going to start investigating this crime but we don't honestly expect anyone involved to be alive by the time we've finished' , which shows you how far French justice has come from the days when they just used to go around butchering everybody in sight on the basis that God will know who is innocent and who is not, so what the hell.

I didn't have time to check but you don't have to be a French logician to know that around a corner somewhere or other is also their own local equivalent of the famous, or rather infamous, Parisian restaurant La Coupole on the Boulevard Montparnasse, or better still Lapérouse, with its private dining-rooms, its heavy red velvet curtains and its oh-so-discreet waiters who would never dare think of going in and serving the guests unless the buzzers sounded the all-clear first. Personally the other thing I liked about the place – who says the French are not subtle? – was that it was on the Quai des

Grands-Augustins, bearing in mind the original Grand Augustin's comments about wanting whatever it was but not yet.

As for the main street – you can guess what it's called – it couldn't be more French. Apart from all the hotels and bars and restaurants anyone could ever ask for, it's full of *pâtisseries, coiffeurs* and *parfumiers*, all run by *femmes d'un certain âge* who look as though, because of the heat, perspiration is about to break through the second layer of their foundation cream.

The bookshops, no doubt because of the absence of any decent readable French modern literature, seem to be full of nothing but comics about their legendary heroes Asterix and Obelix and riveting titles such as *Etymologique du Français, Synonymes et Contraires* and even the universally acclaimed *Proverbes et Dictons*.

The video shops are packed to overflowing with all the most boring, heavily state-subsidised French films you can imagine. In black and white.

Chemists' windows are crammed with displays for pills and powders for a million different kinds of '*flatulences*'. Phew. See what I mean about as fresh as a day-old Camembert?

Fashion stores are naturally full of traditional French fashions: les sweats, les pulls and les T-shirts.

Everywhere there are huge posters advertising the most important news of the decade, maybe of the century. Some new kind of saucepan has just been launched in France. Even as we speak, supplies are on their way to Cayenne. Fresh deliveries will then be made weekly. Impressive, what!

The back streets, however, are a bit like the Marais, the old, crumbling, decaying quarter of Paris. Before they started doing it up. The buildings, mostly wooden, are all in desperate need of some garlic to bind them together. The swing doors swing a bit too loosely. The old-fashioned metal balconies look none too steady.

There are piles of washing all over the place, a million missing manhole covers and – phew – why don't they get someone to do something about the drains?

But no matter how many times I've been all over Cayenne, or I suppose I should say *le tout* Cayenne. I still keep expecting to turn a corner and stumble on Ernest or Albert or even Jean-Paul sitting casually outside a café (on the left-hand side of the street, naturally), sipping absinthe, smoking Gauloises and moaning about Simone going on and on about women's lib and how he thinks it'll never catch on. Or better still, Claude Lévi-Strauss scribbling away on his book, *Tristes Tropiques*, the story of his swing through South America, which began with the immortal words, 'I hate travelling' . And in the background Edith Piaf belting out, 'I did it my *chemin*'.

But it's not just the buildings and the streets, it's the people as well. Everything they do is French. They drive Peugeots or Renaults; read *Le Monde*, watch Canal Plus, drink French wine; dream French dreams; pray to the one true God of all mankind – in French, His very own language. They also hope to goodness nobody asks them too many questions about Marshal Pétain, the extent of French collaboration in Vichy from 1940–44, or how well they knew Drancy, Klaus Barbie or Paul Touvier.

Their style of driving is definitely French. High speed. Overtaking on the inside. Carving everybody up on the corners. Trying to knock people down on zebra crossings. Their parking is French too. All over the place. On pavements. In front of signs saying '*Prière de ne pas stationner*'. Especially in front of signs saying 'Prière de ne pas stationner SVP'.

Cayenne's taxi drivers are especially French. Many's the time I've got a cab around town. First the driver, who has lived there since Louis XIV first started taking his annual bath in the fountains at Versailles, doesn't know where I want to go. This, don't forget, is in a town about the size of the Place de la Concorde with a population of forty thousand people. Then, because he doesn't know where to go, he has to stop and ask everyone the way there. Once he's satisfied he knows where to go, ie has to stop and ask everyone the way there. Once he's satisfied he knows where we're going, he then takes the longest possible route to get there, hooting and shouting and swearing at everyone in his way; dodging around corners; climbing on to the pavement and finally dropping me the other end of the road to where I want to go because he's just spotted some *jeune fille* who is obviously an entr'acte dancer and wants to chat her up instead.

Even more frightening, they're already making certain the next generation and the next and the next also know their *oignons*.

Every kid in town can recite, without batting an eyelid, whole chunks of Baudelaire, Musset and Verlaine by heart; explain in perfect detail why perfidious Albion should never be forgiven for burning Joan of Arc at the stake; tell you why Napoleon should never have been exiled; list the three causes of the French Revolution and discuss the strengths and weaknesses of Cardinal Mazarin, the French Minister who believed in Richelieu's policy of a strong monarchy, and in spite of enormous opposition from the nobles did everything he could to strengthen the role of the kings and queens of France. Some people even say that if it wasn't for him there would never have been a French Revolution. Others, of course, disagree. But then the French disagree about everything.

Ask any kid under, say, the age of 69 about mildly more relevant things such as why the great Montaigne, Pascal, Voltaire, Rousseau and Hugo were actually in two minds about la France, and how come the strongest military power in Europe collapsed in 1940 in just six weeks and then went on to collaborate far more comprehensively with the Nazis than any other country in Europe, and they'll stare at you as if you're mad. Or Anglo-Saxon. Or both.

To be fair, which is something I hate being, I also came across a number of grown-ups who actually believed we let them down by not surrendering ourselves in 1940. It's the same with the role of the Allies and especially that of the Americans. They'll go on and on about the Resistance, but very few of them ever say anything about the Allies and the relatively minor role they played in the war, compared, that is, to the heroic efforts of the Resistance. And never, ever, have I heard a single Frenchman or woman ever acknowledge the fact that de Gaulle, who came to London as a colonel and somehow or other ended up as a general, was able to march into Paris only thanks to the Br-t-sh and the Am-r-c-ns. It's almost as if they're more ashamed of that than they are of giving in to the Nazis in 1940.

Maybe that is why when it comes to the past the French prefer to concentrate on the future. The last time I was there, the place was crawling with French mediums and fortune-tellers. To save you consulting your crystal ball, I'll tell you now Monsieur Gassam was in the Rue du Docteur Barratt, at number 23. Monsieur Nakamady, 'un des plus grands médiums', could be contacted care of 21 Rue Louis Blanc. But you knew that already. Madame Siham could be found at 6 bis, Rue de l'Ebène. And I cannot tell a lie, Roxanne was holed up at the Hôtel Phigarita with, it must be said, James. But you probably saw that in the cards anyway.

My own reason for going to Cayenne you'll be surprised to hear had nothing whatsoever to do with the future. It was more simple than that. It was because of Baudelaire. At the time I was desperately trying to put into practice his philosophy, 'It is essential to be drunk all the time'. What better, I thought, after dragging myself around the Caribbean gagging on such rich, exotic delicacies as cinch cornflakes, soggy BLT sandwiches, and weak cups of coffee and for dinner whooping it up on salades fatigués, chicken-head soup, wiri-wiri hot jerk wings buried in cinnamon, market fruit salad and coconut custard than to give it a whirl in Cayenne. I was certain that there I could enjoy some plain, ordinary, no-nonsense eating as well as some plain, ordinary, no-nonsense drinking. I also wanted to see whether I could tear myself away from the bitter realities of this world such as calories, carbohydrates, saturated or polyunsaturated or any other kind of fat and instead concentrate on what to Baudelaire were the frivolous things of life such as sin and degradation.

Day after day therefore, purely in the interests of philosophy, I forced myself to have ordinary everyday things for lunch, such as hand-reared wild Burgundian snails, *millefeuilles de foie gras et bananes jaunes, terrine de pigeons* and I forget what else. Similarly for dinner. Night after night it was a struggle to decide whether to have huge bourgeois dishes of *lapin à la fleur de thym* or *confit de canard au port* or *langouste flambée au rhum vieux* or whatever they had left over.

And to drink? Nothing extravagant. Just your run-of-the-mill Krug 69s to get the juices going. Then with the first course, usually an ordinary bottle of, say, Corton Charlemagne 1986 or a Puligny-Montrachet 1988. For the main courses, though, I did tend to go for something a touch more exciting: a Petrus 1964, a Leoville Lascases 1978, a Lagrange 1982 or a couple of Haut-Brion 1975s, 1976s or 1978. Then, with the Roquefort, I had to force myself to have a d'Yquem 1937. Goodness me, it was tough, I can tell you. But not once did I have the *tête de Nègre.* Well, somehow it didn't seem right. Just coffee and a couple of Delamains.

I had no alternative (will the accounts lady please note when she's checking my expenses). There was no McDonald's, no chip shop, no Kentucky Fried Chicken. There was a Restaurant Kentucky, which was completely unlike any other Kentucky restaurant I've ever seen. It was all red and white stripes. When I went in there to check it out I asked for a Pepsi. Guess what? They didn't have any. But I could have a Pernod, a Ricard, chablis, champagne or even an Orangina.

Seeing as, in my dedication to the philosophy of Baudelaire, I put my liver at risk by visiting all the bars and restaurants I could, if you break open a bottle of champagne, say a plain old Krug 1973, I'll give you my own somewhat punctured Michelin Guide to the best places to eat and drink in Cayenne. But instead of stars, I'll award them flat Michelin tyres. Old Charles-Pierre would like that, seeing as he believed in poetic symbolism, the mysteries of city life and all that.

Okay. *On y va*, as he whispered, sick and paralysed, as they took him back from Belgium to Paris, where he died a year later.

Hôtel Les Amandiers. My favourite. Not quite Le Bamboche, the Fer Rouge or La Coupole, that fantastic temple to art deco which also doubles as a restaurant in the Boulevard Montparnasse. But good enough for me. Red and white tablecloths, fans, lots of lattice work. Dogs prowling about. But the food is superb, the wine is superb, the service is superb. As an extra, if she thinks you're a good boy, the lady with good connections and perfect cheekbones or was it good cheekbones and perfect connections, who runs the restaurant, will even clean your glasses for you. Which is more than they'll do in Le Bamboche, the Fer Rouge or La Coupole. What she'll do if she thinks you're a bad boy I have no idea. But I'm definitely going back there again the next time I'm in Cayenne and I'm going to take two pairs of glasses with me.

Flat Michelin tyres: five.

La Caravelle. This place is excellent. *Tripes. Coq au vin. Andouillette. Huîtres. Cassoulet.* Not your ordinary *cassoulet*, but your genuine *cassoulet Toulousain*. You could be anywhere in France. The only trouble is, the food is so good you feel you can only drink good wine with it. Phew.

Flat Michelin tyres: four.

Hôtel Amazonia. First things first: there aren't any. Or if there are, I certainly didn't see any, although I did have my suspicions. Apart that is from the *vieille carcasse* who looked as though she'd been cooking asparagus and beef-in-jelly every day for the last hundred years. Given that, therefore, I can be perfectly honest. It's okay. The dining-room is nothing special. A bit bland. But they do a wide range of fancy fish dishes. It's the only place I've come across where the French really know their plaice.

Flat Michelin tyres: three.

Hôtel Centrale. Pleasant. About the centre spot in the range.

Flat Michelin tyres: three.

La Croustine. Just down the road from the statue of Victor Schoelcher, who was responsible for the abolition of slavery in the country. Not, I hasten to add, slavery to good food and drink. To be honest, I only went in there because they were serving what they called 'hog dogs'. Whatever they were, they were good.

Flat Michelin tyres: four.

Cuisine Creole. Look, I know it's just a van parked by the main square, but it's great fun. Better than most of the snack food I've had in and around the Caribbean. Although I must say I'll never forget that dish I had in that bar in Caracas that night.

*

Flat Michelin tyres: three.

Novotel. Ideal for breakfast. Plenty of coffee, plenty of flaky, buttery croissants, naturally. Plenty of typical French breakfast conversation. Who slept with whom? Whose turn is it next? That kind of thing. Oh yes – cough, cough – plenty of cigarette smoke. Two problems. I had to wait ages for a calvados. Well, that's what the French have for breakfast, isn't it? It's also a bit of a way out of town, but still well worth it. Don't forget, if you really want to be French, dunk your croissant in your coffee. Ugh.

Flat Michelin tyres: four.

La Peixade. Cayenne's answer to the Café de Flore in the Boulevard St Germain where, for some reason or other, Trotsky and all the others got the idea the world was crumbling to pieces while they munched away on their croissants (flaky and buttery, *naturellement*) for hour after hour while the rest of the world was trying to earn a living. Right on the main square, opposite the glorious, ramshackle wooden public library where one morning I asked them if they had anything on the Dreyfus case. Dreyfus being a local, so to speak. But they pretended not to understand my bad French. Ideal for a quick snack. The restaurant, that is, not the library.

Flat Michelin tyres: four.

Hôtel Phigarita. Looks great from the outside, but, I promise you, this is no fun. The swimming pool might look like a giant ice bucket but, don't tell Ernest or Albert, let alone Jean-Paul, there's no bar. Just a machine in reception. But at least the toilets are on the inside. A word of caution: beware of mediums. For some reason or other they seem to prefer this hotel to any other. Maybe it's got the right vibrations. Or maybe they can just foretell they're going to get a special deal. Either way don't ask anyone for their card. You might get the one with the hangman on it.

Flat Michelin tyres: you tell me if you say you can see the future.

Pom Cannelle. It might look basic – when I was there the walls were bare concrete – but the *pâtisseries* were fantastic. The ideal place to relax after three buckets of *cassoulet. Toulousain,* of course.

Flat Michelin tyres: three. Sick bags: one.

Hôtel de la Ville. Undoubtedly the best in town. The entertainment is superb. Especially if you tell them you're a foreign investor and you want to build this enormous hi-tech factory on that bit of land that just happens to be owned by the ... what do they call him in French? But be warned: however much money you've got, however much you want to spend and however much land you want to buy, they visibly wince at the sound of anything as uncivilised as even a single word in English. *C'est vrai.* I was okay, though. I told them the joke about Edward Heath being interviewed on French television, when he described how his past life was divided in two between politics and music. Speaking in that glorious French of his (who am I to talk?), he said, '*Quand je vois ma derrière, je vois qu'il est devise dans deux parties égales.*' Laugh? They almost gave me a luxury flat as a thank-you present.

If Cayenne is the *plat principal,* then Kourou without any doubt is the *dessert.* Officially, it's the home to Arianespace, the fifty-company European commercial satellite-launching consortium. Unofficially it's, forget the others. Having given the world such delicacies as saddle of lamb *Belle Otero* and *soufflé Rothschild* this is how we, *les Français*, not only invented but went on to lead the world in space, space exploration and space technology. (Incidentally, making a good saddle of lamb *Belle Otero* let alone a *soufflé Rothschild* is a million times more difficult than sending anything into space.)

Drive to Arianespace from Cayenne and you pass nothing but tiny little bars and restaurants the whole way. The nothing is rough scrubland and Amazonian rainforest which covers ninety per cent of the country, where there is no such thing as electricity let alone mobile telephones. This means that the last people actually to benefit from having the European Space Agency on their doorstep is, in fact, the French Guianans themselves. On the other hand, the forests are home to a million monkeys, half a million agoutis and goodness knows how many Frenchmen trying to kill them so they can experience the authentic taste of French Guiana. What they're not home to are beetles. They're all at the airport. It's true. When I landed there the place was crawling with them. I reckon I saw every single one of the 400,000 species of beetles they say are on earth. Twice over. They were everywhere. All over the runway. All over the terminal building. You had to literally crunch your way through them.

As for the best, or rather the most authentic bars and restaurants we careered past – I did say all the taxi drivers are French – the three I liked the most were Le Boeuf Couronne, Dynastie and Le Grand Blanc. (I may have missed some of the others because I fell asleep as a result of taking my philosophical studies too seriously the previous evening.)

Le Boeuf Couronne. Which I'm afraid I couldn't find. There's a sign by the edge of the road, then a long dirt track. We drove up and down the track several times, but nothing. Somebody must have moved either the sign or the restaurant. Which was a pity, because it came highly recommended.

*

Flat Michelin tyres (in anticipation): four.

Dynastie. Well would you believe it? A Chinese restaurant in the Amazonian rainforest. In Macouria, a tiny little township. It was very swish, very smart and very popular. Lots of people drive out from Cayenne for a meal here. Bearing in mind what they've got on offer in Cayenne that's really something.

Flat Michelin tyres: four.

Le Grand Blanc. No, it is not named after me, thank you very much. Although I must admit that French Guiana was one of those countries from which, because of the nature of my studies, I returned home whiter than when I arrived. Come to think of it, more of me returned home than when I arrived. The restaurant is about fifteen or twenty kilometres out of Cayenne. Set back off the road, it has even got its own helicopter pad if you fancy dropping in. Try as I might, I'm afraid I can never seem to let go whenever I drop in. Probably because just outside is a giant-sized display reminding you how many people so far have been killed on the roads that year. Incidentally, this is where I heard the helicopter joke for the first time. Ready?

    Englishman: *Voilà. La hélicoptère arrive.*
    Frenchman: *Non, monsieur. It's le hélicoptère, not la hélicoptère.*
    Englishman: *Mon Dieu.* You've got good eyesight.

Flat Michelin tyres: four. One for the joke.

    Then suddenly, looming out of the rainforest in front of me, is this enormous, beautiful, slim, elegant, gleaming, glistening 420-metric tonne, 50-metre high bottle of wine with two smaller bottles of mineral water strapped either side of it pointing towards the ... No, sorry, I mean, rocket. It's just that to me all rockets look like bottles of wine. Must be something to do with Baudelaire. Or the shape of the thing, I suppose. Now where was I? Oh yes. There was this huge bottle of wine pointing towards those Elysian fields in the sky.

I went there to see the blast-off of Ariane 5, which – after they had proved to the world that they could blow US$3 billion by building a 35,000-tonne nuclear-powered aircraft 12 feet too short for planes to take off from and land on – was the spectacular French bid, after ten years and over 50 billion francs of research, to grab the lion's share of the 200 billion-franc commercial satellite launching business. But I'd no sooner arrived than it was announced that the launch was delayed. That damned European rocket, French officials now said. In spite of more than ten European years of blasted European research it still needed more time for European 'final qualification', whatever that was. The previous European one launched seventeen months before had blown up less than forty European seconds after take-off. Now the French, no doubt with their Yves on the ball and utilising the very best French brain power, the very best French technology and goodness knows how many bottles of French wine, were planning to dig Europe out of the dirt.

My guess was that the launch wasn't delayed by any need for 'final qualification' at all. It was just the French being French. They didn't want the rocket to go off when the Europeans said it should go off. They wanted it to go off when they said it should go off. I couldn't have been more grateful to them. Because had the European launch gone ahead at the time planned I would never have had the chance of visiting what must be one of the most hilarious displays I've ever seen in my life: the European Space Centre, the world's business commercial satellite launching station. Sorry, I mean the French Musée de l'Espace, where I promise you, as sure as Monsieur Chauvin was a Frenchman – come on, you didn't think chauvinism came from Papua New Guinea, did you? - you get a unique view of space and space exploration you would never, ever see in any other country in the world. Not only is it cringe-making, it's cringe-making on an inter-galactic scale. If you believed everything you see on display you would think that if it wasn't for the French the rest of us poor dumbos wouldn't even have got round to inventing the wheel.

Okay, so which great man inspired the world to search for the stars? The Greek philosophers? Copernicus? Da Vinci? Galileo? *Non*. It was, according to one of the more historically accurate and totally objective displays I saw, some guy or rather monsieur called Camille Flammanon - not Asterix, Tintin or even Obelix but Camille Flammanon - who in 1880 in some magazine called *L'Astronomie Populaire*, came up with the immortal, earth-shattering words 'One looks at the stars'. Go on. Admit it. I bet you could hear the strains of 'The Marseillaise' in the distance as you read that.

Who was the first to come up with the principles of space travel?

Tsiolkovsky? Hermann Oberth? Wrong. According to another historically accurate display, it was Esnault Pelterie. Now, now. The fact that it was a good few years after the other guys produced their studies is irrelevant. What are you, some kind of troublemaker?

Who was responsible for the first manned flight? The Wright Brothers? Wrong. It was Clement Ader. Goodness me. Don't you know anything?

Okay, so now a really difficult one. Who actually undertook the first real flight in the whole history of the world? A Frenchman, do I hear you cry? Wrong. Much as it may be impossible to believe, it was not, definitely not, I repeat not, a Frenchman. It was - are you ready? - a French dog. This happened, according to yet another historically accurate display, in 1797 when André-Jacques Garnerin threw his dog out of a hot air balloon hovering over the Parc Monceau in Paris. Attached to the dog was - two more spectacular firsts for the French – not only the world's first parachute but also the world's first dog parachute. All three landed safely *dans le parc* and in the history books: French only of course. What Monsieur Garnerin had for lunch to celebrate I shudder to think. Probably the dog.

I know you don't believe me but, honestly, wandering around the European Space, oops, I mean the Musée de l'Espace, I don't know why, but you get the distinct impression the French are responsible for the whole thing. Expeditions to the Moon? Rockets to the stars? The Apollo programme? Sure, all these get a brief mention. But then the text goes on to talk about 'present-day rockets which allow us to launch satellites and send probes to explore other planets'. Not a word about who is *sending* the expeditions to the moon, the rockets to the stars or whatever. Not a word about *whose* rockets allow us to send probes to explore other planets.

But *les petits* Russians. The even more *petits* what-were-their-names? Didn't they do something, anything, in space?

Well, yes they did. And I must stress that in no way at all do the French go out of their way to denigrate Russian efforts. In fact, on the first floor of the Space Centre, I mean the Musée de l'Espace, in one of ten major galleries, in a tiny little cabinet there is a passing reference to the Russians and their Mir space programme. There is also a single, solitary reference to all the fantastic achievements notched up by the Americans in the history of space exploration: 'In 1967 three US astronauts die in a fire on Apollo 1.'

And that's it. Honestly, it's unbelievable. What's even more of a laugh is that these revered French pioneers were the guys who originally refused to accept Newtonian mathematics and physics which, I suppose you could say, were the real basis of all space flight – not because they thought they were wrong but because they were not French. Obviously the French have never got over the fact that the apple wasn't even a Golden Delicious.

What does surprise me though, having seen this glorious history of French space exploration in what is after all the European Space Centre financed by, don't forget, fifty companies throughout Europe, is that the French didn't go the final step and insist on giving the rockets different names like the Americans do. I mean ordinary, everyday European place names like Austerlitz, Fontenoy, Wagram, Rivoli, Magenta, Iena, Trocadew, Solférino or even Alésia, where somebody, I forget who, happened to defeat the Romans way back in 52 BC. Or if not ordinary boring European place names, names of the world's most famous people such as, for instance, Comte de la Motte-Piquet, the naval commander who virtually blew the English out of the water in Martinique in 1779; de Saxe, the French general who helped the Americans beat the British in the War of Independence; Hoche, Suchet, Ney; Maréchals Joffre and Molitor; Colonel Fabien and, of course, General de Gaulle and, what was the name of that little guy from Corsica?

My own nominee would be André Coyne, who is known in France as 'the father of thin-arch dams' , and who I think typifies the unbelievable, breathtaking genius of French engineers. Virtually a legend in his own lifetime, he was responsible for building the famous Malpasset dam near Fréjus in 1954. Five years later, in 1959, the whole thing collapsed.

I think I'll write to them and suggest it.

As for Kourou, the local town, all I can say is if Cayenne is a typical example of an old French town that hasn't changed since the birth of the Second let alone the Third Republic, then Kourou is a typical example of an old French new town that hasn't changed since its birth twenty years ago. It's clean. It's orderly. It's got plenty of shops and mile after mile of houses. Some okay, the rest pretty nondescript like, I suppose, any new town anywhere in the world. As for quality of life, the only excitement seems to be standing outside the Foreign Legion barracks, the - would you believe, Quartier Forget - early in the morning when a phalanx of crewcut joggers come pounding out for their regular daily exercise. The way the ground shook I thought another rocket was suddenly taking off.

But enough of this travel stuff. Back to Baudelaire and the important things of life: the bars and restaurants. This time of Kourou.

Au Metro. A piano bar. Pleasant. Discreet. So discreet I'll say no more.

Flat Michelin tyres: A discreet four.

Le Baraka. Superb. The only restaurant I've been in where they give you the bottle and let you pour as much as you like. I always sit on the terrace outside and keep pouring and pouring and pouring. From what I can remember the food is great. Lots of North African specialities, huge portions, very friendly service. You've got to try it. Now, how about another drink?

Flat Michelin tyres: 95 per cent proof.

Le Citron Vert. Pleasant. Friendly. Good for a quick beer. Wouldn't recommend it for much more.

Flat Michelin tyres: three.

Hôtel Atlantis. I went in there for a meal and nearly came out with a mountain. For some reason or other the woman in reception kept on at me to hire one. It's not, I admit, the usual thing women in reception areas in French hotels keep on at me to hire. But I kept saying *non* until eventually she got the message.

Flat Michelin tyres: four (for trying).

*

Les Jardins d'Hermès. Funny place, this. No whisky. No food. No people.

Flat Michelin tyres: none.

Hôtel des Manguiers. Right on the very edge of the beach. Palm trees. Beautiful views of Devil's Island, *alma mater* to Alfred Dreyfus, Papillon, Dustin Hoffman, Steve McQueen and, in accordance with its role as probably the most notorious of all the French overseas penal settlements, birthplace of the now internationally acclaimed *nouvelle cuisine* style of French cooking. Maybe not so much in terms of quality, but certainly in terms of quantity. I tried to get there in order to pay homage. But I was out of luck. It is now home to a down-range satellite tracking station and as difficult to get to today as in the old days it was difficult to get away from. Unfortunately, for some reason or other, the hotel actually looks like a prison. There are bars on the windows and doors. There is an electric locking system to get in. Then when you're in the building there are more gates and more bars to get into the hotel proper. Not, I'm afraid, my hammer. I like bars, but not that type.

Flat Michelin tyres: none. They've been stolen.

Hôtel des Roches. Almost opposite the Hotel des Manguiers. Beautiful views of Devil's Island. On the beach. But no bars – on the doors and windows, that is. The Coconut Bar, however, is a great meeting-place for people at the Space Centre. I forget how many rum and whatevers I had, but it was great.

Flat Michelin tyres: four (hic).

Hôtel Mercure. Near the Space Centre, on a lake. Nice

setting, the service is terrible. I'm not saying they're slow, it's just that the bottle of champagne I ordered when I called in there I'm still waiting for.

Flat Michelin tyres: none yet. They're still waiting for them to arrive.

Les Palmistes. Great place, great food, great atmosphere. The only drawback is it's impossible to get into. It's always crowded with *énarques* from the Space Centre. In the end I only got in by quoting Victor Hugo at them:

> Where then will this rebel rest?
> Space watches with furrowed brow
> Man's footprints in the sky.
> Treading unknown paths
> He scales the surrendering abyss
> And bestrides the reaches of infinity.
> Where will this tireless insurgent
> Halt his onward rush?
> How far from Mother Earth?
> How far from Destiny itself?
> Know thine enemy.

Works every time.

Flat Michelin tyres: four.

Restaurant Képi Blanc. Not very big, which surprised me. It thought every French képi was extra big. But pleasant, friendly. Not the kind of place to make any complaints. Not that I would dare.

Flat Michelin tyres: four.

So that's my definitive list of restaurants in Kourou.
Overall, therefore, is Cayenne to be sneezed at? The answer is no. Definitely *non*. It's a great place. So is

Kourou, especially the restaurant which is famous for it's Vieux Fagots, which I'm not allowed to mention. (Vieux Fagots is, you may recall, a table wine from Marjolaine in the Gironde. Why, what were you thinking?)

Admittedly, you don't see many Guianese there. They've all adopted another French habit: going on strike for no reason at all. At a moment's notice. Regularly, every two months. But they've learnt well from their masters: whenever they go on strike they straight away cut off the electricity, try to set fire to the police station and then camp in front of the court house until the riot police arrive. After that they disappear very quickly.

So when it comes to my admiration of the F-word, I'm afraid I'm not prepared to give an inch. Which, of course, was not what the French did in 1914 and 1940, but never mind. All I can say is, the longer I'm away from them, the more I miss them, even though I've since discovered that when Baudelaire said 'It is essential to be drunk all the time', he went on to qualify his remark by adding that you could get drunk on wine, poetry or just 'being good'.

It's obviously a case of absinthe makes the heart grow fonder.

Georgetown

You want to destroy your liver?

Go to Georgetown. No, not Georgetown, Washington, although I'm sure you can destroy many things in Georgetown, Washington. Like your honesty, your integrity and your resistance to all those little bags of white powder. I mean Georgetown, Guyana, which, ironically, means the land of water. If, however, you want to destroy it immediately, go on a Friday afternoon. Any Friday afternoon.

You think the old six o'clock swill in Australia was rough? You should see the guys pouring off the sugar plantations and the farms along the banks of the Demerara and out of the factories on the edge of the Garden City itself and into the rum shops scattered all over town. Talk about lemmings with one hell of a thirst. The six o'clock swill, let me tell you, is for kids. The Georgetown Friday afternoon rush is for real grown-ups. Because it's not beer they're after but rum. And not your ordinary rum, either – they're after the real stuff, the 100 per cent 69 per cent stuff, if you see what I mean. Which, oddly, if I can remember correctly through the haze, is called High Wine.

One bottle? No problem. That's kid's stuff. Two bottles? Now you're talking. Three? Well, of course, you are one of the grown-ups...

These guys think nothing of knocking back one

bottle, maybe even two or - heaven help their livers - three bottles over a weekend. If they're stuck at home with the wife and kids, that is. If they manage to get out and really start enjoying themselves, it can be more. Five or even six bottles. Each.

I think I can honestly say I've never been anywhere in the world where I've seen so many people knock back so much of the heavy stuff in such a short period of time. And I mean heavy stuff. The stuff they drink doesn't just explode inside you like a mixture of sodium chlorate and nitrobenzene, it makes paint-stripper taste like orange juice. On the other hand, to be fair, the blood you cough up as a result will never, ever congeal. It's probably only because Guinness is Guinness that Georgetowners haven't been given five-star, or rather five-bottle, rating in their *Book of Records* for the ability to enjoy themselves while they are so completely out of the window.

Originally they probably hit the bottle because of all the things they have had to put up with. The Dutch. The British. The British and French. The British again. Evelyn Waugh. *A Handful of Dust.* Tony Last. Dr Messenger. Independence. Near civil war. Forbes Burnham. Marxism. Socialism. The nationalisation of everything in sight. Collapse of economy. The highest debt per head of population of any country in South or Central America - higher than Brazil, higher than Argentina, the two most famous debtors in the region.

Then suddenly everything was slammed into reverse. Deregulation. Divestment. Privatisation. Companies started making money. Not much, but some. People started getting jobs. Not everyone, but more than before. Goods began appearing in the shops. Families started to eat again. Even more significant, roads started being repaired.

But the ironic thing is that the more things get better, the more they start to worry. Worry that it won't last, that their present leaders will foul it up. And that they'll become another Falklands Islands.

'Another Falklands Islands?' The idea seemed absurd.

'Not so,' according to one of the officials I met at the Ministry of Finance who was so smooth he looked as though he could stab you to death and stitch you up again without you realising.

'Venezuela claim that we are not a country in our own right,' he oozed. 'But a province of theirs. After all this time there's still no road between our two countries. There are still no flights, no official flights, either. When we were down and out they were not interested. Why should they be? But now...'

Which I suppose is as good a reason as any for getting bombed out of your mind. Especially as it costs so little. A bottle of rum? Around – eat your liver out – US$2. Yes, US$2 for a whole mind-blowing, body-numbing, liver-collapsing, life-destroying, tooth-melting, bottle of 69 per cent proof rum. Hence the crowds pushing and shoving and jostling for the stuff in the rum shops in and around Georgetown.

One guy in a rum shop about the size of a small-time grocery store, piled floor to ceiling with booze, told me he regularly drank two bottles over the weekend. Minimum.

'Man. This ent no time to stop drinkin' jus' to go to work,' he shouted at me, in that sing-song West Indian type accent of theirs, as he staggered off to oblivion.

An Indian-looking man said that was nothing. His mother-in-law drank a bottle, maybe two bottles a day. Every day of the week. Every week of the year. If he didn't already own a string of rum shops then he should. A customer like that could make him a fortune. Someone else, a young guy with a collar and tie and one of those purses under his arm, was buying five bottles of the stuff. He told me he wasn't an alkie. It was just that suddenly he was in the money. The trouble was, it was other people's money. He had just pulled off his biggest-ever dodge: the immigration officer dodge.

Dragging myself around the world as I'm forced to do

for a living, I've come across thousands of ever helpful chloroform-rag to ripe-banana dodges as well as a million different dodgers. For example:

The customs officer dodge. The customs officer grabs whatever he wants from your suitcase; says he thinks it's illegal to bring it into the country; says to be on the safe side, before he has to charge you an arm and a leg, he'll check first with his superior officer. He then disappears behind a screen or into some scruffy corridor. Forever.

The lost luggage dodge. Your luggage doesn't arrive. Airport officials tell you they'll find it and deliver it to your hotel. But would you please leave your keys with them so that they can check it through customs for you. And if and when it ever arrives...

The airport dodge. As soon as you land, a million guys rush up to you, shouting 'Taxi, taxi,' grab your suitcase and walk straight out of the terminal. Never to be seen again.

The money on the ground dodge. You see some money on the ground. You come over all Boy Scout and pick it up. Within seconds you're surrounded by a gang of guys all shouting and claiming it was their money and that you're stealing it from them. You try and hand it back. Again they start shouting and screaming, this time that you're handing it back to the wrong person. They're going to call the police, unless you're interested in doing a deal. Like buying back everything they've lifted from you while you've been arguing and shouting with everybody in sight: your wallet, your watch, your braces, your underpants...

The taxi dodge. You arrive at midday. You pay what it says on the meter. But the meter is set not only on the night-rate but on the weekend night-rate as well.

The changing money dodge. Somebody stops you in the street and asks you to change some money. Out of the kindness of your heart you take a wad of notes out of your pocket. Depending on how much it's all worth and whether the guy reckons he can get away with it, he'll either grab the lot and run or start yelling and screaming saying you short-changed him; you gave him dud notes or whatever. Because it's all Monopoly money, because you're not certain of the notes anyhow, because you don't want to make a fuss, you give in. The guy walks away with US$20. Plus the extra he made changing money with you.

The throwing-a-rat-in-your-car dodge. A variation of the common throwing-water/beer/paint-in-your-eyes dodge. This is for advanced level students only. Either you're about to get into your car. Or you're driving along slowly, the windows open. Or you're waiting at the traffic lights. Whoosh. In comes a big black rat, or in Africa, a big fat agouti. Everyone, but everyone, panics. They just throw open the doors and run. A group of community-conscious citizens, all offering to catch the rat for you, then surrounds your car. When they've finally caught it and leave to dispose of it, they say you're lucky if you're left with the chassis and at least three of the four wheels of your precious car.

Then, of course, there is the most popular and probably the most profitable dodge or con of all: the Nigerian-send-us-your-bank-account-number-and-we'll-send-you-£36-million-by-return dodge. Don't ask me why, but I've had letters and faxes from Dr Frank Chidozie of the Nigerian National Petroleum Corporation, Mr Morris Otis Kute, Prince Arthur Nweze, Dr Awele Chukwuma and a million others all offering me untold riches if all I do is 'render the needed assistance morally, financially, and otherwise' so that the readies can be 'speedily processed and fully remitted' into my account. And up yours too, sunshine.

Georgetown is probably the dodge capital of the world. Some people say it's because they've all suffered so much in the past. The only way they could survive was to dodge for a living. Now as times are slowly getting better they're finding it difficult to kick the habit.

Myself, I blame television. If the programmes weren't so boring people wouldn't want to go wandering round the streets looking for trouble. They'd stay at home and watch films of other people wandering around the streets looking for trouble.

Now if you change this genuine nine-bob Guyanese note for a brand new US$20 bill, the one with President Andrew Jackson set off-centre on the front, I'll tell you all about some of the tried and mistrusted ways of Georgetown. Just in case you ever go there. Just in case you ever go there, hit the rum and get completely carried away – on a stretcher.

The country is full of gold mines, although a big chunk if not most of the gold is smuggled across the borders into Venezuela, Brazil and Suriname. So wherever you go guys keep shuffling up to you offering you lumps of the yellow stuff. One morning as I left the Tower Hotel, where the executive chairman and general manager and all the other big shots have their personal parking places right outside the front door while we guests have to drive around town for hours on end every night looking for somewhere safe to park, some smart young man in a blue tracksuit offered me a handful of what he said were gold nuggets. To me they looked like bits of dirt. Which they probably were.

Another day, as I was clutching my head one morning, late and stumbling up Main Street to the Bank of Guyana, the scruffiest-looking guy in the world shuffled up to me by the Cenotaph and offered to double any money I gave him.

'Ten dollars. Hundred dollars. Thousand dollars. Give me. Give me. Give me, I'll double it for you,' he kept screaming at me.

I gave him the name of a guy in financial futures. I told him to contact them. I guessed they could use someone with his particular expertise.

Outside Guyana Airways office I saw another guy working the sick/blind mother/father/son/daughter/

whatever dodge. He stopped a couple of Americans, showed them some grubby photograph and collected two US$10 notes in all of thirty seconds. Which on an hourly rate must put him up there with your average auditor or accountant – not that he would probably want to be compared with the likes of them.

Along the Avenue of the Republic, another Guyanese, a tiny, wiry little man with a greasy T-shirt, spiky hair and a face that looked as though he was already wearing a nylon stocking over it, tried to catch me with the religious dodge.

'My brother, my brother.' He thrust out his hand in welcome.

'Good morning,' I grunted, with all the usual civility that we English are supposed to display on such occasions.

'Welcome to Guyana,' he said, stepping it out beside me because we all know the last thing you do is stop and establish eye contact. If you do that, you might as well hand over the keys of your house there and then.

'The Lord is good,' he gasped, as I tried to quicken the pace hoping he wouldn't notice.

'Er, yes.'

'The Lord wants you to have a nice time in Guyana.'

'Oh, thank you. It's very kind of …'

'But the Lord also wants you to avoid certain places.'

'Oh really?' I said, stopping and searching for a bit of paper. 'Which ones?'

Damn. He'd got me.

'The Lord wants you to avoid the railway terminus.' He came closer to me and began whispering in my ear. 'And also the hotels along Main Street. And whatever you do, don't go near the National Park.'

'That's very interesting,' I said, scribbling furiously. 'I will certainly do my …'

'Of course, I haven't got a job,' he whispered earnestly. 'I work for the Church. The Seaman's Mission.'

'Very good,' I mumbled.

'And the taxis. Avoid the taxis outside the hotels,' he continued, trying to grab my hand to shake it. 'They're very expensive. About 90 per cent more expensive than the town taxis.'

'Did you say to avoid the—'

'Of course, I don't need money for myself.'

'—railway terminus? That's by the Ministry of Finance, isn't it?'

'I need it to further the work of the Church. To continue our mission on earth. Help the Good Lord and the Good Lord will...'

I put my pen and bit of paper back in my pocket. I turned round to him. I shook his hand as warmly as my chilly English blood would allow me.

'Tell me,' I said, trying to sound earnest and concerned and dedicated. 'What is more important in this life; prayer or money?'

'Prayer,' he said immediately.

'In that case,' I said, as piously as I could, 'I'll pray for you.'

Vroom. I was gone.

When I got back to my hotel that evening, there waiting for me was the guy with the so-called gold nuggets. He wanted to know if I would give him English lessons. He'd pay for them, of course. Oh yes, I thought. There's me down here giving you English lessons while your mate is upstairs going through my room. Pull the other one.

The immigration officer dodge, however, was a new one on me. What it needs, the smart young man in the tie told me, is three guys and a High Court judge, an accountant or just some innocent schmuck who has not had a life. Foreign, maybe, just arrived, wandering around aimlessly. Preferably in the centre of town and ideally around Stabroek Market, a vast, cast-iron aircraft-hangar of a building with an ornate clock tower on the banks of the Demerara where you can buy everything under the sun, and the moon as well.

One of the three looks all wild and scruffy and pretends he is crazy. As soon as he sees an innocent tourist or businessman, he starts barking and shouting and screaming and swearing at him. Number two guy then approaches. He pretends he is an innocent passer-by just coming to the aid of a stranger. 'Well, surprise, surprise. Don't you recognise me? Last night/two nights ago/a month ago. At the airport. I was the immigration officer. I let you in.' Zap. He's immediately accepted. The innocent is rolling around in gratitude. Some knight in shining armour has come to his rescue. What's more, he's an official, an immigration officer. Wowee. 'Is this guy troubling you? Don't worry. Don't trouble yourself. I'm armed. I'll protect you.' Out comes a knife. Zap. Zap. Zap. He waves it at the crazy guy. The crazy guy retreats to a safe distance but still carries on shouting and screaming. Makes it seem authentic. Right?

Now number three arrives. 'Hey,' he says to the immigration officer. 'Where have you been, man? Haven't seen you for ages, man. Whatdyadoin', man?' Two old buddies meet up again and babyface Mr Innocent/High Court judge/accountant/schmuck goes all gooey because he's not only safe, he's part of the scene, he's accepted. Number three buddy then says to the immigration officer, 'Hey man, want to make some money?' Immigration officer protests. 'No, no, man. Not my scene. Go try somebody else.' Mr Innocent begins to melt into the ground. Not only has he been rescued, he's been rescued by a good guy as well. 'Come on, man,' says number three, pulling three black plastic disks out of his pocket and shuffling them backwards and forwards. 'Choose one. I won't charge you. You're my friend.' Immigration officer chooses one, turns it over and – surprise, surprise – it's the winner. 'Hey man!' screams number three. 'You've won!' and he slaps a thick wad of notes into the Immigration Officer's hands. He protests. How perfect can this man be? But number three insists. His word is his bond. His friend won. He must keep the money.

Now they move in for the sting.

'Hey, you,' says Mr Hero Immigration Officer to Innocent Schmuck. 'I didn't even bet any money and I won. See what you can do.'

What happens? In a split second, Mr Innocent Schmuck is waving his wallet all over town. Mr Immigration Officer grabs it. 'Don't do that,' he gasps. 'Are you crazy? There are thieves everywhere. What do you want to do? Get robbed?' At the same time, of course, he is busily extracting a fistful of notes and slapping them in the hand of number three.

What is Mr Innocent Schmuck going to do? Protest? Grab the money back? Mr Shining Whiter-than-white Immigration Officer has just rescued him. In any case, he's just played the game and won a fistful of ...

'Choose a disk! Choose a disk!' both of them are now yelling at him. Mr Innocent Schmuck looks lost. He's got his wallet back. There's God knows how much money in the other guy's hands. There's no way he's going to get it back. Start shouting and screaming? No way. Like it or not, he's placed a bet. He's surrounded by a crowd. Even good guy Mr Shining White Immigration Officer is shouting at him to choose a disk.

He points to one. Number three turns it over. It's a blank. And – vroom – the whole town is suddenly empty. Gone is Mr Shining White Immigration Officer. Gone is number three. Gone is his fistful of money. And gone is the whole crowd, except, standing over there, eyeing him up and down, is Mr Crazy. Just one word, one attempted cry for help and Mr Innocent Schmuck knows Mr Crazy will be all over him.

So he turns round and heads back to the safety and security of his lonely hotel room, hoping like mad that they've left him enough money to get half a cup of coffee.

How do I know that's what they do? I watched them at it. First under the archways opposite the entrance to Stabroek Market. Then round the corner in the unofficial bus station. Finally along the Avenue of the

Republic by the junction with Charlotte Street where they're building the new High Court. They were so good at it, so smooth and so professional it was a joy to watch. Such acting, such timing, such professionalism. I swear that even Queen Victoria's statue outside the High Court was amused.

The first time it happened, by Stabroek Market (which means 'standing brook' although I would have thought fetid, stinking puddle would have been a better description), I was talking to a couple of burnt-out American missionaries.

'What with casting out seven or eight devils a night, after five weeks I'm exhausted. I've just got to go home,' said missionary number one, who had a beard and for all the world looked as though he could have been the President of Coca-Cola.

'Seeing all those blind people seeing again and all those cripples walking again, it's so boring,' sighed missionary number two, who was younger, much younger, and looked like a tennis coach. 'I've been doing this too long. At first it used to be a rollercoaster. It used to leave me on a real high. But now...'

They started to tell me a story about a voodoo man they had come across who could suck the blood out of a baby at a hundred paces. He took a straw, put it into his mouth, pointed it at a baby, took a deep breath and...

Then I saw our Immigration Officers move in on this guy, who looked maybe Dutch or German. Young. Smartly dressed. The eager young accountant type. What he was doing anywhere near there, goodness only knows. He should have been back at his hotel, in his room, playing with his laptop. He had just strolled past Kentucky Fried Chicken when Mr Crazy started his act. At first the young guy tried to ignore him. But as he got more and more aggressive you could see the poor chap trying to back away. A small crowd stopped to watch which, intentionally or unintentionally, blocked his escape route. Now he was well and truly trapped.

Then out of the crowd arrived our hero, the Immigration Officer. Within a second they were lifelong buddies. Within two seconds the card player was on the scene. They were all shaking hands and slapping each other on the back. Within three seconds Mr Innocent was standing there with a whole stack of dollars in his hand and the Immigration Officer was yelling at him to try his luck. Within four seconds they were all jumping up and down screaming with excitement. Within five seconds Mr Innocent is standing there all alone staring at an empty wallet. It was beautiful.

Round the corner it was a different kind of bedlam. A thousand tiny white mini-buses were packed on to a patch of ground half the size of a polo field. A thousand bus drivers were yelling and screaming and hustling for passengers. A million people were fighting to get on and off them.

I wandered up and down trying to improve my knowledge of one of the world's more exotic languages.

'Yug jiss pick up yuh lil backside and climb into mah bus,' a young Indian-looking driver was screaming at an old lady who looked as though she could be an elder of the church of whatever.

'Eh oh, fancy boy, wha' de rass yuh sayin'? Yuh got a lot o' nerves, yuh know. Yuh go out walkin' an' git lost,' she screamed back at him.

'Miss Lady. Miss Lady. Dis bus wan' one mo'.'

'It ent got no boom boxes.'

'Okay, Miss Lady, Miss Lady. Now dis bus, it ent got no boom boxes. Okay. Okay. We go. We go.'

She climbs in.

'Moving now. Moving now,' screams the driver. But, of course, it doesn't. He's filled all ten seats in the van, now he's looking for some standing-only passengers. About 237 if the other buses are anything to go by.

'Hey. Dis ent how yuh does run a bus service,' I can hear the old lady screaming at him. 'Yuh know yuh ent suppose to, hey.'

Another bus driver is giving up the ghost.

'Oh, Lawd. Give me de strength to go through wid dis,' he is wailing. 'Ah really ent in no mood fuh nonsense dis afternoon. Dis bus is now off-duty.'

'Come si'down.' Another driver comes up to him. 'Dran worry, me go git yuh somethin' fe drink.'

'Me na t'ink me could ...'

'Fuh a lil while.'

The first bus driver sits down on a pile of wooden crates. On one of them I noticed somebody had scrawled, 'Full respect for slackness'.

'I is a sick, sick man,' he is whimpering.

A young, stroppy guy comes up to him.

'Hey, boyfren. He deh 'pon crack or what?'

'Hey. Why yuh don't close dat septic tank!' the driver leaps up and yells in his face.

'Is who you talking to?' The young guy is now dancing up and down and screaming at the top of his voice. 'I could cut you up, you know. I could give you de digits.'

Another old lady, who looks as if she's going to some red hot gospel service, all straw hat and fancy white shoes, now appears on the scene and starts yelling at the driver too.

'Hey. Dis ent how yuh does run a service. Drive dis bus.'

'Tell meh how much people in de bus.'

'Hey. De damn bus full.'

Then suddenly I notice that our Three Musketeers have got another hit. This time the guy is probably American. Loud, Hawaiian-type shirt, baggy shorts, no socks, cigar. You know the type. I can hardly believe my eyes. Before the Immigration Officer has even introduced himself this guy is waving US$100 bills all over the show. They hardly play the game before he is emptying his wallet on top of them.

Outside the High Court it was the same story. This time an Indian-looking guy. Not so much shouting and screaming, but again the same result.

Another day like today, I thought, and instead of celebrating with just five bottles of High Wine they'll be able to buy the whole distillery,

In fact, with so much lyin' and cheatin' and boozin' going on it's a wonder that Georgetown, which at one time must have been one of the most beautiful wooden cities in the world, has lasted as long as it has. After all, one breath of practically raw alcohol has only got to hit one lighted match for one split-second and – whoosh – the whole place would be up in flames. Take my advice, therefore. If you're into wooden buildings go there while it's still matchless. Well, almost matchless. It's a bit run down and scruffy. But don't risk missing the whole thing.

Top of the tinder box is the Anglican St George's Cathedral, the tallest wooden building of them all. Not just in Georgetown but in the world. Inside, however, it looks like a cross between a mediaeval banquet hall and one of those new, modern pubs complete with a table selling souvenirs. When I asked the old lady falling asleep behind the table what souvenirs they had of the tallest wooden structure in the world, she replied, 'Tea towels'. Whatever they are.

The first cathedral was built of wood – not in rock, you notice – in 1811, because no doubt the Guyanese recognised that being Anglican it was probably to their advantage if their church could splinter easily into goodness knows how many pieces. All sharing the same common heritage, of course. No sooner was it completed, however, than they realised it wasn't quite what they believed in so instead of going back to their foundations and re-examining everything again from square one they decided to change the whole thing altogether. They moved to the present site with completely different foundations. But having built the church a second time, they still found they didn't believe in it. In any case, what with all the compromises they were forced to make in building it they very quickly discovered the whole thing was somewhat shaky. Hence the need for selling tea towels.

You think I've got a thing about Anglicans? Okay, let me ask you a question. If you had nine children who kept leaning out of the window of your house and throwing things at passers-by, what would you do? That's right, you'd take the constructive, positive caring approach: you'd belt the living daylights out of them. Not the Bishop of Guyana. With glorious Anglican logic he decided that instead of preaching the Fourth Commandment to his children as he did, no doubt, to everybody else, it was up to them to decide whether they believed in it or not. So what did he do? He had the whole building, all three storeys of it including his private chapel complete with stained glass windows, moved back from the edge of the pavement so that if his nine kids believed they should continue throwing things out of the window they could do so without any risk of them hitting passers-by.

You don't believe me? Go and have a look at Austin House – Austin after the name of the Bishop, William Piercy Austin – in High Street between the Red House, where Cheddi Jagan used to live when he was prime minister, and the head office of Demerara Distillers. You can see quite clearly that it is set back from the pavement.

There are no compromises and shilly-shallying about City Hall. It is quite straightforwardly, no nonsense about it, crazy. Imagine a Bavarian Castle designed by an Italian with his mind on other things and you've just about got it. It's all towers and twiddly bits and fancy icing. But at least they didn't keep chopping and changing and moving around and believing in one design one minute and something else the next. What they decided, they believed in. What they believed in, they got. The architect? Oh, didn't I tell you? It was a Jesuit priest. Incidentally my friend, the con man (he's my friend because I've still got my wallet) told me that however many windows there were in the City Hall you would never catch a civil servant staring vacantly out of one all morning. Because if they did they wouldn't have anything to do all afternoon.

My other favourite wooden buildings are the Supreme Court and two churches, St Andrew's Kirk and the Catholic Cathedral. Look at the Supreme Court. To me it's two styles in one. The ground floor is Italianate with lots of fancy windows. The first floor is Tudor. English law being built on the foundations of Roman law, perhaps. See what you think. Incidentally, if you do, be warned. There's usually a couple of guys playing the Two-Up game on the pavement outside. You know the one: they throw two coins in the air and you've got to guess which side they'll come down. The answer, of course, from your point of view, is always the losing side.

St Andrew's Kirk, the oldest building in town and the oldest church in the country, is the responsibility of the two most generous peoples on earth: the Dutch and the Scots. The Dutch are responsible for the roof. The Scots for the funny-looking cone-shaped steeple.

The Catholic Cathedral, on the other hand, is half and half. Half wood. Half concrete. The first all-wood cathedral burnt down in 1913. See what I mean about their rum and lighted matches? Work started on the present building just two years later. But it was not fully open again for ten years. Why do I like it? Because there are signs inside telling you not to lean your bicycle against the pillars. Now I ask you, who takes their bicycle to church and then takes it inside and leans it up against the pillars? Obviously the law-abiding Guyanese do. A word of advice. Whenever I go there, among the beggars outside there is usually a young woman sitting on the steps, holding a baby with blood dribbling from its mouth. Don't worry. Whatever it may look like, it's not blood. It's the juice from some kind of nut which just looks like blood. Another dodge.

But these aren't the only wooden buildings. There's a whole string of them. The Museum of Anthropology, which seems to be nothing but jazzy shutters, windows and elaborate woodwork, The Park Hotel, your typical Victorian-style hotel. The National Library, and Umana Yana, or the Benab, as everybody calls it, although it's not perhaps strictly a wooden building. More bamboo and vines and troolie and ite, palm leaves to you, and a couple of million nails. A copy of a communal house of the Wai-Wai tribe, the original plan was to build it entirely of traditional materials. Trouble was when they did that the non-traditional high coastal winds kept blowing bits off it. Hence the nails. To me, it looks like a giant, slightly misshapen Chinese coolie's hat on stilts.

Then there is one of my favourites, the stall between the Sacred Heart and the Tower Hotel, which does a nice line in wooden African memorial plaques of all kinds of traditional gods and spirits. Their best seller: a huge wooden plaque of Mrs Thatcher. I was going to buy one. But every time I went back to get it the whole place was blocked by this enormous refuse lorry which had plastered all over it London Borough of Bromley. Which means that either the London Borough of Bromley has suddenly turned generous or some clever Guyanese has gone sour on cigarettes and booze and come up with a new line in smuggling.

I also, I must admit, spent a lot of time at police headquarters. No, not because I was caught playing Find the Lady and taking money off the locals which would never do, but because I discovered in their chamber of horrors, tucked away behind a motley collection of Sam Browne belts and helmets and rusty old trumpets, this wonderful display telling you exactly how to set up your own illegal distillery – which I must say has proved very useful over the years. But just to show you the triumph of the Guyanese human spirit even in the depths of police headquarters, one afternoon as I was leaving a policeman tried to tell me the colour of my car was illegal in Guyana. He would have to charge me, unless I could see my way to, you know what.

But I think my favourite place of all was not one of the rum shops but the downstairs bar at the Pegasus Hotel. One guy I met there kept on insisting I went to the local Botanical Gardens not to see the flowers but to visit the mausoleum of Forbes Burnham, the wild, left-wing Marxist who led the country to independence in 1966 and then afterwards straight to the knacker's yard. Apparently they wanted to embalm him and put him on display there forever like his hero, Lenin, but even in death he slipped through their fingers. Something went wrong. Either the sun got to him first or the electricity broke down and the body decomposed like mad. In the end they just scooped him up and buried him there as quickly as possible. Which didn't sound like my idea of fun.

Someone else I met there, who looked just like a Dickensian lawyer, all striped pants and black jacket, kept offering to get me completely free of charge a passport for the low-cost, tax-free island paradise of the Dominion of Melchizadek, not to mention all the banking certificates, university degrees, legal indentures and Rotary Club certificates I wanted.

'Dominion of Melchizadek? I've never heard of it,' I kept saying to him. 'Melchizadek, yes. But not the Dominion of Melchizadek.'

'Look at our website – www.melchizadek.com. It's all there. You agree, yes?'

The whole thing was another elaborate con. There is no Dominion of Melchizadek. It's all the figment of someone's imagination. The website? That makes it all seem legit. Clever, eh?

There was another old boy there who looked like Evelyn Waugh without the bowler hat. He kept telling me he could still remember what he was doing the day Princess Margaret visited Georgetown 'when she was pretty', which tells you how long ago it was. Standing by the edge of the pavement, that's what he was doing, waving his little Union Jack in the air. There's loyalty for you.

Then, when I could break away, I was having tutored rum tastings with this wiry little man who reckoned he could tell a whole range of different rums even if he was blindfolded. He put different glasses in front of me of what looked like different flavours of liquid nitro-glycerine.

Were they dangerous? I asked him.

'Wha' yuh really know 'bout dis? Look: Drink dis do do right t'ing,' he said.

Or at least, I think that's what he said, not being an expert on Georgetown-speak, or rather, slur. Was he worried about the damage all that drinking was probably doing to his liver?

'Wha' wrong? Is wha' yuh t'inking. Nobody na know nuttin' 'bout dis. Well, ah t'ink yah should an damn well whey de hell.'

Which I think meant, I've got only half a liver left. So what the hell. But then again I may be wrong.

So we had another one and another one and ... each one less tutored than the one before. There was no doubt this guy liked his drink. He liked mine as well, because no sooner had he finished his than he was after finishing mine too.

'Wha' happen. Wha yuh doin' me dis fuh?' I suddenly found myself slurring.

'Me had to put ...'

'Na do dis to meh.'

'You wid yor IMF nose.'

'My IMF nose? Look if you're not careful, me go put my ...'

'De police. Don't deh roun fuh see dem?'

But we made it up – 'Sorry, man. Sorry.' Then had another. By the time we'd finished, I don't know about a bottle, I reckon we'd drunk a whole shop full of the stuff.

But before I completely collapse on the floor, I'll give you a chance to double your money. Now here's three cards. Okay. Choose one. Go on, just one. If it's the Queen of Hearts, I'll pay you double your money. Couldn't be simpler, could it? Go on. I know you're going to win, I just know it.